CITIES AND NATURE

A Handbook for Renewal

Edited by Roger L. Kemp

McFarland & Company, Inc., Publishers

Jefferson, North Carolina, and London

LIBRARY OF CONGRESS CATALOGUING-IN-PUBLICATION DATA

Cities and nature : a handbook for renewal /
edited by Roger L. Kemp.
p.   cm.
Includes bibliographical references and index.

ISBN 0-7864-2214-9 (softcover : 50# alkaline paper) ∞

1. Urban ecology — United States.   I. Kemp, Roger L.
HT243.U6C575   2006   307.76 — dc22   2005016995

British Library cataloguing data are available

Cover photograph by Jonathon Herman

Manufactured in the United States of America

*McFarland & Company, Inc., Publishers
Box 611, Jefferson, North Carolina 28640
www.mcfarlandpub.com*

For *Alexandra* and *Joanna,*
who will make the world a better place

ACKNOWLEDGMENTS

Grateful acknowledgment is made to the following organizations and publishers for granting permission to reprint the material contained in this volume.

American Planning Association
Congressional Quarterly Inc.
Government Finance Officers Association
International City/County Management
  Association
Landscape Communications

Nolan Media LLC
PRIMEDIA Business Magazines & Media
  Inc.
The Next American City, Inc.
Urban Land Institute
World Future Society

CONTENTS

Part III: The Future

PREFACE

Citizens, nonprofit organizations, and local public officials, in increasing numbers, are restoring nature as a vehicle to improve their downtowns, as well as to enhance general economic conditions within their communities. Public officials especially are learning that they can plant the seeds of urban renewal and, at the same time, restore nature. Not only do they renew their neighborhoods and downtowns, but they also attract tourists as well as private investment. The return-to-nature movement is becoming a fact of life in our communities as our nation and its cities enter the 21st century.

The types of investment in nature that are taking place in our cities and towns include those projects and programs related to creating, protecting, preserving, and restoring nature. The major projects and programs described in this volume in each of these categories are highlighted below.

- "Creation" projects include the development of computer models to prevent urban sprawl, the establishment of open spaces to improve downtown living, and the purposeful networking of inner-city greenways and trails.
- "Protection" programs include maintaining local climate patterns, positively impacting the environment through proper planning techniques to guide development, and ways to safeguard animals from the automobile.
- "Preservation" efforts include maintaining existing urban corridors, wildlife refuges, open spaces, and nature areas.
- "Restoration" initiatives encompass both water-related and downtown-oriented programs. Water-related programs include rivers, watershed areas, and beaches. Downtown-oriented projects include restoring public parks, plazas, open spaces, and greenways.

This new type of community renewal process represents the efforts of citizens and local public officials to invest wisely in their downtowns and neighborhoods with the goal of revitalizing them through nature, and to bring citizens back downtown in record numbers. This volume focuses exclusively on local government and nonprofit organization revitalization efforts that emphasize those public works projects to create, protect, preserve, and restore nature in America's cities and towns.

The realities of modern economic life have shown us that, when investment focuses on enhancing the natural aspects of our communities, business, commerce, and tourism will follow shortly thereafter. A new eclectic economic development model is evolving that is beginning to work in a number of politically, economically, racially, and culturally diverse communities. An investment in "nature" now yields positive community-wide benefits, both tangible and intangible–for residents and tourists alike.

This volume is broken down into four sections for ease of reference. The first section introduces the reader to this new subject, "cities and nature." The second section, and by design the longest, includes numerous case studies, or best practices, on how cities and towns are investing in nature to stimulate downtown and neighborhood revitalization. The next section focuses on the future of this "back-to-nature" movement as our nation enters the 21st century. Several appendices included in the last portion of this volume provide important information in this new subject area. Based on this conceptual schema, the four primary sections of this volume are highlighted below.

- *Cities and Nature.* Chapters in this section describe new approaches to managing urban growth, evolving environmental management systems, and the movement to create "new" Main Streets in our cities and towns. The last chapter describes the economic benefits of creating parks and open spaces.
- *The Best Practices.* The cities and towns examined in this volume, including the states in which they are located, are listed below categorically in alphabetical order. The case studies represent an important effort to obtain a body of knowledge on the best practices available in this dynamic new, and still evolving, field.

  ...Cities: Atlanta, Baltimore, Boston, Cambridge, Camden, Charlottesville, Chattanooga, Chicago, Denver, Fairfield, Fort Collins, Gainesville, Grand Forks, Hampton, Harmony, Hartford, Irvine, Lafayette, Lake Worth, Lancaster, Mattituck, Miami Beach, Minneapolis, New York City, Petaluma, Philadelphia, Phoenix, Port Aransas, Portland, Riverhead, Saint Louis Park, Saint Paul, San Francisco, San Jose, San Rafael, Silver Spring, and West Des Moines.

  ...States: Arizona, California, Colorado, Connecticut, Florida, Georgia, Iowa, Indiana, Illinois, Maryland, Massachusetts, Minnesota, New Jersey, New York, North Dakota, Ohio, Oregon, Pennsylvania, Tennessee, Texas, Virginia, and Washington.
- *The Future.* This section examines the likely future of the "back-to-nature"

movement in our nation's cities and towns. Chapters included in this portion of this reference work focus on the ecological revolution taking place in America, the trend to search for economic growth that does not bring destruction to nature in the process, the importance of placing landscaping in the urban manmade environment, and the return of urban parks and public plazas to our inner-city areas. The concluding chapter examines the impact of nature on the human spirit, and how important nature is to our "living" environment. These readings reflect the fact that initiatives related to the creation, protection, preservation, and restoration of nature to man's urban environment are here to stay.

- *Appendices.* Several appendices are included in this volume. They include a regional resource directory of all of the cities and towns included in "The Best Practices" section of this volume, and a national resource directory of all major professional associations and research organizations in fields related to "cities and nature." Lastly a comprehensive bibliography on this new subject is provided, with listings under the headings of books, monographs, articles, and other sources.

The case studies in this volume represent state-of-the-art practices on how citizens, nonprofit organizations, and local public officials alike are using various aspects of nature to promote neighborhood and community renewal. All of these projects related to nature now represent a new discipline within the traditional field of municipal economic development. The term "nature" in this volume is used in its broadest sense, and is meant to include those improvements to land and water that encompass the creation, protection, preservation, and restoration of nature in the very core of our communities. The case studies selected for this work fall under this definition.

The practices reflected in the case

studies contained in this volume are typically applied in a piecemeal and incremental fashion in cities and towns throughout America. For the most part, citizens, nonprofit organizations, and local public officials are busy doing their own thing within their own communities. They do not have the time to find out what other neighboring cities and towns are doing in this area, let alone what other communities are doing in far away places located throughout the nation. For this reason, the case studies selected for this reference volume represent an important codification of knowledge in this rapidly evolving field.

This reference work assembles, for the first time, materials based on a national literature search, and makes this information available to citizens and public officials throughout the United States. The goal of this volume is to help educate the public on how to best use aspects of nature as an economic stimulus for downtown and neighborhood revitalization. If additional information is desired to follow-up on any specific case study in this volume, every city, town, county, special district, and nonprofit organization listed for each case study is included in the Regional Resource Directory. Additional information can easily be obtained from this directory by contacting individuals at those sources listed. Important state, regional, and national resources are also brought together for the first time to help readers become more informed about the new field of "cities and nature."

Roger L. Kemp
Vallejo, California
January 2006

Part I
Cities and Nature

CHAPTER 1

A NEW APPROACH TO MANAGING GROWTH

Maryann Froehlich

Competing demands are a daily fact of life for local governments. Simultaneously maintaining great schools and low taxes, good transportation and clean air, rising property values and affordable housing are just a few of the balancing acts that local governments are expected to perform. The field of development embodies these tensions. Development can create a better tax base, provide jobs and amenities for residents, and enhance a community's livability. It also can add to traffic problems, disrupt neighborhoods, and detract from the character of the community. To avoid the pitfalls and to capture development's benefits, local governments are increasingly turning to the policy of "smart growth."

Smart growth invests time, attention, and resources in restoring community and vitality to center cities and older suburbs. New growth is more town-centered and transit- and pedestrian-oriented; includes a greater mix of housing, commercial, and retail uses; and preserves open space and other environmental amenities. Examples are springing up in communities across the United States.

Portland, Oregon, with its longstanding urban growth boundary and well-developed transit system, is one of the best-known and most frequently cited examples of smart growth. A recent groundswell of efforts around the country has been changing development patterns for the better. Over the past 18 months, 11 cities in California have enacted urban growth boundaries.

The city of Fort Collins, Colorado, is expediting permitting for exemplary developments with superior environmental performance. Charleston, South Carolina, is creating dispersed affordable housing that actually revitalizes neighborhoods and spurs private investment. Lancaster, California, is encouraging investment in town by reducing development impact fees. And the city of St. Louis, St. Louis County, and the state of Missouri are using their new transit system, Metrolink, as a potential focus for new development.

This movement is not about no-growth, or even slow growth. People want the jobs, tax revenues, and amenities that come with development. But they want these benefits without degrading the environment, raising local taxes, worsening traffic congestion, or busting budgets. More and more local governments are finding that current devel-

Originally published as "Smart Growth: Why Local Governments Are Taking a New Approach to Managing Growth in Their Communities," *Public Management*, Vol. 80, No. 5, May 1998. Published by the International City/County Management Association, Washington, D.C. Reprinted with permission of the publisher.

opment patterns and practices often fail to provide this balance.

The Right Time for Smart Growth?

In communities across the nation, there is a growing concern that current development patterns — dominated by what some call "sprawl" — are no longer in the long-term interest of our cities, existing suburbs, small towns, rural communities, or wilderness areas. Though supportive of growth, communities are questioning the economic costs of abandoning infrastructure in the city, only to rebuild it farther out. They are questioning the social costs of the mismatch between new employment locations in the suburbs and the available workforce in the city.

They are questioning the wisdom of abandoning brownfields in older communities, eating up the open space and prime agricultural lands at the suburban fringe, and polluting the air of an entire region by forcing more people to drive to get anywhere. Spurring the movement for smart growth are demographic shifts, a strong environmental ethic, increased fiscal concerns and more nuanced views of growth than in the past. The result is both a new demand and a new opportunity for smart growth.

Demographics and Preferences

Consumer preferences change as demographics and values change. A demographic study by the marketing firm American LIVES indicates a growing desire for community, open space, and town-centered living, with less reliance on the automobile. Demographic shifts underlie and support these trends. The phrase "typical family" — meaning a married couple with children — described 40 percent of all households a generation ago; it now accounts for only 26 percent.

Homebuyers are getting older, too. A third of the homebuying market is over the age of 45. In surveys published by the National Association of Home Builders, most of this market segment wanted to live in communities with a diversity of ages and thus a diversity of housing sizes and types. Three of their top four location priorities were based on ease of transportation and access — to shopping, family and friends, and medical care.

And most of the mature homebuyers who intend to move will move to smaller houses with smaller yards, to reduce cleanup and yard work. Mature buyers' preferences, in combination with the overall trend in the United States toward smaller households, will mean a greater market for smaller houses on smaller lots, especially where density's perceived problems can be solved through smart design.

Environment

It seems that everywhere you look, from Portland, Oregon, to Portland, Maine, and from Toronto, Canada, to Miami, Florida, people are concerned about vanishing farmland and open space. Yet loss of open space is not an inevitable outcome of growth. Smart growth scenarios such as the New Jersey redevelopment plan show that a 43 percent reduction in the loss of open space can be achieved by better directing growth. Support for plans that preserve open space is evident. Open space initiatives and bond issues fared well on voters' ballots in the last national election and often have won support at the local level.

Water quality concerns also are affecting the development industry. Contaminated urban runoff increases as rainwater pours off newly constructed roofs, driveways, roads, and parking lots and into lakes, rivers, and bays. Increasingly, developers and local governments seek development designs that protect water resources. Town-style developments designed with stream buffers and lots of open space can cut runoff by over 40 percent, reducing contaminants and avoiding potentially costly upgrades at the local treatment plant. Projected treatment-plant cost savings drove New York City and upstate New York to an agreement sharply curtailing development in upstate watersheds.

Time, Air Quality, and Traffic Congestion

Getting stuck in traffic is a ubiquitous phenomenon in America. In fact, Americans lose more than 1.6 million hours a day mired in traffic. And delays only are expected to lengthen, as traffic congestion is projected to get worse. For a suburban mother interviewed by the *Wall Street Journal*, the cost of being stuck in traffic is already high. Asked what social reform would most improve her quality of life, she replied, "Lower the driving age to 10." She had put 40,000 miles on her minivan in the previous 18 months by ferrying her three kids around the suburbs.

Costs to the nation also are high. Traditional fixes — involving building more roads — seem to be less effective. Congestion levels have risen an average of more than 22 percent between 1982 and 1994 (just under 2 percent per year) according to a 10-year study recently completed by the Texas Transportation Institute. Many localities have experienced a much greater increase in congestion during this time, including two with greater than three percent increases per year. Of the 50 cities in the study, only two (Houston and Phoenix) had lower congestion levels in 1994 than in 1982. Metropolitan planning organizations like the one in greater Washington, D.C., predict that even massive, costly building programs will only be able to slow the worsening of traffic conditions on area roads.

The connection among development patterns, transportation, and air quality is receiving increased attention. There is a growing recognition that the auto-oriented development patterns of the past 50 years have contributed to the need to drive more and farther. While Americans averaged 4,485 automobile-miles per person in 1970, this number increased to 6,330 miles per person in 1993, a 41 percent increase.

Between 1983 and 1990, almost every segment of U.S. society increased its trips and mileage. According to the national personal transportation survey conducted by the U.S. Department of Transportation during that time, the average trip for all purposes went from 8.68 to 9.45 miles. EPA's Office of Air and Radiation predicts that by the year 2005, growth in vehicle-miles traveled will begin to overtake the improvements in air quality gained from using cleaner fuels and less-polluting cars. In other words, after 30 years of steady improvement in air quality, we will begin to lose the battle because of burgeoning growth in automobile travel.

These trends are stimulating a search for development alternatives that will provide more choices, better accessibility, and less auto dependence. Advocates for alternative means of transportation believe that air quality, community livability, and transportation choice all can be improved through smart growth and through supporting transportation investments. This means that the traditional opponents of development are increasingly seeing development as part of the solution.

And local governments are agreeing, particularly when they have the opportunity to combine more intense, compact, mixed-use development with access to transit. Rail transit service is a new feature in a dozen cities, including St. Louis, Tampa, Salt Lake City, San Diego, and Dallas. An amazing

100 new transit project startups are currently proposed in the United States.

Fiscal Concerns

Fiscal conservatives and antitax groups have been increasingly vocal players in development debates. They object to the dynamic of subsidizing costly development at the fringe while previous investments in neighborhood infrastructure go underused or unmaintained. This phenomenon can be seen at work in the state of Maine: between 1970 and 1995, the state lost 27,000 students but spent $434 million on new schools in outlying locations. During this same period, school-bus costs rose from $8 million to $54 million, a 65 percent increase in inflation-adjusted dollars.

And in Prince William County, Virginia, officials estimate they collect about $2,100 a year in real estate and other taxes on the average house. That same house, however, costs the county $3,700 a year in services to its occupants.

Scattered development also can bring higher infrastructure and public capital costs as development takes place beyond the local service area. A major source of the higher costs for "leapfrog" developments is the need for longer trunk lines and connecting roads. The Urban Land Institute has reported that for residential developments of three to five dwelling units per acre, which are located 10 miles away from the service area, utility costs are almost $10,000 per unit, compared to less than $5,000 for developments that are five miles away.

Concentrating development along service corridors or in a specific area can reduce costs. A study of the forms of similar land uses and levels of service in Florida, conducted by James Duncan and Associates, showed that public capital costs were between $16,000 and $17,000 per unit for corridor and nodal developments and almost $24,000 for scattered developments.

Another study of two alternative growth patterns in New Jersey conducted by the New Jersey Office of State Planning found that following the dispersed pattern of growth would cost approximately 9 percent more in infrastructure capital costs than following a planned development pattern. Other studies have found similar outcomes.

Thus, while previous efforts to redirect growth have often been driven by a desire to protect open space and the environment, the new concern in many communities is increasingly about the fiscal impacts of development patterns.

Local Competition

To relieve fiscal pressures and bring in jobs, virtually every local government pursues what it calls economic development. According to former Pasadena (California) Mayor Rick Cole, in the vast majority of cases, what that essentially boils down to is sales tax development. Cities, particularly those in California, depend on sales tax revenue to pay the bills for police, fire, library, and other basic services.

Unfortunately for local governments, the escalating subsidy war is stealing more and more revenue from these services. For instance, in the past several years, New York City has provided subsidies to corporations to keep them from moving to New Jersey or Connecticut: $235 million to Chase Manhattan Bank, $98 million to the National Broadcasting Company, and $97 million to Citicorp. As long as one jurisdiction offers incentives, others must follow suit.

Local officials know that this type of competition often is a loser for the public. And more and more taxpayers are questioning it, too. Stadium bonds are facing tougher scrutiny, and local jurisdictions are seeking solider assurance that the promised jobs, taxes, and other benefits will materialize. But some jurisdictions have taken steps to make more fundamental change. They are seeing a common interest in ensuring the health of their nearby neighbors.

Minneapolis/St. Paul has an innovative tax base-sharing arrangement. Corporate executives in the Pittsburgh area have proposed a metro-wide sales tax, including the outer suburbs, to finance new riverfront development projects downtown. In greater Cleveland, a regional consortium of older suburbs has joined forces with the city, civic, and business leaders to lobby state officials to stop building new roads and start repairing older ones, and to push for legislation that would encourage families and businesses to reclaim vacant land near the urban center rather than undeveloped farmland farther away.

Projects at Loggerheads

Unease over current growth patterns has spread among suburbanites, environmentalists, fiscal conservatives, alternative-transportation advocates, and civic activists. As a result, pitched battles over approvals of new infrastructure and development projects have become more and more the norm.

Win or lose, developers and local advocates pay a higher and higher toll — in the form of lost time and piecemeal, ad hoc solutions that often fail to satisfy any group. Proposals to stop all growth, to cap property taxes permanently, and to close off schools to new residents have gained currency in some locales, illustrating one extreme of the spectrum of community reactions to growth.

Surprising, some good is coming out of this seemingly intractable impasse. Frustrated with the business-as-usual, project-by-project fighting that has prevailed, developers, fiscal conservatives, local governments, environmentalists, and suburbanites are finding common ground in the philosophy of smart growth.

No Special Formula

Smart growth shifts the terms of the debate away from the pro- and anti-growth context of the past. It seeks growth, recognizing the crucial role that development plays in maintaining and improving communities. But smart growth also acknowledges the fiscal, environmental, and other concerns that are dominating current discussions of growth, and it asks the fundamental question, not of whether to grow but of how to grow.

There is no one-size-fits-all formula for smart growth. It takes different forms in different communities. Smart growth, however, shows common features in each of the communities that have adopted it. Wherever it occurs, smart growth:

- Enhances a sense of community.
- Protects investment in existing neighborhoods.
- Provides a greater certainty in the development process.
- Protects environmental quality.
- Rewards developers with profitable products, financing, and flexibility.
- Decreases congestion by providing alternative modes of transportation.
- Makes efficient use of public money.

Following smart growth principles, developers, environmentalists, affordable housing providers, and alternative-transportation advocates are able to agree on a surprising range of development questions. The most consistent agreement occurs over the need to enable development that meets smart growth criteria — to make it easier to permit, easier to finance, and easier to build.

Many local governments have found that they play a crucial role in bringing barriers down and offering incentives for smart growth. For example, some communities have discovered that their zoning ordinances actually raise barriers to the type of growth they want to attract, requiring unnecessarily wide streets, deep setbacks, large lots, and excessive parking.

Ordinances often forbid mixing retail and commercial uses with residential ones. In addition to changing zoning, many local governments have had success in using tax increment financing, public/private partnerships, coordinated transportation and land use policies, and other approaches to encourage smart growth.

Although smart growth is not the answer in every locality, an increasing number of local governments are using it to create good neighborhoods, reduce traffic, and preserve open space. And, these localities are not only finding solutions. By encouraging development that serves the economy, the community, and the environment, they also are helping to build consensus and broad support among community constituents.

CHAPTER 2

ENVIRONMENTAL MANAGEMENT SYSTEMS

Michelle Wyman Pawar and *Christopher Rissetto*

The economic boom of the past decade has led to explosive growth and has strengthened local tax bases in communities. Though the growth has benefitted local governments in many ways, some old challenges have remained while new challenges have emerged.

Exponential growth has required new construction and often new and expanded local government services and operations like wastewater collection and treatment, solid waste management, pesticides storage and use, management lubricants and fluids associated with garage or fleet operations, and regulatory and land use oversight.

Through these examples, one can see the extent to which local government operations and activities impact the environment and public health, thus creating immense liability exposure. Few tools like an environmental management system (EMS) provide local administrators with effective methodologies for practically and systematically managing the health, financial, and regulatory risks associated with their responsibility as stewards of the environment.

An EMS is a set of management processes and procedures that allow an organization to analyze, control, and reduce the environmental impact of its operations and services to achieve cost savings, greater efficiency and oversight, and streamlined regulatory compliance.

Local governments seek innovations that improve performance in public health and environmental protection, risk and liability reduction, and service efficiency and effectiveness. Programs must be implemented without a reduction in a community's quality of life or significant impact on limited budgets. Over the long term, an effective EMS can achieve these objectives.

An EMS, for example, offers accurate tracking of regulatory compliance, a reduced public health risk and liability, improved public understanding of management decisions, streamlined organizational processes, better relations with community stakeholders (citizens, businesses, and special-interest groups), and environmental leadership.

EMS Advantages

Gains realized by a local government through an EMS may include:

Originally published as "A Tool for Improvement: Environmental Management Systems," *Public Management*, Vol. 83, No. 11, December 2001. Published by the International City/County Management Association, Washington, D.C. Reprinted with permission of the publisher.

- Increased operational and administrative efficiencies.
- Cost savings, including economic and environmental ones.
- Improved public health and environmental protection.
- Reductions in risk and liability.
- Improved tracking of all types of permits (health, water, fire, building).
- Streamlined processes for regulatory compliance.
- Enhanced interaction with community stakeholders.
- Improved internal and external communication and education.
- Higher levels of employee participation and stewardship.
- Innovations in environmental solutions.
- Better public relations.

Self-Audit Policies and Immunity

One of the early steps of an EMS is an effort to identify and comply with an organization's regulatory requirements. A local government might be hesitant to audit its operations for fear of finding a regulatory violation, consequently facing legal and financial liabilities.

The U.S. Environmental Protection Agency (EPA) and a number of states have developed self-audit policies in an effort to dispel the fears and encourage local governments to promptly disclose and correct violations that are discovered through a self-audit process. This statement has been copied from EPA's self-audit policy:

"Under the final Audit/Self Policing Policy, EPA will not seek gravity-based penalties and will not recommend criminal prosecutions for companies that meet the requirements of the Policy. Gravity-based penalties represent the 'seriousness' or punitive portion of penalties over and above the portion representing the economic gain from

non-compliance. The policy requires companies:
- To promptly disclose and correct violations.
- To prevent recurrence of the violation.
- To remedy environmental harm.
   The policy excludes:
- Repeated violations.
- Violations that result in serious actual harm.
- Violations that may present imminent and substantial endangerment."[1]

EPA's audit policy is designed to protect human health and the environment, while providing an incentive for entities to voluntarily discover, disclose, and correct violations of federal environmental requirements regardless of how they were detected.[2]

States often have their own self-audit policies that may provide protection to disclosing entities through application of an "audit privilege and immunity" law.[3] State audit policies typically only protect entities that are in violation of state requirements. Some states are working with EPA to gain federal immunity benefits for entities that have been granted immunity under the state audit policy.

A successful EMS must reflect recognition and compliance with federal and state statutes as well as other requirements that may impact a local government. Managers first should check with state regulatory officials to determine if an audit policy exists, and if so, they should further determine if a grant of immunity under the state policy also protects that entity from federal prosecution.

What Is ISO 14001?

ISO 14001 isn't the name of a new software package! It is an environmental standard developed by the International Organization for Standardization to meet the need of both governmental and private sector organizations and to monitor their environmental performance and their impacts on natural and finite resources like water, air, soil, and raw materials. The elements of ISO 14001 thoroughly integrate environmental thinking into all levels and processes of an organization and enable environmental concerns to become integral to overall performance.[4]

It is important to clarify that ISO 14001 is just one model of an EMS, although many organizations choose to initiate a more modest level of EMS implementation. The primary concern is that if an organization aims to achieve ISO 14001, third-party environmental audits must be completed to receive ISO 14001 certification. Many organizations, however, set up and implement an EMS without seeking ISO 14001 certification. This approach allows greater flexibility in EMS design and execution.

ISO 14001 is recognized in the domestic marketplace, in both the private and the public sectors. Many companies mandate that their suppliers and service providers are certified under the ISO 14001 standard.[5] Application and use of ISO 14001 by European and Asian companies and public sector organizations are somewhat advanced.[6] In recent years, ISO 14001 and other EMSs have become increasingly common in both the public and private sectors of the United States.

Using ISO 14001 Specifications

ISO 14001 outlines specifications for five steps that should be taken in the process of EMS development. These steps are generally applied by organizations even if they are not seeking certification. Here are the essential elements of an EMS as set forth in ISO 14001.[7]

1. Environmental policy. Develop a statement of the organization's commitment. This policy should be used as a guide for planning and action.

2. Planning. A detailed analysis of existing functions, processes and policies, including regulatory requirements, should be completed; establish objectives and targets that are aligned with the environmental policy.

3. EMS implementation. Roles and responsibilities should be designated and resources, including training, should be provided to employees who are involved in the EMS.

4. Oversight and improvements of the EMS. A consistent flow of information on the EMS should be collected and maintained to monitor key activities and to track performance improvements.

5. Annual assessment of EMS performance and value. Records should be kept to periodically verify that the EMS is operating as intended and to ensure compliance and continual performance improvement.

These five steps are the broad-strike guidelines for developing and managing an EMS. As long as the five are included, the detailed process of implementation varies based on the organization's demographics, culture, commitment, service, or product.

Added considerations. Based on the experiences of local governments that have implemented EMSs, several critical elements should be noted: stakeholder participation is fundamental to maximizing the potential for continual improvement within the organization (and is even more so within the community). Not only is management buy-in requisite to an EMS, but also employees must be engaged from the earliest stages to ensure that the EMS is integrated into the organizational culture.

A useful EMS also should strive to build upon and enhance the existing organizational machine and its processes, not to replace it. And an EMS should be promoted beyond its environmental benefits. It should encompass employee empowerment, improved communication, stronger account-

---

FIGURE 1
Basic Elements in an Environmental Management System[8]

Initial Task
Design and
  Development

- Establish an environmental policy for the organization.
- Identify operations, functions, permits, and policies of the organization that impact the environment.
- Review legal and regulatory compliance requirements and current status.
- Set environmental objectives and targets that aim to improve environmental performance and lessen environmental impacts.

Implementation
and Action

- Develop an EMS framework, including the five basic elements.
- Establish an EMS team and designate management and staff responsibility.
- Designate an external stakeholder group comprised of citizens, business and industry, school districts, and non-profits.
- Provide training and education of EMS team and external stakeholder group.
- Disseminate marketing materials internally and externally to promote EMS; educate and demonstrate the organization's commitment to the environment.

Tracking and
Adjustments

- Set performance measures to assess and monitor EMS performance.
- Establish process for reporting and audit system.
- Develop and maintain records for external and internal reporting.

Continual
Performance

- Complete periodic management reviews.

---

ability, streamlined operations, cost savings, and performance improvements.

A local government can focus an EMS on a single function or service (wastewater treatment) or on a single department (public works), or it can implement one that encompasses the entire organization. The scope of an EMS often is referred to as the "fence line."

Basic EMS criteria. The basic elements of a standard EMS are detailed in Figure 1. Although the methodology of an EMS varies, the criteria are standard and provide the foundation for the EMS. How the criteria are applied and how the EMS evolves

are determined by the types of services offered by the local government, the scope of EMS application, and the management resources available for the execution of an EMS.

Costs of Implementation

If a local government elects to implement a comprehensive EMS (as, countywide), the cost will be more substantial than if it elects to implement an EMS in a single department (as, in public works). Cost of development and implementation also de-

> ## FIGURE 2
> ## Sampling of Participants' Focuses in the 1998 EPA Initiative
>
> | Participant | EMS Focus |
> |---|---|
> | Wayne County, Michigan | Wastewater Treatment Facility |
> | Scottsdale, Arizona | Municipal Government |
> | Lowell, Massachusetts | Wastewater Treatment Facility |
> | Gaithersburg, Maryland | Public Works |
> | Lansing Board of Water and Light, Michigan | Electric Generating Facility |
>
> Source: U.S. Environmental Protection Agency, Final Report. *"The U.S. EPA Environmental Management System Pilot Program for Local Governmental Entities."* Spring 2000.

pends on the size of the organization or fence line and the number and complexity of the operations that impact the environment.

This is why a strong starting point for an organization would be to identify the functions, policies, or programs somewhere in the organization where success is most likely to be achieved. Starting with a small fence line to establish credibility for an EMS can lead to successful cost savings and to subsequent application on a broader level within the local government. It also creates momentum and further buy-in.

EMS cost checklist. A small community that typically has smaller operations and fewer resources can rely on current staffing to develop and implement a basic EMS. For resources that assist in the establishment of an EMS, see page 18.

Here is a checklist of the essential items needed for development and implementation. All items, of course, are contingent on the scope of an EMS, but these items can be used as key categories for developing direct and indirect cost estimates.

1. Management. Representation from top-level management, as well as elected and appointed officials, is critical to provide the necessary leadership, motivation, and oversight. Costs here are primarily related to time expended by management and elected and appointed officials.

2. Core team. The core team is composed of vertical representation from all relevant departments, to ensure program integration from all levels of the organization; members are to be appointed as dedicated staff to provide EMS implementation, maintenance, and identification of gaps needing continual improvement. In a small community, the core team can consist of a council member or mayor, manager, and facility managers. Small communities must develop their core teams with a high degree of flexibility given their diverse nature of governance.

3. Policy. This item refers to the development of an initial environmental policy or enhancement of an existing policy. Possibly, amendments should be made to the appropriate existing ordinances and policies. An environmental policy is a statement that articulates the philosophy of the community regarding the protection of its environment and public health. As in the steps above, the major costs are related to staff time associated with policy development.

4. External services. Subcontracted services for technical guidance on EMS, particularly in the initial development and implementation stages, often is required for localities with many and/or complex operations. The services may consist of federal and state regulatory audits and process and operations reviews to determine pollution prevention opportunities and cost savings, or implementation of process changes.

5. Materials. Costs for materials, which are generally minimal. Usually, there

is no need for capital expenditures. Larger fence lines, however, may choose to implement significant education programs that may require an investment in the development of signs, brochures, maps (used to provide directions on the appropriate way to store or dispose of product), training pamphlets, and the like.

6. External auditor. If an organization is seeking ISO 14001 certification, third-party auditors must be hired to complete the EMS audit, as during the annual financial audit process.

A general guideline for assessing initial start-up costs for an EMS is the "18-month rule." Generally, cost savings begin 18 months after EMS implementation. They comprise savings both in direct costs (manpower, insurance, energy savings) and in indirect costs (natural resources, community and employee relations, streamlining of operations). Important savings are liability claims that will not be sought because there is a systematic process in place to reduce and eventually eliminate those risks.

The value of an EMS can and should be quantified through performance measures. By streamlining operations, improving employee morale, and increasing accountability within the organization, an EMS extends beyond the environmental focus and has measurable positive impacts on non-environmental functions within an organization. A local government can substantiate the value of an EMS with real numbers by tracking and quantifying selected criteria.

Local Experience

In 1998, EPA established a two-year project to assess the effectiveness of ISO 14001 EMSs in local governments. Nine local governments in the 1998 *U.S. EPA Municipal Environmental Management System Implementation* initiative reported the

overall effort to be successful. Benefits cited by the participants included:[9]
- Improved efficiency and reduced costs.
- Increased internal communication and education through demonstrated environmental stewardship.
- Positive effects on environmental compliance and performance.
- Better relationships with regulators.
- Improved environmental awareness and competency throughout the organization.

The EPA initiative described was successful enough to merit a follow-up. In April 2000, EPA selected 14 public sector organizations to participate in its second EMS study. Though this program does not provide direct funding support, it does provide on-going training and technical assistance.

ICMA has started the Local Government Environmental Assistance Network (LGEAN) to give local governments clear, concise, and relevant information on environmental management, planning, and regulatory issues of concern at no cost to local governments. LGEAN also serves as a resource to answer the technical questions that local officials have in developing EMSs and other environmental concerns.

Through the Environmental Liability Outreach project, LGEAN has partnered with the International Municipal Lawyers Association (IMLA) to respond to local government inquiries on environmental risk and liability. This effort is funded by the nonprofit Public Entity Risk Institute, Fairfax, Virginia.

It is essential to be creative in seeking funding and technical support for an EMS initiative.

Assistance

Federal agencies have initiated programs that offer both technical assistance and in some cases funding to support EMS initiatives in local government. Among the agencies that offer assistance are the U.S. Department of Transportation's Community and Systems Preservation Program, EPA's Livable Communities program, and the U.S. Department of Commerce. Some programs also offer assistance administered and supported by joint agreements between several federal agencies.

Private foundations should be considered possible sources of funding for EMS-related initiatives. The strength of the stock market in the past five years has sent foundation portfolios to enormous levels, increasing the amounts they are required to give annually to retain nonprofit status.

Corporate sponsorships also are possible funding sources, particularly at the local level. Community stakeholders should be encouraged to generate initiatives in partnership with local businesses and industry to strengthen their participation in an EMS process.

A Tangible Solution

As the realities of growth and resource management, as well as the lag in infrastructure capacity, continue to challenge local governments, an EMS can offer a dynamic management tool both for environmental protection and for cost savings. In an era when economic development pressures, community infrastructure problems, and environmental concerns are leading priorities and challenges for local governments, an EMS can offer solid and practical solutions. An EMS has the potential to take a local government to a new level of environmental stewardship. The value of being proactive, rather than reactive, is the freedom to innovate and to strengthen local controls.

Notes

1. Protocol for Conducting Environmental Compliance Audits under the Comprehensive Environmental Response, Compensation, and Liability Act, EPA Office of Enforcement and Compliance, EPA-305-B-98-009, December 1998, page iii.

2. "Incentives for Self-Policing: Discovery, Disclosure, Correction and Prevention of Violations," 65 *Federal Register*, Part VII (April 11, 2000), at 19, 619.

3. EPA addresses its opposition to state audit privileges and immunity laws, 65 *Federal Register*, at 19, 623-19, 624. Discussion of these differences, and strategies to address conflicts, is beyond the scope of this article.

4. Schaarsmith, James H., "The ISO 14001 Environmental Management System Specification." May 1999.

5. In 1999, three of the largest automobile manufacturers mandated their suppliers have ISO 14001 certification.

6. The European Union promulgated an EMS system known as the Environmental Management and Audit Scheme (EMAS) that extends beyond ISO 14001 in its specifications for certification.

7. Based on the most commonly used framework for an EMS, the ISO 14001 standard developed by the International Organization for Standardization. ANSI/ISO 14001-1996.

8. *Ibid.*

9. U.S. Environmental Protection Agency, Final Report. *The U.S. EPA Environmental Management System Pilot Program for Local Government Entities.* Spring 2000.

CHAPTER 3

CREATING "NEW" MAIN STREETS IN OUR CITIES

Charles Lockwood

Throughout the 1980s and 1990s, hundreds of towns — both large and small — embarked on main street revitalization programs to strengthen their communities. Now, post–World War II suburbs throughout the United States are building main streets from scratch in a bold attempt to give identity to an anonymous suburban sprawl. By doing so, they hope to gain an edge in competing with other towns for future development and increased tax revenues.

Several dozen new main streets are under construction or in the planning stages in suburbs across the country. They are *not* intended to be outdoor shopping malls masquerading as main streets. Like pre–World War II, small town main streets, they contain a full range of everyday uses and activities — including office, retail, entertainment, hotels, housing, and civic institutions such as public libraries — all integrated within a pedestrian-friendly environment.

New suburban main streets are sprouting up in virtually every kind of postwar community — from unplanned, sprawling suburbs like Schaumburg near Chicago, to new towns like Valencia outside Los Angeles, and to picture book new urbanist communities like Haile Plantation in Gainesville, Florida, and Disney's new town of Celebration, Florida. These new main streets take many forms — from streets several blocks long to tree-shaded town squares and village greens.

These developments mark the wane of an old trend and the emergence of a new movement. Since World War II, most suburban development has ignored the broader, historic role of the street as a key component in a shared public realm. Rather, development patterns have reduced the street to a pedestrian-intimidating, single-purpose traffic arterial. The last few generations of Americans rarely have had the experience of coming togther on a tree-lined street to shop, to walk after dinner, or to talk with friends.

Today, the pendulum is swinging another way. More and more people want to return to the traditional main street, particularly as their lives become more mobile, more global, and more computerized. Despite all the talk about "going virtual," people still need to feel they belong to a community.

Originally published as "Retrofitting Suburbia," *Urban Land*, Vol. 57, No. 7, July 1998. Published by the Urban Land Institute, 1025 Thomas Jefferson Street, N.W., Suite 500 West, Washington, D.C. 20007-5201. Reprinted with permission of the publisher.

Why Retrofit Suburbia?

Why are a growing number of suburbs, which previously celebrated their shopping mall/automobile-dominated lifestyles, building new main streets?

The "Tin Man" Syndrome. Like the Tin Man in *The Wizard of Oz*, more and more American residents are complaining that their postwar suburban towns have no heart. They feel cast adrift, with nothing to hold onto except a steering wheel. A main street, whatever its scale or architectural style, is the heart of a community. Reston Town Center in the new town of Reston, Virginia, for example, serves not only as a downtown that brings the Reston community together but also as a regional center for residents and workers from neighboring suburban communities that lack multiuse public gathering places.

Identity. As look-alike suburbs increasingly compete for residents, jobs, conventions, and tourists, many of them are regarding the addition of new main streets as one way to create an easily recognizable — and marketable — identity and character that will attract new businesses, development, and shops, as well as generate increased sales tax revenues.

Suburban Renewal. Many 1950s and 1960s inner suburbs are declining, just as urban neighborhoods did a generation or two ago. The suburb of Park Forest outside Chicago watched its population decline by 14 percent in the 1980s and its median household income shrink by 3 percent when the nation was enjoying a 7 percent increase in median income. The 695,000-square-foot Park Forest Center regional mall has been plagued in recent years by a 70 percent vacancy rate. Now, most of the mall buildings have been bulldozed as Park Forest builds a new main street in its place to help revitalize its community.

Program Overload. Many people are turning away from over-structured, formulaic places that look alike to the diversity of traditional main streets. Big buildings, small buildings, a few ugly buildings, and some standout ones work together to make main street a real place where people can feel connected.

Changing suburban retail trends are another key factor fueling the new suburban main street trend. Medium-sized, higher-end stores like William Sonoma, Barnes & Noble, and Crate & Barrel no longer want to locate inside typical suburban malls. They prefer a separate identity, which means having their own building on a pedestrian-oriented main street. According to *Stores* magazine, "The revitalization of main street has caught the imagination of retailers, who see neighborhood locations as a viable means of growth.... Main street stores are answering shoppers' demands for convenience, efficiency, and something new while avoiding the sense of sameness that frequently seems to fill many suburban centers."

The Gap, Saks Fifth Avenue, Sears, Limited Stores, Express, Victoria's Secret, Bath & Body Works, and Abercrombie & Fitch are a few of the increasing number of retailers that have rediscovered the profit potential of main street. But not all retailers are appropriate for a new suburban main street, or for any main street for that matter.

"You cannot have major stores or big-box retailers on a pedestrian-oriented street," notes Kalvin Platt, chairman of the SWA Group, an international land planning and landscape architecture firm. "Their buildings and their parking lots are simply too big for the pedestrian-oriented main street scale."

Blazing the Trail: Three Pioneers

Construction of one of the first suburban main streets began in 1987. Fields Point

Development Company hired architects Andres Duany and Elizabeth Plater-Zyberk to redevelop the circa–1960 New Seabury Shopping Center in Mashpee, Massachusetts, into a three-block-long, pedestrian-oriented town center called Mashpee Commons, complete with stores, housing, a library, and a church.

In 1991, Crocker & Company completed the first phase of pedestrian-oriented, mixed-use Mizner Park in Boca Raton, Florida, on the site of the failing 420,000-square-foot Boca Raton Mall. Architects Cooper Carry & Associates created an instant community hub by designing a two-block-long village green ringed by low-rise buildings with shops and restaurants and entrances to them on the ground floors. The upper floors have offices or apartments.

In 1991, Mobil Land Development Corporation completed the first phase of Reston Town Center — the "big city" version of a traditional main street. The town center includes 530,000 square feet of office space, 200,000 square feet of stores and restaurants, an 11-screen movie theater, a 514-room Hyatt Regency Hotel, and a one-acre central plaza with a fountain. Parking structures and surface lots are located behind the buildings.

Schaumburg, Illinois: Municipality as Main Street Developer

Sometimes, a municipality — rather than a developer — is the catalyst behind a new main street. In recent decades, Schaumburg, Illinois, near Chicago's O'Hare International Airport, became one of the nation's largest, most successful edge cities. However, it had no town center, no unifying core. Then, several years ago, Schaumburg's village government purchased a run-down, half-empty retail center at Roselle and Schaumburg Roads, the community's traditional crossroads, along with several nearby parcels.

Land assemblage for this 29-acre site took several years. "Although we initiated condemnation proceedings on some properties," says Mayor Al Larson, "we did not go to court. Instead, we ended up negotiating the prices, using money from the larger tax-increment financing (TIF) district to purchase and redevelop the land." After completing site assemblage in 1995, the village of Schaumburg began selling parcels to developers. "We didn't want to own the center," Mayor Larson explains. "We just wanted to create a development plan to reflect our vision for the site and the community, and then sell the parcels to developers who would build our vision."

The key was attracting strong anchors to Town Square. Larson wanted one of these to be the Schaumburg Township Library, the second busiest library in the state. He knew the library wanted to relocate, and he sold it on Town Square. A 70,000-square-foot grocery store serves as the second anchor. Together with the library, it will generate strong retail traffic for the restaurants, stores, and other businesses that will surround the central square. A nearby residential project, with more than 100 upscale townhouses and some single-family houses, will bring additional foot traffic.

Schaumburg's new Town Square, designed by Hitchcock Design Group, is rapidly taking shape. An amphitheater, a park, ponds, and waterfalls have been built in the central square. A 55-foot-tall clock tower, the traditional icon of town squares for centuries, is already standing. The grocery store is open, and the shops and professional space on the south side of the square are completed and 80 percent occupied. Parking has been placed behind the buildings, so that visitors are not confronted by an ocean of parking when they arrive. The library, which will open this September, is expected to attract an estimated 1 million patrons a year.

Village Commons: Vernon Hills, Illinois

Several postwar Chicago suburbs are following Schaumburg's lead by planning and building a wide variety of new main streets. One of these is Vernon Hills, 35 miles northwest of Chicago. Incorporated in 1958, Vernon Hills has more than 3.5 million square feet of retail space. With a population of 20,000 and rising, it has been one of the fastest-growing municipalities in the state for the last two decades. Still the village wanted to improve its ability to compete with surrounding historic towns.

Vernon Hills is reviewing plans for the Village Commons, which will have a village green, a library, a hotel, retail space, residential uses, and a senior center. "We are trying to create some history and a sense of place," says Craig Malin, the village's assistant manager.

Part of the funding for Village Commons is coming from a $200,000 CMAQ (congestion mitigation air quality improvement) grant, which uses federal Intermodal Surface Transportation Efficiency Act (IS-TEA) funds. Using CMAQ formulas, the village was able to show that reconfiguring land usage and constructing a town square would reduce automobile emissions in Vernon Hills. The Chicago Area Transportation Study, CMAQ's Chicago metropolitan planning organization, is funding this new approach to pollution reduction.

Town Center Drive: Valencia, California

In the new town of Valencia, 30 miles north of downtown Los Angeles, the Newhall Land and Farming Company is now building a half-mile-long, pedestrian oriented main street called Town Center Drive, directly adjacent to the enclosed Valencia Town Center regional mall, which opened in 1991.

"The Valencia master plan, which was completed by planner Victor Gruen in 1965, designated this location as the community hub," explains James S. Backer, senior vice president of Newhall Land's commercial and industrial real estate division. Many industry leaders were thinking of an outdoor retail mall for this location, but Thomas L. Lee, Newhall Land's chairman and CEO, Tom Dierckman, president of Valencia Company, and Backer were main street boosters from the start.

A key component of the site plan was linking Town Center Drive with the Valencia Town Center regional mall. John Kriken, a partner with Skidmore, Owings & Merrill, LLP, had advised Newhall Land to break the traditional ring of mall parking and set aside an area for the mall's main entrance, with movie theaters, a working carousel, and fountains — all waiting to connect to Town Center Drive.

Wide sidewalks, shade trees, and benches line the new main street. The first two Town Center Drive buildings already are open and seven other buildings are under construction, including the 250-room Valencia Hyatt Hotel, an entertainment/retail complex, and office buildings, as well as several hundred apartments on the western end of the street.

Haile Village Center: Haile Plantation, Florida

In 1992, architect and developer Robert B. Kramer and his partner Matthew Kaskel began building a five-block-long main street at Haile Plantation, a master-planned community outside Gainesville, Florida. Kramer laid out Haile Village Center and designed about three-quarters of the relatively small white clapboard, tin-roofed professional buildings, most of which have apartments on the second floors.

The 50-acre project uses a network of bike paths to link Haile Village Center to the surrounding subdivisions. Popular events like a weekly farmers market help to lure residents to the new village center. More than 40 buildings already line the street. About half of the commercial property is owner occupied.

"We have the traditional mix of main street uses — plenty of shops, including a corner grocery store, a dry cleaners, a post office, a dentist, a stockbroker," says Kramer. "We didn't create a list and say 'We've got to have those people.' They came to us, so there must be a demand for our kind of main street." Future development projects include a town hall, a 100-unit apartment complex, an assisted-care facility, and a 75-unit lodge and conference center.

Roadblocks to Success

For all its benefits, the new suburban main street trend faces several roadblocks, including:

Expense. Many developers and municipalities cannot afford to fund such large, long-term development projects, particularly when they must pay today's high prices for land even as municipalities struggle with dwindling tax bases.

Site Assemblage. Like Schaumburg, most suburban cities will have to assemble their own main street sites. Will other municipalities have sufficient political support — and funds — to assemble these sites through negotiation or eminent domain?

Traffic Codes. Many jurisdictions require overly wide streets that spoil the intimate scale of pedestrian-oriented main streets and introduce high-speed traffic into their roadways.

Too Many Clones? The real estate industry's mania for formulas also threatens

the success of the new suburban main street trend. Developers and municipalities are notorious for replicating successful projects, rather than creating a distinctive streetscape that reflects their area's market, history, and demographics. Others take the main street "formula" and strip it down to cut costs, leaving residents with a cheap outdoor mall. "Big developers are already jumping on the main street bandwagon," warns Plater-Zyberk, "without understanding or appreciating the many intricate components that can make or break a public realm."

Too Little Too Late? Finally, trying to create a traditional, pedestrian-oriented main street in the midst of sprawling, automobile-dominated postwar suburbia may be impossible for most communities. Without careful planning, the results can be little more than nostalgic window dressing, like the faux turn-of-the-century storefront in a typical suburban mall.

But there is more upside than downside for this development trend. Touring developers and architects, for example, are flocking to Haile Plantation. "They come here," say Kramer, "and tell me, 'We don't have Disney's money to do something large and all at once, like Celebration. But if you can do it in small, market-driven increments, I guess we can do this kind of main street development, too.'"

Equally promising, developers of some vast mixed-use complexes are making new suburban main streets a key feature in their projects. The focal point of the Winmar Company's just-completed Redmond Town Center outside Seattle is a five-block-long new main street. Built on the site of a former golf course in Redmond, Washington, this 1.375-million-square-foot, mixed-use project, designed by LMN Architects, contains retail space, office buildings, multifamily housing, restaurants, an eight-screen cinema complex, a hotel, and 40 acres of parks and open space.

Main streets also are being included in

large downtown redevelopment plans. Rockville, Maryland, is in the beginning stages of replacing a failed downtown mall that physically divided its central business district with a $300 million, 1.5 million-square-foot, mixed-use development. Designed by Hellmuth, Obata & Kassabaum, the project includes a new four-block-long main street whose purpose is to unite and revitalize the downtown and create a community hub for the entire city.

"Building a main street from scratch," says Philip J. Enquist, a partner at Skidmore, Owings & Merrill, LLP, "take a total commitment from the city, the developers, and the community. Fortunately, dozens of communities are making that commitment. We are the only American generation to live without main streets. We may not have to live without them for much longer."

CHAPTER 4

DEVELOPMENT FOR PEOPLE AND WILDLIFE

Donald L. Elliott, AICP

America's wildlife is increasingly important to its citizens. As major urban and suburban areas have grown out into open lands, people are noticing that they can no longer see the large and small animals that they once took for granted. In addition, many communities have concluded that the protection of native wildlife is important to local and regional tourism, and to their ability to attract good jobs and a trained workforce. Those who enjoy recreational hunting and fishing have added their voices to the growing chorus asking for increased respect for wildlife, its habitat, and the ecological forces that sustain them. The focus on wildlife has quickly led to a focus on habitat, since that is one of the most important factors in the animals' survival, and one over which local governments have some degree of control.

All this attention has required that local planning staffs and planning commissioners become smarter about how to plan for the protection of wildlife and how to implement those plans. Fortunately, many land developers are becoming increasingly sophisticated about the incorporation of open spaces into their developments. They have learned that well-designed open space more than

pays for itself in terms of increased values on surrounding lots and parcels. However, successful strategies for protecting wildlife require more than just open space. They require at least a basic understanding of some of the principles of wildlife biology and an ability to apply those principles to different types of land and different scales of development.

Last year, we worked with wildlife biologists from Colorado State University to develop a handbook to help planning commissioners in Colorado understand these issues and apply them to both planning and development activities. The result, Managing Development for People and Wildlife, won a 1996 award from the Colorado chapter of the American Planning Association (APA). We later developed a national version of the handbook for the APA Planning Advisory Service as Where the Wild Things Are. This chapter presents some of the information from those reports in a condensed format; information on how to order the PAS (Planning Advisory Service) Report is found at the end of this volume in the National Resource Directory under the publisher's name.

Originally published as "Planning and Development for People and Wildlife," *The Commissioner*, Spring 1998. Published by the American Planning Association, Chicago, Illinois. Reprinted with permission of the publisher.

General Principles of Wildlife Planning

Like all fields of science, wildlife biology requires large amounts of data from expensive and time-consuming field research. It also requires very careful analysis and high standards of accuracy. As a result, the body of knowledge advances slowly, and it is seldom possible to "prove" that a specific action will, in fact, preserve a given species of wildlife over the long run. America's real estate market, on the other hand, operates in the "here and now," and constantly requires planning commissioners to make decisions whether or not they have all the information they want. To be effective planners and regulators of land use, we need to be able to summarize what we think we know about wildlife protection on the basis of available experience, even if it may later turn out to be wrong.

Working under these constraints, biologists from Colorado State University developed the following principles.

Seven Operational Principles of Habitat Protection

Principle 1 Be willing to use rules of thumb based on scientific findings that may someday prove to be false.

Principle 2 Understand that complex environmental problems do not have a single, scientific solution founded on "truth."

Principle 3 Begin all conservation plans with clearly stated, specific goals for wildlife protection. Identify what species are most important, and whether you are trying to make sure that some of the animals remain, or that many of the animals remain, or that the animals remain over a wide area of land.

Principle 4 Insist that the analysis used for setting conservation priorities can be understood by everyone who is affected by it.

Principle 5 Realize that all models are wrong, but some are useful.

Principle 6 Make plans adaptive by evaluating the consequences of actions. Learn by doing.

Principle 7 Seize opportunities to enhance wildlife habitat by intelligent design of developments.

The Question of Scale

In addition, it is important for commissioners and local decision makers to understand the importance of "scale" in wildlife planning. We found it most helpful to think in terms of two different scales: (1) the Landscape Scale — such as a valley, a city, or a region, and (2) the Site Scale — such as an individual PUD or development project. Different approaches to planning, and different tools for implementation, are necessary depending on the scale of the project being considered. Some of the differences are summarized below.

Protecting Wildlife at the Landscape Scale

At the landscape scale, many opportunities are present to protect wildlife because there are many ways in which development and infrastructure can be planned to protect major areas of habitat and the connections between them. In many cases, this is the most effective scale at which to "design in" wildlife habitat protection, because if major habitat areas and linkages have been protected, then the details of Site Scale planning become easier. To guide the thinking of local decision makers, we described the following "Seven Biological Principles for Habitat Protection at the Landscape Scale."

Principle 1 Maintain large, intact patches of native vegetation by preventing fragmentation of those patches by development. If all other values of habitat are equal, larger patches of habitat should be protected in preference to smaller ones.

Principle 2 Establish priorities for species protection and protect habitats that constrain the distribution and abundance of those species.

Principle 3 Protect rare landscape elements. Guide development toward areas of landscape containing "common" features.

Principle 4 Maintain connections among wildlife habitats by identifying and protecting corridors for movement. Identify and protect small patches of vegetation that provide "stepping stones" among large, core patches described above.

Principle 5 Maintain significant ecological processes in protected areas. Examples of ecological processes include periodic fires, floods, and scattering of habitat materials by wind.

Principle 6 Contribute to the regional persistence of rare species by protecting some of their habitat locally. In other words, local communities need to "think regionally, and act locally."

Principle 7 Balance the opportunity for recreation by the public with the habitat needs of wildlife. Assure that some protected areas remain in private ownership not open to the public, in order to reduce intensity of use by recreationists. Regulate recreational use of protected habitat on public land to minimize impacts on sensitive species.

Protecting Wildlife at the Site Scale

A different set of principles apply when planning or development reviews are conducted at the Site Scale. Different principles are necessary because the opportunities to protect wildlife habitat are more limited at this scale. If Landscape Scale planning has not preserved the large intact patches, connections, or rare vegetation that some species need to survive, then Site Scale planning cannot build on that foundation. Instead,

Site Scale planning often needs to focus on protecting smaller areas and linkages, on minimizing the "differentness" of the built environment, and on controlling the day-to-day impacts of human presence.

Five Biological Principles for Wildlife Conservation at the Site Scale

Since planning commissioners spend a lot of time reviewing specific proposed developments, we developed the following principles.

Principle 1 Maintain buffers between areas dominated by human activities and core areas of wildlife habitat. Limit human activities to one or more buffer zones surrounding a core area, with more intense activities restricted to more distant zones. If people must pass through the core area on foot or bicycle, limit them to a well-defined trail.

Principle 2 Facilitate wildlife movement across areas dominated by human activities. Provide alternatives to crossing busy roads, such as underpasses, especially during road construction. Minimize fencing types that inhibit the movement of wildlife species that are likely to occur in the area.

Principle 3 Minimize human contact with large native predators. Prevent wildlife from associating food with humans by exercising tight control over potential sources of nourishment such as garbage or food for domestic animals.

Principle 4 Control numbers of mid-sized predators, such as some pets and other species associated with human-dominated areas. Prevent domestic pets, especially dogs and cats, from roaming freely. As an alternative provide designated areas where people can exercise or "run" their pets.

Principle 5 Mimic features of the natural local landscape in developed areas. Keep levels of disturbance to trees, the understory, and other structural features to a minimum during construction. Design house lots in a fashion consistent with local natural habitats — by using native vegetation, for instance.

The Question of Location

In addition to the scale of planning and review, local staff and planning commissioners should think about the location of the proposed action: Is it rural, suburban, or urban? Wildlife habitat can often be protected in rural areas through the use of both Landscape Scale and Site Scale tools, since the abundance of open space and presence of the species affords many opportunities for creative design. On the other hand, wildlife protection in urban areas often has to be done at the Site Scale, because most of the land has already been developed in ways that are either friendly or unfriendly to the species in question. One exception, however, is planning for urban park and trail networks, where careful design and management can often allow wildlife to thrive along the open spaces that weave themselves through an urban area.

Planning for wildlife protection in suburban areas is particularly important — and sometimes challenging — because it draws on both Landscape and Site Scale tools. These challenges must be met, however, because suburban areas are the fastest growing areas in the U.S., and the areas in which potential habitat land is being lost at the fastest rate. Failure to use all of the tools available to protect habitat in suburban areas may have the largest impact on wildlife within a typical planning horizon of 20 years.

Opportunities and Challenges

Depending on whether the planning commission is considering a plan or project at the Landscape Scale or Site Scale, and depending on whether it is located in a rural, suburban, or urban setting, some of the principles of wildlife protection will be relatively easy to achieve, and some will be hard. The opportunities and challenges created by the scale and location of activity are summarized above.

This matrix can help guide planning commissioners, staff, and citizens as they consider how to protect wildlife in a given plan or project. For any given scale and location, the "opportunities" in the matrix represent those principles that should be able to be achieved without undue effort. These can serve as the baseline for solid wildlife habitat protection. The "challenges" for each scale and location represent those extra steps that should be incorporated to go beyond the baseline towards a strong system of protection. We hope that the approach, principles, and tools identified in this article will help result in better decisions for wildlife habitat protection in the years ahead.

CHAPTER 5

THE ECONOMIC BENEFITS
OF PARKS AND OPEN SPACE

Margaret C. H. Kelly and *Matthew Zieper*

In the past several years local, county, and state election results have clearly demonstrated that protecting open space is an issue of growing importance to American voters. In fact, voters will not only support land conservation initiatives, they also will authorize public funds to pay for such efforts.

The election returns speak for themselves. In 1999, 102 referenda to commit public funds to protect open space were placed before voters in 22 states. Ninety percent (92 referenda) passed, generating more than $1.8 billion in open space acquisition funds.[1] Voters accomplished this by authorizing new property taxes, sales taxes, real estate excise taxes, and general obligation bonds to protect special or unique landscapes.

These statistics, however, tell only part of the story. State and local governments across the United States also launched open-space initiatives that did not require referenda. For example, Illinois Governor George Ryan signed a bill that gave communities $160 million to buy open space and Montgomery County, Maryland, announced a $100 million program to fund open space.[2]

Development of open space is hardly a new phenomenon; however, it has experienced a renaissance of extraordinary scale in the post–World-War-II era. During this period, there has been a trend away from older communities and a demand by the middle class for newer, single-use housing on individual lots. While open space everywhere is being converted to other uses, fast-growing corridors clustered near metropolitan areas perhaps have seen the most pressure for housing and other development. For example, total population of the biggest cities in the United States' 39 largest metropolitan areas has grown by one million over the past 20 years. During this same period, however, total suburban population of these 39 metropolitan areas has grown by 30 million.[3]

These new tracts of suburbia and industry arrive mostly at the expense of an ever-shrinking reserve of public and private open space. Currently, the United States has 400 million acres of land in agricultural production — 20 percent of the total land base. Likewise, 600 million acres — 30 percent of the United States — is comprised of forests and wetlands.[4] These figures represent significant acreage, but they are dwindling at a rapid and steady pace. According to the American Farmland Trust, between 1982

Originally published as "Financing for the Future: The Economic Benefits of Parks and Open Space," *Government Finance Review*, Vol. 16, No. 6, December 2000. Published by the Government Finance Officers Association, Chicago, Illinois. Reprinted with permission of the publisher.

and 1992, 400,000 acres of prime agricultural land were lost to urban and suburban development. On average, this works out to 45.7 acres per day.[5]

The pressure on open space is unprecedented and apparent to a general public that for more than a century has been reluctant to abandon the pioneer-era mentality that American resources are boundless and inexhaustible. The recent groundswell of public opinion that has moved local, regional, and state governments to action on behalf of remaining open space is fueled by the public's desire to have a say in the rate and location of future development.

Arguments for Open Space

Each community, county, or state has its own reason or reasons for deciding to fund open space acquisition or enhance existing open, but unproductive, space (e.g., brownfields). Several of these reasons are discussed in more detail below.

The Costs of New Development Often Exceed Local Tax Revenues. Community leaders generally expect that taxes generated by local growth will pay for the increased costs of development, but in many instances this is not the case. A 1998 study by the Trust for Public Land (TPL) examined the relationship between land conservation and property taxes in Massachusetts. The study found that in the short term, property taxes generally rose after a land conservation project. In the longer term, however, those Massachusetts towns with the most protected land enjoyed, on average, the lowest property tax rates.[6] It is entirely possible for the longer-term costs of development — roads, schools, sewer and water infrastructure, fire and police service — to exceed the revenues from increased property taxes.

The conclusions drawn in the TPL Massachusetts study have been replicated in other parts of the country, as well. In Louden County, Virginia (the fastest growing county in the Washington, D.C., area), the costs to service 1,000 new development units exceeded their tax contribution by $2.3 million.[7] In fact, when long-term costs are considered, towns often conclude that they cannot afford *not* to buy some of their prime remaining open space.

Other studies done in DuPage County, Illinois, and Morris County, New Jersey, suggested that even commercial development may cost taxpayers in the final analysis. In addition to making demands on community resources, commercial development often attracts residential sprawl and puts further strain on local services.[8]

To implement smart growth, a community must decide what space needs to be protected for recreation, community character, the conservation of natural resources, and open space. These decisions are unique to each community and are often controversial. After all, few, if any, communities can afford to save every neighborhood field or woodlot. However, making these decisions helps shape growth appropriately and control costs.

Open Space, Parks, and Outdoor Recreation Opportunities Attract New Businesses and Increase Real Estate Values. In a 1995 poll conducted by the Regional Plan Association and the Quinnipac College Polling Institute, respondents cited low crime with safe streets and access to greenery and open space as the major criteria for a satisfactory quality of life.[9]

The parks/open space quality of life factor provides at least two more benefits to communities. First, communities that make parks, open space, and outdoor recreation a priority generally have enhanced property values. This is particularly true of the properties near or adjacent to the open space, parks, or recreation sites. For example, in Oakland, California, a three-mile greenbelt around Lake Merritt added approximately

$41 million to surrounding property values.[10] Likewise, in Seattle, Washington, homes bordering the 12-mile Burke Gilman trail sold for 6 percent more than other homes of comparable size.[11]

Second, quality of life and easy access to outdoor recreational opportunities attract new businesses to a community or region. This is evermore true as the United States moves toward a mixed economy based on services, light industry, consumer goods, and new technologies. Businesses and their employees are no longer tied to traditional industrial centers. Instead, businesses look for an appealing location that suits both work and leisure needs. In fact, corporate CEOs say that quality of life for employees is the third-most important factor in deciding where to locate a business, behind access to domestic markets and availability of skilled labor.[12]

Chattanooga, Tennessee, is a good example of a city that thrived following a late 1980s collaboration by local governments, businesses, and community groups to rebuild deteriorating quality of life and fight rising unemployment and crime. The environmentally progressive redevelopment of Chattanooga's downtown riverfront was funded by $356 million of public and private investment. Between 1988 and 1996 the number of businesses and full-time jobs in the district more than doubled and assessed property values rose by at least $11 million (127.5 percent). In this same period, the combined city and county property tax revenues grew by $592,000 (99 percent).[13]

Urban Open Space Rejuvenates City Neighborhoods and Attracts Businesses and Tourist Dollars. In the 1850s, famous landscape architect Frederick Law Olmsted argued that the purchase of land for New York City's Central Park would be justified by the increase in value of adjacent properties, and hence increased tax revenues. He was right. By 1864, there was a nearly

$60,000 net return in annual taxes beyond what the city was paying in interest on the land and improvements. By 1873 the park — which had cost the city $14 million overall — was responsible for an extra $5.24 million in taxes per year.[14]

Central Park, however, has done more than raise property values and city taxes. The park also draws millions of residents and tourists to its attractions and those of nearby hotels, restaurants, and businesses.

Other cities have similar — and more current — tales of urban rejuvenation. Many involve brownfields — former industrial sites that have some level of contamination from their industrial pasts and will require cleanup before they can be put to new use. Even with the costs of environmental cleanup factored in, a recycled parcel is often less expensive to develop than virgin land because it already is serviced by roads, utilities, and other infrastructure. Brownfield development also reduces the pressure to develop farms and other open space. For example, in North Birmingham, Alabama, an abandoned steel mill has been reclaimed by an industrial byproducts resale business. With 30 employees, this business is the first tenant on the 900-acre brownfield. Eventually, additional new businesses on the site may employ 2,000 people in this economically depressed neighborhood.[15]

Not all urban renewal projects involve brownfields. In Boston, Massachusetts, in the early 1980s, a public-private partnership demolished a 500,000-square-foot concrete parking garage in the heart of the financial district and created a privately funded underground parking facility topped with the Park at Post Office Square. This park features a formal garden and lawns, a walk-through sculpture fountain, and café — and is visited by as many as 2,000 people each day. Furthermore, the city receives $1 million each year for its ownership interest in the underground garage and another $1 million in annual taxes. After the construction debt is paid off, the ownership of the garage and park will revert to the city.[16]

The American Tourism Industry Is Heavily Dependent on Local, State, and National Parks and Other Open Space of Scenic, Ecological, or Historic Importance. Nationwide, parks, protected rivers, scenic lands, wildlife habitat, and recreational open space contribute to a $502 billion tourism industry. As one of the country's largest employers, tourism supports seven million jobs.[17] Outdoor recreation (hiking, biking, paddling, fishing, etc.) generated at least $40 billion in 1996 and accounted for 768,000 full-time jobs and $13 billion in annual wages.[18] In fact, river rafters on only one of West Virginia's famous white water rivers — the Gauley — pump $20 million per year into the local economy.[19] Similarly, river rafting, and kayaking contribute $50 million per year to the Colorado state coffers, while the state of Arkansas reaps $1.5 billion annually from all types of outdoor recreation.[20]

Many communities recognize that their natural resources have value to outsiders that translates into local economic benefits and are protecting these resources accordingly. In Stowe, Vermont, for example, people come to vacation year round, drawn by the mountains and the traditional rural and agricultural vistas. For these reasons, Stowe requires that developers seeking building permits guarantee the preservation of scenic views and signature landscapes. Many developers have supported these stringent requirements, believing that by preserving the area's character they also are protecting their investments.[21]

Protected Farm and Ranchland Generate Economic Stability for Agricultural Communities and Preserve Historic Open Landscapes. Not only does agricultural open space represent a traditional American way of life, it also provides a steady annual inflow of dollars to host communities. In 1998, the Growth Alternatives Alliance in Fresno County, California (the nation's top producing agricultural county), issued a report entitled, "A Landscape of Choice: Strategies for Improving Patterns of Community Growth." According to the report, each acre of irrigated land produces between $6,000 and $12,000 per year for the local economy. Thus, each acre lost reduces the local domestic product accordingly.[22]

Of course, development often brings new sources of local revenue in the form of property and other taxes. However, more than 40 studies in 11 states have found that farms often save communities money by contributing more in taxes than they demand in tax-supported services. For example, in Hebron, Connecticut, farms required $0.43 in services for every dollar they generate in taxes. In contrast, residential properties in the same town required an average of $1.06 in services for every tax dollar. Similarly, in Dunn, Wisconsin, farmland required $0.18 in services per tax dollar, and residential development cost taxpayers $1.06 for each tax dollar collected.[23]

To combat the loss of farmland, states and communities are increasingly turning to the purchase of development rights to agricultural land and restricting this land to farm, woodland, or other open space use. Purchase of Development Rights (PDR) programs began in the eastern United States and spread west across the country. Fifteen states and dozens of county and local governments now sponsor PDR programs. State PDR programs have protected more than 470,000 acres. Maryland, alone, with one of the oldest state PDR programs (1977), has protected almost 140,000 acres of farmland.[24]

Watershed, Wetland, and Floodplain Open Space Protection Enhance Drinking Water Quality and Minimize Economic Damages from Flooding. According to the U.S. Army Corps of Engineers, flood damages in the United States average $4.3 billion per year.[25] However, protected floodplain contains no property to be damaged and serves as a "safety valve" for flooding by reducing destruction to downstream areas. A 1993 study by the Illinois State Water Survey found that every 1 percent increase in protected wetlands along a stream corridor reduces peak stream flows by 3.7 percent.[26]

Since 1960, floods along California's Napa River have caused an average of $10 million per year in property damages ($500 million total). For years, engineers have attempted to mitigate the damages with levees and concrete fortified banks, yet seasonal floods still risk lives, damage property, and disrupt the valley's lucrative tourist trade. To break this cycle, in 1998, county voters allocated $160 million to acquire 500 acres of floodplain, raise bridges, lower levees, and purchase and demolish homes, businesses, and a trailer park that lie on the floodplain.[27] This newly created floodplain will provide the additional benefits of open space, wildlife habitat, or even farmland as the community sees fit.

Other Benefits

In addition to the benefits of open space previously discussed, open land enables nature to perform life-sustaining services that alternatively might be provided technologically (at great expense). These services include:

- degradation of organic wastes;
- filtration of pollutants from soil and water;
- buffering of air pollutants;
- moderation of climate change;
- conservation of soil and water;
- provision of medicines, pigments, and spices;
- preservation of genetic diversity; and
- pollination of food crops and other plants.

Many communities are facing issues related to water quantity and/or quality. Widespread development often results in increased coverage by impervious surfaces (e.g., roads and rooftops) that shunt water away from aquifers and into culverts and streams. As communities nationwide face the cost of treating polluted drinking water, or looking to new sources of water for local needs, there is a growing realization that keeping water clean is almost always cheaper than cleaning it post-contamination. Recognizing this, Congress has authorized the use of a portion of federal clean water funds for watershed acquisition.

New York City's resolved water supply crisis is a good example of one of the many ways that protected open space can provide a cost-effective and life-sustaining service. Manhattan's primary sources of drinking water are located upstate. These traditional sources of water, however, were seriously threatened by encroaching development. To protect its clean drinking water, the city agreed to spend $1.5 billion to preserve 80,000 acres of an upstate New York watershed. The alternative to the open space solution involved construction of an $8 billion water filtration plant with an operating budget of $300 million per year.[28]

Conclusion

From New York to New Mexico, California to Connecticut, state and local governments are coping with the challenges of growth — namely, how to balance the need for continued growth with consideration for preserving natural resources and quality of life. Instead of dismissing parks and open space as unaffordable luxuries, savvy government and civic leaders are embracing them as ways to grow smarter, foster economic development, and protect the fiscal bottom line while conserving critical natural resources. This trend has been gaining steam in recent years, with voters across the country approving billions of dollars to protect land for parks and open space. The choice is clear — parks and open space pay big dividends for state and local governments.

Notes

1. *Voters Invest in Open Space, 1999 Referenda Results*, The Land Trust Alliance, Washington, D.C.

2. *Ibid.*

3. The Smart Growth Network — see http://www.smartgrowth.org/ISSUEAREAS/regionalism.html.

4. The Smart Growth Network — see http://www.smartgrwth.org/ISSUEAREAS/landuse.html.

5. *Ibid.*

6. Brighton, Deb, "Community Choices: Thinking Through Land Conservation, Development, and Property Taxes in Massachusetts" (Boston, MA: Trust for Public Land, 1998). Also see http://www.tpl.org/tech.

7. Parks and Open Space. Orig. footnote: National Park Service, Rivers, Trails and Conservation Assistance Program, "Economic Impacts of Protecting Rivers, Trails, and Greenway Corridors," 4th ed. (Washington, DC: National Park Service, 1995), pp. 8–14.

8. Parks and Open Space. Orig. footnote: Elizabeth Brabec, "On the Value of Open Spaces," *Scenic America*, Technical Information Series, Vol. 1, No. 2 (Washington, DC: Scenic America, 1992), p. 2.

9. Lerner, Steve and Poole, William, "The Economic Benefits of Parks and Open Space — How Land Conservation Helps Communities Grow Smart and Protect the Bottom Line" (San Francisco, CA: Trust for Public Land, 1999), p. 14.

10. *Ibid.*, p. 13.

11. *Ibid.*, p. 13.

12. Parks and Open Space. Orig. footnote: National Park Service, 1995, pp. 7–13.

13. *Ibid.* Orig. footnote: Statistics from Chattanooga News Bureau and Hamilton County, Tennessee, tax assessor.

14. *Ibid.* Orig. footnote: Tom Fox, "Urban Open Space: An Investment that Pays," A Monograph Series (New York, NY: Neighborhood Open Space Coalition, 1990), pp. 11–12.

15. Lerner, Steve and Poole, William, "The Economic Benefits of Parks and Open Space — How Land Conservation Helps Communities Grow Smart and Protect the Bottom Line," p. 19.

16. Parks and Open Space. Orig. footnote: Harnick, Peter, "The Park at Post Office Square," in Garvin and Berens, 1997, p. 150.

17. *Ibid.* Orig. footnote: National Park Service, 1995, pp. 3–5.

18. *Ibid.* Orig. footnote: Outdoor Recreation Coalition of America, "Economic Benefits of Outdoor Recreation," State of the Industry Report (1997) — see http://www.outdoorlink.com/orca/research/97SOI.

19. *Ibid.* Orig. footnote: National Park Service, Rivers, Trails and Conservation Assistance Program, "Economic Impacts of Protecting Rivers, Trails, and Greenway Corridors," 3rd ed. (Washington, DC: National Park Service, 1992), pp. 5–6.

20. *Ibid.* Orig. footnote: National Park Service, 1995, pp. 2–8.

21. Lerner, Steve and Poole, William, "The Economic Benefits of Parks and Open Space — How Land Conservation Helps Communities Grow Smart and Protect the Bottom Line," p. 24.

22. Parks and Open Space. Orig. footnote: The Growth Alternatives Alliance, "A Landscape of Choice: Strategies for Improving Patterns of Community Growth" (Fresno, CA: The Growth Alternatives Alliance, April 1998), pp. 7–8.

23. *Ibid.* Orig. footnote: American Farmland Trust, "Saving American Farmland: What Works" (Washington, DC: American Farmland Trust, 1997), p. 150.

24. *Ibid.* Orig. footnote: Daniels, pp. 182–183.

25. *Ibid.* Orig. footnote: U.S. Army Corps of Engineers, Total Damages Suffered in FY 1997. http://www.usace.army.mil/inet/functions/cw/cecwe/table2.htm.

26. *Ibid.* Orig. footnote: Demissie, Misganaw and Khan, Abdul, "Influence of Wetlands on Streamflow in Illinois" (Champaign, IL: Illinois State Water Survey, October, 1993).

27. *Ibid.* Orig. footnote: Egam, Timothy, "For a Flood-Weary Napa Valley, A Vote to Let the River Run Wild," *New York Times* (April 25, 1998), p. A1. Statistics updated by Howard Siegel, project planner, Napa River Flood Control Project.

28. *Ibid.* Orig. footnote: Trust for Public Land, "Watershed Initiatives, Introduction," http://www.tpl.org.

Part II
The Best Practices

CHAPTER 6

ATLANTA BUILDS PARKS TO CREATE OPEN SPACES

Barbara Faga

Big downtown parks are back, Atlanta's Centennial Olympic Park — the largest new inner-city park built in the last quarter of the 20th century — and San Francisco's Yerba Buena Gardens soon will be followed by a major urban central park at Denver's Stapleton airport redevelopment, and comparable public spaces in Pittsburgh and Chicago. Projects in such cities as Chattanooga, Tennessee, and Modesto, California, are more limited in scale, but equally keyed to an urban core. Meanwhile, historic spaces like New York's Bryant Park and Washington, D.C.'s, Franklin Square have been rescued from decay and revamped as lively urban focal points.

There have been a number of changes over the years in the revitalization of downtown parks, including more private and public/private funding, and an emphasis on activity and a sense of place rather than a focus on pastoral escape. The ability of a well-timed, well-conceived park to generate both short- and long-term value is in keeping with the experience of more than 200 years.

While American cities have never stopped building parks, between World War II and the 1990s parkland was often treated as a utilitarian recreational amenity and often begrudgingly maintained. New parks typically involved preserved watersheds and woodlands left by suburban development, or narrow riverfronts abandoned by industry and not fit for much else. Older city parks, including the great "icon" parks designed by the Olmsteds and others between about 1870 and 1920, often seemed lost to decay and crime. Mid-century modern architects rarely considered parks interesting in themselves. By 1961, even the humanist critic Lewis Mumford could publish the 650-page *The City in History* with barely one mention of "park" in the index.

It took another generation — excited by preserving and exploring urban history, and revitalizing rather than reforming cities — to see parks once more as centers of urban design and urban life. William H. "Holly" Whyte, like Central Park codesigner Frederick Law Olmsted, a prolific journalist, led the way by observing and recording how people actually use urban open space. The neighborhood meetings and workshops that exist today reveal similar specific wish lists of both active and passive uses for parks. These days, parks seldom serve as escape valves for overcrowded industrial cities;

Originally published as "Parks Downtown," *Urban Land*, Vol. 60, No. 7, July 2001. Published by the Urban Land Institute, Washington, D.C. Reprinted with permission of the publisher.

more often, they help inject life into low-density cores, as in the pioneering culture parks at Yerba Buena and Paris's La Villette.

Amid renewed interest in cities, public life, and public places, urban parks are in. Architect/writer Witold Rybczynski made parks a major topic of his recent book *City Life*, depicting their openness and mobility — and decay and rebirth — as keys to understanding North American cities. In the Urban Land Institute's recently published *Inside City Parks*, author Peter Harnik surveys 25 representative U.S. cities and finds that they spend more than $500 million a year on capital building and rebuilding.

The new attitude toward downtown open space has plenty to do with the renewed competitive energy of inner cities as places for knowledge and service professionals to live and work, and as destinations for entertainment and tourism. At the same time, this renewed energy goes back 200 years or more to English designer/developers like John Wood (Bath's Royal Crescent), John Nash (Regent's Park in London), and their successors.

How much value parks add always is hard to quantify, admits Atlanta's Dan Graveline, whose Georgia World Congress Center Authority (GWCC), a state agency, created and now owns and manages Centennial Olympic Park. Employing an ad hoc 501(c)3 catalyst group named Centennial Olympic Park Area, Inc., (COPA) and using no public money, Graveline and his team assembled 60 acres of parking lots and other semi-brownfield downtown land fronting the GWCC's key sports and convention locations at pre–Olympic prices no higher than $2 a square foot.

Partly developed as the six-acre, $18 million centerpiece for the 1996 Olympics, the 21-acre park was finished the next year for an added $12 million, with the remaining land made available for private, mixed-use development. With about half the park frontage now committed to projects ranging from super-luxury condominiums and a hotel to new facilities for CNN and the Coca-Cola Company, the value of that development today is near $1 billion. Property values now are $200 a foot and climbing.

As good as that is, however, there are added direct and indirect economic benefits to the owners and to Atlanta — less quantifiable and taking longer to mature, but also less dependent on the national economic boom. In fact, the most successful such projects have long been a multifaceted overlay of art, social purpose, and commerce, as the granddaddy of big U.S. city parks still reminds us.

Central Park, which (with the Brooklyn Bridge) *New York Times* design critic Paul Goldberger calls New York's greatest work of architecture, may also be its greatest real estate investment. Considering only land, the city's purchase of 843 acres of distinctly suburban land for $5.8 million, a gamble in 1856, in effect generated the incremental land values and rents of Fifth Avenue and Central Park West, where today apartments with park views alone sell for $5.8 million. But how can the value of Central Park be quantified as a tourist attraction — enhanced after two decades of restoration of architect Calvert Vaux's buildings and enforcement of higher standards of cleanliness and safety? Or its value as a photographer's favorite — consider the advertising value to the Plaza hotel alone? Or as a venue for public celebrations and events, a place for free Shakespeare and free rock concerts? Or as a site for such profitable restaurants as Tavern on the Green? Or — as Olmsted predicted — a social safety valve. Large and small, these and other benefits from Central Park have contributed for decades to New York's real estate and business economy, and its intangible leadership among world cities. Yet, none of this was preordained or permanent.

Although clearly in the path of development, in the 1850s the site of Central Park was a semirural brownfield of shacks and tanneries. More than a little vision was required. Far from simply preserving nature, Olmsted, as both superintendent and codesigner, and Vaux took the land apart and reworked it with a thoroughness, and artifice, rivaling modern theme parks. The project's instant success helped Olmsted launch what became the country's first national-scale design firm, preceding the first large architecture and engineering firms by decades, and create vast, sophisticated park systems throughout North America at a time when few cities employed a trained planner.

To be sure, not all parks have proved to be real estate bonanzas. Beyond design lies maintenance, and beyond that, real stewardship. From the beginning, Olmsted fought encroachments on Central Park as well as mismanagement and neglect, and it has weathered many crises since, as both patterns of use and the city's commitment to the public realm have changed.

More than a century later, and on a far different scale, Centennial Olympic Park is still recognizable as a revival of the Central Park idea, with its own mix of short- and long-term, and tangible and intangible rewards and challenges. As a prototype for the current downtown park revival, its key ingredients include:

• The initial opportunity to acquire underused, semibrownfield property near the core — an ingredient of many low- and medium-density U.S. cities. (In current projects in Dayton, Ohio, and in Pittsburgh, the sites involve a riverfront, but the locations are still closer to the center of town than the edge.);

• The need to provide a better setting and better access for existing properties, in this case the Georgia Dome, the convention center, and Phillips Arena; as Graveline point outs, this need alone justified replacing derelict blocks with a park;

• The challenge and the opportunity of presenting the 1996 Centennial Olympics,

which was a galvanizing force that accelerated and focused the effort;

• The attraction of a "pure" real estate venture, allowing an imaginative leap from a wasteland to a prime parkside address that can, and here did, succeed handsomely;

• The chance to create a public amenity with 100 percent private funding through the quasi-public COPA as development agency and broker, and the quasi-private Georgia World Congress Center as park owner/manager;

• The unusual status of the property as a Georgia state park, which enabled special tax and zoning tools, and the possible use of imminent domain;

• The existence of well-funded, interested neighbors like CNN and Coca-Cola;

• The unfulfilled market for downtown luxury housing, quality hotel rooms (always logically located next to the convention center, but previously scared off by the setting), and other upscale mixed uses;

• The market for revenue-generating activities in the park itself, from one-time outdoor fairs and corporate receptions to daily vendors, with natural synergy created by the adjacent sports and convention facilities — an example of what Whyte disciple Fred Kent, president of the nonprofit Project for Public Spaces, would call "triangulation"; and

• The city government, tourism/hospitality industry, business community, and general public all eager to boost Atlanta's image — and promote their own interests — with a new, photogenic urban setting.

Additional aspects of the project might be thought of as post–Olmsted design. Most fundamental, perhaps, is the shift from the idea of park as refuge from the city's bustle, to parts that — at least in some places — actually add bustle, although in fairness, Olmsted designs often provide lively open areas like Central Park's Bethesda Terrace where people can see and be seen. This comes in part from today's more active tastes in recreation, and in part from the need to prime the pump of downtown revival with visible urban excitement.

In cities where lack of density and isolation have replaced crowding and noise as major problems, new parks like Atlanta's must often double as plazas, making physical and visual connections among previously separated streets and neighborhoods, and providing a variety of magnet stages for daily activities and special events. Centennial Park's design device of a quilt is a metaphor for community and a symbol of regional history — part of today's interest in narrative urban landscapes that celebrate a city's particularity, rather than support a rural fantasy. But it also is a fairly direct expression of the pedestrian routes that now cross and meet at the park.

Connection and visibility also serve the need for security, an ever-changing but constant concern for America's open, democratic parks, as it was in Olmsted's time. Today's park designs not only omit the shadowy bosques and crags of Victorian landscapes, they also avoid all sharply elevated or sunken areas to increase both real and perceived safety. Bright, even theatrical lighting where appropriate, as with Atlanta's light towers, can also make places feel both more secure and more engaging.

Centennial Olympic Park is still a place in progress, already evolving from its Olympic fame toward becoming the center of a downtown residential and commercial neighborhood. As for its economic value, the evidence can be seen in more than mere statistics. CNN, for example, has in effect moved the front of its building around to face the park.

As for the next evolution of the Central Park model, the new urban neighborhood on the site of Denver's former Stapleton International Airport provides an example. At 4,700 acres, the project is less a neighborhood than a town (12,000 housing units, 3 million square feet of retail, 10 million square feet of office and tech space) about to be attached to adjacent downtown Denver. An 1,100-acre open-space plan, which includes a 250-acre first phase of neighborhood squares, playing fields, and connecting greenways, will feed into a true central park — in fact, "Central Park" is its working name — roughly 1,000 feet wide and nearly a mile long. While built on the almost blank slate of Stapleton's former runways, the park and its design will grow out of several influences. One is a streambed, long hidden under the airstrip, which will be restored. Another is Denver's tradition of fine old Olmsted-designed city parks, which this added "central park" will explicitly recall. Overall, this Stapleton park will expand the city's park system by 25 percent. A third influence is the expansive view of plains and distant mountains from the large open site, which has led to the design of both rolling mounds and a flat, prairielike meadow.

And yet, with all these influences, the park still will clearly be the result of design, rather than pure forces of nature. A bold diagonal connector, a central gathering space, a music bowl, and a clearly human-planted "urban forest" that will act as a "stroll garden" for adjacent office workers suggest a purpose-created space targeting active, sports-minded families — clearly an artifact of the 21st century.

"A great object of all that is done in a park, of all the art of a park, is to influence the minds of men through their imaginations," Frederick Law Olmsted wrote back in the 1800s. After 150 years, Olmsted's insight that parks could define the city, increase the value of property within it, and enhance the quality of life of its citizens still holds true.

CHAPTER 7

BALTIMORE USES LINEAR TRAILS TO LINK NEIGHBORHOODS TO HARBOR DISTRICT

Martin J. Rosen

Until several years ago, the meandering stream corridor in the Gwynns Falls Valley, in Baltimore, Maryland, was scoured by floods, piled with trash, and all but abandoned by the residents of the middle- and low-income neighborhoods through which it passed. Back in the early 1900s, the sons of Frederick Law Olmsted had envisioned the 14-mile-long stream corridor as a linear urban park to be anchored by the existing 1,400-acre Gwynns Falls/Leakin Park. But the vision was never realized and the downward spiral of the stream corridor escalated over the last 30 years.

Now, thanks to funding from local philanthropies, state and municipal government, and the federal Intermodal Surface Transportation Efficiency Act (ISTEA) for the park's construction — along with the acquisition of an additional 35 acres — the Gwynns Falls Trail soon will link Baltimore's neighborhoods to the city's redeveloped harbor district — and, just as important, to a new spirit of urban possibility.

This park project and other similar projects reveal a major shift in the way parks and open space are being created and revi-

talized in U.S. cities. Since the early 1980s, federal government support for local parks and open space — through the Land and Water Conservation Fund state grant program — has been slashed, even in the face of rising need. A 1994 study by the National Recreation and Park Association showed that $30.7 billion of state and local recreational investment would be needed between 1995 and 1999 in order to meet public demand. With the decline in federal support and the tendency of cities to cut park budgets when money is tight, many of our urban parks are in dire need of repair and rejuvenation, and money is simply not available.

Recognizing that the need for parks does not go away, cash-strapped states and cities are scrambling to raise local money and take advantage of private funds. At the same time, there is a growing belief that the most successful parks emerge from broad community participation and contribute bankable value to nearby residential and commercial districts. This confluence of forces is leading to new public/private partnerships to create, rejuvenate, and sometimes manage urban parks and open space.

Originally published as "Reviving Urban Parks," *Urban Land*, Vol. 56, No. 11, November 1997. Published by the Urban Land Institute, Washington, D.C. Reprinted with permission of the publisher.

In 1994, The Trust for Public Land (TPL) created the Green Cities Initiative to help cities meet the need for more parks by providing assistance in real estate acquisition, finance, and negotiations, and by exploring new ways of involving communities in public finance strategies and park management. While every park is different, successful park efforts share two or more of the following characteristics:

- A formal planning and "visioning" process involving a broad spectrum of public and private stakeholders;
- Catalytic leadership from the public and private sectors;
- A strong connection between parks and open space and broader goals such as economic development, community identity, neighborhood renewal, and provision of needed services;
- A mix of private and public funding, with public funds often coming from state or local sources;
- The advice and assistance of nonprofit partners such as academics; urban planning groups; local civic, community gardening, and "friends-of-parks" organizations; and conservation real estate specialists such as TPL.

Such stakeholder-driven, public/private partnerships will be a primary force in America's future urban park efforts. The challenge of the modern urban parks movement is to ensure that these partnerships develop productively and equitably. From what has been accomplished so far, successful parks will depend on visioning, team building, broad community support, and creative financing and real estate skills. Just as important, new public/private partnerships will have to be forged to maintain and manage parks, so that the great parks created today will remain great parks tomorrow.

If there is a single danger in the public/private approach, it is the risk of sending the wrong message about the need for public sector funds and leadership. Private money can no more bear the entire cost of park creation than public money can, and in a time of rising need, governments need to appropriate more funds for parks, not less. Similarly, the public sector must take the lead in creating change. It is the public sector that must call for community investment in parks, create the visioning process, and invest in the master plans and documents that will get private partners involved. Healthy partnerships cannot be sustained without a substantial public commitment.

Successful Parks/Successful Partnerships

A successful park is more than an island of green space marooned in the concrete of the city. Its success emerges from its relationship to surrounding development and from the special features that attract users and make the park central to a city's image and personality. Its success is also related to the value it provides to the community — be it economic or qualitative value. Success depends not only on good planning and sound execution of park design, but also on continued public/private support for and involvement in park programming and management. In most cities, the era when a simple purchase of land by the city would lead to the creation of a city-envisioned and -designed park is gone. Instead, park creation and redevelopment involve putting together a development team, assembling land (often from multiple and diverse owners and users), raising funds from sources outside the city budget, and ensuring participatory planning every step of the way.

Significant strides have been made toward building productive partnerships. In communities across the country, committed and visionary leaders are beginning to understand the power that parks have in knitting together the frayed urban fabric. But no matter where the impetus comes from, the most successful partnerships include the widest range of stakeholders. The most obvious of these are government, business, and charitable foundations, who may together provide the major financial support for a park project. One significant national foundation partner is the Lila Wallace-Reader's Digest Fund (LWRDF), which has invested $15 million to create and improve urban parks in 11 cities and to share lessons with public and nonprofit leaders about best practices in the field. The LWRDF supported TPL's research on urban park needs in the early 1990s. In 1994, with the foundation's continuing support, TPL launched its Green Cities Initiative to bring its deal-making, fundraising, and park-planning skills to a wide range of public and private urban partners.

But the most important partners in any park plan may be nearby residents and neighborhood groups. The time should be long past when political leaders and professional park designers create parks for — instead of with — neighborhoods. The success of any park depends on how it is used; to ensure neighborhood involvement and support, professional designers and facilitators can use community meetings, written surveys, and individual interviews to lead local residents — the ultimate users — through the visioning process.

What is sometimes not understood about the park visioning and planning process is the extent to which it can transcend creation of a specific park or open space and deal with larger questions about community identity and purpose: What kind of city do we want to become? What role will parks play in our community? How do we want open space resources to be distributed in our city? What social and economic benefits do we want parks to provide? How will park programs serve city residents? And how will residents resolve conflicts over these issues?

There are success stories worthy of examination across the country. For example,

the creation of Cedar Lake Park and Trail in Minneapolis, Minnesota, reveals a city that prizes nature, bicycle transportation, active recreation, and citizen initiative. Similarly, the process that created Downtown Park in Bellevue, Washington, suggests a city that has used a park to create a sense of place and encourage a pedestrian-friendly, densely populated center. Mill Race Park, in Columbus, Indiana, shows that the city prizes volunteerism and cooperative effort. And in Spartanburg, South Carolina, Flagstar Corporate Plaza and Jerome Richardson Park are examples of a city committed to downtown revival.

In some instances, a major park project simply cannot get off the ground until a community answers larger questions about how the park might shape and confirm its future. In Seattle, voters have twice rejected efforts to create an 86-acre "commons" in a lower-income, light-industrial neighborhood north of downtown. Seattle Commons has been supported by the mayor and city council, generous contributions from corporations and philanthropies, and enthusiastic volunteers and professional staff. But other Seattle residents have worried about gentrification, rising rents and land prices, and the diversion of city resources from smaller neighborhood parks. If and when this park is created, it will be stronger and more successful because the process has addressed these issues to the satisfaction of most residents.

Whether Baltimore would become the kind of city that links its neighborhoods to larger community resources is a question to be answered, in part, by the creation of the Gwynns Falls Trail. For two decades, Baltimore had been working to rejuvenate its downtown harbor district as a cultural, recreational, and retail showplace. In this context, Baltimore officials and residents began looking toward the western neighborhoods, which are joined to the harbor by the lush — though trash-strewn — ribbon of

Gwynns Falls. Plans for the prime open space began taking shape in 1988, when the late Ralph Jones, Baltimore's park director, challenged the Yale School of Forestry and Environmental Studies to help create a new vision for Baltimore parks. Inspired by this work, the city soon forged a partnership with two organizations — TPL and Parks and People, a local nonprofit — to link that vision to a revival of Baltimore's neighborhoods. The visioning process to revitalize the Gwynns Falls corridor, which took more than four years, included contributions from 16 community groups, 11 nonprofit organizations, and eight city agencies. Residents were polled on their open-space needs, properties were studied, and a master plan was created. Since then, trash has been cleared, boardwalks have been built, and a schedule for major trail construction has been set — all to answer the larger question about what kind of a city Baltimore would become.

Assembling Urban Parkland

Assembling land for today's urban parks is complicated by the involvement of various stakeholders and multiple jurisdictions, complex ownership patterns, and the frequent need for extensive environmental assessment and cleanup. Razing abandoned buildings and cleaning up contaminated "brownfield" sites can turn economic sinks into economic engines for a city, but such projects are also complicated by myriad federal, state, and local regulations that can make the politics of a project as complicated as the economics. Rarely do city park departments have the staff or financial resources to take on assemblages and cleanups. Completion of these new parks often requires interdepartmental teams within a public agency and the support of nonprofit and for-profit development partners.

In Winston-Salem, North Carolina, for example, civic leaders have long de-spaired of salvaging the city's southeast gateway district, a blighted patch of abandoned warehouses adjacent to the Old Salem historic park — Winston-Salem's major tourist attraction. An eyesore at the very doorway of a bustling downtown, for years the southeast district has offered no shopping, lunch spots, or gathering places for Old Salem visitors — or for students from the four surrounding prep schools and colleges. And easy access to a greenway along Salem Creek and a "strollway" along a former trolley line was blocked by a public road (which is now slated for closing).

In the early 1990s, local business leaders, educational institutions, and civic groups joined to forge the Southeast Gateway Council, a private nonprofit organization dedicated to renewal of the southeast district. In 1992, the American Institute of Architects sponsored a two-day design workshop to envision a plan for the area, which involved a land assemblage. But as a relatively small city, Winston-Salem lacked the staff and expertise to complete the ambitious project. At the request of the city, TPL researched the feasibility and costs of assembling almost nine acres of commercial properties west of Main Street for a proposed public plaza and retail village. The organization contracted for title searches, environmental audits, appraisals, and an economic feasibility study, and also negotiated with the eight area landowners to secure options to purchase their properties. Working together, TPL, the city, and a group of civic leaders came up with a financing package for the project: approximately $1 million will come from the site's developer, and several million more will come from the county, the city, and private donations from individuals, foundations, and corporations. Plans call for a new visitors' center for Old Salem, a pedestrian shopping plaza, and completion of the two greenways.

Creating parks from urban sites often requires such multiple and complex partnerships. Sometimes a development component is built in to support the park, and the developer becomes part of the partnership. Outside planning and design groups may donate their expertise; an example is the work undertaken by the American Society of Landscape Architects to help create a vision for a greenway along the Los Angeles River. Private funding for the planning stage may come from local philanthropic foundations that hope to leverage a public commitment in the form of a bond act or tax measure, as was the case in Los Angeles County, where a bond measure — the Los Angeles County Park, Beach, and Recreation Act — was passed in 1996 that will provide about $319 million for acquisition and capital improvement projects, including $9 million dedicated to improving and restoring the Los Angeles River with a greenway. This is at a cost of about $7 per year for an average household.

Other models are emerging, particularly in urban areas where vacant, underused, and often contaminated urban lands and buildings offer cities key resources for the revitalization of their waterfronts and neighborhoods.

TPL, with seed funding from the James Irvine Foundation, recently launched the California Center for Land Recycling (CCLR), whose mission is to foster land recycling as a way to redirect growth away from the fringes of metropolitan areas and to revitalize the urban core. To assist in the development of new policies and strategies for rejuvenating urban centers, CCLR supports and documents model projects that incorporate community participation, economic development efforts, and brownfield remediation.

Understanding the assets and roles of public and private partners is key to building successful and strategic partnerships. Nonprofits may bring short-term efficiencies to a project, taking advantage of the dynamic real estate market on behalf of a public agency that cannot move quickly; flexible

funding and financing from creative and entrepreneurial sources that can leverage public sources; organizational flexibility to build staff around projects, hire consultants, and track down the expertise needed; and community credibility, through their contacts with broad constituencies and their goal of working on behalf of the public's interest. The public sector can add stability and legitimacy to a project, grounding it with a stable base of funding, a long-term commitment to public use and management, and the ability to link the project to a broader city vision or plan, which can support and leverage the project.

Raising Money and Forging Transactions

Usually, the first question park advocates and public officials ask about any park or open space project is, how will we pay for it? An analysis of nearly 100 land acquisition cases that TPL has completed with local public agencies showed close to 20 different sources of acquisition and development funding, including sources at the state and federal levels. And these numbers showed few projects with single sources of support: 58 projects relied on at least two sources of funding.

Funding sources are as varied as the projects themselves. Sometimes private stakeholders bear all or most of the costs of park development, as was the case for the Park at Post Office Square in Boston and the Flagstar Corporate Plaza and Jerome Richardson Park in Spartanburg, South Carolina. More often, private stakeholders such as businesses and foundations provide capital grants, indirect capital (through fundraising campaigns), management assistance, and publicity — or, in the case of developers, an influx of residents or workers to use and support the park. In exchange for these private contributions, governments may contribute free or discounted land, tax and financing concessions, and city support services for the park or open space.

In 1995, officials and residents of Santa Fe, New Mexico, hoped to buy a 50-acre former railyard — the last major open parcel in the city's booming downtown. The Catellus Development Corporation — the successor of the Atchison, Topeka & Santa Fe Railroad — did not lack prospective buyers for the land, which was appraised at $29 million. The city of Santa Fe wanted at least a portion of the parcel for a park and other public use, and it wanted some control over how the balance of the property was developed, but it was not sure how it would pay for the land. At the city's request, TPL stepped in to bargain with Catellus. By offering a tax benefit to the corporation, TPL acquired the land at an $8 million discount. As part of the arrangement with TPL, the city agreed to dedicate at least ten acres of the property to a public park.

Funding and support for a single park project may come from many sources: federal, state, and local governments; foundation funds; corporate grants; developer concessions; and donations of land value by landowners. Often a nonprofit partner serves a coordinating and brokerage function — raising funds, combining funds, and structuring the final transaction. A nonprofit partner may also be able to maximize funds, reducing the cost of a property by offering a tax break to a landowner — as in Santa Fe — or accepting a donation of land for a city. In Boston, TPL accepted the donation of a 1.2-acre rail corridor from Consolidated Freight Corporation (Conrail) for a new greenway in East Boston, one of the city's most densely settled neighborhoods. To enable the city to accept the property, TPL agreed to have an environmental assessment and cleanup performed.

New Public Funds for Parks

Nonprofit partners can also help by building community support for open space protection. One of the most heartening developments in recent years has been the public's willingness to help fund new parks and open space acquisition. As is the case in all aspects of park creation, effective public fundraising is based on effective team building: when enough stakeholders show enthusiastic support for a project, a community will often commit new funds to parks and open space.

In the late 1980s, Austin, Texas, faced a serious open space crisis when development west of the city began to pollute Barton Springs, a downtown swimming hole that is one of the city's best-known natural and recreational features. Austin environmentalists had been trying to protect the creek corridor for decades, but the pollution of Barton Springs sparked wider community concern. In 1991, TPL began working with government and community groups to quantify Austin's open space needs. Questionnaires distributed to residents revealed that a majority would support new local taxes for recreation and park facilities. In 1992, in the wake of a TPL-organized campaign for the measure, voters approved a $20 million bond act to establish the Barton Creek Wilderness Park.

It is no accident that Austin's support for park facilities coalesced around a specific place. Citizen support for well-conceived financing measures with explicit goals for land acquisition continues to have good outcomes in cities. The "market share" of parks and recreation bonds in the municipal bond market increased in recent years from 1 to 1.5 percent. The municipal finance industry has noted the public's willingness to pay for parks. Voters are also more likely to approve new spending for parks if a property or properties have already been designated and optioned for acquisition. This not only protects a valuable park property while funds are being raised, but also provides a tangible focus for voters evaluating an open space tax or bond measure. While governments are usually prohibited from risking public funds to option properties in advance of voter approval, a nonprofit partner is not, and TPL has been asked to provide up-front financing in many communities.

Nonprofit partners can also help government and community groups by polling voters on open space needs and conducting funding and direct-mail advertising campaigns. Using such techniques, TPL has helped pass funding measures in Portland, Oregon; King County (Seattle), Washington; Dade County (Miami), Florida; Los Angeles County; Austin, Texas; and Pima County (Tucson), Arizona.

Even after a measure is approved, a public agency may ask a nonprofit partner to hold land until funds accumulate, structure a special lease-purchase agreement, or arrange for the land to be transferred in several phases to meet budgetary or legal requirements. A lease-purchase agreement can be particularly helpful if a city has decided to acquire land and does not have up-front funds. For a new park in Lakewood, Colorado, TPL structured a 30-year lease-purchase transaction. The lease is renewable year by year, and the city has reserved the right to purchase the property before the 30 years have passed.

In other instances, a public agency may ask a nonprofit partner to assemble properties for a planned unit development (PUD), so that park or conservation lands can be transferred to the public agency and the remaining land can be sold to private developers for cluster development. After voters in Austin, Texas, approved a $20 million bond initiative to acquire land along Barton Creek, TPL used a portion of those funds to purchase a 1,000-acre historic ranch for the Barton Creek Wilderness Park. The city's PUD ordinance allowed TPL to sell 240 acres to private developers for cluster development; the remaining acreage was sold to the city for the wilderness park. The subsidy provided by the development purchase allowed the city to acquire the conservation land for approximately a quarter of what city planners had expected.

Partnerships in Ongoing Management

Public/private partnerships have proven highly effective in generating vision, creating public support for new parks, raising and maximizing funds, and structuring workable land-acquisition transactions. The greatest need for the future is to enlarge the focus of partnerships to include park management. In uncertain budgetary times, some cities hesitate to create parks because of the ongoing obligation to manage and maintain them. But there is no reason to assume that the creativity and energy that partnerships bring to park creation cannot also be applied to park management and maintenance. The public sector, which can no longer run the nation's urban park systems alone, must call on the ideas, skills, and strengths of private partners, not only to create parks, but also to guarantee their long-term health and usefulness.

Many successful park projects continue to depend on private support. In some instances, this support is monetary. In Spartanburg, South Carolina, the Flagstar Corporation pays to maintain the plaza and park it largely created. Management of Manhattan's Bryant Park is funded mostly by proceeds from the park's restaurant and café and from assessments of a business improvement district — an increasingly popular way for businesses to return to the public some of the wealth generated by urban open space. And at the Park at Post Office Square in Boston, fees for private parking support park management.

But just as important as financial support are the energy and vision private partners bring to parks. In the most successful park processes, the same partners who help envision and build parks stay involved to help fund and manage them. Through continuous evaluation, planning, programming, and use, these committed private partners seek not only to create but also to sustain valuable parks.

At Cedar Lake Park in Minneapolis, park neighbors organized as the Cedar Lake Park Association have continued their involvement — not only by raising more than $1.2 million for the park's support, but in hands-on efforts to restore natural ecosystems absent for 100 years. In Pinellas County, Florida, groups and communities along the Pinellas Trail have raised money for plantings, benches, water fountains, and other amenities, and have also donated greenery and planted demonstration flower boxes. One community along the trail has created a bicycle and pedestrian plaza, organized musical performances where the trail passes through downtown, and is making it possible for its segment of the trail to be used at night. Such measures draw users to parks, who come to value them in a whole new way. Through such efforts, the real meaning of a park emerges, one user-day at a time.

The largest and most productive public/private park partnership in the nation is the partnership between the New York City Parks and Recreation Department and the Central Park Conservancy, which was established in 1980. In its first 15 years, the conservancy raised $110 million to restore and reclaim Central Park from decades of declining maintenance and increasing vandalism. In addition, the conservancy contracts with the city to help develop programs for the park. And the nonprofit's 175 staffers bear many responsibilities traditionally borne by city employees. Not only has Central Park been largely rejuvenated through the conservancy's ministrations, but the effort has freed the city parks department to devote funds and staff time to smaller neighborhood parks.

In Philadelphia, declining public monies and a venerable philanthropic tradition have led to a three-way partnership between the Philadelphia Recreation Department, the Fairmount Park Commission (manager of one of the nation's largest urban parks), and Philadelphia Green, the inner-city division of the Philadelphia Horticultural Society. The organization also assumes broad responsibilities often borne by a city parks department: it plants, prunes, and removes trees; beautifies boulevards and neighborhoods; fights graffiti; and organizes environmental education programs. Some of the more than $3 million the horticultural society spends on such projects each year is raised through its annual flower show; the balance is from traditional philanthropic sources. Although staffing remains half of what it was in the early 1980s, the city recently responded to this private energy by incrementally restoring staff to the Philadelphia Recreation Department.

The experiences in New York and Philadelphia bear important lessons for the urban parks movement. The first is that great parks are not created once, but are recreated over and over again, as is happening in New York City. The experience in Philadelphia teaches us that, despite the worries of some observers, private efforts can be solidly democratic, can forge strong community partnerships, and can create important open space resources in low-income neighborhoods.

The promise of the new public/private partnerships is that they will remain flexible and open to new approaches — constantly reinvigorated by their mix of governments, businesses, charitable and stakeholder groups, and nonprofit consultants. Such partnerships represent the greatest hope of the urban parks movement.

CHAPTER 8

BOSTON, OTHER CITIES, CREATE URBAN PARKS ON EXISTING PUBLIC FACILITIES

Christopher Leinberger and *Gayle Berens*

It is easy to forget that each generation has different open-space needs. Like fashion and music, parks and park design become outdated. Recreational preferences also change: 30 years ago, no one used in-line roller skates, and few Americans played soccer. City, state, and federal funding priorities shift. The public sector often forgets what successful private sector entrepreneurs never do: responding to market preferences is critical to success.

How individual Americans value their parks and open space changes from generation to generation and does not always reflect public sector budgeting priorities. The nation's parks have never had as many visitors as they have now, and many suffer from overuse and insufficient public funding. Many large city parks have been allowed to deteriorate, in large part because they came to be regarded as unsafe environments and city budgets were inadequate to counteract real or perceived security issues. Usable open space, however, is an invaluable amenity that most people instinctively desire. The emotional attachment that people have to open space (and the idea of it) is often the catalyst for revitalizing parks over and over again.

For urban residential neighborhoods to survive and prosper, parks and open space have to work with and unify the built environment. Walking access to parks and community gathering places is one of the few reasons that urban neighborhoods continue to be meaningful alternatives to the suburbs for middle-class households that have the option of moving. To maintain their middle-class tax base — a necessity for remaining fiscally viable — cities must focus on the things that they can do better than the suburbs, and one of the most important is to provide parks and open space within walking distance of every household, reinforcing the urban neighborhood's viability in the automobile age.

While each city, each piece of land, and each parks department is unique and each effort must be started anew, lessons can be learned from other cities' efforts.

Originally published as "Designing for Urban Parks," *Urban Land*, Vol. 56, No. 12, December 1997. Published by the Urban Land Institute, Washington, D.C. Reprinted with permission of the publisher.

Lesson 1: Involve the neighborhood.

Encourage — do not bureaucratically resist — the active participation of neighborhood groups in planning, funding, and maintaining parks. In virtually every case study, residents provided input (and often resistance) that ultimately made the park a better place.

Lesson 2: Design with a vision.

Do not underestimate the power of imaginative design. Park design is more than a matter of recreating the soft, pastoral, "Olmstedian" spaces beloved in many American cities. Visionary design can affect a park's safety, viability, and usability — and it most certainly affects its long-term success.

Whether the dangers are perceived or real, safety concerns are among the biggest contributors to the downfall of urban parks. But even in neighborhoods where safety has been a long-standing concern, changes in design, landscaping, and use patterns can make parks viable once again.

Using art as a fundamental feature of a park can give it a special quality that will endure over time. Incorporating old uses and structures into the design of a park also can add character and create an inexpensive link to the past. The history of a site may suggest an unusual and visually interesting theme, and building on it may be less expensive than clearing the site and developing a theme from scratch.

Lesson 3: Revive underused or unused space.

Underused, unused, or unusual space — such as underground parking garages, piers, air space, and floodplains — can be success-

fully transformed into viable parks and open space. In Harlem, the state of New York provided much-needed recreational facilities by building Riverbank State Park atop a wastewater treatment plant. Careful planning of load capacities and the use of lightweight materials did not compromise the integrity of the park's design. In Boston, the Park at Post Office Square rests on top of a seven-level underground parking garage. Park users relax in peace, barely aware of entrance and exit ramps for the many vehicles that use the garage daily, and the revenues from the garage support upkeep of the park.

Formerly underused or abandoned floodplains — particularly when they are adjacent to expensive downtown real estate — can be transformed into parks and open space that recover easily after flooding. Instead of fighting Mother Nature, it is wise to consider accommodating the low-cost, flood-prone land that may be adjacent to some of the highest-priced land in the region. Mill Race Park, for example, was successfully reclaimed through a design that allows all elements to withstand annual flooding. Among other features, the park has an automatic shutoff for electric power that goes into effect when the water reaches a certain height and restroom walls begin eight inches above the ground to allow easy drainage. While a park that is not in a floodplain would not incur the costs associated with the process of flood cleanup, the cost of cleaning or rehabilitating flood-damaged open space is almost too small to measure when compared with the cost of rebuilding flood-damaged residential or commercial neighborhoods.

Lesson 4: Program park activities.

Make a concerted effort to program activities in the park, insofar as programming is manageable and appropriate for the type of park and open space. Steady use has been shown to enhance revenues, and, as Page Gifford in the Mill Race Park case study puts it, "A high level of activity is the cheapest security."

Lesson 5: Remember that cleanliness equals respect.

Keep public open spaces clean and well maintained. Several factors can influence the cost and relative ease of maintaining a park: first, the availability of adequate operating funds, whether from public, private, or civic sources; second, strategic use of maintenance staff; and third, a design that is not only attractive but also inherently low maintenance. Users tend to respond to a pleasant, well-designed space by exhibiting orderly behavior.

Lesson 6: Be creative in funding parks.

By "pushing the envelope" of possibilities, resourceful public and private sector groups have been successful in finding money to develop and maintain parks. They have, for example, taken advantage of federal programs that may not be intended for parkland per se. For example, the Intermodal Surface Transportation Efficiency Act (ISTEA), due for reauthorization and probable modification in 1997, has been an important source of funds for rail-to-trail conversions. Linear park development can be a particular boon to a region because it not only adds recreational space but also adds to the transportation network of a region or community. While obtaining such funds may involve cumbersome bureaucratic procedures, a certain percentage of ISTEA money spent in every metropolitan area must be spent on nonhighway, transportation-related projects.

In addition, groups like the National Endowment for the Arts have various public arts program funds that can be applied to parks and open space. The sale of shares at the Park at Post Office Square was an innovative entrepreneurial approach to funding that jump-started that project and provided purchasers with a real benefit: access to parking in a dense city center. Private sector donations for a successful first phase may spark increased public support for subsequent phases.

Lesson 7: Consider using parks as organizing elements.

An urban park can create a sense of place, a landmark, and a community focal point, which may in turn increase property values and create incentives for new development. Since few great downtowns have evolved without some connection to nature, an urban park should be an important component of any successful city redevelopment.

Lesson 8: Parks departments must play a leadership role.

Most parks departments in the country have the capability, but for many reasons may lack the motivation and leadership, to play a strong role. Sometimes leadership must come first from elected officials. But regardless of whether the impetus comes from an elected official or a city department, the public sector needs to reclaim its leadership role in protecting parks, which are among the most valuable assets of the nation's cities.

Riverbank State Park

The 28-acre Riverbank State Park, located in West Harlem, Manhattan, is built atop the North River Water Pollution Treatment Facility. Paid for with public funds, this park and recreational facility represents the transformation of an unwanted but necessary facility — a sewage treatment plant — into a heavily used community resource. Like most public projects of this scale, this project had a percentage of total costs set aside for beautification. Although the community, which was actively opposed to the plant, was not won over by promises of beautification, the state moved forward to secure an easement for the air rights above the plant to develop a park.

The initial project proposal, commissioned from Philip Johnson in 1968, involved flooding the roof and building a series of fountains that would spring from the resulting pool. When community residents discovered that the pool was going to use clean New York City water, they were outraged. Then-Governor Nelson Rockefeller subsequently committed the state to constructing a state park on the roof instead.

Numerous alternatives were evaluated; ultimately, in 1980 a committee of state officials and community representatives chose architect Richard Dattner to spearhead the design and development of a rooftop state park and recreational facility. Between 1980 and 1993, when the park finally opened, the project was designed and redesigned and shown to every community group imaginable. According to Dattner, "The decision to locate in Harlem results in 25 years of community protest, political struggle, and a variety of efforts to assuage the community by balancing the pain of locating a sewage treatment plant in its front yard with the benefits possible from its construction."

"We met with the steering committee every two weeks," noted Dattner. "We started with six schemes and a list of design criteria to use in evaluating and ranking the schemes. The design criteria included things like protection from north winds, orientation to the sun, energy conservation, prox-

imity to access points, flexibilities of use, views of the river, preservation of views from surrounding buildings, and so on. The steering committee and design team then ranked the six schemes against the design goals and assigned numerical scores. Based on their scores, two schemes were chosen for further development."

Most design problems were related to the limited amount of weight that the building below the park could support. Concerns included the load-bearing capacity of the plant's caissons, columns, and roof spans. Load equations also had to take into account expected live loads (people, vehicles, and snow). Adding to the project's complexities was the fact that much of the construction had to take place without interrupting the sewage treatment plant's operations.

To comply with load-bearing criteria, the park's buildings had to be made of lightweight steel with metal- or tile-faced panels. The 28-acre roof, which is almost a half-mile long, consists of 14 separate sections that move independently as the roof expands and contracts with changes in temperature. To avoid damage from movement at expansion joints, each of the park's buildings is completely contained within one roof plate. Every column in a park building is located directly over a corresponding sewage plant column. Original plans called for the roof to carry 400 pounds per square foot throughout, but the design team was able to shave $10 million off the project's cost by identifying those roof plates that had to support that much weight and designing other areas for lighter loads.

Weight limitations also made it necessary to limit the depth of the pool to four feet, to use wood instead of concrete for the walls of the handball court, and to clad the facade of the buildings in prefabricated brick tiles (five-eighths of an inch thick) instead of whole bricks. Because pipes, drains, and electrical conduits had to run over the plant's roof, utilities required special attention. Stormwater collected by the park's sophisticated drainage system is channeled through the sewage plant for treatment.

Riverbank State Park includes five major structures: a 50-meter pool with two movable bulkheads that allow it to be divided into three areas; a covered skating rink for ice skating in the winter and roller skating in the summer; a cultural center; a multiuse athletic building designed for basketball, volleyball, gymnastics, and martial arts; and a 150-seat restaurant with a 100-seat outdoor terrace.

Outdoor facilities include a 25-yard lap pool; a wading pool 18 feet in diameter; four basketball courts; four handball/paddleball courts; four tennis courts; a waterfront amphitheater; a running track surrounding a football/soccer field; a community garden and greenhouse; picnic areas; and a children's playground.

Because of the treatment plant's location on the riverbank, decisions on how to site the park's buildings had to take into account a number of factors, including wind exposure and the potential for flooding. For protection against winter winds blowing off the Hudson, four major park buildings are clustered inward around a south-facing courtyard. In addition, the buildings needed to offer views of the river without blocking river views from nearby buildings.

"We designed the project to be as flexible as possible," explained Dattner. "Everything is multipurpose, to adapt to different sports trends." The park is ringed by a promenade high above the Hudson. A knee-high, striated concrete barrier along the promenade discourages graffiti. To shield neighbors from noisy concerts and events, a boat landing and an outdoor amphitheater are located 50 feet below the athletic building, at the river's edge. From there, the sewage treatment plant is highly visible, but its design is inconspicuous. Clad in concrete, the plant has arched openings that reflect the form of a nearby bridge.

Operated and managed by the state, Riverbank State Park has become the second most heavily used state park in New York: over 3.7 million users visited it in 1995.

Mill Race Park

Mill Race Park is a park of high ambitions. Its planners and designers intended to reclaim a floodplain and toxic waste site for community use, to provide support for downtown revitalization efforts, and to leave a legacy to the community on the 500th anniversary of Christopher Columbus's voyage to America. If that were not enough, they were determined to match the world-class level of design for which Columbus, Indiana, is nationally known — and to accomplish all of those goals without major capital funding from the city.

The resulting 85-acre park, located at the west end of downtown Columbus, substantially succeeds in realizing its ambitions. Dedicated in 1992, the park is now a focal point for concerts and community activities and a source of civic pride. The park's design has attracted national attention, and the once swampy, sleepy bottomlands have been recalled to life with minimal public investment.

Located "at the meeting of city and river," as project landscape architect Michael Van Valkenburg described it, the park's built forms and landscapes range from urban to wild, its uses from communal to solitary. Along the park's urban edge, the landscape and hardscape tend to be rectilinear — parking lots framed by the remnants of old concrete floodwalls, rows of Kentucky coffee and hackberry trees, and an 80-foot observation tower, axially sited in line with the primary park entrance and the downtown area. The urban edge soon gives way, however, to softer forms, terminating in the natural vegetation of the meandering riverbank, which borders the park on three sides. Taking advantage of the site's proximity to water and the abandoned gravel pits from its industrial past, the landscape also includes two lakes: 450-foot-diameter Round Lake and the previously existing North Lake.

Interspersed throughout the park is a series of red-painted structures designed by architect Stanley Saitowitz — an amphitheater stage, an arbor, picnic shelters, fishing piers, a boathouse, and restrooms. Park facilities also include a playground, a basketball court, a horseshoe pit, a wetlands interpretive area with a raised boardwalk, a wildflower area, and the scenic Riverwalk, which connects to the city's People Trail outside the park borders.

According to Van Valkenburgh, designing Mill Race Park was a matter of editing the landscape. "It was both additive and subtractive, like putting paint down on a canvas and taking it up," he said. The design process included a four-month master-planning period, during which Van Valkenburgh met with community leaders, interested citizens, groups such as the River Rats, and even elementary-school children. The very public consultations and design presentations "allowed people to feel an involvement in the process," he said, and aided him in creating a vision for the park.

With the site's riverfront location and long history, there were a variety of positive elements and memories to draw upon, as well as "found objects" that had been brought to the site over time. To maintain a sense of continuity with the past, old tannery floodwalls were retained, as was an old gravel-pit lake. Similarly, four old bridges representative of early wood and steel bridge technology, which had been brought to the site, were incorporated into the design.

Despite its rich history, Mill Race Park was "like the Tin Man looking for a heart," commented Van Valkenburgh. To remedy this, he designed a new lake in the shape of a grand circle, formally ringed by old-

fashioned lampposts and ornamental trees. The "civically scaled" and "democratic" Round Lake, as it has come to be known, stands in deliberate contrast to the nearby river and North Lake.

Several landscape mounds also were added to the site. One crescent-shaped mound forms the amphitheater, with concrete-and-grass benches carved out of the slope. A second grassy mound flanks a basketball court, giving the court a strong presence in the otherwise flat and open plain. The mounds echo those built by Native American tribes indigenous to the Midwest. They also served as disposal sites for earth excavated in the construction of the lake.

The principle of "editing" was applied to the landscaping as it was to other park features. More than 700 trees were planted at Mill Race Park, and some 200 were removed. Of those removed, some were dead or diseased; others were removed or pruned to open up vistas and create connections to the water. New trees were added strategically to complement the existing landscape, to protect park structures from flood-borne logs and debris, and to create the formal landscapes desired for Round Lake and the "city" edge of the park.

The flood-prone character of the site was accommodated in other ways as well. Drainage was planned carefully to minimize ponding and retention of floodwaters; pathways were made strong enough to resist flood scouring and wide enough to accommodate standard cleaning machines; and off-the-shelf playground equipment was selected because it could be easily replaced in the event of flood damage.

The park's structures also had to accommodate the annual flood cycle. The structures, which serve a variety of purposes, contain many of the same materials, including steel tubing, wire mesh, perforated metal, concrete, and glass blocks. The design intention, according to Saitowitz, was to "establish a family." Though each structure is specific in function, "all share the same genetic structure." The "family" includes three picnic shelters, the Custer-Nugent Amphitheater structure, an arbor, a boat pavilion, two fishing piers, restrooms, and the lookout tower near the park entry.

All of the picnic shelters are circular in form, though each varies in detail from the others. "The marking out of a circle," explained Saitowitz, "is the most primitive and universal way of claiming territory." Within the circle, the picnic tables, benches, barbecue pit, and trash receptacle are poured-in-place concrete. Roof coverings over the shelters are designed as warped planes supported on red metal tubing.

The amphitheater has both architectural and landscape components and resulted from a collaboration between Saitowitz and Van Valkenburgh. The open-stage structure, which is topped by a red steel canopy shaped like an inverted curve, plays on one side to the concrete and grass terraces, which seat approximately 600. On the opposite side, the stage plays to an open lawn capable of supporting 10,000 or more concert patrons.

The design of the restrooms addresses not only the threat of flooding, but also the more routine problem of bringing light and air into typically damp and dark spaces. The restroom walls are made entirely of translucent glass blocks and are raised approximately eight inches off the ground to allow floodwaters to drain more easily. The walls also stop short of the roof, maximizing natural ventilation within the restrooms. In a bit of whimsy, the steel-tube and corrugated-metal roof structure is bent into the shape of a "W" on the women's side and an "M" on the men's.

According to the master plan objectives, the design of Mill Race Park provides multiple recreational environments and opportunities for a broad range of experiences, from solitary walks along the river to rock concerts for 10,000. Facilities are provided

that appeal to children (playground), teens (basketball court), and families (picnic shelters). Several facilities, such as the amphitheater, the boat rental, the fishing pier, the lakes, and the trails, attract a wide range of users.

The highly popular amphitheater and programmed events attract the largest number of park visitors. From June through September, nearly every weekend is programmed. The amphitheater is the site of the Mill Race Park Live Concert series, which includes rock concerts, country-and-western concerts, and performances by the Columbus Philharmonic as well as Count Basie. The amphitheater also is the site of a noon concert series for kids and the Family Film series.

In addition to the concerts, films, and major events, the park hosts several other smaller programs and camps. Responsibility for planning and staging the myriad events and programs resides jointly with the Columbus Arts Council, a nonprofit organization, and the Columbus Parks and Recreation Department.

Park at Post Office Square

Boston, the city that in 1634 presented America with its very first urban civic space — the Boston Common — has broken new ground again, this time with an innovative park that has the potential to change public thinking about creating new greenspace among downtown skyscrapers.

At 1.7 acres, the Park at Post Office Square is barely large enough to hold all the awards it has won. Its conception and design have led it to be called "the perfect park," and it has become the focal point for the city's dense, serpentine financial district. Because the park has the feel of a comfortable living room, most visitors — and many Bostonians — have trouble believing that it has not always been there.

The park's centerpiece is a walk-through sculptural fountain. A couple of yards away is a 143-foot-long formal garden trellis, supported by granite columns, draped with seven species of vine and lit internally by computer-driven minibulbs that perform a subtle nighttime show. The Great Lawn, raised above the walkways by a granite curb, provides a relaxed retreat, even furnishing a grassy entrance ramp for wheelchairs. Post Office Square includes an airy, copper-and-glass garden pavilion that houses a year-round café. It features wrought-iron fencing and specially monogrammed drainage gates. Seating styles range from stately teak benches, curving steel settees, and movable cast-iron café chairs with tables to hundreds of linear feet of inviting polished granite wall and half an acre of lawn. Under it all are seven floors of parking spaces for 1,400 cars. In an unusual twist, the Park at Post Office Square is supported — both physically and financially — by a 500,000-square-foot parking garage, the largest in Boston.

"The garage functions like a gusher," wrote *Boston Globe* architecture critic Robert Campbell, "spuming people and activity continually upward." More than 2,000 people enter and leave the garage's gazebo-covered escalators daily. The garage also generates about $8.6 million a year — enough to make a sizable payment on the $76 million cost of developing the park and parking lot, manage a $2.9 million annual operating budget, pay a $1 million local tax bill, and, if things go well, contribute to a maintenance fund for neighborhood parks all over Boston.

Two matching, gazebo-type structures rest on the surface of the garage; one houses the Milk Street Café, and the other serves as the escalator entrance to the garage. Constructed of copper and glass, the café building is airy, yet movable doorways and glass panels make it flexible enough to handle the extremes of Boston's weather. These structures and the garage were designed by Ellenzweig Associates of Cambridge, Massachusetts.

The garage includes a complete car wash, repair services for minor automobile problems, numerous security cameras, and backlit walls for better visibility and security. It also houses a marble lobby that features amenities such as fresh flowers, music in the elevators, a shoeshine, telephones and restrooms, 24-hour attendants, a free phone connection to a traffic hotline, and free downtown maps for tourists. "You can even give someone a gift certificate to park here," Harry Ellenzweig noted. "We have a couple of suburban-based repair companies that rent spaces for their service vans, use our phones, eat in the park, and don't even need an office in the city — they're just based at Post Office Square, a couple of minutes from everywhere."

Ironically, the only reason there is a park at Post Office Square is that parking in Boston is so expensive. The reason parking is so costly — more than $25 a day — is that Boston, responding to a U.S. Environmental Protection Agency mandate to control air pollution, instituted a freeze on the number of parking spaces allowed in the central business district. The final tab for constructing each parking space at Post Office Square was $34,000.

Leverage in Value Gained

The character and civility of cities can be vastly improved through the development and adequate maintenance and operation of parks — and for relatively little money, compared with the amount of other public and private urban investments. Moreover, parks and open space can significantly increase the private capital base. The leverage in value gained through properly developed and maintained parks is one of the great unexploited opportunities in cities today, yet it takes effort to create a space that works and provides value. Most often, that effort is best made by taking advantage of the skills and initiative of the public, private, and civic sectors. Relying on the public sector alone risks limiting the resources and creativity that can be brought to bear on development of urban parks and open space and diminishing the sense of ownership and interest that communities can feel in their greenspace.

CHAPTER 9

CAMBRIDGE DESIGNS OPEN SPACES TO IMPROVE DOWNTOWN LIVING

Terry J. Lassar

In 1634, Boston created what would become the nation's first large-scale urban civic space, the Boston Common. Now, 365 years later, another grand civic space, the Common at University Park, has been added to the cityscape. A common ground for neighborhood residents, university scientists, and office workers, the 1.3-acre park is the centerpiece of a new, mixed-use neighborhood developing next to the Massachusetts Institute of Technology (MIT) in Cambridge.

More than 25 years ago, MIT began acquiring land adjacent to its campus for the development of a corporate office research and development (R&D) park that would help accelerate the transfer of technology into the commercial marketplace. In 1983, MIT selected Cleveland-based Forest City Enterprises to develop University Park at MIT. Forest City also owns and operates the development under a long-term lease.

Unlike some suburban-style, corporate research facilities affiliated with universities, such as those at Stanford and Princeton, University Park at MIT is decidedly urban and urbane. The 27-acre corporate campus,

located in the heart of Cambridge, is a lively, integrated community of offices, laboratories, restaurants, shops, a hotel, residences, and parks. The first office/R&D space opened in 1987 in a rehabilitated shoe factory. Two office buildings followed in 1989 and 1990, together with 142 loft-style residences in a renovated cookie bakery. Subsequent development was put on hold for nearly a decade until the economy strengthened. In 1998, an additional phase opened, including an office building, hotel, and retail services. A full-service supermarket, which had not been contemplated in the original master plan, also was included in this phase in response to community demand. Located on the second level of the hotel, the supermarket has its own street-level entry as well as direct access from the adjacent parking garage.

The latest development phase — 270,000 square feet of office/R&D space in twin buildings, a parking facility, and the landscaped 1.3-acre University Park Common — opened this past spring. The primary occupant is Millennium Pharmaceuticals Inc., a biotech company that relocated its

---

Originally published as "On Common Ground," *Urban Land*, Vol. 58, No. 10, October 1999. Published by the Urban Land Institute, Washington, D.C. Reprinted with permission of the publisher.

headquarters to the research park. Cereon Genomics, LLC, a collaboration between Millennium and the Monsanto Company, also has established its headquarters there.

The Cambridge market has long been propelled by technology companies that are attracted to the area because of the presence of MIT and Harvard. Forest City's strategy for University Park was to develop buildings that would be sufficiently flexible to address the evolving needs of high-tech companies as they matured, while responding to fundamental shifts in the high-tech industry over time.

The first University Park buildings targeted the high-tech industries that had populated Cambridge for the past 30 years, such as defense, computer, and software firms. In the late 1980s, however, just as the park's buildings were delivered, the region's high-tech market sector, along with New England's overall real estate market, entered an economic tailspin. At the same time, though, a new technology-based industry — biotechnology — was emerging from university research laboratories and beginning to establish itself in the commercial sector. Many early-stage biotech companies require a decade to achieve significant revenues, let alone a profit, and the cost of tenant improvements, which typically ranges between $75 to $100 per square foot, is significantly higher than for traditional office space. Moreover, the city's supply of research laboratory space was severely constrained and unable to meet the needs of emerging biotech firms. Initially, the economic downturn left few developers and lenders favorably disposed to risking their capital to build for the biotech industry. It was in this uncertain environment that Forest City recognized an opportunity serve a developing market niche.

The flexibility built into the structures at University Park — high floor-to-ceiling heights, large ventilation shafts, and higher-than-average power capacity — was originally geared for high-tech users but also met the functional needs of the growing biotech sector. MIT scientists were involved in many of the startup companies and were attracted to University Park because of its proximity to the institute. The MIT "halo effect" helped draw other Cambridge-based biotech startup firms. As the number of firms grew over the years, some expanded into additional space at University Park.

By the late 1990s, the industry was beginning to mature, and some larger firms, such as Millennium Pharmaceuticals, which leased space in several buildings throughout the Cambridge area, were looking to consolidate. University Park was the logical choice for two reasons. First, Eric Lander, one of Millennium's founders, runs the genomics center at MIT's Whitehead Institute, and other company scientists also have close ties to MIT. Second, Millennium selected University Park for its new headquarters because no comparable facilities were located nearby. Although other universities in Boston have started developing biotech-related facilities, none is as extensive as University Park and none offers a similar academic campus environment.

Although Forest City did not start out to develop a biotech park, biotech firms now occupy 90 percent of the 700,000 square feet of the park's existing R&D space. "It was a marriage of need and opportunity," explains Peter Calkins, vice president for planning and project development with Forest City. "With an expanding biotech industry competing for a limited supply of suitable space, these value-added buildings generate attractive returns. At full build-out — within the next four to five years, according to Calkins — University Park will encompass 1.3 million square feet of office/R&D space, a 212-room hotel and executive center, 150,000 square feet of retail space and restaurants, 650 housing units, structured parking for more than 3,000 cars, and seven acres of parkland. The development is currently 50 percent completed.

University Park is built largely on blighted, unused industrial land in the Cambridge neighborhood. Located across the Charles River from Boston, Cambridge was once a thriving manufacturing district. As with many other communities in the northeastern United States, Cambridge's economy flagged after World War II when most of the city's blue-collar industrial base moved to the suburbs, leaving behind a jumble of derelict warehouses and neglected parking lots.

The city of Cambridge, after working for several years to spark developer interest in the vacant site, welcomed Forest City's mixed-use concept. In 1988, the city approved the master plan and passed the requisite zoning and design guidelines. In addition to the planned commercial space, the developers agreed to provide a minimum of 400 residential units, including a significant affordable housing component. Some of the affordable residences are located in the renovated F. A. Kennedy Steam Bakery, original home of the Fig Newton cookie. Additional affordable housing is included at Auburn Court, a family-style development on the neighborhood edge of University Park. A community-based nonprofit developer is building this residential phase under rights sublet from Forest City.

In addition to the special zoning district created for the development, the developer, the city of Cambridge, and MIT entered into a series of development agreements governing specific issues — including traffic generation and mitigation, housing obligations, and roadway improvements — that may be changed only by mutual consent of all three parties. University Park represented the first use of development agreements to augment the city's zoning process. The city's community development department views University Park as the new paradigm for large-scale development and will likely employ similar agreements for future projects.

Like many dense neighborhoods in mature urban centers, Cambridge has a scarcity of parks. The public voiced strong concern that large-scale developments such as University Park should provide plenty of green open spaces for the neighborhood. "Because we're in a dense, urban location," says Calkins, "our intent was to create a research park with its own identity that, over time, would knit into the adjacent neighborhood structure." In the master plan for University Park, Koetter Kim & Associates, a Boston-based architecture firm, used a framework of street edges and axially related parks and open spaces to integrate the development into the surrounding community. The centerpiece of the interconnecting open-space system — and the heart and soul of the master plan — is the University Park Common. Located alongside Sidney Street, the main north/south thoroughfare, the common will eventually take the form of an outdoor room defined by eight different buildings.

As designated in the master plan, the central open space has always been envisioned as a common ground for both Cambridge residents and University Park office and scientific workers rather than as a corporate enclave, isolated from the neighborhood. The developers hired a Boston landscape architecture firm, the Halvorson Company, Inc., best known for its design of Post Office Square, a park built above a parking garage in Boston's financial district. Halvorson's office worked closely with community representatives on the common design. The community was concerned that the initial concept designs were overly formal, with too much paving and not enough lawn areas to support passive recreational uses. They also felt that the common appeared to be a frontyard to the private office buildings.

In response, the designers reconfigured the plan, minimizing the building entries and making room for a larger green open space at the park's center. To encourage active use of the common as a destination park, the landscape architects integrated attractions — including a ministage area that turns the central green space into an amphitheater — as well as enclosed nodes for picnicking and reading and, most important, an abundance of seating. Its large open spaces make the common an ideal setting for neighborhood festivals. A system of meandering pathways runs diagonally through the common, inviting residents in the adjacent Brookline Street neighborhood to stroll through the park on their way to work at MIT or to pick up groceries at the supermarket.

The Brookline Street community actively participated in developing the art program for the common. The first art phase, Traces of History — a series of plaques and three-dimensional sculptures — depicts the history of the University Park site. Once part of the Charles River, the site was filled to expand Cambridge's land area. A variety of industries operated on and around the area, including Simplex Wire and Cable, shoe factories, a book publishing firm, a bakery, candy makers, audio products, and a telescope manufacturer. The new industry at University Park focuses instead on producing various pharmaceuticals and biotech products such as replacement materials for bone and cartilage.

Also featured in the public art program and placed throughout the park are 18-inch square granite blocks with sand-blasted letters and symbols of hydrogen, lithium, and other elements of the periodic table. Some are freestanding on the lawn; others are laid out in a row near the main entryways to the buildings.

As a focus of the second art phase, neighborhood representatives encouraged the landscape architects to design a fountain for the common. Because Boston's frigid winters make it difficult to operate a fountain year round, the team came up with the concept of a fog fountain, designed not to freeze. The system is powered by a compressor pump that boosts water through a hydraulic line under high pressure and forces water out of nozzles to produce fog.

A major challenge for Boston architects Tsoi/Kobus & Associates was to create a building design for the Millennium Pharmaceuticals buildings that was compatible with the adjacent residential neighborhood, located due west of the 45/75 Sidney Street buildings. Since each building is 70 feet high and 200 feet long, scale was an important issue. On the service side facing the residences, the architects articulated the building facade into smaller components to reduce the scale and visually minimize the large plane of the wall. Likewise, the loading bays were buried inside the building and designed to reduce the number of external overhead doors. Residential bay-style windows on the west ends of the buildings — facing the residential neighborhood — frame the courtyard between the two structures that lead into the common. Ornamental street lights, trees, and planters along the west street edge also helped humanize the scale.

Several traffic-calming devices protect the residential neighborhood from the increased flow of cars and trucks to the Millennium buildings. For example, a Woonerf-style road near the exit from the parking garage discourages vehicles from cutting through the Brookline Street neighborhood and instead channels traffic to Sidney Street. This curvilinear road, which resembles an oversized walkway, is large enough to accommodate emergency vehicles in compliance with the city's access requirement.

The skybridge connecting the two Millennium buildings was controversial. Initially, some members of the planning board maintained that the bridge disrupted an important cross axis in the master plan. They were also philosophically opposed to the idea of taking people off the street. The architects responded by designing the bridge as a ceremonial gateway that reinforces rather than disrupts connections to the adjacent residential neighborhood. In addition, the mullions and ornamental curved arch design strengthen the gateway concept.

Unlike the self-conscious presence of many corporate headquarters, the Millennium buildings are deliberately unassuming. "They were intended as background buildings to the common," says Carol Chiles, who headed the design team for Tsoi/Kobus. For this reason, the entry facades facing onto the common were designed asymmetrically with the entryways shifted to the side streets. The entryways — curved glass and metal atriums — project into the park to welcome employees and visitors arriving from the garage or side streets.

"In this business, where change is a constant," says Chiles, "flexibility is critical. Research projects change over time; funding expands and contracts. Labs must be designed with ultimate flexibility to respond to these changes." In particular, modular planning and standardization accommodate changing needs. "You don't want a lab bench that is designed so specifically for one research group that it can't be adapted later for a different group," she adds. The architects created a template for each floor and designated general zones for office or laboratory space. As Millennium's space needs change, "it will be more cost effective to convert office to lab space, rather than the other way around, to avoid wasting expensive lab infrastructure," notes Chiles. In fact, some completed laboratories were substantially modified even before the first scientists moved into the buildings.

In addition to flexibility, Millennium wanted its new facilities "to encourage communication between the different research groups," comments Janet Bush, Millennium's vice president of finance. So the architects designed a number of informal break-out spaces that permit employees to meet for spontaneous brain-storming sessions. On every floor, 20-foot-long white writing boards are strategically placed near the coffee and snack kitchens. The ground-floor cafeteria, which features large glass windows facing the common, also serves as an off-hours meeting space.

The mixed-use development concept has been an important draw for many anchor tenants, including Millennium. "The central location and proximity of the hotel makes University Park attractive for recruiting purposes," says Bush. In addition, nearby public transit and on-site housing, along with such conveniences as the supermarket, daycare facilities, and restaurants, appeal to prospective employees, she adds.

In the next development phase, a market-rate apartment building rather than the originally planned R&D space will be constructed on the south end of the common. Forest City concluded that a residential building would better enhance the development's open space and encourage greater use of the park after business hours. Furthermore, the area's robust housing market, along with Cambridge's repeal of rent control three years ago, is prompting Forest City to build 246 additional residences beyond its original obligation of 400 units. Besides offering employees nearby living accommodations, a number of University Park companies lease apartments for use by out-of-town employees, consultants, and customers.

"It's rare that designers have the opportunity to work on such a large vacant site in a dense, older city like Cambridge," notes Boston landscape architect Robert Krieg of the Halvorson Company. "University Park, with its mix of residences, offices, laboratories, restaurants, shops, hotels, and parks, challenged us to create a whole new integrated community — a mini-village — within an existing city."

CHAPTER 10

CHARLOTTESVILLE, OTHER CITIES, RESTORE THEIR WATERSHEDS

Michael Burger

Diane Easley lives in Nelson County, population 14,000, just south of Charlottesville, Virginia. Big pieces of land were once used to grow tobacco here, but all that remains of this agricultural heritage is some dairy farming and a small lumber industry. The growth industries here now include a ski resort, second homes, and speculation on land ready to accommodate more second homes. It is a prototypical exurb in transition. Charlottesville has been creeping closer for a decade. And if fears of living in a nearby target city like Washington, D.C., intensify following another 9/11, Nelson County's permanent population could double overnight. Already, the population in some parts of the county is growing at ten percent per year.

To retain the area's tony charm — and its water quality — Easley and other residents are trying desperately to keep sprawl at bay.

The construction of new roads and bridges has led to soil erosion and siltation of rivers and streams, and an informal survey of groundwater tables revealed some po-tential contamination in shallow wells. The equation is simple and common: more houses and roads create more impervious surfaces and human uses; these in turn increase the rate and amount of polluted runoff into rivers and streams, deteriorating the water quality.

Just a few years ago, the forty-something Easley was not by her own account an environmental activist. She was not even especially political. But when the University of Virginia received a "small watershed" grant from the U.S. Environmental Protection Agency to develop a pilot program in her area, she started showing up at meetings. She has since taken charge and expanded what was a 5-person citizen task force into an 80-person organization, the Friends of the Rockfish Watershed, and is now spearheading a campaign to make water quality a top priority in Nelson County.

The campaign represents a change in the way people respond to clean water issues. While much of the modern environmental movement is built on lawsuits and top-down enforcement of federal and state

Originally published as "A Watershed Moment: A New Urban Environmental Movement is Born," *The Next American City*, Issue 4, October 2004. Published by The Next American City, Inc., New York, New York. Reprinted with permission of the publisher.

statutes and permitting programs, Easley and groups like hers, known as community watershed organizations, take a more collaborative, bottom-up approach. Their strategy, essentially, is to mobilize individual citizens to participate more directly in the law-making process. "We're extremely local and governed by what people that live here want," Easley says.

More than 2,000 groups adopting similar approaches have materialized across the country, and many more are in various stages of formation. Through these organizations, some half million people participate in activities that range from tree planting and river bank clean-ups to canoe and kayak trips to public education in schools and parks. In recent years, these watershed groups have taken on a more political bent. A changing legal landscape has raised their profile, and they've become more vocal in city, county, and state legislatures by participating in a collaborative form of decision-making called watershed management planning.

Easley and her Friends of the Rockfish Watershed, for instance, have built informational kiosks in local parks and tried to raise general awareness of the issues surrounding water quality by sponsoring events and programs. But they have also sat at the negotiating table with county officials, local business interests, individual farmers, scientists, and engineers to draft a "watershed management plan" for 258 square miles of land that drains into the James River at Howardsville. Like many such plans, it employs clustered zoning — bunching together new developments on small parcels of land in order to preserve parts of the natural landscape in large open spaces — in conjunction with conservation easements — covenants that forbid any future building on these open spaces. These practices help to preserve vital habitats and maintain agricultural uses. The management plan would also, for the first time, regulate area storm-water-drainage systems and require buffer zones free from development along stream banks. Finally, the plan encourages local monitoring of water quality by citizens groups.

The local county government has responded by incorporating various elements of the draft into its Comprehensive Plan and its zoning ordinances. Easley and her group have thus managed to infuse water quality concerns into local politics without having to sue anyone.

The Challenge of Urban Watershed Management

Easley's success with the cooperative watershed planning model of regulation may not translate to all locales, however. Watershed management planning in a metropolis is a different beast than in exurban or small city environments. The politics are more complex, and environmental concerns compete against a slew of other social problems for top billing. The city of Baltimore, for instance, "has a horrible history of trashing the environment," says Richard Hersey, executive director of the Herring Run Watershed Association. "It's the legacy of our industrial background, these contaminated lands and waters. Up until three years ago [and the election of Mayor Martin O'Malley] we couldn't even get the environment onto a list of the city's critical urban ills."

But watershed management planning also represents a potentially fresh angle from which to approach urban environmental problems. According to Hersey, watershed management planning is integrally connected with open space preservation, "brownfield" (industrial site) redevelopment, and remediation of Superfund sites. He believes that an adequate citywide plan in Baltimore could help retire 200 to 600 acres from the development market, and integrate that land with restored streams returning to the river's headwaters.

Baltimore is divided into three watersheds — Herring Run, Jones Falls, and Gwynns Falls. As with many urban rivers and streams, much of the water is buried under the city's infrastructure, making it difficult to access, never mind manage, says Christel Marie Cothran, program director at the Jones Falls Watershed Association. And even if Baltimore could map out a vision for the city's watersheds, integrating it into zoning ordinances and comprehensive plans would prove difficult. "I don't really know where the system breaks down, but I think it breaks down everywhere in Baltimore," says Hersey.

Jurisdictional boundaries that have no relation to watershed boundaries pose particular difficulties. Surrounding Baltimore County has developed a watershed management plan, and has been acknowledged as one of the most aggressive counties in the state in pursuing its design. The plan, however, does not include anything inside the Baltimore city line. The city, in turn, has looked at its three primary watersheds and wants to develop plans for each. Predictably enough, the city and county are acting on different sets of facts, and for any number of institutional reasons have difficulty communicating, although they have at least signed an agreement to cooperate on the issue.

Ultimately, the success of watershed management planning depends on community buy-in, and there are quite simply many differing interests in Baltimore that may prove contentious — at least 8 universities, 8 golf courses, and 26 private schools, for instance, as well as all of the building owners, homeowners, and tenants. "We are trying to work with them to think about ways to change land use practices," Cothran says. Her group has been trying to promote the use of rain barrels — to collect rainwater and prevent it from overwhelming the stormwater system — and bayscaping, which uses native plants in gardens and yards to reduce the amount of pesticide and fertilizer likely to enter waterways.

New Front Lines for Clean Water

Watershed groups have become more prominent in the last half-decade because they are particularly well-adapted for solving a set of problems that environmental law is now addressing after decades of neglect. Since the 1972 Clean Water Act, the United States has most successfully reduced pollution from "point" sources — the ends of sewage and industrial pipes. But more than half of all the nation's water pollution comes from "nonpoint" sources, such as urban and agricultural runoff and discharge from storm sewers, construction sites, and logging operations. Pollution from these sources accounts for nearly all the sediment deposition and the vast majority of nitrogen and phosphorous reaching the nation's waters. In fact, the U.S. Environmental Protection Agency and many states have reported that nonpoint source pollution is the primary reason a high percentage of the nation's waters remain unswimmable and unfishable. Yet, because the problem is so diffuse and difficult to regulate, it remains largely outside the reach of federal and state authorities.

But many cities now have no choice but to deal with it. The Clean Water Act's monstrously-named Phase II National Pollutant Discharge Elimination System (NPDES) Stormwater Program requires operators of municipal storm sewers in urbanized areas with populations under 100,000 to start controlling polluted stormwater runoff, most of which can be attributed to nonpoint source pollution. The patterns of urban and suburban sprawl that accompanied the economic boom of the 1990s increased the number of local governments subject to the regulations even while they made the nonpoint problem worse. "The 1990s were a crazy time for development," says John Rozum, the national network co-ordinator for Nonpoint Education for Municipal Officials (NEMO), a confederation of programs that educate local decision-makers on the connection between land use and water quality. "You had people buying all these houses, developing all this stuff. Now we're looking at it, and thinking, is this really how we want to be?"

The problem is particularly acute around the Chesapeake Bay, which does not meet the federal clean water standards — in regulatory lingo, the region is a "non-attainment area." The EPA has given the Chesapeake Bay Program, an agency shared by the Bay's watershed states of Maryland, Virginia, and Pennsylvania, until 2010 to clean it up. If the Bay Program fails, the feds will force the states to significantly tighten their regulation of both point and nonpoint pollution sources. The states are loath to take on this Total Maximum Daily Load program. They would have to calculate how much pollution each water body that feeds into the Bay could absorb and then divvy that load among all the players who need or want to discharge into it. The process would be technically challenging and politically terrifying. Under the auspices of the Bay Program, the states are making great efforts to clean up the Bay and avoid regulating daily loads. Maryland, Virginia, and Pennsylvania have each committed to work with local governments, community groups, and watershed organizations to develop and implement watershed management plans in two-thirds of the Bay watershed by the year 2010.

The Chesapeake Bay states have taken different approaches to meeting their commitments, but watershed groups play a role throughout the region. In Maryland and Virginia, watershed management planning is mostly done at the county level, with some participation from state agencies, com-munity watershed organizations, and individual landowners. By contrast, in Pennsylvania watershed management planning is an entirely grassroots affair, where community watershed organizations develop plans with little government oversight. Despite their prominence, the groups have a strained relationship with Bay Program staff. Paul Sturm of the Maryland-based Center for Watershed Protection says that Bay Program personnel's "perception of local 'friends of' groups is that they are limited in scope and competence." The disdain works both ways: "The Bay Program people are ... often perceived as people that live in ivory towers and are asserting their values into local communities," says Steve Talley, watershed coordinator at the Canaan Valley Institute, a nonprofit group that works in West Virginia and Pennsylvania.

An Undefined Future Role

Watershed management planning and other collaborative approaches to environmental decision-making are now being championed not only by progressives and liberal pragmatists, but also by Interior Secretary Gail Norton and other proponents of deregulation and private rights. Ambiguities in the current watershed planning process have temporarily brought together forces that want very different outcomes from the process. It remains uncertain, for instance, whether these plans create the enforceable regulations that environmentalists want or merely encourage the voluntary efforts by businesses and citizens that conservatives often promote. It also remains unclear just who is beholden to them, and what impact they actually have.

How these watershed planning processes turn out will determine whether this new trend becomes primarily an educational tool, or a new kind of political force for the environmental movement. The Canaan Valley Institute's Talley thinks of watershed management planning in broad, educational terms. "The fundamental essence of watershed management planning," he said, "is really nothing more than an effort to get local folks to differently value natural resource conservation." Tom Schueler, executive director of the Maryland-based Center for Watershed Protection, stakes out the alternative perspective; he derides what he calls "pleasant structure" — voluntary programs that spur citizen participation — and thinks that watershed activists need to push full force into local legislatures, and into the law, as the Friends of the Rockfish have. "A lot of people just want to get people to talk and think that's going to be enough," Schueler says. "I think we need to raise a little hell."

CHAPTER 11

CHATTANOOGA CREATES
PUBLIC PARKS AND GREENWAYS

Richard Bailey

The city of Chattanooga's most recent urban revitalization project is not urban at all. After years of successful downtown redevelopment along the city's 200-acre riverfront and more recently in the 640-acre southern end of the central business district, Chattanooga has broadened its focus with a project to revitalize four square miles in the inner suburban ring anchored by the city's oldest suburban mall, long in decline.

When Eastgate Mall opened 35 years ago, it drew shoppers, stores, and economic vitality from downtown Chattanooga to the developing suburbs. Ten years ago, the cycle continued as the larger Hamilton Place mall opened several miles further out, drawing economic vitality away from Eastgate and the surrounding area. But last year, with a new mayor and a new mall owner, the fortunes of Eastgate's declining mall and surrounding suburb began to change. Now "urban" redevelopment is following in the aftermath of suburban sprawl.

Chattanooga's Mayor Jon Kinsey, a real estate developer before his election last March, described Brainerd, the area surrounding the declining Eastgate Mall, as "an older suburb with the same concerns as most downtowns. We need to make sure that we do something about our core city," he stressed, "and Brainerd is clearly part of our core city." After taking office last April, Mayor Kinsey requested that the Chattanooga-Hamilton County Regional Planning Agency develop a plan to revitalize Brainerd. The following summer, the idea acquired reality and momentum when AT&T leased one of the mall's former anchor store sites for a call center and a new owner purchased the southern half of the mall where AT&T would be located.

By fall, a consulting team had been selected for a planning study to be managed by the regional planning agency but funded primarily by the stakeholder group the agency assembled. The winning proposal was submitted by Miami-based Dover, Kohl & Partners Town Planning. The new urbanist firm proposed creating a multidisciplinary team that included Water Kulash, a principal of Glatting Jackson Kercher Anglin Lopez Reinhart in Orlando, to oversee traffic planning and economic planner Robert Gibbs of the Gibbs Planning Group, based in Birmingham, Michigan, to handle retail planning. Private sector stakeholders funding 80 percent of the study included 40-percent-leased Eastgate Mall, fully leased

---

Originally published as "Mall Over," *Urban Land*, Vol. 57, No. 7, July 1998. Published by the Urban Land Institute, Washington, D.C. Reprinted with permission of the publisher.

Brainerd Village strip center next door, Osborne Office Park adjacent to the mall, and other businesses and banks in the area.

Designing in Public

In January, after preliminary field evaluation and market research, a public design charrette was held by the regional planning agency that drew 300 residents and business owners to help create a new vision for the mall and the surrounding area. The heart of the week-long process was a six-hour "designing in public" event in which 150 community members gathered in an empty storefront inside the mall and broke into groups to create separate plans for the area. Over the next few days, elements of these plans were evaluated and combined to form a composite draft plan that was presented at the end of the week to an audience of about 250. The high level of participation in the charrette and participants' positive emotions surrounding the failed mall surprised planners, local officials, and mall owners. The charrette also was unusual in other ways.

Victor Dover, of Dover, Kohl & Partners, noted that the plans created by 11 groups of "citizen planners" all had a prodevelopment theme. "They envisioned more development, building their way out of the problem instead of downsizing. That was interesting, because in some communities the reaction to development is much cooler. In many other places, folks have given up on the idea that development can make things better and have adopted a not-in-my-backyard (NIMBY) attitude," he said. "We really didn't see any of that here, which says that folks realize this place has to be more like a town, rather than less like a town, to be successful."

Even more unusual was that expectations for what could be accomplished rose dramatically during the charrette, particularly for the new mall owner. According to

Gibbs, "something very interesting happened at the charrette. The plan kept getting better and better and better in terms of design standards," he said. "I've never seen that before — when the planners started showing sketches, the developer got motivated and said things that made the planners raise the bar. The mayor said some things, and the standard kept rising higher and higher. It ended at a very sophisticated level."

Norie Harrower, who leads Eastgate Mall, LLC, the Hartford, Connecticut-based investment group that purchased half of the mall at the same time that AT&T became a tenant, approached the charrette process with considerable skepticism. "I tend to believe a lot of those things are exercises in futility," he said. "Everybody gets all excited, and the visionaries come into town and spin the wheel and then leave. Nothing happens — and it costs a lot of money."

Owning a mall was not on his mind when, acting as a real estate consultant, Harrower suggested Eastgate as a location for AT&T's new 65,000-square-foot call center. New York Life owned the southern half of the mall, which included the space he recommended to AT&T. But when Harrower proposed that, in return for a ten-year lease, New York Life pay for a $2 million renovation of the empty anchor store in which AT&T would be located, the insurance company would not consider investing in the property. Harrower ultimately assembled a group of investors and bought New York Life's share of the mall, primarily to help AT&T get the space it wanted but also because the price was so low that he could break even without bringing any new tenants other than AT&T to the mall.

When the mayor told the new mall owner that he was integral to the kind of comprehensive revitalization of Eastgate that the city had accomplished earlier downtown, Harrower was not enthusiastic. He had expected only to improve the mall property and sell it for a modest profit. But, at the urging of the mayor and other local officials, Harrower agreed to host the charrette in the mall.

"That was when I got hooked because all of a sudden I saw hundreds of people. I thought 20 or 30 irate citizens would show up and say, 'Tear the damn place down.' I saw some real articulate people coming in who cared. What I picked up on first was the emotion," he recalled. "And the mayor was there. I began to see that the city was really behind this process. It is important to a developer to have a city behind you," adds Harrower. "The citizens were behind it. They didn't want to tear it down. They actually wanted us to revive it. Of course, that was what we wanted to do."

A draft plan was presented in public at the end of the week-long charrette. Harrower had worked extensively with the consultants as they created the composite plan from designs proposed by the citizens. What he asked for in exchange, he says, was that "whatever we came up with had to be doable. It had to be achievable."

Over the next few weeks, the plan was polished and the realities of funding, traffic engineering, and the real estate market were considered. The plan did not change substantially from the January draft, but it gathered so much support from the city, the mall, and prospective tenants that the final public presentation in April — made soon after Harrower's group acquired the rest of the mall in a second transaction — included not only the finalized plan but also announcements of the first projects to implement the plan.

Connecting the Pieces

The new plan calls for creating a town center by turning the mall literally inside out and embedding it in a street grid with new office, retail, and residential construction. The mall's exterior will be refaced with new outward-facing storefronts in one- and two-story urbanistic designs. Much of the 50 acres of parking will be used for new housing, parks, civic buildings, and a town square. The plan also reshapes Brainerd Road, the pedestrian-hostile arterial street on which the mall fronts, which currently has seven lanes and no sidewalks.

One of the plan's most dramatic and symbolic recommendations will be the first to be implemented. Brainerd Town Square is intended to create a signature space for the revitalized district, what planner Dover calls "a center for the town center." The traditional town square will replace the main entrance to the mall — now simply a right turn past a small sign that is difficult to see from the road — with one acre of grass and trees in an unused parking area. Two- and three-story mixed-use retail and commercial buildings will surround the square on three sides.

Before the ink was dry on the new plan — indeed, before the consulting team had provided a final, written plan — construction on Brainerd Town Square was announced. At the final public presentation of the plan in April, Mayor Kinsey announced that the mall owners would donate one acre of parking for the town square and that he would ask the city council to provide $250,000 to build the public park. Mall owners revealed at the same time that construction would begin on three buildings along one side of the square. Retail space in two of the buildings already had been leased by a delicatessen and a dry cleaners.

Urbanism and Economics

Gibbs sees the planned conversion of Eastgate from a mall to part of a mixed-use town center as an example of a new category of shopping center — a hybrid of a main street and a mall — that is beginning to be built in significant numbers. "There is a huge movement right now in retailing to go back to main street. Today all the national chains are looking for space on main street. The shopping centers are learning from the cities."

For now, because these hybrid main streets or village shopping developments remain less common, they command trade areas two to two and a half times the norm, said Gibbs. "We're at the very tip of that wave. Tenants are demanding that developers do it, and brokers are saying that it's not doable, that no one will shop there. But tenants and developers are ignoring them and they're being leased out." Under Gibbs's influence, rather than simply defining the highly visible and symbolic Brainerd Town Square as a green space surrounded by mixed-use buildings, the plan calls for five to seven stores totaling 15,000 to 20,000 square feet. This level of detail emerges from Gibbs's "void analysis" of potential retail development in and near the mall. Based on the number of households in the trade area, typical expenditure per household based on demographics, and current spending in stores within the trade area, Gibbs develops an estimate by retail category of spending that can be captured by new stores.

Gibbs notes that preliminary interviews with local brokers and developers were consistently negative about the area's ability to support any new development but that his research strongly contradicted those views. "We found a very viable market area. There is a solid neighborhood, a mature residential community, a lot of office space, excellent visibility, and vehicular access. All the elements you need for a good stew were there. The region had developed a bias against the area that was not true."

Even before redevelopment, there were bright spots. Although the mall had few tenants, some were very successful. A Gap Outlet store that predated the new owners is one of the chain's top performers, and a Goody's discount clothing store has been successful.

Both stores face outward. Within several blocks of the mall, Chili's and Bennigan's restaurants, a Lexus dealership, Staples, and other businesses are doing well. According to Gibbs, "The money is here. The potential is here. A lot of businesses are doing well here. It just doesn't look like it."

The plan's overall retail mix recommends a "town center commercial" area around the new Brainerd Town Square and designates most of the northern half of the mall and some new buildings in the eastern parking lots as a "core retail" area, while most of the southern end of the mall is devoted to office, hotel, and recreational uses. Neighborhood retail and services will occupy most of the refaced western edge of the mall, on both north and south ends, as well as an area of new construction between the mall and Brainerd Road.

Connections Within the Town Center

The boldness of building a traditional town square next to a stereotypical suburban strip-commercial street is matched by another dramatic feature of the plan: a new road that cuts the mall in half and connects it with existing residential and office development on either side and with a proposed greenway.

As it cuts through the mall, the new road will pass new outward-facing, neighborhood-oriented retail stores and a new hotel with an attached conference center built in a former anchor store. At the mall's western edge, the plan envisions a second green square surrounded on three sides by new residential development built in a former mall parking area next to existing postwar single-family housing. Immediately east of the mall building, in what is now parking, the road will pass through new office buildings that will include a proposed transit transfer center, then enter the existing

Osborne Office Park. The plan proposed in-fill office buildings close to the new road to define a boulevard-like passage, encouraging pedestrian and vehicular traffic between the mall and office areas. Similar connections are proposed between the office park and adjacent strip commercial development along Brainerd Road. While the 100 percent-leased Brainerd Village currently turns it back to the Osborne Office Park, the town center plan proposes new pedestrian connections and a new road to pass through the back of the strip center and into the office park.

In addition to humanizing the pedestrian-hostile Brainerd Road arterial street, the plan is notable for what it does not do in terms of transportation planning. The study calls for no new highway access for the mall, despite local conventional wisdom about the necessity for new interstate access from nearby I-75 and I-24. "Eastgate is an example of the departure from allowing infrastructure, in this case a major interstate, to determine how a community grows and regrows," said Ann Coulter, executive director of the regional planning agency. "The community said, and the market and transportation analysis confirmed, that access to I-75 was neither necessary nor desirable for the success of the project."

What Happens Next?

With strong public input, a visionary plan has been created for the future town center that guides its physical design and economic development. Partnerships and working relationships have been established among local government officials, planners, and business owners. The first projects to implement the vision have been announced. If all the pieces fall into place, what happens now and over the next few years?

According to Kulash, "With real success it would look like a true town, no longer auto-dominated. The overriding impression would no longer be that of moving and storing automobiles, which it is now."

In five years "the mall will be a very profitable, highly active center with many strong national and local tenants" and potentially a complementary shopping destination for out-of-town visitors to Warehouse Row, believes Gibbs. This designer label outlet mall built downtown in 1989 in renovated turn-of-the-century warehouses attracts shoppers from as far away as Atlanta.

Harrower envisions "a mall that no one will really recognize here in another 12 months. In five years you'll see a vastly different terrain." He describes a scene with outdoor cafes, streets that have sidewalks and grassy medians, and acres of asphalt broken up with plantings and water features — a place built to human scale, "where people could spend the day and not be in a car."

Dover sees 100 years of sustained economic development and a beautiful, livable community, but he cautions that the vision is just the first step in a long transformation. "We can't predict everything that will happen. The vision should allow you to do anything at any size and know that your piece of it will fit the greater whole that we're attempting to build over time. A single property owner, a small developer, or a subdivision developer can do that with great confidence because they control all of the land. But here, with a variety of property owners, small and large, the only common manager of the whole process is the community, the city. That's why the city is involved in the planning, because no one else is responsible for the big picture."

The task in this suburban area is the same one Chattanooga is addressing successfully in its downtown: restoring a lost center for the community. The pieces are there — community services, stores, offices, homes and walking trails. Under the guidance of the new plan and its stakeholders, those pieces will be pulled together to create a vital town center.

CHAPTER 12

CHESTERFIELD COUNTY PROTECTS NATURE TO PRESERVE QUALITY-OF-LIFE

Thomas Jacobson

There's still enough of the rural South left in Chesterfield County, Virginia, to attract new residents and corporate offices. Newcomers are drawn by the county's tall forests, its rivers, its historic houses, and its laid-back life style.

But Chesterfield County, which stretches south and west from Richmond, has many of the same characteristics as growing suburban counties all over the U.S., including standardized subdivisions and ungainly commercial strips. Already up to 250,000 residents, the county is expected to add another 100,000 people within the next 20 years.

Moreover, surveys of prospective home buyers indicate a strong preference for large lots in a country setting — with urban conveniences readily accessible. New buyers want to be close to shopping centers, office parks, and cultural and recreational facilities while still living in the countryside.

Resolving this dichotomy between rural dreams and urban needs is the focus of our planning efforts. Our approach is based on a synthesis of urban form and rural char-acter, with particular attention to the preservation and creation of special community places.

Our design program has evolved from an appreciation and understanding of our suburban "customers" — a diverse group that includes people who prefer urban-type settings and people who seek rural home sites.

Basic Beliefs

We've based our program on these principles:

- Land-use relationships will be improved by integrating land use and infrastructure development, locating mixed-use centers in central locations, and discouraging development outside planned urban development areas.
- The suburban land-use pattern should provide for a variety of development densities, with some areas designated very low density.
- Rural visual characteristics should be preserved. Forests, stream valleys, and scat-

Originally published as "Suburban Design: One Step at a Time," *Planning*, Vol. 64, No. 5, May 1998. Published by the American Planning Association, 122 South Michigan Avenue, Suite 1600, Chicago, Illinois 60603-6107. Reprinted with permission of the publisher.

tered farmsteads should provide the design foundation for new suburban development.

- Special places deserve particular design attention. Renewed towns and villages, and new, well-designed mixed-use centers can provide a focus for nearby residents.

Setting Standards

Throughout the 1980s, Chesterfield County grew in a typical sprawl pattern with subdivisions scattered randomly throughout the countryside. Within the last few years, however, several amendments to the comprehensive plan have steered development to designated planned growth areas.

The plan identifies appropriate areas for continuing development (infill and redevelopment areas), for new fringe development, and for deferred future development.

A key feature is the flexible urban service boundary. The plan sets restrictive standards for exurban residential development (five-acre minimum lot size, 300-foot frontage on existing rural roads, no subdivisions) beyond the boundary.

Within subdivisions, the plan's standards for developer-financed public water and sewer lines foster a more compact and orderly development form. All development within the planned growth areas must connect to public water and sewer lines. The plan also calls for a modified grid arterial road network and interconnecting pedestrian paths.

A key element of our planning is to steer new office, retail, light industrial, and multifamily residential development into mixed-use activity centers. Our aim is to shift from the traditional suburban commercial strip to a nodal pattern.

Our zoning ordinance establishes a hierarchy of activity centers based on market area (regional, community, neighborhood, sub-neighborhood). Design standards focus

on pedestrian and vehicular circulation, and the integration of building and site design.

Rural Flavor

Maintaining the county's rural character is a key goal of our planning efforts.

We started by identifying some of the hilltop views, tree-lined corridors, and idyllic ponds that we hope to save. In 1993, we adopted zoning and subdivision ordinance amendments that specifically require preservation of such visual resources to "the maximum extent practicable." We have encouraged the preservation of historic plantations and farmhouses, which ideally provide the architectural theme for surrounding new development.

An extensive area has been designated for large lot development (generally two acres or more). This area had many rural amenities and its soils and hydrology are suitable for septic tank drainfields. No future sewer extensions will be built here. Our hope is that we will avoid the pressure for increased development density that often occurs in unplanned exurban development.

Throughout the county, we are encouraging the use of landscaping features, such as wood fences and gates, that add to the rural flavor of suburban development.

Keeping Green

Hardwood and pine forests cover much of the county's rural area, and the tree-lined roads are a major aesthetic asset.

Protecting this asset has been a key goal of county planning efforts. Tree preservation has been relatively easy to accomplish in residential and office areas. Forested residential lots and office parks have proved to have strong market appeal. The job is harder in commercial areas where merchants insist on visibility from public roads.

In 1989, after considerable debate, the county adopted a zoning ordinance provision that requires preservation of the mature tree canopy along major public roads. The ordinance allows low-growing vegetation to be cleared to provide visibility to adjacent commercial developments. A 50-feet setback along arterial roads is required to preserve large trees and insure that view corridors will be maintained.

Special Places

We have designated a series of activity centers as community focal points. These "places of special design character" include the county's historic courthouse area, five village centers, and several new shopping centers.

Unlike other parts of Virginia, Chesterfield County has few intact historic villages. In most cases, the 18th and 19th century buildings within the village's commercial core are scattered among more recent buildings.

Nevertheless, the five existing villages — Bon Air, Chester, Ettrick, Matoaca, and Midlothian — have a special place in the hearts of county residents and thus are worthy of special design consideration.

Our design standards specify that the form and texture of new structures in the villages should be compatible with their older neighbors, and that the traditional street pattern and setbacks should be maintained.

Chester is an example. The village was established in the mid–19th century at the intersection of two railroads. In recent years, subdivisions and shopping centers have grown up along Route 10 at the edge of the village.

The village plan adopted by the county in 1989 proposed that a new village center be created adjacent to the commercial core.

Now under construction is the first phase of the 85-acre Chester Village Green project, an outgrowth of that plan and the work of local developers. Eventually, the development will include 300 units designed in a neotraditional fashion, with shops, offices, and restaurants. A new public library will anchor the new commercial core, which will be oriented around a village green. An art center has also been proposed, along with a new post office.

Heads Up

There's no shortage in planning journals of recommendations for rehabbing typical suburban areas like those in Chesterfield County. I think it's important to realize, however, that no single design philosophy — neotraditionalism, for instance — will do the trick.

Each suburban jurisdiction should guide its building form in a way that is consistent with its own environment, history, form, and character. In our case, we've focused on four things: expanding in an orderly way, maintaining urban form, enhancing our rural features, and creating special areas of unique design character. The result has been satisfying both to us and to our suburban customers.

CHAPTER 13

CHICAGO CREATES "GREEN" INFRASTRUCTURE

Jessica Rio, Suzanne Malec, Steve Bylina,
Joe McCarthy, Glenda Daniel, and *Eric Emad*

Chicago has developed a well-deserved reputation for urban greening over the past ten years, and its best-known proponent is the city's mayor, Richard M. Daley. Born on Arbor Day, Mayor Daley has a fondness for trees and greening that goes well beyond beautification. In Chicago, urban greening is not undertaken with the sole purpose of aesthetic improvement; it also is an important and recognized component of the city's urban infrastructure and is considered imperative for good quality of life in all of Chicago's 77 communities.

In Chicago, greening provides a source of new job skills, brings communities together to work toward a common goal, calms traffic, reduces heat and air pollution, improves habitat, and contributes to scientific knowledge of natural systems. From a range of agencies in the city of Chicago, to nonprofit conservation agencies, green-industry businesses, and a professional arboriculture association, the reason that Chicago is so green, and so well known for being green, is the many successful collaborations that exist.

Creating Caretakers

The city of Chicago became caretaker of its trees in 1909 when the 30-member Chicago Tree Committee was established. Since then, various government agencies have assumed forestry-related responsibilities within the city. In 1961, the Chicago Bureau of Forestry committed to caring for the city's forest through planting, trimming, and removal operations. Granted authority in the municipal code of Chicago, the bureau inspects, determines the condition of, and performs work as needed on all vegetation growing on public property within the city.

In 1980, however, disaster struck forestry operations when fiscal shortfalls resulted in a budgetary reduction of more than 50 percent. During most of the 1980s, Chicago forestry operations were almost nonexistent. The nails in the bureau's coffin were almost completely embedded when in 1988 the budget was reduced further, and the bureau's responsibilities were shifted to another city bureau. Cutting municipal forestry operations because of budgetary constraints is common in large cities across the country.

Originally published as "The City in a Garden Goes Green," *Urban Land*, Vol. 59, No. 9, September 2000. Published by the Urban Land Institute, Washington, D.C. Reprinted with permission of the publisher.

However, the winds of change breathed new life into forestry activities when Richard M. Daley came into office in 1989. Regaining its independent bureau status in January 1990, the forestry bureau has been one of seven under the jurisdiction of the department of streets and sanitation. Bureau personnel include 275 full-time employees funded by a budget of close to $20 million. Unlike other large municipal forestry programs across the country that continue to suffer budget cuts, the Chicago Bureau of Forestry has enjoyed consistent support, and even growth, during the past decade.

The city of Chicago's geographical boundaries encompass 3,676 miles of streets and 450 acres of boulevards with more than a half-million public trees. The city also manages 180 flowerbeds and the shrubs on its boulevards. Currently, the bureau removes 7,000 to 9,000 dead or hazardous trees each year, while planting 7,500 trees. In addition, the bureau trims approximately 100,000 — or one-fifth of the city's trees — yearly and mows 300 acres of boulevard every seven days. On any given day, 35 to 40 mobile towers with chippers can be deployed throughout the city. Hydraulic clam loaders, semitrailers, and trucks add to this motorized armada.

Greening is more than a philosophy in Chicago. The city's high-profile Green-Streets program promotes public/private partnerships to plant Chicago's expressways, boosts green space for school and commercial sites, and generally encourages greening programs. GreenStreets enlists private support and financial commitment and collaborates with many organizations to accomplish important projects. The Chicago Gateway Green Committee, the Chicago and the Illinois Department of Transportation, the Chicago Park District, and others have collaborated with GreenStreets on projects such as planting Lake Shore Drive medians, landscaping school campuses, and incorporating new trees into sidewalk construction.

The Chicago Department of Transportation also manages an innovative program that installs traffic-calming devices throughout the city in the form of median planters, traffic circles, and curb expansions. Each of these treatments is planted with trees, shrubs, and perennial plants that provide an aesthetic and cooling benefit, as well as slow traffic in commercial and residential areas. In addition, the Chicago Park District plants 2,000 trees per year in parks throughout the city. The district has undertaken a major effort to rehabilitate the parks' lagoons and ponds, introducing native vegetation. Many acres of turf are being turned into meadows to reduce mowing and increase habitat for local wildlife.

Constant Vigilance

While tree planting and greening efforts are admirable, they can easily go for naught if not properly cared for and protected. The bureau of forestry has eight degreed foresters and six training agents to ensure that projects are professionally executed and staff professionally trained. Currently, the bureau has 69 certified arborists, making it the largest single employer of arborists certified by the International Society of Arboriculture. The city has been designated a "Tree City USA" — a leader in urban forestry — by the National Arbor Day Foundation since 1982, has received Tree City USA Growth Awards for the past nine years, and has been an accredited forestry department of the Society of Municipal Arborists since 1991.

Many factors affect tree health. One of the major roles of the bureau of forestry's staff is to review construction plans and to make recommendations on tree preservation, removal, and planting. Root pruning, protective fencing around critical root zones, and tree pruning to minimize damage from construction equipment are just a few of the tools of the trade.

With the advent of federal highway programs such as ISTEA and TEA-21, local communities have been provided flexibility in roadway design. This legislation has greatly assisted the bureau of forestry in preserving trees by allowing city engineers to modify roadway design standards. In one instance, a one-mile section of an arterial street, which was turned into a one-way malled street 30 years ago, was slated for restoration to two-way traffic. The original plan called for the street to be widened from its existing 38 feet to 42 feet, requiring the removal of close to 95 percent of the street trees. After reviewing the proposal, city foresters worked with engineers from Chicago's department of transportation to save the majority of the trees by maintaining the existing road width.

In addition to construction, other forces can threaten trees. Recently, the city's trees have come under attack from exotic invaders such as the gypsy moth and the Asian long-horned beetle. Because the gypsy moth has long been approaching the Chicagoland area from Wisconsin and Indiana, the forestry bureau began working with the Illinois Department of Agriculture in 1992 to conduct a citywide program monitoring the spread of such destructive insects. As a result of this cooperative effort, the city of Chicago was in an excellent position to combat the attack of the Asian long-horned beetle.

Since the discovery of the invader in the area in 1998, the bureau of forestry — along with the Illinois Department of Agriculture, the United States Department of Agriculture, and the citizens of Chicago — have worked together to eradicate the Asian long-horned beetle. Within days of the discovery of the beetle, Mayor Daley committed the city to removing and replanting not only the public trees but also the private trees that were affected — a decision that was made before securing funds from the federal government and without knowing the full extent of the infestation. As a result, public involvement was enhanced because residents no longer were deterred from reporting infested trees on their property because of the cost of replacing them.

The city of Chicago and the United States Forest Service together developed a plan to compensate homeowners for the loss of infested trees. The majority of residents chose an option that allowed them up to three trees along with a landscape subsidy for additional woody plants, spending an average of $1,000 in additional landscaping. A maximum of $3,000 was provided for each household. To date, 239 properties have lost trees and 154 homeowners have participated in the program, with more than 300 trees planted and about $140,000 requested for landscape subsidies. More than 1,300 infested trees have been identified in Chicago, plus 75 trees in two Chicago suburbs.

Community-Based Work

In addition to the green infrastructure projects already mentioned, the city and others are working to engage Chicago's residents in the planting and care of their neighborhood green spaces. The Greencorps Chicago program of the Chicago Department of Environment (DOE) provides horticultural instruction, materials, and employment opportunities to enable Chicagoans to improve the quality of life in their neighborhoods.

Each year Greencorps selects 25 crew members with the help of two social service agencies. Crews receive hands-on horticultural training and job-skills training. Horticultural instruction includes plant identification, installation, and maintenance. Then Greencorps takes to the field, helping communities with neighborhood gardening projects in three ways. First, Greencorps's horticulturists visit community gardens to provide advice and to measure progress. Second, Greencorps provides groups with plants, soil, and tools to install and maintain their gardens. Third, crews provide technical information and assist with building or maintaining the gardens. Greencorps crews and horticulturists also work with 400 high school students and DOE interns to improve grounds at schools through the Greencorps summer program.

The Greencorps crew members also serve internships with private industry and acquire job skills training, river restoration skills, and brownfield remediation skills as part of the nine-month program. As a result, they are well prepared for placement in private-industry jobs after graduating from the program.

Greencorps also promotes greening through its citywide plant distribution days, when groups receive plants for community open spaces. Greencorps gives away seeds in March, annuals and vegetables in June, and bulbs in October. The City Wide Plant Divide in October is an opportunity for gardeners to thin out or diversify their perennials. Landscaping companies with overstock also donate plants. Distribution and division centers are conveniently located throughout Chicago.

With a twist on the traditional vision of urban green infrastructure, Chicago's model projects not only improve aesthetics, but also provide ample environmental benefits. From river restoration, to urban heat island mitigation, to greening brownfields, ideas and enthusiasm abound.

From the air, one can see how the Chicago River curls through the city, linking residential, commercial, and industrial neighborhoods to each other and to Chicago's downtown Loop. Crossed by nearly 70 bridges, the Chicago River is always near, a highly visible natural feature, habitat, and recreational resource.

The Chicago DOE is working with an interagency team to stabilize and beautify the banks of the Chicago River. The team has chosen four model sites where engineers, working with ecologists and hydrologists, will demonstrate techniques to improve water quality, enhance habitat, and improve recreational and habitat access. Treatments include "naturalizing" the riverbank and stabilizing built structures or eroded banks where appropriate. Other projects will create a visual buffer of green space between the river and an industrial site.

Besides making the river's edge more attractive, greening can have additional benefits, such as reducing noise, lowering heat, and inhibiting dumping or littering. Green sites also can contribute to knowledge of the river, serving as locations for water-quality monitoring and habitat studies. The interagency team working to improve the river consists of representatives from the Chicago Department of Energy, the U.S. Army Corps of Engineers, Chicago Department of Planning and Development, Friends of the Chicago River, and community members. The department of transportation also is actively involved in carrying out recreational improvements to the river edge, installing bicycle and hiking paths where possible. And the department of planning and development created and enacted design guidelines that provide for a 30-foot setback and specific landscape requirements for any river-edge development.

Green Spaces and Brownfields

The Chicago DOE is out to reduce temperatures in the city. Urban heat islands occur in areas where pavement and dark-colored roofs absorb heat, causing temperatures to be higher than in surrounding areas. Urban heat islands are a concern because they contribute to air pollution. First, high temperatures and sunlight react with industrial, automotive, and household pollutants to create ground-level ozone, or smog; in high concentrations, ozone may cause or aggravate respiratory problems. Second, when heat builds up around a building, more energy is required to cool it; producing that energy creates more pollution.

Chicago's Urban Heat Island Initiative is demonstrating ways to mitigate these results. For instance, buildings absorb less heat if their roofs have reflective surfaces or green space. When these techniques are concentrated, they can have a greater impact. Planting trees and other plants in parking lots and along major streets also helps cool an area.

To demonstrate the benefits of reducing urban heat islands, the department of energy has launched numerous model projects in the city. The most intriguing and exciting is the development of a large rooftop garden on top of City Hall. This garden will trap rainwater and use it to irrigate plantings, attract birds and butterflies, and demonstrate the ability of vegetation and appropriate materials to reduce the temperature of the surrounding air and thus to reduce the cost of cooling the building. Future neighborhood projects include replacing large expanses of concrete and asphalt with green spaces, painting roofs lighter colors, lightening colors of concrete and asphalt, and developing additional rooftop gardens.

The city also is actively cleaning and remarketing abandoned industrial brownfields. A special brownfield in the West Pullman community on the South Side will demonstrate green technology as part of the redevelopment, which is assembling 140 acres for a model urban industrial park. The city will develop the park as an industrial conservation community, where parts of the area will be used to grow native plants to improve the interim aesthetics and provide a seed harvest for additional plantings across the city. Stormwater will be pretreated by natural filtering of runoff through wetlands developed on site. Development incentives will include energy-efficiency projects that,

in combination with the habitat and pollution-prevention projects, will save on infrastructure and operating costs for site users.

Working in Partnership

It is clear that the city of Chicago and its sister agencies have multiple efforts underway to improve Chicago's green infrastructure. However, many partners have contributed to Chicago's successes. From green businesses to conservation organizations, the city's efforts have been leveraged and expanded with the support of some key groups.

The International Society of Arboriculture (ISA) has been a strong supporter of Chicago's efforts to improve its green infrastructure. From supporting the arborist certification process to lending support through its many ISA-certified companies, ISA has helped the city plan and implement major projects that have become sustainable, sound investments. ISA and its Chicago-based companies work side by side with the city to ensure that ordinances are enforced and that Chicago's public and private trees are preserved and cared for.

Openlands Project, a nonprofit conservation group, supports city greening with two programs that enlist citizen participation in establishing, protecting, and maintaining public open space in Chicago. More than 600 TreeKeepers now have graduated from Openlands's rigorous seven-week course, taught by volunteer faculty members from Hendricksen the Care of Trees, city agencies, area institutions such as Morton Arboretum, and local universities. TreeKeepers mulch, prune, plant, and monitor the health of city trees on public parkways and boulevards, in city parks and forest preserves, and in their own backyards. TreeKeepers also have been recruited by the city to help identify and to provide public education about trees damaged by Asian long-horned beetles and gypsy moths.

Openlands's Neighborhood Open Space Planning program takes city greening a step further. It responds to requests from city neighborhoods to help them plan for permanent open space in their communities at the same time they work with city agencies and other groups to plan for housing, improved schools, economic development, and other needs. The communities help locate and design community and school gardens, mini-parks, recreation fields, and play lots; Openlands then helps them install the gardens and parks and develop ways to organize their block, church, or school to provide on-going care for their new green space. Openlands also puts communities in touch with city agencies like the Chicago DOE's Greencorps program or the bureau of forestry, with other greening groups, or with a nonprofit called NeighborSpace, set up by the city to hold title to and maintain community-managed green spaces on a permanent basis.

To spread the message of public greening even further, Openlands teaches three courses each year in addition to its Tree-Keepers course. "Teaching through School Gardens" offers continuing education credit and practical assistance to city school teachers interested in developing multidisciplinary classroom curricula they can use in connection with school gardens as outside learning laboratories. "BUG (Building Urban gardens)," taught in partnership with another nonprofit, the Garfield Park Conservatory Alliance, teaches basic gardening techniques in a course open to backyard gardeners as well as to community and school garden groups. And the "Neighborhood Open Space Planning" course focuses on helping staffed community development corporations and other community-based organizations incorporate open-space planning into their broader agendas for the city's many neighborhoods.

The city of Chicago's official emblem depicts a number of trees and includes the motto *Urbs in Horto* (City in a Garden). The heritage represented by this statement must be properly preserved. The Chicago experience should encourage other organizations and cities to realize that green infrastructure goes far beyond the task of simply planting trees. Simply feeling that trees and other landscaping are beautiful will not suffice, especially during lean budgetary years. Like Mayor Daley, city administrators must remain resolute in their commitment to their green infrastructure.

CHAPTER 14

DENVER NETWORKS WITH GREENWAYS AND TRAILS

Robert H. Searns, AICP

If you stay in a downtown Denver hotel, you can walk a few blocks to Cherry Creek, get on a landscaped path, and follow a remarkable network of greenways and trails that will take you just about anywhere in the metro area.

Cherry Creek is, arguably, Denver's ancestral greenway. Its creation can be traced to Robert Speer, who served as mayor at the beginning of the 20th century. At the time, the creek, a tributary of the South Platte River, was seen as a "sandy and miserable waste," and there were plans to put it in a trunk sewer.

Speer, who once said "every time a private citizen, by gift or otherwise, adds to a city's beauty, he rekindles the spirit of pride in other citizens," had a different idea. He had been to the 1893 World's Fair in Chicago and came back captivated by the Burnham and Olmsted vision of grand buildings along landscaped waterways.

He began acquiring land along Cherry Creek and stabilized its banks with retaining walls and landscaping. The Cherry Creek corridor — later to be known as Speer Boulevard — was the crowning achievement of Denver's 19th century legacy of parkways planned by Reinhard Schuetze and others.

While the park and parkway system was inspired by civic leaders seeking to add a genteel side to Denver's raw, Wild West image, the greenway network had its roots in a natural disaster, or two to be exact.

One evening in May 1965, a torrential rain struck the city, combining with runoff from snowmelt in the mountains. The result was massive flooding of the South Platte River, which had been neglected and abused for decades. A second flood in 1973, along with pressure to redevelop obsolete railyards in the Central Platte Valley, finally brought action.

Then-mayor Bill McNichols, a Democrat, and state senator Joe Shoemaker, a Republican, organized a nine-member task force to reclaim the river as a major community asset. The city council approved a $2 million seed grant, and the city secured matching funds from a variety of federal, state, and philanthropic sources.

The first efforts were modest: Several demonstration sections of trail were built along the river. A few small parks were added. Unsightly rubble and trash along the banks were hauled away, and the many (and dangerous) small dams were notched to create chutes for kayaks, rafts, and canoes.

Originally published as "Happy Trails: Greenways Put Their Stamp on the Denver Area," *Planning*, Vol. 69, No. 1, January 2003. Published by the American Planning Association, 122 South Michigan Avenue, Suite 1600, Chicago, Illinois 60603-6107. Reprinted with permission of the publisher.

In the years that followed, the project grew until a continuous trail and string of parks lined the South Platte's 10-mile stretch through the city's heart. Local residents began to use the trail — and the river. The concept soon caught on in the suburbs, and virtually all of the metro area communities began building connecting trails and greenways.

Developers joined in, linking new planned communities to the system. In the central Denver area, this basic greenway infrastructure, along with a booming economy in the 1990s, led to more than $1 billion in spin-off development.

Private-sector projects included REI's award-winning flagship superstore, where customers can try out bikes and boats just outside the door, and housing advertising "a trail at your doorstep." Popular suburban developments like Ken Caryl Ranch in Littleton and Highlands Ranch in Douglas County also boast trails and greenways, which, according to local real estate brokers, have enhanced property values by as much as 15 percent.

Today, metro Denver has well over 400 miles of interconnected trails and greenways and many thousands of acres of protected open space, and the system continues to grow. Meanwhile, the idea has spread to the other cities up and down the Colorado Front Range.

Cooperation the Key

Implementation of the metro Denver greenway system was a rather informal affair, relying on nonpartisan cooperation and leadership. "If no one tells you what you can do," Shoemaker liked to say, "no one is telling you what you can't do." Early in its evolution, Mayor McNichols's Platte River Development Committee evolved into the nonprofit Greenway Foundation. Nonprofit status turned out to be a good way to avoid political and interagency squabbles. It also made it easier to raise philanthropic and corporate donations.

The Greenway Foundation's partnership with the city government was largely based on goodwill and a common mission — to get the greenway built. There was also a formal agreement that all new riverfront projects proposed by the foundation would be subject to city council approval and the city's capacity to maintain them. The city handled the actual construction contracting.

This model was replicated in the suburbs. The Mary Carter Greenway, winner of a 1986 APA Current Topic Award for "doing more with less," was spearheaded by a similar nonprofit group called the South Suburban Park Foundation. This group, about to celebrate its 24th year, secured $4 million in funding from nine jurisdictions to complete an eight-mile link along the South Platte, from the Denver city line to Chatfield State Park and the 400-mile Colorado Trail.

Nonpartisanship

In 1992, Colorado voters passed the Tabor Amendment, which substantially limited taxation. In the same election, they created the Great Outdoors Colorado Trust Fund (GOCO), directing hundreds of millions of dollars raised through the state lottery into open space, trails, and park projects.

The GOCO fund is a key to the success of greenway systems throughout the state. It is also indicative of the will of Colorado's citizenry to protect open space and outdoor recreation. Although there have been both subtle and not-so-subtle attempts to raid the GOCO kitty, the program has endured, to date investing over $250 million to preserve more than 350,000 acres of open space and create more than 500 miles of trails.

GOCO echoes the bipartisan effort of McNichols and Shoemaker, who had transcended political lines two decades earlier. By putting up a united front, they overcame the naysayers, raised the money, and built a project that had no precedent. In Denver, the alliance lived on through two subsequent mayoral administrations.

There have been similar partnerships elsewhere in the metro area. In the late 1960s, civic leaders and trout fishing advocates in nearby Littleton teamed up to convince the Army Corps of Engineers (with a little help from Congress) to shift funding originally earmarked for channelizing the Platte River to acquiring the floodplain.

Not long after that, voters in suburban Jefferson County approved a half-cent sales tax, leading to the preservation of 30,000 acres of open space in one of the metro area's most populous counties. Also around that time, the state legislature created the Denver Urban Drainage and Flood Control District, a metropolitan authority for stormwater management, with control over trail development and stream conservation. Each of these endeavors transcended party lines and political philosophies and each set a national precedent.

One Thing Led to Another

The greenway phenomenon in metro Denver is noteworthy for the lack of formal planning. So how do we account for its success? One factor is the combination of clout and leadership demonstrated by Shoemaker and McNichols. Together, they could get things built quickly and set an example.

Another factor is the simplicity of the original greenway concept. River cleanup, small parks, boating improvements, and a continuous trail from city limit to city limit were easy to understand and hard to oppose.

Once most of Denver's system was in place, the surrounding communities had a model to emulate and a system to connect with. Soon similar projects sprang up in the suburbs. It became a goal to have the greenway reach the larger reservoir-based parks and other destinations on the periphery of the metro area.

Key public agencies also chimed in, adding a greenway or trail element to their infrastructure. The Colorado Department of Transportation added a trail to its beltway highway system, and the Urban Drainage and Flood Control District included trails (a.k.a. floodway maintenance roads) along stream corridors in their capital and maintenance funding programs. Developers also picked up on the process and added trail and greenway corridors to their projects.

The system took on a life of its own, spreading, replicating, and integrating into the nation's most extensive regional urban greenway network. Now plans are afoot to link the greenway and trail systems of the Colorado Front Range into a 300-mile-long network that will eventually run from the Wyoming to New Mexico borders, connecting Fort Collins, Denver, Colorado Springs, and Pueblo. Although there is no formal plan, a similar east-west system linking Grand Junction, Vail, Denver, and other places is also in development.

Wake-up Calls

A few years back, someone — presumably a graduating senior at the nearby high school — spray painted a big "97" on the rock face of the Dakota Hogback, a geological formation that helps define the western edge of the metro area. The neighborhood newspaper called for the prosecution of the wayward adolescents.

If you stood facing west to look at the vandalism, and raised your eyes to the mountains beyond, you noticed an enormous new trophy home cut into the top of the ridgeline. It was painted white and floodlit. But this time the press was silent.

A few years later, in the spring of 2002, a huge column of smoke filled the sky behind that huge house. That was the beginning of the wildfires that plagued the West much of last year.

Events like these are wake-up calls. People in Colorado still live on the edge of untamed nature, made manifest by storms, fires, droughts, and floods. A legacy of spectacular beauty draws people here, but they don't always recognize the terms of the gift.

Greenways, I suggest, are a way to help people recognize the thin line between nature and development, a place where they can walk along a trail and observe natural processes, or perhaps participate in a tree planting or wetland reclamation. Indeed, a greenway, where a strand of the wild is preserved in a city or suburb, can be an ideal outdoor classroom.

Legacy

Although popularly used by William H. Whyte in the late '60s, the term "greenway," meaning a major multiuse urban corridor, was probably first applied in Denver. Today, it's a household word used to describe an emerging form of urban infrastructure that combines the benefits of conservation, stormwater management, resource stewardship, and recreation. It sends the message that there is value in setting these open spaces aside, not only for recreation but to buffer a floodplain, unstable hillside, or wildfire zone.

Denver led the way in creating the nation's first interconnected metropolitan urban trail and greenway system. It's a model that many communities have emulated for over two decades and one that we hope will be followed for years to come as a way of dealing with environmental and urban growth challenges.

CHAPTER 15

FAIRFIELD USES TOWN GREEN TO PRESERVE NATURE DOWNTOWN

Arthur Pizzano

Quality of life evidences itself in a variety of ways from one jurisdiction to the next. In Fairfield, Ohio, a community approaching 45,000 residents, this intrinsic value is best manifested in the city's newly emerging downtown. When Fairfield incorporated itself as a city in 1955, its land use pattern was typical of many post–World War II suburbs, in that it developed several, disparate commercial areas but had no identifiable downtown business district to call its own. Forty years later, city officials began to take concerted steps to embark on a program that would provide a central focus for residents.

Thoughtful Planning: A Critical Element

Planning for the Fairfield Village Green started almost a decade ago, and development began in earnest over the past five years. The village Green is envisioned as the first of four quadrants, all in the geographic center of the city that will ultimately compose Fairfield's downtown. The commitment to public and private coordination, targeted investment, and high quality has brought about a distinctive destination that has emerged as a true community gathering place.

The Village Green also is a source of intense civic pride and provides a much-needed citywide focus and "sense of place." It has been a key element in Fairfield's overall strategy to establish itself as a sustainable city, so that it can remain a community of choice as the city continues to mature.

Initial public funding occurred when the city council authorized the creation of a contoured and heavily landscaped central park, or Green. The two-acre park site had been donated as a condition of a planned-unit development (PUD) process by a local developer of what once was a 120-acre farm, bypassed by development for almost five decades. The parcel is strategically located at the city's historic crossroads and adjoins the Fairfield Municipal Building.

The Green contains a lake, meandering creeks, an assortment of water features and

---

Originally published as "The Fairfield Village Green: A New Downtown for a Sustainable City," *Public Management*, Vol. 85, No. 11, December 2003. Published by the International City/County Management Association, Washington, D.C. Reprinted with permission of the publisher.

fountains, walking paths, an outdoor amphitheater, and a tots' playground. Construction costs for the park's development totaled $2.1 million, financed from accumulated annual cash balances from the city's general fund, which were then systematically transferred to its dedicated Downtown Development Fund. The Green lies between two parcels of land (3.0 and 4.8 acres) that were later purchased by the city to showcase two new signature public facilities.

One of these, the 25,000-square-foot Fairfield Lane Library, which opened in September 2001, is technologically advanced and features a prominent clock tower, a Vermont-slate roof, and interior vaulted ceilings. Circulation has increased 83 percent since the new facility opened, and library patron usage is up 132 percent. The library site is juxtaposed with that of the 40,000-square-foot Fairfield Community Arts Center, scheduled for completion in early 2005.

The arts center will feature a 250-seat performing arts theater, a senior citizens' lounge complete with doublesided fireplace, a child-care facility, an art gallery, and spaces for dry and wet crafts, dance, aerobics, and other individual and group activities. The facility also will contain leasable space for large gatherings and receptions in a three-section multipurpose room. There, groups will enjoy access to an adjacent, outdoor second-story deck from which to overlook events being held at the park and the amphitheater within it.

Return on Investment: Getting Down to Business

A variety of private development investment has occurred in response to this targeted use of public capital. In turn, this investment has had significant and positive economic effects on the community; 160 units of single-family residential housing have been developed within the PUD, and lot sales have exceeded expectations, particularly given the fairly unconventional nature of the project's somewhat denser, in-town subdivision configuration. The detached housing caters to a broad mix of lifestyles, including those of young families, empty-nesters, and seniors.

A 120-unit, independent-living complex was later built within the overall master-planned project area to meet the specialized needs of its occupants. Clientele of this facility have found the pedestrian-oriented, one-stop aspects of the mixed-use residential, civic, and commercial Village Green area to be user-friendly.

Attractively designed commercial development has added desirable character and balance to the downtown as well. A new 72,000-square-foot, full-service Kroger supermarket and 195,000 square feet of adjacent retail stores and offices have become fully occupied in just two years. Uses included the 400-seat Symmes Tavern on the Green restaurant, the Village Green Coffee Shop, the Pottery Place, a bank, and lawyers' and doctors' offices.

While the anticipated negative traffic impacts on the existing residential areas initially met with protests, the careful attention to traffic mitigation, buffers, lighting, and so forth has enabled the community to embrace the commercial component as integral to the overall fabric of the neighborhood.

Meeting the Implicit Goal: A Sense of Community

Most significant has been the community spirit and activity evident within the Village Green. Annual July 4th activities have drawn thousands to the area, and arts festivals have been promoted regionally. The Thursday-night "Groovin' on the Green" concert series at the outdoor amphitheater has been supplemented with community theater events, as well as by Friday-night "Movies in the Park," sponsored by the Fairfield Fire Department.

An award-winning sculpture acquisition program has added nine life-size bronze pieces to the downtown, thus providing a comfortable yet urbane, hands-on exposure to the arts. Plans for a major, annual fall event that will be uniquely Fairfield are in the works. It is likely that the venues will include international food (Fairfield is home to the nationally acclaimed Jungle Jim's International Market), along with art, crafts, and a variety of music and performing groups.

Resiliency: Staying on Course

However, things have not always gone smoothly. Residual effects of the city's rapid 1960s through 1980s suburban growth boom continue to be evident from time to time. For example, while substantial efforts and public expenditures have been made by the city to deal with water and sewer management issues, problems persist within the community despite more than $22 million in remedial public improvements to the utility systems. The city is in the midst of considering pre-disaster mitigation measures, including the outright purchase of a number of homes that lie within flood-affected areas.

Also, during the course of the city's development, in 1989 Fairfield lost its major employer, which had been housed in a 1.3 million-square-foot General Motors-Fisher Body industrial plant. While the facility had employed 5,100 people at its peak, its use has since been reinvented, and it now accommodates a variety of smaller tenants, much as a business incubator does. But the loss of the substantial local earnings tax revenues that had previously flowed to the city was a major blow to Fairfield's financial underpinnings. (The municipal income tax is the principal source of general-fund revenue for Ohio cities.)

Fortunately, Fairfield's subsequent concerted efforts to attract replacement industry on its abundantly available and well-located land have been rewarded. These steps have also demonstrated the city's resiliency and resolve. Over the past 15 years, Fairfield has diversified and broadened its tax base and is now home to a variety of light-manufacturing, warehousing, research and development, and, increasingly, service sector businesses.

Daytime employment is currently estimated at 26,000. The earnings tax has seen more than a decade of steady and substantial growth. Another byproduct of this metamorphosis is that the city has shed its "company town," single-industry image and is considered a leading and progressive center of commerce within the region.

Today, the city competes favorably for market share in the burgeoning Cincinnati/Dayton corridor, as a part of booming Butler County in southeast Ohio. Fairfield includes the home offices of the Cincinnati Financial Insurance Corporation, Ohio Casualty Insurance, and Skyline Chili. Pella Windows, Medco Health Solutions (formerly Merck Medco Pharmaceuticals), and DNA Diagnostics Center also are members of the city's corporate family.

The combination of a growing and stable financial base and a record of responsive and responsible service delivery has enabled Fairfield to enhance its offerings beyond the provision of basic services. The city's nationally accredited police department, highly competitive utility rates, and aggressive street maintenance program are a few of the municipal offerings that stand out.

Community Results = Community Support

As Fairfield readies itself to celebrate the 50th anniversary of its incorporation in 2005, it has positioned itself to build strategically on its strong foundation. It is prepared to reinvent itself to help sustain its neighborhoods, business community, and tax base. Fairfield's ability to fund new quality-of-life facilities and programs has enabled this maturing suburb to offer residents and businesses an environment and lifestyle not readily available elsewhere in the region.

What's important is that residents also sense an enhanced level of respect from the surrounding metropolitan area. The community now has a distinct and distinguishing image. Fairfield is enthusiastic about its evolving reputation as a progressive city with a vibrant downtown center. The synergy that exists among a highly focused mayor and council leadership team, a supportive public, and a dedicated staff is evident. It's for these reasons that the city's economic development literature carries the tag line "Fairfield Works."

CHAPTER 16

FORT COLLINS TAKES STEPS TO PROTECT AND PRESERVE ITS CLIMATE

John Fishbach and *Lucinda Smith*

While greenhouse gases (GHG) play a vital role in maintaining the necessary conditions for life on earth, rapidly increasing concentrations of these gases are causing a rise in global temperature, or climate change. During the past decade, the issue of climate change has received greater attention in scientific and political circles, as well as in the media.

With the sharpening focus on this issue, local government officials have found themselves asking, "What is the appropriate role for local governments to play? What impact can local governments have on this broad, global issue of climate change? What are the risks of action or inaction?"

This chapter offers a perspective on how Fort Collins, Colorado, decided to tackle the issue of climate protection. Like other growing communities, Fort Collins (population 115,000) faces multiple management demands. Transportation challenges, infrastructure needs, and environmental concerns all compete for resources and attention. The city's decision to embrace climate protection was not an attempt to solve global warming but rather a deliberate effort to find ways to address multiple community needs and goals.

First, an Overview

It is helpful to begin with a brief overview of the global warming issue. Human-caused greenhouse gases, primarily carbon dioxide, are produced when fossil fuels are burned to produce energy. Deforestation also increases atmospheric carbon dioxide, through the burning or decay of vegetation, as well as the removal of an important carbon dioxide sink. Methane, the second most common human-caused greenhouse gas, is generated as organic matter decays in landfills.

Since the Industrial Revolution, atmospheric concentrations of GHGs have increased 30 percent. Assuming that no actions are taken to reduce emissions, computer models predict that average global temperatures will rise between 1.8 and 6.3 degrees Fahrenheit by the year 2100.

These models suggest that the conse-

Originally published as "Climate Protection: Fort Collins Likes the Idea," *Public Management*, Vol. 82, No. 8, August 2000. Published by the International City/County Management Association, Washington, D.C. Reprinted with permission of the publisher.

quences of global warming could be serious both for human beings and for the ecosystems that support all life on earth. Average sea levels may rise, rainfall patterns may change, agriculture may be harmed by unusual temperatures, and soil and moisture conditions and water resources may be threatened.

While unanimous agreement does not exist on the effects of increased GHGs, the mainstream scientific community does agree that global warming is taking place. The Intergovernmental Panel on Climate Change (IPCC; Web site, http://www.ipcc.ch), which was formed jointly in 1988 by the World Meteorological Organization and the United Nations Environmental Program, is a group of more than 2,000 leading scientists and technical experts from around the world. The IPCC asserted in 1995 that "...humans have made a discernible impact on the climate."

IPCC's latest assessment on climate change reports that global temperatures have risen between 0.7 and 1.5 degrees Fahrenheit since 1860, to about 0.2 degrees higher than their immediately previous evaluations. Because the balance of opinion supports the climate change theory, more and more local governments are evaluating their roles and responsibilities in this complex issue.

Fort Collins's Approach to GHG Reduction

In 1997, Fort Collins joined the Cities for Climate Protection (CCP) Campaign. Sponsored by the International Council for Local Environmental Initiatives (ICLEI) and EPA, the campaign helps local governments achieve lower GHG levels by offering technical assistance, training, publications, marketing tools, and grants to support GHG reduction activities. Since its inception in 1993, more than 380 localities worldwide have joined the CCP.

As a member of the campaign, Fort Collins has conducted a GHG emissions analysis and developed a local action plan to reduce emissions up to 30 percent below the worst-case levels predicted for the year 2010. The city's focus was on identifying realistic, cost-effective measures that would provide tangible local benefits. Fort Collins's commitment is voluntary, and the priority of GHG reduction always will be considered in the context of all of the city's needs.

Fort Collins found several good reasons to justify the exploration of climate protection, including the chance to reduce risk, the ability of local government to influence the community's energy use, and the recognition that GHG reduction offers multiple local benefits.

Roles and Responsibilities

Here are three areas in which local governments can show responsibility.

Ability to effect change. Local governments often are the first to confront such environmental issues as waste disposal and air and water pollution. Because local governments greatly influence activities in land use, transportation, building construction, waste management, and often energy supply, they can play a vital role in reducing energy use and GHG emissions. Although they cover only 2 percent of the earth's surface, localities are responsible for about 78 percent of the carbon emissions from human activities.

Risk reduction. In a 1999 report, the American Geophysical Union warned that scientific uncertainty over the details of climate change does not justify inaction by policymakers. In fact, a rising number of governments and businesses around the world are taking a "prudent avoidance" stance on climate change, recognizing that the risks from a changing climate are great and may significantly hurt citizens, businesses, and local government.

In 1999, more than 570 local-government elected officials joined forces to urge the federal government to make domestic GHG reduction a priority. Pointing out the risks to local governments from the severe weather events predicted to accompany climate change, their joint letter cites an estimated $140 billion in property damage that has resulted from heat waves, storms, floods, and other extreme weather events in the United States between 1988 and 1997. As the letter says, "FEMA and other federal disaster funds cannot begin to cover the economic and human losses that have been caused by these weather disasters."

Leadership. Fort Collins's master plan contains a policy stating that "the city will employ strategies to increase energy efficiency and use of renewable energy sources (except residential wood burning), in order to reduce the impact of the Fort Collins community on global warming." This GHG reduction initiative is one concrete way in which the city can show a policy-based commitment to environmental protection. It also sends a message to other community leaders about the importance of reducing GHGs. And because it is the city's desire to lead by example, Fort Collins's plan contains a number of internal municipal actions toward this goal.

Management Benefits

When considering climate protection, Fort Collins also considered the numerous benefits of reduction activities. It already has realized some of these benefits and expects to reap longer-term benefits in the future.

Spotlight on existing programs. As with many communities, Fort Collins began by looking at existing practices that reduce GHG emissions. One of the strongest selling points for Fort Collins's adoption of a GHG reduction plan was indeed the recognition that many existing energy efficiency and waste reduction programs have the added benefit of GHG reduction. Over half of the GHG reduction credits identified in our plan come from the continuation of existing programs.

Key opportunities for cost savings. Enhanced energy efficiency can mean savings for city or county government, businesses, and citizens. Although investments in energy efficiency measures may be capital-intensive at first, they have the potential to deliver significant long-term savings.

For example, communities across the country are converting their traffic signals from incandescent bulbs to energy-efficient LEDs. While LEDs cost more to purchase, they use much less energy and last longer, saving local governments millions of dollars over the long term.

Economic stimulation. Climate protection can stimulate economic development, especially in the area of "green" building products and services.

Increased partnership with business. The U.S. Department of Energy's Climate Wise program offers a fine opportunity for government/business partnership. Climate Wise works with businesses to identify, implement, and report GHG reduction measures that improve their bottom line.

In 1999, Fort Collins received a grant to help recruit city businesses to join the Climate Wise program and to offer technical assistance to ensure that businesses file action plans for reducing GHG emissions. Business interest has greatly exceeded initial expectations: 15 businesses have been recruited into Climate Wise this year. This effort supports city policies identified in the master plan, to develop partnerships that will improve air quality and to act as a resource that will help the community implement pollution prevention strategies.

Environmental benefits. Energy efficiency measures have the direct benefit of reducing the emissions of key air pollutants, including carbon monoxide, particulate matter, sulfur dioxide, and nitrogen oxide. In 1999, the State and Territorial Air Pollution Program Administrators (STAPPA) and the Association of Local Air Pollution Control Officials (ALAPCO) (Web site, http://www. ipcc.ch) released a major report quantifying the air pollution benefits from a variety of GHG reduction activities. Fort Collins has estimated that the five largest measures identified in the city's own GHG reduction plan alone would reduce more than 3,300 tons of key air pollutants by the year 2010.

Increased recycling or waste reduction extends landfill space, as well as reducing methane and carbon dioxide emissions. This benefit can be an important factor for a community whose landfill is nearing capacity, as is the one near Fort Collins. Other environmental benefits can be achieved from GHG reduction, like water conservation and the lowering of toxicity levels.

GHG Credit Trading and Reporting. Quantification of GHG reductions will prepare local governments for eventual emissions trading programs. Voluntary emissions reporting and trading programs exist now. The Leonardo Academy has instituted the Cleaner and Greener Program, which lets consumers, businesses, and organizations buy emissions credits to offset their emissions. Sellers of reduction credits can use the revenue for further investments in energy efficiency efforts.

The Department of Energy's Energy Information Administration (EIA) also conducts a program for the voluntary reporting of greenhouse gases. Quantifying GHG reduction activities has enabled Fort Collins to enhance its reporting to the EIA.

Heightened competitiveness for grant funding. Numerous grant opportunities are available to local governments interested in climate protection. The Environmental Protection Agency, the Department of Energy, the Department of Transportation, and the FHWA all offer funding opportunities related to climate protection. Perhaps because of its stated commitment to climate protection, Fort Collins has successfully competed for two ICLEI-funded grants.

Other Issues

Additional issues that communities may wish to evaluate when exploring GHG reduction might include assessment cost, public opinion, and the role of the utilities.

Evaluating costs and benefits. In developing a prioritized list of reduction activities, Fort Collins has attempted to evaluate its return on investment for proposed actions. Although time-consuming, this semi-quantitative approach has eased councilmembers' consideration of adopting the plan, because a reasonable estimate of costs has been made up-front.

Garnering public opinion. Fort Collins is fortunate to have a clear community mandate that environmental protection should be valued highly. Its master plan contains a specific policy to curb the impact of the Fort Collins community on global warming.

Some communities might turn to local or national surveys to evaluate the public acceptance of climate protection. National polls indicate that such acceptance does exist. According to a recent poll conducted by the Sustainable Energy Coalition, a majority of voters (55 percent) believe that people know enough about climate change and its causes to feel that we should act now to reduce their impact. This past January, at the 30th Annual World Economic Forum in Switzerland, hundreds of government and business leaders voted that climate change was the world's most pressing problem.

Boosting the role of utilities. With the impending deregulation of the electric utility industry in many states, utilities are striving to become as competitive as possible by cutting their expenses. This can mean a decrease in support for energy conservation programs or renewable energy. At the same time, the prospect of deregulation may lead utilities to diversify in order to extend their potential customer base. This can mean the addition of renewable energy sources like wind, despite any added costs.

Local leaders across the United States are recognizing the benefits of green-power energy from renewable sources. Fort Collins Utilities was the first utility provider in Colorado to offer wind power to its customers. Under a voluntary "green pricing" program, residential and commercial customers can elect to pay a premium for wind. The wind-power program offers utility customers a choice, *and* it cuts GHG emissions.

Making the Decision

Perhaps the key issue faced by any locality deciding whether to embrace climate protection actively is: How do you justify this move in a time of inadequate funding for all the programs and services the locality already wants and needs to provide?

An answer lies in seeking the common ground that exists among the concerns for greenhouse gas reduction, energy efficiency, and good community planning and operation. Improving transportation options lowers local pollution levels, enhances energy efficiency, and reduces the amount of combustion of fossil fuels. Improved energy efficiency in businesses boosts the economic

bottom line, along with helping to meet gas reduction goals.

Energy-efficient housing improves housing affordability, as well as aiding in GHG reduction. Fort Collins has chosen to focus on what makes sense now in addressing community needs and goals, while also making an effort to contribute to the solution of a threatening world problem.

Don't Entertain Regrets

For many local governments, the debate over the likely impacts of climate change is not productive. Nobody is likely to be able to prove that climate change is happening until it is too late to do anything about it. The real questions are whether or not GHG-reducing actions will provide tangible local benefits and whether these benefits are worth the price tag.

In choosing to embrace climate protection, Fort Collins has gone with the no regrets approach already adopted by localities and corporations around the world, an approach that entails making economically sound choices to curb GHG emissions, thereby providing multiple benefits to the community and support for existing community goals.

Fort Collins sought solutions that would enhance energy efficiency and waste reduction without the city's having to delve deeply into the scientific debate on climate change.

CHAPTER 17

GAINESVILLE AND HALL COUNTY WORK TO PRESERVE WATERSHED AREAS

Kim O'Connell

For decades, the United States has been fighting with Canada and Mexico over rights to rivers along national borders. In the arid West, rapidly growing cities are competing for water rights along state borders in Arizona, California, Colorado and elsewhere.

Even in regions where water has traditionally been plentiful, bitter battles are erupting. Georgia, Alabama and Florida, for example, are wrestling over two river systems that cross state boundaries.

Nationwide, water battles are intensifying, as booming populations, migration to urban areas and chronic drought conditions strain metropolitan water supplies. However, the same phenomenon that has produced conflict also has given rise to cooperation.

Many local governments have begun planning and managing their watersheds regionally. Working with other local jurisdictions, they are addressing stormwater, wastewater, land use and development to ensure that the quantity and quality of water supplies in their regions remain ample.

Common Goals

Two years ago, acting on a statewide directive issued by the Georgia Department of Natural Resources, three Georgia localities embarked on a watershed assessment study to determine how to best protect the region's beleaguered water sources. Gainesville, Forsyth County and Hall County are — like the rest of metropolitan Atlanta — facing a severe water shortage and a water quality crisis. They assessed three different watersheds, with the primary focus on popular Lake Lanier and the Chattahoochee River watershed.

"Watersheds don't know political boundaries, so from a scientific standpoint, it made the most sense [to work together]," says David Dockery, environmental service administrator with the Gainesville Utilities Department. "We also realized that some restrictions on development and watershed protection measures would come out of this study. We wanted to approach it in a regional fashion to not drive development from one side [of the watershed] to the other."

Originally published as "Regionalizing Watershed Management," *American City & County*, Vol. 116, No. 6, June 2001. Published by the Intertec Publishing Corporation, Atlanta, Georgia. Reprinted with permission of the publisher.

The local governments tested the water chemistry in more than 30 streams. They found that, in urban areas, the streams were affected by altered hydrology, erosion, degraded habitat and sedimentation. Then using the collected data as a baseline, the governments developed computer models that simulated how future development or other changes would affect the watersheds.

The governments also outlined several options that each could use to protect the watershed. For example, they recommended establishing buffer zones around rivers and streams, building regional retention ponds, improving erosion controls, and using trenches and semi-pervious surfaces to aid in stormwater filtration and groundwater absorption.

The results of the watershed assessment can be applied by each locality individually. For example, in a proposed ordinance, Gainesville is calling for a 100-foot buffer zone, while rural Hall County — where residents are concerned about infringement on private property — is proposing a 50-foot buffer.

"All three entities aren't doing exactly the same thing as far as implementing watershed protection, but we're all basically on the same page," Dockery says. "We're [proposing] ordinances that are seeking the same ends, but the means vary a little from entity to entity."

That flexibility helps stave off resentment, which can result when one or more regional partners dictates what the others should do. Public resentment also is possible, which is why public meetings about regionalization are important. During the assessment, Gainesville and Hall County held 26 public meetings — two for each of the 13 community watersheds identified in the region.

"Politically, no one wants to give up their turf, to a certain extent," Dockery says. "There are also cultural issues — when we're dealing with the way rural folks look at

water as opposed to how urban folks look at water. There's a private property rights issue to deal with, and we're sensitive to that."

Dockery notes that the three governments still handle their water supplies separately and that the regional assessment is not part of a source water protection plan. (A separate regional development commission is working on guidelines for source water.) However, he says that protecting the region's watersheds will have peripheral benefits, such as a cleaner water supply.

Inclusion and Education

Cleaning up the water supply was the motivation for forming the Medford Waste Commission early in the 20th century. At the time, the residents of Medford, Ore., were plagued with foul-tasting and odorous water that had tadpoles and other aquatic life floating in it.

Medford is situated within the Bear Creek watershed, which joins the Big Butte Creek and Rogue River watersheds (owned primarily by the U.S. Forest Service and Bureau of Land Management) in making up the Rogue River Valley. Within decades of MWC's formation, the commission had secured rights to groundwater within the Big Butte Creek watershed and rights to surface water within the Rogue Rover watershed. By default, it became the regional water manager.

The jurisdictional mosaic gets even more complicated, however. The Big Butte Creek and Rogue River watersheds cross three counties, private timberlands and cattle grazing areas.

Building consensus among those entities has been an important part of managing the region's water, says Medford geologist Bob Jones. "It's a long, steady process, and you have to keep working at it," he says. "One of the things that will help you achieve success in working together is having all the main entities, people with jurisdictional authority, at the table at the same time." Talking to stakeholders separately opens the door to miscommunication and suspicion, he notes.

The commission is involved with two local watershed councils, which include a cross-section of stakeholders — environmentalists, loggers, landowners and others. The groups meet monthly to discuss project status and proposals.

Sometimes, projects are put to a simple majority vote, Jones says. When parties are unable to negotiate an agreement, opponents are sometimes willing to step out of the proceedings to let the project continue.

The commission also has undertaken efforts to educate the public about watershed management. For example, it has published brochures with other entities in the region, and it has made door-to-door visits to discuss programs with residents.

"So often people say we need an ordinance to stop something from happening, and I'm not saying that's not sometime true, but what happens so often is they don't get enforced," Jones says. "So we've taken the tack that it would be better to do an education campaign."

Rather than correcting harmful behavior with short-term punitive responses, the MWC assists stakeholders in identifying ways to eliminate or modify the behavior to produce long-term improvements. For example, when a private entity recently sprayed herbicides that affected a spring in the Big Butte watershed, the Waste Commission convinced the owner to stop spraying over water and to allow monitoring by the commission. In another instance, the commission helped to work out a master plan for cattle grazing that protected particularly sensitive areas of the watershed.

A Matter of Necessity

Long-term, cooperative relationships are key to successful regionalized management, says Chip Norton, watershed manager for Cambridge, Mass. Massachusetts is divided into numerous watershed regions, with much of the populated area around Boston served by the Massachusetts Water Resources Authority. However, since the mid-19th century Cambridge has had its own water supply, drawn from the city and four nearby communities.

Although Cambridge does not supply water to the region, it relies on regional partners to help protect its watershed. "One of our problems is we own 5 percent of the watershed, so it makes things difficult," Norton says. "A lot of water suppliers own most of their watershed. I think regionalization is a trend that comes out of necessity."

Cambridge has learned to communicate with and rely on the cooperation of other entities and stakeholders in the watershed. As part of the Cambridge Watershed Advisory Committee, the city works with conservation commissions, fire departments, planning boards, sewer departments, health boards and other groups to protect its water supply.

It builds relationships and resolves issues via meetings on a case-by-case basis, and it keeps residents informed through a quarterly newsletter. According to Norton, the city has dealt with a variety of issues, including those related to highway runoff, urbanization and development.

"We're really looking at the next 100 years," he notes. "This water supply has to be here forever."

The Wave of the Future

With chronic water shortages and water quality problems throughout the country, regionalization is likely to become more commonplace, according to Dockery. Instead of staging never-ending turf wars, local governments are now more apt to look for ways to work together.

The process can have several benefits. For example, taking a holistic view of watersheds makes good environmental sense, and, by pooling resources, local governments can implement changes more effi-ciently and less expensively than they could individually.

Regionalization is not always easy. However, by bringing all stakeholders to the table, local governments can reduce conflicts, build consensus and, in some cases, avoid the time-consuming and politically charged process of developing ordinances.

CHAPTER 18

GRAND FORKS REBUILDS DOWNTOWN WITH OPEN SPACES AND WALKWAYS

Kim O'Connell

Even for the hardy and resilient citizens of Grand Forks, North Dakota, 1997 was a tough year. Located at the eastern edge of North Dakota, Grand Forks is home to hard-working Midwesterners who pride themselves on their ability to thrive despite the city's long, harsh winters. The winter of 1996-1997 was extraordinary, however, even by Grand Forks's standards. It lashed the city with record storm after record storm, piling up a total of nearly 100 inches of snow. Spring brought more blizzards, followed by rapid warming and heavy rains. The rains and melting snow caused the rivers to swell and surge. When the Red River rose to 55 feet above sea level (more than double the 26-foot flood level), it broke through its earthen dike. Water flowed freely over the city, until more than two-thirds of Grand Forks was under water and nearly all the city's 50,000 citizens had to evacuate their homes. The city water system was contaminated, and the sewage treatment plant had to be shut down.

Downtown Grand Forks, which is adjacent to the river bank, was especially hard hit. Streets, basements, and the first floors of all buildings were awash with sewage-fouled floodwater, mud, and debris. Fires raged in 11 downtown buildings during the flood, wreaking further destruction. Torrents of water also flooded homes in adjacent neighborhoods and flowed over and beyond the city, across the plains of North Dakota.

When the floodwaters finally receded, the city, under the leadership of Mayor Patricia Owens, began the arduous job of cleaning up and rebuilding. U.S. Secretary of Housing and Urban Development (HUD) Andrew Cuomo moved immediately to help and pledged $171 million in aid to the city. As part of its assistance effort, HUD offered the city the services of a ULI advisory services panel, which visited Grand Forks last September.

Re-Imagining Downtown

The city of Grand Forks began to consider how to organize its recovery effort by taking a hard look at its downtown. Even

Originally published as "Rebuilding Downtown Grand Forks," *Urban Land*, Vol. 57, No. 2, February 1998. Published by the Urban Land Institute, 1025 Thomas Jefferson Street, N.W., Suite 500 West, Washington, D.C. Reprinted with permission of the publisher.

before the devastating flood, downtown Grand Forks, like many U.S. cities, had begun to evolve from being the region's primary office and retail center to being its residential, governmental, and educational center. Over the past 20 years, changes in retail development and spending patterns had resulted in the movement of many stores and services to suburban locations, particularly after a regional mall was built in the southwestern part of the city. Many downtown businesses had been replaced by professional services and entertainment uses, while other storefronts remained vacant. In an attempt to compete with the shopping mall and other retail outlets, an indoor shopping center, City Center Mall, had been developed downtown by closing a street and connecting buildings on either side with a roofed enclosure.

Since the flood, many of the businesses that had remained downtown have relocated, have closed completely, or are in temporary space and have no definite plans for permanent relocation. Although government offices and schools are expected to rebuild in their existing downtown locations, the future of many of the retailers and professional service firms is uncertain.

The flood therefore has presented the city and its citizens with an opportunity to ask basic questions about the role and function of downtown. Some people believed the downtown core was obsolete and that perhaps the city should not devote resources to rebuilding it. Others felt that the downtown should be redeveloped, not simply as it was before, but in a way that reflects today's changed market realities.

With this in mind, the city's charge to the ULI panel was to determine, in the light of current market conditions and trends, what role downtown Grand Forks should play in the regional economy and to suggest rebuilding strategies that would enable it to fulfill that role. A great deal of useful planning work was done before the panel's arrival, including preparation of a report issued by Grand Forks's Re-Imagining Downtown Committee, a plan known as the River Forks plan, an interim business program, and more. In preparing its recommendations, the panel reviewed these reports, briefing materials prepared by the city, and information gleaned from interviews with more than 100 individuals.

Envisioning a New Heart for Grand Forks

The ULI panel advised that downtown Grand Forks be redeveloped in a way that asserts its historic role as the symbolic, physical, and functional "heart" of the region. To that end, the panel envisioned the city core as an exciting gathering place, with restaurants, specialty shops, entertainment, and festivals; public open space along the river; governmental, educational, and financial offices; and housing that offers easy access to downtown amenities, and, when possible, views of the river. The proposal also included a traditional town square that would serve as the main public space and focal point for the entire community.

The panel found that downtown Grand Forks has an essentially strong and stable economy founded on agriculture, retail trade, wholesale distribution, aerospace technology, and education. Key economic forces include the University of North Dakota, which has 13,000 students, faculty, and staff, and nearby Grand Forks Air Force Base, which employs 12,500 people. The city also functions as a metropolitan service center and provides retail stores and services to a 17-county area of 210,000 people in eastern North Dakota and western Minnesota.

The city's urban core seems to have many strengths on which to build. From a financial point of view, millions of public dollars have been invested in buildings, infrastructure, and community facilities downtown, which include a central high school, the city hall, the county courthouse and administrative offices, public safety offices, and a federal building. There also has been significant private sector investment. Despite the flood, underground utilities are in reasonably good condition. There is little crime, and the city is considered safe. The central business district is surrounded by generally stable and well preserved neighborhoods. In addition, downtown Grand Forks has remained a viable and affordable residential location. Before the flood, multifamily housing downtown served the needs of the elderly and university students. These generally affordable units were typically fully occupied, and waiting lists were common.

Downtown Grand Forks remains the geographic center of the metropolitan area and is one of the most accessible points in the entire region. The downtown area is small and well defined, with a grid street system that creates an urban scale and character that is unique in the Grand Forks metro area. The proximity of city and county government offices downtown provides an opportunity for the two systems to work together and employ a large, stable population of workers who represent a potential market for other business activity downtown. In addition, there is significant unmet demand for both replacement and new development in all segments of downtown real estate: residential, office, entertainment, public sector, and hotel uses.

The city also embodies the heritage of Grand Forks, with a collection of historic buildings that is admired throughout the West. Although it lacks a defined physical and social focal point, the downtown area — and particularly the riverbank — continues to serve as the gathering place of citywide community celebrations. Little riverfront infrastructure is in place, however, and little effort has been expended to capitalize on

the river as one of the city's major assets and gathering spots.

Containing — and Celebrating — the River

The panel proposed a conceptual land use plan for downtown Grand Forks that includes a flood protection system; creation of exciting public spaces along the river, including a traditional town square; clustering of land uses by development type; and streetscape and infrastructure improvements.

The first order of business was to recommend ways to contain and celebrate the river. To make the area safe from future flooding, the panel, after consulting with the U.S. Army Corps of Engineers, advised creating a flood wall, part of which would be architecturally integrated into the historic buildings parallel to the river along the east side of Third Street, thereby preserving both sides of that street. All major streets would pass through the wall, allowing physical and visual access to the river. Movable flood gates would secure open passages during periods of flooding. The gates also would present opportunities for public art to mark and enhance the entrances to the river. At the same time, the panel suggested both making the river more efficient in its hydraulic flow and enhancing its value as an aesthetic and recreational amenity by creating a weir, an underwater dam, that would raise and widen the river's surface area. To accommodate the wider flow of water, reconstructing approaches to bridges would enable water to flow beneath them.

According to the panel, the river is the key to establishing a sense of place in downtown Grand Forks. To realize its value, the cities of Grand Forks and East Grand Forks were encouraged to work together to create a bistate Red River Park that would feature a landscaped esplanade anchored by the proposed town square, which is located at what is now City Center Mall. The town square would serve as a formal "living room" for civic and cultural events, provide a balcony overlook to the river basin, and be the point of transition from the flood wall into the park. The park would include regraded shorelines landscaped with natural flora, pedestrian promenades, hard-surface hiking and jogging paths, and, at the upper reaches of the floodway, baseball and football fields. Marinas, bicycle paths, and other amenities also could be included.

Repositioning Downtown

Next, clustering development downtown into three districts was recommended. Each cluster would emphasize a particular type of land use: a residential, retail, and entertainment district in the few blocks near and overlooking the river and the proposed town square; a financial district that would provide a first-class, high-profile home for financial institutions and professional service firms; and two government and educational centers that would build on existing clusters of public uses flanking the proposed financial center location. The activity centers would be connected by street-level retail activity, upper-floor apartments, and civic amenities such as street trees, lighting, paving, sculpture, fountains, and banners. Initial development would be concentrated within a five-block area to create a compact, walkable environment that would be attractive to downtown residents, workers, and visitors.

To reposition downtown Grand Forks so that its market potential would be maximized, the panel recommended that the city embrace the strategic elements of the nationally recognized Main Street Program of the National Trust for Historic Preservation, which consist of economic restructuring, through a business retention and recruit-

ment program; organization, enabling downtown businesses to collaborate; design guidelines and assistance that emphasize historic preservation; and marketing strategies that present downtown as a unit to both investors and consumers. To encourage historic preservation, the city was urged to support retention of cultural landmarks and to work with the Historic Preservation Commission to develop a reuse strategy for individual historic buildings.

The panel suggested that the existing River Forks Commission (RFC) assume responsibility for marketing and promoting downtown, river-related events, and the region, using its delegated legal powers. RFC also would be responsible for developing the bistate Red River Park and ensuring good communication between Grand Forks and East Grand Forks. Also advised was that an autonomous public/private subcommittee of RFC, to be known as the Downtown Development Committee (DDC), be established to create and implement the plans and budget for rebuilding downtown Grand Forks.

Progress in rebuilding downtown Grand Forks was thought to require public/private partnerships. The panel suggested that the DDC encourage a stronger private sector role by preparing and marketing "packaged" development opportunities for desired projects when appropriate.

Both short-term and longer-term strategies to revitalize the downtown area were recommended. Short-term projects include completing demolition of unusable structures; clearing, grading, and seeding lots as an interim measure to prepare them for development; creating a skating rink/farmers market; engaging a historic preservation consultant to prepare site-specific development proposals; and rehabilitating existing housing in key areas. As an important early but highly visible step in establishing confidence and investment momentum downtown, the panel suggested that the city take the first step toward creating the recommended financial center downtown by negotiating an equitable and mutually beneficial lease with First National Bank and interested attorneys and accountants as soon as possible. Longer-term projects include developing site-specific plans for infill and new housing, assembling sites for strategic development, addressing zoning and other regulatory issues, hiring a director of development, and preparing a detailed infrastructure improvement plan budget.

Since most market-rate downtown projects initially will not pencil out financially without some public funding, the panel recommended that the city allocate $50 to $70 million of its community development block grant (CDBG) allocation for the rebuilding of downtown and outlined various ways that the city could leverage its investment. The use of public funds would be essential for stimulating both initial revitalization projects and private investment, and it should be viewed as an investment that will pay future dividends to the entire community.

Taking a Regional View

The panel also looked across the river. East Grand Forks is about to complete its own ambitious comprehensive redevelopment plan, and the community's leadership is prepared to make a significant investment to implement it. In its final comments, the panel stressed that its suggestions for Grand Forks and the proposed plans for East Grand Forks are complementary, interdependent, and mutually reinforcing, and it urged the two cities to work closely together in implementing their downtown redevelopment plans.

Much of what the citizens of Grand Forks are proud of in their downtown was built by an earlier generation at the turn of the century. In about two years, there will be a new source of pride, based on what *this* generation gives to the future citizens of Grand Forks and East Grand Forks.

CHAPTER 19

HAMPTON CREATES ENVIRONMENTAL CENTER WHILE PRESERVING OPEN SPACE

Lawrence O. Houstoun

No longer content to leave economic development to government agencies, tens of thousands of business and property owners in more than 1,200 North American locations have taken the reins themselves by setting up business improvement districts. Their focus: improving property values, adding jobs, and increasing their own profits.

This movement toward self-help management has been going on for 20 years, mostly in the downtowns of major cities. But business improvement districts are now cropping up elsewhere as well — for example, in highway commercial strips, university and hospital clusters, and even industrial areas. The districts described here grew from a local government plan or policy or are designed to implement plans or policies. Each required public-private cooperation.

Edge City

By the early 1990s, the diverse owners of the 1,800-acre commercial center along Mercury Boulevard in Hampton, Virginia, knew they were losing market share to newer, larger retail areas elsewhere in the Tidewater region. Hampton's vast edge city includes Hampton's Coliseum, hotels and restaurants, and more than three million square feet of retail space.

To stay competitive, Mercury Boulevard property owners in 1995 took the advice of Richard Bradley, then president of the International Downtown Association, and decided to work with a consulting team to consider setting up a business improvement district. The city favored the idea because the tax revenue it was collecting from Mercury Boulevard businesses was topping out at $17.8 million and showed signs of slipping. When approved by the city in 1996, Coliseum Central became one of the first districts in the U.S. located in a large commercial area oriented to highway, rather than to central business district, markets.

With an organization and financing in place, the district's executive director, Peter Gozza, convinced his board that the area needed a plan to convert "1,800 acres of as-

Originally published as "Smart Money: New Directions for Business Improvement Districts," *Planning*, Vol. 64, No. 1, January 1998. Published by the American Planning Association, 122 South Michigan Avenue, Suite 1600, Chicago, Illinois 60603-6107. Reprinted with permission of the publisher.

phalt and aging commercial buildings" into a popular center for the entire Hampton Roads area. The 20-year blueprint for revitalization, written in 1996, has five major proposals, one of them being that Mercury Boulevard should be narrowed and landscaped. The other four: a pedestrian mall near a new movie complex, an entertainment-retail center near the Coliseum, an environmental center on 60 wooded acres, and a boat canal. Preliminary plans for the waterway show a canal leading from the lake at the Hampton Coliseum into the heart of the shopping district, after the fashion of San Antonio's Riverwalk.

Gozza is now using the plan to solicit state and federal funds for this $60 million project. One possibility is to link the development with an extension of Interstate 664, which will need stormwater retention ponds.

Like a downtown, Coliseum Central must draw customers attracted to a locale, not just an individual store. So Gozza is trying to create a sense of identity for the area — something that has been missing until now. One innovation is "Courtesy Kids," four teams of four teenagers each, who serve as a hospitality force, carry packages, open doors, sing, and clean up. These talented young people have given merchants a more positive view of teenagers and have made the area friendlier for shoppers.

Some may question why a tool of downtown revitalization should be used to bolster a suburban development. But Hampton's political and business leaders felt there was no competition between Coliseum Central — with its highly mobile regional market — and the city's small, waterfront-oriented downtown (which has its own business improvement district).

It's Institutional

University City District in West Philadelphia grew from a tragedy. Only after a University of Pennsylvania faculty member was killed there in 1996 did the concept of a district emerge.

University City lies immediately west of Philadelphia's popular Center City — a two-square-mile area where many university people live. Center City's business improvement district provides cleaning, security, and landscaping services that are among the best in the nation, enhancing attractions such as theater, nightclubs, restaurants, hotels, office towers, and department stores.

The contrast between the two locations could not be greater. While University City houses the beautifully restored Thirtieth Street Station and three attractive campuses — Penn, Drexel University and the Philadelphia College of Pharmacy and Sciences — most of the remaining 100 blocks there are marginal. Once proud residential streets are poorly lighted and choked with weed trees, and beyond these streets and the campuses are acres of parking lots, roaring traffic, ugly vending trucks, and graffiti.

John Fry, executive vice-president of the University of Pennsylvania, launched the remediation effort in 1996 by hiring consultants and visiting the heads of major nonprofit groups and public agencies, securing their agreement to participate in what soon became cleanup, security, visual improvements, and marketing. So little commerce remained in University City at that point that business representatives were not included at first. But after four months a nonprofit corporation was formed and a five-year budget created.

The University City District's nearly $4 million annual expenses are being shared under a series of multiyear voluntary agreements by the two universities and the pharmacy college, the University of Pennsylvania Health System, the University City Science Center, Amtrak, the West Philadelphia Partnership (an alliance of neighborhood organizations), and several multifamily residential property owners. In addition,

University City District will seek state and federal funding for infrastructure, visual improvements, and signage. Paul Steinke, formerly with Philadelphia's Center City District, was appointed executive director of the University City District in September 1997.

University City District may now be one of a kind — an improvement district that is not dependent on municipal property tax assessments. But inquiries from comparable areas elsewhere in the country indicate interest where several institutions can support a district even when commercial properties are absent.

Industrial Site

The Bunker Hill Special Improvement District in Paterson, New Jersey, is one of the few business improvement districts based in an industrial area. Now three years old, the district's management corporation consists of a nine-member board whose industrial property owners (plus a city council member, as mandated by New Jersey law) administers a $175,000 annual budget. Every member of the group is a volunteer; there are no paid employees.

Both Fortune 500 companies and international firms are represented among the 200 property owners in the district. John Ressie of the Bascom Corporation is chairman of the district's board.

Sixty percent of the group's revenues are spent on security, about 30 percent on sanitation and beautification, and the balance on public relations and special projects. A private security service provides 24-hour mobile service within the square mile service area. When the district's burglar alarm is activated, security guards typically arrive before the police do. Other tasks the district has undertaken include graffiti cleaning, fence repair, and fighting dumping by roofers and others.

When the district was being organized, opposition came from some of the industrial property owners, residents (who were to be charged a $5 annual fee), and one city council member, who objected to business improvement district assessments on principle. Once the district was approved, however, residents were dropped from the project and the idea became so popular that the city formed a second district, this one downtown.

New Jersey law is the most flexible in the nation with regard to assessment formulas, specifying only that there needs to be a relationship between charges and benefits. Some districts use square footage, share of property taxes, or type of use as the basis for assessment. Districts do not have independent bonding authority, although long-term capital improvements can be financed through business improvement district assessments with municipal bonding authority. Ressie says that the board of the Bunker Hill district will seek grants, not bonds, to finance infrastructure improvements there.

Ongoing operating expenses are financed through payments based on assessed valuation, with a minimum annual payment of $125 per property. Each assessment represents the property's share of the district's total assessed valuation. Owners of large properties may pay between $10,000 and $12,000 a year.

Entertainment Venue

Lark Street in Albany, New York — separated from downtown by the massive state office complex — is a pleasant mix of restaurants, specialty shops, residential buildings, and a supermarket. By 1995 this 10-block-long area had become somewhat shabby but still had plenty of energy.

Early support for a business improvement district came from George Leveille, the city's director of economic development. Sharon Ward, a former city alderman, and

Lark Street businessman Tom Rowland co-chaired the planning phase. A consulting team hired by the city found that local people were especially interested in nighttime security, parking improvements, holiday lights, and joint advertising directed at state and private office workers.

When opposition surfaced from the adjacent Townsend Park neighborhood, this area was excluded from the service area. The Lark Street business improvement district, the city's first, was approved by the city council in 1995.

By the fall of 1997 the Lark Street Neighborhood District Management Association had survived the turnover of both the chairman and the director and now has a lot of successes under its belt. Executive director Vicky Stoneman and board chairman Bill Allen have made the district a major force in revitalizing the area, despite a shrinking budget. Property reassessments have reduced the district's annual revenues from $90,000 in 1995 to $70,000 in 1997.

The district contracts with Homeless and Travelers Aid for sidewalk cleaning four hours daily. A local security firm provides uniformed officers, who patrol on foot during the evenings from May to September. The extra security people have been helpful in moving panhandlers, breaking up fights, dispersing teenagers, and responding to merchants' complaints.

Reflecting a common theme among business improvement districts in commercial areas, entertainment and cultural offerings are important here. "Art on Lark" attracts artists and craftspeople for a weeklong event in the spring. In September, "Larkfest" offers three stages of live entertainment with special presentations for children. And holiday events are offered in October and December.

What's Coming Up

Because the downtowns of most large cities already have business improvement districts, the next decade's growth will necessarily include nontraditional settings—very small places, nonprofit clusters, industrial areas, and highway strips. New York City and Philadelphia each already have half a dozen small business improvement districts with yearly budgets of under $100,000.

Look, too, for more partnerships with residents, more concern for public open space, and more programs that serve residential properties where property values are high. These efforts might better be called "civic improvement districts."

Expect more hybrid financing, with greater attention being given to combinations of commercial property assessments and multiyear voluntary agreements, like University City's, where the institutions share common problems and can agree on a unified program to enhance their environment.

Where the conventional wisdom once held that universities, residents, business interests, and industrial firms must be kept apart, planners can now be more ambitious in proposing business improvement districts to solve common problems. The notion that one size fits all is obsolete — if, indeed, it was ever valid. A new generation of business improvement districts is coming.

CHAPTER 20

HARMONY: AMERICA'S LATEST CONSERVATION COMMUNITY

Jennifer Wolch

The surprise is that this gator is a full-time resident of Florida's newest and largest conservation community, called Harmony. It shares the lake with large mouth bass, bluegill, sunfish, and catfish. Monarch butterflies drift overhead.

Harmony, being built on 11,000 acres in central Florida's tourism-dominated Osceola County, is a place whose developers and designers are convinced of the benefits of living harmoniously with nature. They have placed animals (and people) at the heart of the urban design process.

The new town is the brainchild of Jim and Martha Lentz, whose thought was to create a new sort of conservation community. In 1998, Jim Lentz, an investment banker, entered a partnership with a Chicago-based insurance firm, the Arthur J. Gallagher Company, to buy the Triple E Ranch on the southeastern fringe of the fast-growing Orlando metropolitan region. The company agreed to finance the purchase of the $25 million property and to underwrite the project. Lentz took on the role of general partner.

The site includes two pristine, sandy-bottomed, 500-acre lakes (Buck and Cat), cypress-forested wetlands, palmetto prairies, and extensive forests filled with live oaks and pine flatwoods. The land encompasses a variety of rare plants, including bromeliads and a threatened pine lily.

New Urbanism with a Difference

At first glance, Harmony's design seems typically new urbanist, although it's larger than most such communities. Houses are clustered along narrow streets. Setbacks are shallow. The plan includes foot and bike paths, alleys, accessory apartments, and a 30-acre, mixed-use town center. With a total of over 1.8 million square feet of commercial and light industrial uses, Harmony will provide some 6,000 jobs, a plus in a rapidly growing county whose current population of 172,000 is expected to double by 2020.

Like its neighbor, Disney's Celebration, Harmony includes a charter elementary school that already has more than two dozen students. In addition, the developers have donated an 80-acre site for a 2,500-student regional high school, which will open next year.

Originally published as "Two By Two: A Conservation Community with a Twist," *Planning*, Vol. 69, No. 8, August/September 2003. Published by the American Planning Association, 122 South Michigan Avenue, Suite 1600, Chicago, Illinois 60603-6107. Reprinted with permission of the publisher.

And because this is Florida there is also a golf course, or what the developers call a "golf preserve." The course is now the second largest in central Florida and has already held a major tournament. Harmony's first residents are just beginning to move in, although no stores or commercial activities are open yet — except for the golf course pro shop.

In one important way, Harmony is far different from its competitors. That is in its strategy for preserving ecologically functional open space, a critical goal since the site ultimately drains into the Everglades. The lakefronts in the western portion are protected from development. And the golf course wraps around existing wetlands that provide nesting sites for protected sandhill cranes.

Plans for the site's eastern half eventually call for 400 "rural residential" or large-lot home sites in a low-density zone covered by a conservation easement. The long-term management strategy for this section is designed to maximize habitat protection.

The site's wetlands are home to Florida softshell turtles, Eastern Indigo and Florida pine snakes, and several types of frogs and toads. Bobcats, white-tailed deer, and river otters roam the woods. Protected species routinely or periodically spotted include the American alligator, Florida sandhill crane, gopher tortoise, bald eagle, osprey, and Florida black bear.

The bird life is astounding: northern bob-whites, red-shouldered hawks, swallow-tailed kites, downy and pileated woodpeckers, kill-deer, white ibis, green and night herons, double-crested cormorants, anhingas (snake birds), black vultures, and turkey vultures.

Environmental laws required Harmony to include a variety of wildlife protection provisions. But the project plans go beyond state and federal requirements. For example, a gopher tortoise conservation area was established under a state permit that gives developers the option of paying into a mitigation fund that is used to buy land elsewhere for habitat preservation. Harmony chose not to take the buy-your-way-out option, electing instead to preserve 31 acres of otherwise developable uplands as a gopher tortoise preserve.

Another example of going above and beyond is Harmony's approach to its wetlands, which are significant both in their own right and as part of a regional system.

The site's wetlands run in long north-south corridors, which are unprotected by state or federal laws. Harmony's plan protects wildlife along these corridors by limiting road width, minimizing the number of intersections, and instituting speed-control measures. Residents will be encouraged to use electric carts for short trips.

A habitat management plan is now being developed by the town's full-time conservation manager, Gregory Golgowski, AICP, who left his position as deputy executive director of the East Central Florida Regional Planning Council to take up the post. "What makes our habitat plan unique," he says, "is that it addresses a variety of land-use types, from residential back yards to rural pastures. Putting all of that into a single management plan is pretty special."

Eventually, habitat management will be turned over to a nonprofit conservancy. The developer is committed to planting more trees than are removed as a result of the project. And, on the theory that everyone — even the wildlife — needs some downtime, recreation will not be allowed on the lakes one day a week.

The Institute

A key to fulfilling the community's mission is the nonprofit Harmony Institute, which Martha Lentz, a former executive director of the Orlando Humane Society, established before the project was conceived. The institute is dedicated to developing and

Figure 1
Excerpts from Harmony's Community Covenants and Restrictions

The Lakes
- No residential development on the shores of Buck and Cat Lakes.
- No gasoline-powered boats or jet skis allowed.

The Night Sky
- Window treatment guidelines are designed to minimize bird collisions.
- Home lighting guidelines support low-intensity lamps and Dark Sky goals.

Habitat for Animals
- Native plants and "backyard wildlife habitat" encouraged, lawns discouraged.
- Planting invasive species such as Chinese Tallow or Melaleuca is prohibited.
- Residents encouraged to use pesticides only within the context of an Integrated Pest Management approach, and only after biological and other alternative controls are tried first.
- Lawn mowing targeted for midday, when wildlife are apt to be safe in trees or burrows.

Wildlife
- Chemicals specifically used to kill birds (avicides) are banned.
- Residents not allowed to feed wildlife other than squirrels and native birds.
- Animal dens, squirrel or bird nests may not be disturbed.
- Residents may not remove wild bird eggs from nests.
- Trees with nests or dens cannot be cut down.
- Capture or harassment of any wild animal is forbidden as is recreational hunting or trapping wildlife.

- So-called pest species, such as house mice, may be trapped and killed only after other alternatives for "wildlife conflict resolution" have been attempted.
- Pest removal using glueboard, snares, and foothold traps is prohibited.
- Any lethal pest-species control must be accompanied by a plan to address and remediate the causes of infestation.
- Residents warned to avoid antibacterial substances so as to protect beneficial bacteria and avoid the development of antibiotic-resistant bacteria.
- Trash handling guidelines to avoid attracting wildlife and thus cause conflicts.
- Nesting and sheltering boxes, such as bat houses, snake boxes, and toad abodes encouraged.

Companion Animals
- No off-leash cats or dogs are allowed in Harmony — except in off-leash pet parks — to protect birds and herpetofauna.
- Keeping exotic animals is not permitted.
- Domestic animals cannot be confined to crates or cages; nor can they be left unattended for any significant period of time.
- Companion animals must be protected from the weather.
- Commercial activities involving companion animals are not permitted.
- Anyone intending to breed a companion animal must register with the Harmony town board.

testing new ways to foster bonds between people, animals, and nature through supportive community design and programming.

Some of the new town's most innovative features have resulted from the advice offered by the institute's campus advisory board, a group that includes experts from national animal welfare organizations and major academic institutions in fields ranging from veterinary care to environmental sciences.

The board's charge is to provide specific direction regarding environmental and animal issues to Harmony's development team and to help establish a program of research on human-animal relations. The experts have offered advice on designing wetland roadway crossings and developed plans for a community health center that will treat both people and companion animals — sometimes, in the case of pet therapy, at the same time.

From a planning and development perspective, one of the institute's most useful products is a model set of community covenants and restrictions, drafted in collaboration with the Humane Society of the United States and with the help of the campus advisory board.

Ongoing Work

A major goal is to turn Harmony into a virtual "no-kill" community through such programs as Pet Concierge, which will seek foster homes for unwanted animals. The institute also will host a service dog training organization (PAWS with a Cause) and a pet therapy program connecting ponies with disabled children (Personal Ponies Limited).

Another goal is to provide educational resources for local schools and community organizations. Along those lines, the institute is collaborating with the University of Florida on a WildSide Walk program, designed to teach the public about environmental issues through the use of interpretive kiosks, a website, and a wildlife-monitoring program.

The institute is also working closely with the charter elementary school to develop an environmental curriculum based on human-animal coexistence values. And it has developed a partnership with the Connecticut-based Albert Schweitzer Institute to house a campus in the town. It will offer workshops, conferences, and other programs, including continuing education for professional licensing.

Finally, the Harmony Institute's input has led to an important decision. All of the town's public lighting will be designed to prevent light pollution. In April, before a single resident had moved in, the institute held its First Annual Dark Sky Festival, replete with telescopes for star-gazing, astronomy games for kids, and a series of talks by experts on light pollution and its deleterious impacts on wildlife.

Social Mix

At buildout, Harmony will have 7,200 homes on 11,000 acres. That's far larger than other well-known conservation communities. Illinois's Prairie Crossing, for example has 362 housing units on 678 acres. Disney's new urbanist community, Celebration, which also touts its conservation benefits, will eventually have about the same number of units — it's approved for 8,000, although just 3,000 are built so far — but on less than 5,000 acres.

Harmony's conceptual design was developed by the Evans Group of Orlando. The housing is being constructed by D. R. Horton, a Texas-based national home builder, and a handful of local custom builders. Twenty percent of the units, all multifamily, will be set aside for low- and very low-income households, helping to ensure that many of the service workers will be able to live in the town.

That's important because Osceola County has a lower median household income and a higher poverty rate than the Orlando area as a whole. At just under $100,000, Osceola's median home price in 2000 was slightly lower than the regional average, but rents were higher.

The plan is unusual both for the 70 percent share of land set aside for open space and for its emphasis on mixed density. Housing in the town's 10 neighborhoods will range from 11 units per acre in the town center (mostly townhouses) down to three units per acre at the edge.

Most of the residential areas average six units an acre, making Harmony a medium-density development. What is striking is that lots have been distributed not to maximize neighborhood homogeneity, but rather to maximize social mix.

Even in the lower density areas, 35-foot-wide lots are interspersed with 100-foot-wide lots. That means that you might live in a $500,000 home on an 8,000-square-foot lot but be across the street from something distinctly more modest, a $140,000 bungalow on a 3,000-square-foot lot. Each neighborhood has at least one park.

Part of the credit for this arrangement goes to the developers, who have a much longer financial horizon than is typical in such projects. Instead of the usual several-year payout period, they are thinking further ahead, allowing them to build the type of community that will add value over time.

How Green Is It?

How far does Harmony's commitment to coexistence really go? No planned community designed for the general public has laid out such ambitious and thoughtful goals to promote animal-human coexistence.

That is not to say this is a vegan paradise. Cattle will continue to be raised for slaughter by a local rancher who subleases some of Harmony's pasturage. Fishing is permitted in the two lakes. And a "conservation club"—whose activities include hunting—will be allowed to continue operations, although its lease on a remote portion of the property is being phased out.

According to the community's covenants, hunting of deer, turkeys, and quail is a "demonstrated conservation technique" so long as it is done carefully and "humanely"—a claim unlikely to win over diehard animal rights advocates.

Ads for Harmony herald its environmental philosophy. Brochures term the community "environmentally integrated" or "environmentally intelligent." But the developers have shied away from using labels like "green" or "sustainable" because they don't want to position the project too far out in front of mainstream buyers.

Yet Harmony is, in fact, "green" in several important respects, beyond the provisions for lake protection and wildlife habitat. All water will come from two on-site wells. Wastewater will be treated on site, with 95 percent reused for landscaping. The stormwater system is designed for zero runoff.

The golf preserve integrates wetlands, uses native plants, and includes littoral shelves for nesting birds in its retention ponds. Residents are being encouraged to landscape with native plants, and zero-emission electric carts are promoted for in-town travel. There will be community-owned electric boats on the lakes.

The fence along U.S. 192, the two-lane road fronting the project, is made from recycled plastic beverage cartons, and at least one wildlife crossing is included in Harmony's master plan. On-site schools will help reduce traffic generation. And all homes built must meet U.S. EPA Energy Star and Florida Green Building Coalition standards and offer the option of solar hot-water heaters.

Final Score

Most planners would see Harmony's most serious shortcoming as its location on the metropolitan fringe, seven miles beyond the nearest small city and poorly served by public transportation. Not surprisingly, some local environmental advocates as well as regional planners have charged it with contributing to urban sprawl.

Yet, if Jim Lentz had not bought this site, another developer could have come along and legally divided it into 11,000 building lots — allowed by the zoning — obliterating virtually all the wildlife habitat and encircling the lakes with development.

In the context of the county's historical development standards, there's no doubt that Harmony has raised the bar for future projects. Moreover, urbanization is sure to catch up, moving down U.S. 192 (soon to be widened to four lanes) as Osceola County continues on its rapid growth trajectory.

Harmony is a test of whether integrated design and management practices that focus on animals can survive in a world of bottom-line development. Only time will tell if newcomers will continue to practice the co-existence values the community preaches. But if the residents — and not just the gators — bite, Harmony may offer a road-map to more respectful relations between the species.

CHAPTER 21

HARTFORD REVIVES
ITS RIVERFRONT

Steve Starger

You could talk about a long history of tobacco farming; the major transportation hub of Bradley International Airport in Windsor Locks; the jet engine manufacturing giant Pratt & Whitney in East Hartford; the towering financial, insurance and investment home offices in Hartford; the capital city's rich store of nationally recognized arts and cultural institutions; the suburban communities that have transformed Hartford County's diverse towns into class-driven enclaves; the few working farms that still exist here and there throughout the county.

And perhaps the most significant feature of all, the Connecticut River, whose 400-plus miles meander through Hartford County on the way to Long Island Sound to the south. The river, a major navigable waterway that nourished the county's history and growth, gives Hartford its most visible symbol of vitality.

Assets ... and Challenges

In recent history, there have been seismic shifts in Hartford County: Steady migrations from the cities to the suburbs have created new, autonomous societies but have left depleted urban areas in their wake, in effect creating two separate and not so equal societies; the wrenching evolution from a manufacturing to a service-oriented economy has cost jobs and businesses but also has held the promise of new opportunities for those equipped to take advantage of them.

Hartford's plate currently is running over with an embarrassment of new development proposals and visions for revitalizing the city. The recent fever to remake and restore the city to a new version of its former glory has put Hartford into the public consciousness in much the same way that revitalized urban centers like Providence, Indianapolis and Baltimore have. Those cities may in fact be models for Hartford visionaries to consider, but Hartford has its own particular range of assets and challenges.

All of this development excitement has come out of an extended period of struggle by Hartford to salvage what many have seen as a dying city. Hartford has absorbed a number of shocks in the wake of the region's socio-economic sea changes. The city has been plagued by financial downturns, a

Originally published as "Reinventing Downtown Hartford," *CT Business*, Vol. 1, No. 4, November/December 1998. Published by Nolan Media, LLC, Cromwell, Connecticut. Reprinted with permission of the publisher.

school system seen as racially segregated and bereft of resources, reigns of terror by warring gangs, and a steady drain of its population to the perceived safety of the suburbs.

Major Projects Proposed

For all of its problems, Hartford also has such advantages as a rich, multiethnic core population, a thriving arts and entertainment scene, long-established neighborhoods that feed into the downtown sector, and, of course, the invaluable resource of the Connecticut River.

Tallying the pluses and minuses, Hartford in 1998 — although more than three-and-a-half centuries old — remains a work in progress, which can bode well in terms of creating a high quality of life for its citizenry but can also offer a jolting rollercoaster ride.

Hartford is rebounding from its latest thrill ride, the crashing of the heady financial boom times of the 1980s. The last decade in Hartford, like Connecticut and the country at large, was marked by an almost insatiable lust for acquisition and expansion. Corporate mergers and dizzying deal-making created mega-banks and real estate empires that looked great on the surface but which all too soon collapsed like the proverbial house of cards.

From the stock market crash of 1987 on, the party atmosphere quickly turned noxious in the halls of power. Corporations that had expanded as if pumped with helium began to deflate, expelling assets and personnel. "Downsizing" became the favorite euphemism for job loss. The economic landscape resembled a village ravaged by vandals.

But out of that bleak scenario has sprung a series of development projects that, even if a small percentage reach completion, will have enormous impact on the entire city and will have the potential to restore Hart-

ford to a vibrant center of life, culture and commerce.

Among the major proposals on the boards for Hartford are:

- Adriaen's Landing, a billion-dollar, multifaceted development complex that would encompass a good portion of downtown near to and linking with the river.
- Redevelopment of the old G. Fox and Co. site at 960 Main Street as a multiuse facility anchored by the Shaboo Nite Club, a resurrected version of a former eastern Connecticut night club and concert hall that, in its heyday, was one of the East coast's major entertainment venues.
- Purchase and redevelopment of the Hartford Civic Center, a high-profile but problematic downtown mall and arena that has seen more downs than ups in recent times.
- A plan to develop the neighborhood around Trinity College as a cooperative effort between the college and neighborhood organizations, and initiatives to locate Capital Community-Technical College and a University of Connecticut training center in downtown areas.
- A $15 million city bond to renovate and expand the Hartford Public Library.
- A $30 million proposal to build a 950-seat theater addition to the Bushnell, one of Hartford's oldest performing arts centers.
- Six Pillars of Progress, a $300 million plan developed by Gov. John G. Rowland to help fund and generate funding for numerous economic, education, and cultural projects over the next decade.
- Various proposals to build new hotels, offices, and residences throughout downtown to bring a core population back to the city.

Adriaen's Landing: Massive Plans

Proposed by Robert W. Fiondella, president, chairman and chief executive officer of Phoenix Home Life Mutual Insurance Co., Adriaen's Landing is, simply in terms of dollars, the most ambitious plan of the lot.

The plan, unveiled at a meeting of the Hartford City Council last May, includes a convention center and stadium; a 700-room convention hotel; a 14-screen movie complex; a Riverfront Discovery Center with aquarium, space station and history museum; affordable housing; and a network of shops, nightclubs and other recreational amenities.

Also planned is a riverfront pedestrian arcade that would provide walking access to the river, a multiuse sports complex and an intermodal transportation system featuring water, rail, pedestrian, vehicular and air traffic. An underground parking lot with more than 4,000 spaces is also proposed.

Promoters of Adriaen's Landing estimate that the project will generate 7,000 jobs and breathe considerable life to Hartford's economic doldrums. The big consideration, of course, is the price tag.

The current phase of the project involves seeking the needed $500 million in private funding and pursuing some $150 million in federal funding to cover environmental cleanup of the proposed site, housing and transportation costs. A feasibility study also must be done and the city must agree to donate the land, which encompasses the old Hartford Times building, owned by the city's pension committee.

At this point, work is continuing on developing architect's plans, raising the public portion of the funding, and generally drumming up support for the project among business people, community groups and developers, says Jon Sandberg, a spokesman for the project. Sandberg says he expects those efforts to continue into early next year.

The city has applied for environmental cleanup funds on behalf of Adriaen's Landing, and the project's leaders will also be talking about funding with the Capital City Economic Development Authority, the group that also controls the $15 million earmarked for the Civic Center makeover, Sandberg says.

Neighborhood organizations throughout the city "have been genuinely supportive" of Adriaen's Landing, Sandberg says, but added that they also have raised such concerns as traffic congestion and the possibilities for jobs and job training connected with the proposal.

For all of its glittering promise, Adriaen's Landing remains at this point a kind of shining vision on a hill, with some major questions and financial challenges yet to be addressed.

But, Sandberg says, "we're as anxious to get working as people are anxious to have us get working. There's a lot of work to do on a project this complex."

Linking the Resources

The short list that includes Adriaen's Landing and the other major development projects begins to boggle the mind. Add to them ongoing projects by Riverfront Recapture Inc. to link the city to its riverfront and to the riverfront of East Hartford, the continued redesigning of the I-84/91 interchange through Hartford to restore links to the city and some neighborhoods, and initiatives by local and regional arts and downtown councils, planning groups, think tanks and the Rowland administration, and Hartford appears to be a kind of giant Lego set looking for the right builders. That's preferable to being compared to a piece of Swiss cheese, as Hartford has in the recent past.

Why this sudden spurt of activity now?

"It was time," says Rie Poirer, a spokesperson for the Greater Hartford Growth

Council, an economic development agency that serves the Greater Hartford Region. The council created the MetroHartford Millennium Project, a coalition of area business leaders led by Pratt & Whitney President Karl Krapek.

"Over the past few years, there's been a cry for some kind of cohesive strategy" from business leaders in Hartford and surrounding towns, Poirer says. "We finally had the plan when we put together Millennium. It's really a broad mix of people, and it's the people who can get things done."

The group is charged with overseeing the "action agenda for the region," Poirer says. That means bringing the various downtown development plans into a cooperative situation to reach the resources they need to realize their proposals.

"The myriad activity is a happy problem," Poirer says. "Millennium's role is to provide synergy."

As an example, Poirer pointed to the group's receiving requests from developers who want to build housing downtown that would connect the downtown to the city's neighborhoods. "If the neighborhoods aren't connected, then we've failed," Poirer says.

One proposal to link the neighborhoods to downtown is the so-called "Circuit Line" route that would follow historic and architecturally significant sections of the city and ultimately tie together not only peripheral neighborhoods — such as Asylum Hill, North Meadows, Armory, and South Green — but many of the development proposals for downtown as well.

The Study

That idea was generated by a survey of downtown development activity by Ken Greenberg, a consultant with Urban Strategies Inc. of Toronto, Canada, who was hired by the Hartford Downtown Council under its Action Strategy Plan, developed with the Millennium Project. Greenberg began his study last March and was expected to complete the task by the end of September, according to Anthony M. Caruso, executive director of the Hartford Downtown Council. Greenberg interviewed more than 400 organizations, businesses and individuals to "get a feel for what the situation is in Hartford," Caruso said. Greenberg also looked at the Hartford Civic Center and the concept of a new downtown convention center in the context of Adriaen's Landing.

In terms of the Civic Center, Greenberg had worked with LaSalle Partners, a real estate development company that had been given exclusive rights by Hartford city government and Aetna Inc. to propose development plans for the Civic Center mall. Aetna owns the mall. Fifteen million dollars in state funds were earmarked for the mall's renovation.

But uncertainty about how the money would be used resulted in the city and Aetna reopening the search for a developer. The city is rebidding the project, but LaSalle Partners could still be in the picture, Caruso said.

Despite the stalling of that project and the snail's pace on others, Caruso is optimistic about the downtown activity.

"I think we're on the brink of some significant development," he said. "Obviously, these kinds of projects don't happen immediately, but this is the first time in a long time that we're on track to bring a good portion of these projects to fruition over the long term."

The Importance of the River

Perhaps the most visible reclamation project in Hartford — short of the impossible-to-miss construction on the I-84/91 interchange — has been in the works for nearly 20 years: Riverfront Recapture's massive effort to reunite the river with the city.

Driving through Hartford on the interstates, one can see real evidence of progress in the form of a walkway down to the riverfront on the Hartford side and continuing construction of a promenade to span the river and connect Hartford to the East Hartford side of the river.

Also planned with the walkway is a landscaped plaza over I-91, which will allow pedestrians to access the walkway to East Hartford. The walkway will be 18 feet wide and will be open to pedestrians, bikers and joggers, says Joseph Marfuggi, president and chief executive officer of Riverfront Recapture.

Other plans call for grassy terraces descending to the river from the plaza on the Hartford side, areas that could seat up to 2,000 people for performances and other special events. A bulkhead is also planned to be built along the river's edge to allow excursion boats and water taxis to operate from downtown, Marfuggi says. That construction is scheduled to be completed next summer, he adds.

Since the group was formed in 1981, Riverfront Recapture has raised about $42 million for design and construction, Marfuggi says. The organization was formed out of a public forum held at Hartford's Old State House in 1980 that focused on how the city could take advantage of its waterfront as other cities had done.

The river had been cut off first by flood-control dikes in the downtown area after the floods of 1936 and 1938. A flood-control system was installed in the 1940s that protected the river but also became a barrier between the city and the river, Marfuggi says. The construction of the I-91/84 interchange "finished off the job and made the river inaccessible."

Since the early '80s, Riverfront Recapture has built a network of public parks and riverwalks in Hartford and East Hartford, "literally taking people by the hand and showing them how to use the river," Marfuggi says. The river has been the site of numerous activities, such as the annual July 4 celebration, which attracts thousands to the riverfront, and such nationally profiled events as a big-money bass tournament held this past summer.

Marfuggi says, "The river is becoming a destination for visitors from outside the region. We're showing that we can use the river as a magnet to attract people. That's a new kind of economic development."

Making Use of Existing Resources

All of these visionary proposals for turning Hartford's economic vitality around are certainly exciting in the abstract, but they're also a bit dizzying. It seems basic that to have any kind of successful urban center, you need to start with an existing population that supports itself and its neighborhood with its own resources.

Hartford evinces vitality through numerous merchants' associations scattered across the disparate sections of the city. Whether in the north, south, west, east or downtown areas, these organizations of local businesspeople share a mission of addressing challenges by adopting a general mission to the specific needs of their communities.

To connect the merchants' organizations and help them take care of business, Hartford's Office of Economic Development contracts with about a dozen different merchants' associations throughout the city, groups that already exist as independent entities usually affiliated with nonprofit organizations in their neighborhoods.

The city makes available $30,000 to each association from Community Development Block Grant funds, according to Hector Torres, Hartford's acting director of economic development. Typically, the money is used to hire a full- or part-time merchant coordinator who works directly with the associations on a near-daily basis.

How do such associations meld with the big development proposals saturating the city?

"The media are interested in the mega downtown projects," Torres says. "In reality, I've found that the majority of economic development in Hartford — and in most urban areas — with internal, existing businesses and the entrepreneurial activity that comes out of that."

But Torres also feels that the redevelopment picture is a good one for local businesses.

"These projects will certainly provide more life and more economic activity, not only for downtown, but for the neighborhoods," he says. "When you look at the entire picture, if we're able to generate economic activity downtown, that would certainly spill over into the businesses in the neighborhoods."

And, Torres notes, along with those developments come jobs. "If people in the neighborhoods can get jobs, they'll be spending some of their dollars at local businesses."

When all of the dust settles on the development frenzy in Hartford, the city will certainly be transformed. Exactly what the landscape will look like is still unclear. One thing is certain — to be successful, a transformed, economically vital Hartford must be conscious of all of its citizens and users, whether they live in Enfield, Avon, Manchester or within the city limits.

As the comedian Mort Sahl liked to observe: The future lies ahead. In Hartford and Hartford County, the glow seems to be brightening.

CHAPTER 22

IRVINE TURNS MILITARY BASE INTO PARK AND NATURE PRESERVE

Christopher Swope

Ever since the federal government told the Marine Corps to abandon the El Toro airbase in 1993, residents of Orange County, California, have been bickering about what to do with two crisscrossing runways and the valuable land surrounding them. One side wanted to see a commercial airport at El Toro. The other side was open to almost anything — so long as it wasn't an airport. Several ballot initiatives and many lawsuits later, in March 2002, the "anything but" faction finally won out. After years of pushing lackluster schemes for offices, shopping malls and housing developments that would only add to Orange County's congestion, they came up with a winning plan that a majority of people could agree on: turning the base into a humongous park.

When it is finished, the park at El Toro will be four times the size of San Francisco's Golden Gate Park. The new park's name — Great Park — has a straightforward ring to it. Now that the basics have been decided, however, there are new arguments breaking out in Orange County. Parks mean different things to different people. So what should a park of almost 4,000 acres look like?

Citizens' ideas for how to paint Orange County's giant green canvas are pouring in. Some want a nature preserve where sprawl-weary souls can relax. Others would like a county fairground. There are proposals for sports stadiums and museums, rock-climbing walls and places to fly model airplanes. "There's a desire for just about anything you could think of," says Michael Ray, chairman of the nonprofit Great Park Conservancy. "Soccer is the most popular, but there's also people who want facilities for basketball, baseball, softball, rugby, skateboarding, bicycling, motorcycling. You name it, there's a subgroup of people here doing it. And they all have legitimate needs."

The good news is that in a park of this size, it's possible that every constituency may get what it wants. Great Park is among a handful of gigantic municipal park projects in the works from coast to coast. Some 150 years after New York's Central Park set the standard for mega-parks, ambitious plans are on the drawing boards in Denver, Fairfax County, Virginia, and even once again in New York City itself. In each of these places, park planners are seizing one-time opportu-

Originally published as "Green Giants," *Governing*, Vol. 17, No. 3, December 2003. Published by Congressional Quarterly Inc., Washington, D.C. Reprinted with permission of the publisher.

nities to add huge additions to their park systems and enhance the quality of life in their communities. The circumstances of each case are very different. But all of the localities to some degree share the view that the modern mega-park can function as something like an attic for recreation: It'll all fit in there somehow.

In Denver, which is redeveloping the site of the old Stapleton Airport but has set aside 1,800 acres for parks, some of which is being restored as wild prairie, paying homage to a local landscape that has otherwise disappeared in the city. As New York converts the Fresh Kills landfill on Staten Island into a 2,200-acre park, planners are eyeing trails for mountain biking and all-terrain vehicles — activities that have no home in Midtown Manhattan. "Every kind of active recreation will have a place there, particularly things that are hard to do in the city," says Candace Damon, a consultant working on the Fresh Kills park. "The site is so large."

Yet planning these mega-parks — not to mention paying for them — is a monumental task. And as Fairfax County is discovering while it plots out a park on the grounds of a defunct prison, promises can add up quickly even when you're talking about a space that covers 2,400 acres. With a master plan for the site that already calls for a golf course and lots of undisturbed open space, Fairfax has only about 430 acres left to make decisions on. "We're struggling through this process," says park planner John Pitts. "It's viewed as the community's panacea, that all this land is the answer to all of our prayers. But we have to balance the needs with what's good planning."

For all the opportunistic ambition, some experts caution that thinking huge with parks may also mean thinking backwards. Are giant land deals the best way to plan for parks? "Ideally when you plan, you get out a map and ask which part of the county is well-served with parks, and you build parks in the underserved areas," says Peter Harnik, director of the Green Cities Initiative with the Trust for Public Land. "You think it out just like libraries and schools. But you don't just respond to a group of people saying we don't want anything else here; let's just build a park instead."

Thinking Long Term

Orange County, to be sure, came around slowly to the idea for Great Park. Airport politics slogged on for years before county voters overwhelmingly approved the definitive ballot initiative last year setting aside El Toro as parkland. Relieved to have the airport war behind them, many residents are just now realizing how great Great Park might be. Located dead in the center of the nation's third-most densely populated county, the park will connect with forests and open space to the north and south, making it possible to hike all the way from the beach to the mountains through a continuous corridor of green.

The city of Irvine, which sits adjacent to El Toro and annexed the airbase into its borders in November, is taking on the complicated task of planning the park. Early next year, the U.S. Navy is set to sell the land to private developers in four chunks. In exchange for the right to build around the fringes of the property, developers will cede the heart of the site for the park and pay $350 million toward building it. "We'll have the land and have the money," says Irvine Mayor Larry Agran. "The essential elements of Great Park will be landscaped within five years."

Agran thinks of Great Park as though it is 10 parks in one. A preliminary master plan shows a large central park in the middle for passive recreational activities such as picnicking or frisbee. Riparian and wildlife corridors are planned, along with a 1,000-

acre nature preserve. About 160 acres are set aside for sports fields, 580 acres will become golf courses, and in a bow to Orange County's farming roots, about 300 acres are to be used for agriculture. There will also be land for a university campus, land for a museum district and land for a veterans' cemetery.

Great Park's founders say they are looking to New York's Central Park as something of a model, and have crafted quasi-public agencies similar to the Central Park Conservancy to look after the park. The Great Park Corp. will handle construction and maintenance, while the all-volunteer Great Park Conservancy will act as an advocate and fundraiser, and will help arbitrate fights between joggers, cyclists, dog walkers, equestrians and other enthusiasts who all want their space. "East coast parks are steeped in tradition, but where we are everything is new," says Michael Ray. "The joy of this is we get to be the founders of something we hope will truly be world class and be around for hundreds of years."

They're also thinking long term in New York when it comes to Fresh Kills. The landfill is the nation's largest, and after 50 years of continuous use was finally closed in 2001. From the tops of four grass-covered trash mounds, one sees a stunning, if paradoxical, view of city and nature: Manhattan and New Jersey on the horizon and marshes and creeks below. Some parts of the site were never used as dumps and can be converted to park use soon, but turning the mounds into parkland could take as long as 30 years since the garbage underneath needs to settle and release plumes of methane gas.

The completed park will be almost three times the size of Central Park. If that goal is still distant, however, the process to decide what the park will become is well underway. The city sponsored an international design competition to come up with an overall vision for the site. Now, as a master plan is being drawn up, a public outreach process is beginning to enlist suggestions for specific park uses. "There's such a sense of relief on Staten Island that the landfill is closed that people haven't had a chance to think about what it could be," says Candace Damon. "That will happen over months and years."

Competing Proposals

Much like Fresh Kills, Fairfax County's future mega-park is healing a one-time sore spot in the community. Nobody in Fairfax much liked having a federal prison in their backyard, especially since the inmates weren't from there but from Washington, D.C., 30 miles up the road. Congress closed the Lorton prison in 2001 and the following year sold Fairfax the buildings and grounds for $4 million. There was one condition: that the site be maintained mostly as open space.

Today, nobody in Fairfax calls the prison site Lorton anymore. The new name is "Laurel Hill." It is a beautiful area with rolling hills and ponds, and large portions will stay that way. Some of the prison buildings are historic landmarks, designed as gothic fortresses, and the county board of supervisors is considering turning them into a facility for the performing arts. For other "programmed" parts of the park, the county parks authority is sorting through competing proposals from various sports and recreation groups. For example, a youth soccer association wants to build a 35-field soccer complex; another group prefers athletic fields that can be used for multiple sports.

These are the sorts of fights Denver has, for the most part, already gone through. Park planning for the Stapleton redevelopment began back in 1989, six years before the old airport closed. Builders are already putting up a mix of housing, offices and retail there, but about one-third of the site was set aside for parkland. The most significant park at Stapleton, currently known by the planning designation "major urban park," is about 175 acres — much smaller than the other mega-parks. But in total, Denver stands to gain about 1,800 acres of parkland by the time the bulldozers leave many years from now.

With tens of thousands of people expected to live and work around the Stapleton parks, Denver had a unique challenge: How do you plan for parks whose prospective users aren't there yet? Denver relied heavily on the input of citizens in adjacent neighborhoods. A citizens' advisory board still meets regularly to discuss what Denver's newest parks should look like and how they should be used. Happy Haynes, a former city councilwoman who co-chairs that board, believes that when this much land is in play, parks can indeed be all things to all people. "These parks can serve a lot of needs, from athletic fields to picnics and strolls through the park to a let's get out of the city and pretend we're not even there kind of an experience — and a whole bunch of things in between," Haynes says. "When you start from scratch, you can make those all work."

CHAPTER 23

LAFAYETTE, OTHER CITIES, USE PUBLIC PLAZAS TO REVIVE MAIN STREETS

Chris Dimond

In the 1970s, a tangle of transportation problems prompted Lafayette, Ind., officials to begin planning for changes downtown. At the time, Amtrak trains ran down the middle of a central city street, requiring passengers to load and unload on the street, and the local bus station was situated on Lafayette's courthouse square, causing traffic delays and interfering with nearby business operations.

Officials decided to reposition the railroad tracks and create a junction using the city's historic train depot, which would have to be moved. The facility would not only serve as a transportation hub, but it also would stand as the centerpiece of a public plaza for Lafayette's 45,000 citizens.

In purpose, Lafayette's plans were similar to countless others in cities across the county. Driven by a desire to bring people — and dollars — downtown, local officials are implementing a variety of ideas to beautify their streetscapes, calm traffic and create pedestrian-friendly pathways and venues.

An Historic Hub

The Lafayette Railroad Relocation project included the 1902 Big Four Depot from the start. The building had served as an active railroad station for 70 years prior to its closing, and citizens wanted to preserve it as part of the city's heritage. The rails were relocated, and the depot was moved four blocks to a spot adjacent to the Wabash River near the heart of the city's downtown.

In 1996, the restoration was complete, and today the depot provides rail, inter-city and local bus service for more than 7,000 passengers per week. It also serves as the crossroads for pedestrian traffic traversing the historic John T. Myers Pedestrian Bridge, which joins Lafayette to West Lafayette.

As the depot underwent restoration, Lafayette began building James F. Riehle Plaza, an outdoor venue directly in front of the depot. Constructed of brick pavers and featuring extensive landscaping and a fountain, the plaza is a popular site for festivals, concerts, art fairs and receptions. A textured concrete wall on the east side screens the plaza from nearby trains and noise.

Originally published as "Made for Walkin'," *American City & County*, Vol. 113, No. 8, July 1998. Published by Intertec Publishing Corporation, Atlanta, Georgia. Reprinted with permission of the publisher.

Since completion of the $7.8 million project, Lafayette residents have embraced the depot and plaza. New development, including retail establishments, restaurants, offices and housing has sprung up within three blocks of the site. The project also has encouraged redevelopment in West Lafayette, across the Wabash River.

"The railroad relocation was vital to business development in Lafayette, but it couldn't be done at the expense of the riverfront environment," says Liz Solberg, Lafayette's manager for the railroad relocation project. "We used the track relocation as an impetus for creating a vital, exciting civic resource."

"Driving" Development

Lafayette citizens are drawn downtown by the ambience of the riverfront, open space and the retail surge created by the James F. Riehle Plaza. In Glendale, Wis., officials are creating a similar draw by implementing a new streetscape plan that incorporates pedestrian-friendly, unifying elements.

West Silver Spring Drive, a straight, 1-mile stretch of heavily traveled arterial, is lined with parking lanes and surrounded by vacant properties and underused land parcels. In its place, the city is constructing a gently curving roadway that will produce larger land parcels for office and retail development. The improvements also will slow traffic (which routinely exceeds the posted 35 mph speed limit by 10 to 15 mpg) and remedy an accident-prone intersection.

Neighborhoods to the north and south of the new roadway will benefit from additional upgrades to the area, says Glendale City Administrator Richard Maslowski. "The neighborhoods will be united by the new configuration," he notes. "In addition to traffic being slowed, a number of new features will enhance [residents'] experiences."

For example, signal light intersections will increase from two to five; green spaces and pedestrian lighting will be added; and benches, bus shelters and rest areas will be installed. Overall, the city intends to produce a safe and inviting place for residents and visitors to stroll and shop.

The West Silver Spring Drive project will be completed this fall at a cost of $24 million. As it progresses, officials are ensuring that subsequent development will create a harmonious character for the area.

A landscaped entrance will open the west end of the project, and the city has established development guidelines that define acceptable architectural materials and building placement. For example, the guidelines specify that front entrances for commercial buildings must face the roadway. Side and rear entrances can be provided to enhance pedestrian access, but they must be less dominant visually than the front entrances.

Concrete Continuity

While Glendale is reconstructing a neighborhood to make it more attractive to new businesses and patrons, Waco, Texas, is using the streetscape concept to update its image citywide. The goal is to create an environment that offers downtown visitors easy access to an already-developed retail and entertainment base.

"Development came first in Waco," says Bill Falco, city planning director. "Rather than implementing the streetscape program to spur development, we were focused on enhancing the progress that was already being made.

"We have created a program that links Waco's various downtown areas," he explains. "People will be able to travel in a more friendly pedestrian environment between shops, restaurants, hotels, apartments and clubs."

The $4.1 million project kicked off two

years ago, when Waco hosted a four-day de-sign workshop in which city representatives, downtown business leaders and Baylor Uni-versity staff shared ideas about the new streetscape. The city then analyzed primary vehicular and pedestrian linkages, develop-ment characteristics, existing sidewalks and other features.

Measuring 9,600 linear feet, the pro-ject incorporates lighting, furniture, paving, signage, landscaping and other features to help create an attractive and functional pedestrian environment. Work is under way, and residents already are seeing signs of transformation.

For example, as sidewalks are improved or replaced, they are inlaid with brick pavers and Texas stars that establish continuity yet provide some variation among the districts. Streetlights, trees and furniture have been installed, and the city has improved parking areas with the addition of pedestrian path-ways and lighting.

Residents have responded favorably to the changes, as have developers. State and federal offices, hotels, loft apartments, res-taurants and specialty shops have been added to Waco's downtown, and even more enhancements are in the works. For exam-ple, state symbols may be integrated into the sidewalk design and correlated to a map of key city sites. The city also is installing a bi-cycle/pedestrian trail along the Brazos River to connect with the downtown improve-ments.

Finally, Waco residents and visitors will have a new place to relax and play when the city celebrates the 150th anniversary of its founding in 2000. Heritage Plaza, which will connect the retail district to city hall, will be completed that year. Spanning 115,000 square feet, it will include fountains and shaded areas.

Waking the Waterfront

Balancing commerce with a sense of community is a recurring characteristic in local revitalization projects. Although new developments emphasize spaces that will en-tice commercial interests and the traffic they generate, they also incorporate elements that take the squeeze off pedestrians. As demon-strated in Lafayette, Glendale and Waco, such projects are changing the feel of down-town districts, ensuring that the public does not pass them by.

In Boston, officials are taking the pedestrian-friendly concept and extending it beyond the downtown perimeter to connect urban districts with some of the city's nearby natural resources. The City of Boston Beach Access Plans will improve public access to the beaches and parks along the Boston Harbor coastline, as well as to the harbor is-lands.

The plans are backed jointly by Mass-achusetts, Boston and the Boston Harbor Association. With them, the parties intend to reintroduce the vitality of the waterfront to Boston's urban neighborhoods.

Key elements of the plans include the Dorchester Project, which will connect and update pedestrian routes in the Dorchester Bay area, and the Long Island Project, which will open access to one of the harbor islands and create a new circulation route. Both projects emphasize convenience for pedes-trians and cyclists.

The $5.2 million Dorchester Project comprises an area that is bordered by the University of Massachusetts to the north, an expressway to the west, Boston Harbor to the east and the Neponset River to the south. Existing pedestrian routes are dis-jointed and difficult to use, and the plan seeks to turn that around by connecting ex-isting arteries and by introducing consistent design elements and signage.

When completed (a target date is not available), the Dorchester Project will provide a critical link in Boston's HarborWalk, which was initiated in 1986. Extending from east Boston through Dorchester to the Neponset River and Greenway, HarborWalk eventually will connect 43 miles of public and private space via a network of continuous walkways and green spaces.

Along with the Long Island Project, the Dorchester Project ties into "Back to the Beaches," a $30 million program to develop and restore 8.5 miles of urban shoreline and harbor beaches. Launched in 1993 by the city, Back to the Beaches is a long-term project, like Boston's other beach-related ventures.

"The Boston Harbor waterfront is one of the city's most valuable recreation, cultural and educational resources," says Lorraine Downey, director of Boston's Environment Department. "Boston's Beach Access Plans are an important component of HarborWalk and the Back to the Beaches programs. Together, these projects are providing access to and linking miles of open space along Boston Harbor."

Similar to the Dorchester Project, phase 1 of the $8 million Long Island Project specifies enhancements to existing infrastructure. It focuses on a 214-acre island that is physically connected to Boston's mainland but closed to the public. The project will open access to the island, which offers spectacular views of the city and Boston Harbor.

Additional phases for the Long Island Project call for design and construction of new facilities to create an extensive circulation route along the island's shoreline. As in Dorchester, consistent design elements and signage are included in the plans, as are connections with Boston's transportation network. Overall, the project is intended to create a direct, efficient intermodal transportation system and to strengthen recreational and cultural possibilities for the region.

There is no single way to revitalize downtowns; successful projects have included everything from streetscaping to reconfigurations of existing districts. However, cities across the country appear to be focusing on a need for pedestrian-friendly elements that create a sense of convenience, safety and community. And in doing so, they are stretching the old definitions of redevelopment and changing the urban landscape.

CHAPTER 24

LAKE WORTH RESTORES ITS PUBLIC BEACHES

Paul M. Twitty

The term civic architecture often conjures up visions of important community buildings such as libraries, courthouses, or town halls. But in the city of Lake Worth, Florida, some of the most important civic structures are on the beach. A 19-acre site, Lake Worth Beach is 1,240 feet long and 560 feet deep. Unlike many Florida beaches, this site encompasses parking, a pool, restaurants, retail shops, and a fishing pier between State Road A1A and the ocean.

Although the beach has been a center of Lake Worth community life since before the city was founded in 1913, the existing beach facilities were not constructed until 1949.

A Mediterranean/revival-style casino and bath built on the site in 1922 were largely destroyed by a hurricane in 1947. Remnants of the original gambling casino survive within the shell of the 1949 casino-style replacement building, but the current structure has no historical significance. Also in 1949, the entire beach was scraped clean of native vegetation and converted to a vast surface parking lot to accommodate large numbers of tourists; today, 80 percent of the beach is paved. A freshwater pool was added in 1971 to replace an original saltwater pool

that was filled in behind the casino building the same year.

The effects of more than a half century of use are evident in the shabby condition of most of the beach facilities. Over the years, there have been several efforts to rally public support to improve its appearance. In 1981, the Lake Worth City Commission solicited a comprehensive redevelopment plan, which was debated, changed, and ultimately abandoned four years later. Conditions continued to deteriorate until the mid–1990s, when the beach again became a matter of public discussion. Subsequent inaction has stemmed from a lack of agreement within the community about what the beach should become. At long last, through the efforts of both a determined mayor and the city commission, a shared vision for the beach has finally emerged — a core master plan produced by the Treasure Coast Regional Planning Council (TCRPC) and refined by a specially appointed beach steering committee, as well as Lake Worth residents.

"The redevelopment of our beach is truly a grass-roots project; it's what our citizens want," notes Mayor Rodney Romano. "When I was mayor from 1993 to 1997, I

Originally published as "Beach Structures," *Urban Land*, Vol. 60, No. 10, October 2001. Published by the Urban Land Institute, Washington, D.C. Reprinted with permission of the publisher.

was courted by a developer who wanted to redo the beach, but the resulting shopping mall concept was rejected. After I left office, the city went through the process again, as several hotel/resorts vied for the opportunity to develop the site. At a public meeting at Lake Worth High School in December 1998, our citizens rejected the various plans and clearly informed elected officials that the beach should be considered a public space and not be turned into a mall or hotel resort," he adds.

A charrette organized by the TCRPC was held with designers, planners, and various public interest groups in March 2000, and a preliminary plan was drawn up three months later. The city embraced that plan, and in September 2000 appointed a beach steering committee to improve it. Local planner Frank Palen led the 16-member committee, with the nine-member city planning and zoning board at its core, augmented by a mix of professionals and interested citizens.

"The beach appeals to a lot of people," points out Palen. "Yet initially, it was not clear how the beach was perceived by people. We conducted a survey and discovered there are many different perceptions. Some people want to sunbathe; others like to fish or just stroll on the pier. Then there's the group that sees the beach as a place to meditate and watch the sun rise. We have surfers, kids who clearly love to 'cruise' the beach, and tourists and residents who like to come to the beach to eat. We have one of the area's top restaurants: John G's is an institution. All these groups don't mix together, but each has an interest in what is going to happen at the beach."

Between September 2000 and this past May, the beach steering committee met 17 times to consider the TCRPC plan and the issues identified by the city commission, before presenting its report on May 23. "It is not a physical plan, it's a policy plan," emphasizes Palen. "We brought in experts on

parking, finance, fiscal impact analysis, and we asked them all to assist us in making rational judgments and help validate the design.

"We had to come up with a shared vision and look at the beach as an economic asset, not just a physical asset. It is also a social asset, a gathering place in an urban setting. People get very passionate about the beach," Palen adds with a smile. "While there is a tendency to get caught up in side issues, the steering committee was committed to keeping the process moving. We needed to get people with very different views together and focus them on the main issue—what to do about the beach. My main concern was getting people to commit to the planning and design process. The plan is more likely to be accepted if people feel they have a real opportunity to participate and get their questions answered. That was not always true in the past, and I am pleased with the nearly unanimous consensus the steering committee achieved."

Romano was reelected mayor of Lake Worth in March after a campaign in which he focused on the beach plan and neighborhood revitalization, and he says he is intent upon moving beach redevelopment forward. In July, the city commission voted unanimously to accept the conceptual designs produced by West Palm Beach–based Schwab, Twitty & Hanser Architectural Group (STH), which is responsible for the final design for the beach redevelopment. Rather than wait for construction drawings, STH suggested to the mayor that he and the design team expedite the process and go immediately to the state of Florida to begin a dialogue with various state permitting agencies, especially the Bureau of Beaches and Coastal Systems zoning agency, and get them on board from the beginning. The city task force now is eager to market the project to the general public.

The design team recognized the beach — with its small-town attributes and charm —

as the jewel of Lake Worth. The new plan calls for strengthening these attributes and improving and preserving the character of the beach as a historic focal point for the city and as an important amenity for its residents, which comprise a diverse community of first-, second-, and third-generation Americans, including African Americans, as well as Guatemalans, Jamaicans, Haitians, Finns, and a sprinkling of others of varied ethnic backgrounds. The new public entrance and proposed facilities are designed to announce an arrival to a unique public place.

Included in the project will be the casino building, a two-story structure comprising retail; John G's restaurant; conference and banquet space; and a common area. An upscale restaurant is planned for the second level. Another mixed-use group of buildings will feature retail, public locker rooms, a lifeguard station, and a common area. Also included in the plan are a parking garage, a picnic pavilion, restrooms, a fishing pier, and a pool equipment building. The total building space is about 145,000 square feet, but retail and restaurant space has been limited to 22,000 square feet.

"There will be a lot of open space, a simple circulation plan, and the area will be barrier free," explains design architect Ron Wiendl. "It was a conscious decision to create interaction among spaces. The retailers will have high exposure to visitors coming from the garage, but retail is limited to avoid competition with downtown Lake Worth."

The design of the new structures is Mediterranean/revival, reminiscent of, but not a replica of, the architecture of the original casino building. STH has recalled some of the architectural features of the original casino building — e.g., domes, gables, etc. — and there are a lot of similarities to the old facility because the city and the citizens want the new buildings to reflect the character of the past. But there is no gambling; the casino name remains for historical purposes.

The existing Olympic-sized pool will remain in its present position, with the casino building at one end, and the new mixed-use building, locker rooms, and lifeguard station, which flank the children's pool, at the other end. "This allows for more visibility and pedestrian circulation, and provides a direct connection between the pool and the beach," notes Wiendl. "Bathers will enjoy the use of the freshwater pool rather than the ocean on a windy day."

Currently, the road along the beach has multiple traffic lanes. But the new beach promenade will no longer be an automobile circulation area conducive to cruising; it will be a tree-lined, old-fashioned single-lane avenue where pedestrians can feel more secure and welcome. The 500-foot-long promenade also can be closed off for festivals and other cultural events.

The parking garage in the STH plan will hold 200 cars, which will eliminate a lot of surface parking and enable the creation of open space — something the public demanded. Some beachfront parking will remain for seniors and emergency vehicles; a total of 650 spaces will be available, with 120 off-site spaces at the entrance to the beach complex. According to Romano, plans call for Lake Worth citizens to be able to purchase yearly parking passes, while tourists and other visitors would pay a daily fee to use the beach.

The garage, located midway between the casino building and the other mixed-use buildings, will have the character of a retail structure, with tower pods for vertical circulation at the corners. A trellised area will be visible from State Road A1A and from the Lake Worth Bridge. An effort also has been made to make the parking garage visually appealing since it is so highly visible. Visitors approaching over the Lake Worth Bridge will have views of the entire complex and the beach.

Public buses and the Lake Worth Trolley can drop visitors off at the main entrance, and the Lake Worth Bridge provides walking access from downtown Lake Worth. A traffic roundabout proposed for the main entrance to the beach on State Road A1A requires further coordination with the state department of transportation.

John G's restaurant will have an outdoor dining patio connected to a large park on the south. Another elevated terrace with a view of the pool will be located on the north side of the building. From this area, visitors can be seen coming from the garage to the beach and retail patrons can visit the beach and pool. The second-floor conference facility is intended for use by city residents as well as to support the city's hotel and motel industry, which currently lacks comparable meeting space. One of the city's directives is that John G's restaurant stay open during construction. Phasing the redevelopment calls for keeping the existing structure open until the new building is complete, then the old casino building will be demolished.

The fishing pier — one of only two such piers in Palm Beach County — with its restaurant is an important component of the beach complex. While the pier will remain untouched, several options were considered for the pier entrance/restaurant complex, including demolishing and rebuilding it, or renovating it. Plans currently call for creating direct pier access, a new restaurant, and an entry kiosk, providing a gateway to a more inviting and attractive public space.

The beach site's landscape plan, created by West Palm Beach–based Glatting, Jackson, Kercher, Anglin, Lopez & Rinehart, aims to integrate the new buildings and swimming pool into a lush Mediterranean garden alongside the ocean. According to landscape architect David Barth, mature trees and other foliage will be used to enhance the promenade and the pool and to shade walkways. Decorative concrete block paving will be used to link the buildings to the ocean and pier. The main entrance will be planted with avenues of palms and ornamental shrubs to help create a grand entryway.

"The obvious citizen concern will be how we pay for all this," points out Romano. "We wanted to do the beach redevelopment ourselves," he notes. "I feel financing is best served by a bond issue. A workshop has been scheduled to discuss financing options, and if we all agree the best way to finance is with general obligation bonds, a referendum will go before the voters next March. Everyone agrees we have to do the project and we have to raise the funds. We plan to ask our citizens for $19 million. If we can go to Washington and get a $1 million endowment or obtain money from a private source, that will be wonderful, but we must be committed to raising $19 million."

The preliminary budget of $19 million is the actual cost of doing the project. This estimate includes the $14.5 million construction cost escalated over two years at the rate of inflation, a contingency fund to protect the citizens from unforeseen environmental conditions, plus fees, permits, and the actual cost of producing the bond referendum. "We need to consider how much more use will occur with the improved facility. We anticipate generating $1.5 million in revenue against the needed $1 million for maintenance and staffing. This would give us a half million dollars to put back into the general fund," adds Romano. "The fact that the city is retiring an old bond before this new one starts is helpful. A family with a $125,000 house with homestead exemption will pay only $70 more a year in taxes.

"The process has been long and tedious, but at last consensus reigns, and the redevelopment of Lake Worth Beach is nearing realization," says Romano. "Downtown revitalization began five years ago, and the citizens were very involved. They took it upon themselves to be involved in the beach revitalization planning, too."

Romano says he is optimistic about the

beach plan, but not complacent, noting that he plans a very active community sales campaign. "Historically, our citizens have said they don't want to spend money. But, as we have gone through this process, their support has been overwhelming. Their approval will be reflected in the passage of the bond issue next March," he adds. "I think of Lake Worth as an 80-year-old debutante. Our city has a lot of charm and history. It's time to strut our stuff."

CHAPTER 25

LANCASTER REVITALIZES INNER-CITY PARK

Jane Deel

The Design

The entire park is comprised of three individual areas on differing levels that flow seamlessly from one to the other and span the width of the city block. Each section of the park is unified with the overall design through the use of common elements such as brick paving, curbing, seatwalls, lighting, and plant materials.

The first area, the entrance promenade, opens to the street and is furnished with benches, lanterns, and columnar trees. Here there are wrought iron gates and a one-of-a-kind bronze sculpture by J. Seward Johnson, Jr. The sculpture depicts a man reading a copy of the *Lancaster Sunday News* as copies of the *New Era* and *Intelligencer Journal* wait by his side. He invites passersby to follow his example, enter the park, and rest for a while. The headlines on the papers add to the unique character of the space as they memorialize events that truly shaped our time: Neil Armstrong's walk on the moon, the disaster at Three Mile Island, and the first issue of the *Lancaster Sunday News* that reports registration figures as the highest ever.

The second area in the park is the flag-pole court. This area serves as a gathering space as well as a central plaza which is surrounded by entrances to the adjacent buildings. The edges of this area are softened by plantings and benches.

The third and most important area is the three-level inner park which is terminated by a 20-foot waterfall, a water column, and pools. The area is enclosed by buildings and plantings all around and overhead by a tree canopy. This portion of the park is furnished with tables and chairs which can easily be removed when using the space as an amphitheater or for any large-scale events.

Design Elements

Many elements are employed in the park to create a truly timeless design. Quality was the focus when selecting materials for the hardscape, plant materials, site furnishings, and signage. Brick was used throughout the park because it's a very warm material, it fits well with the existing buildings, and it carries on the character of the urban atmosphere.

Original plant material selection in-

Originally published as "Steinman Park: An Oasis in Lancaster," *Landscape Architect and Specifier News*, Vol. 20, No. 3, March 2004. Published by Landscape Communications, Tustin, California. Reprinted with permission of the publisher.

cluded Armstrong red maples to line the entrance promenade, green lustre hollies, 'Mohave' fire thorns, and rosebud azaleas in the flagpole court, Japanese scholartrees to provide a canopy over the benches along the building walls, and a second canopy of Halka honey locusts to enclose the inner park area. Seasonal color is introduced into the space with daffodils, narcissi, muscari, crocus, impatiens, and begonias.

Through careful selection of these plant materials, the hard surfaces of the surrounding buildings were softened. The flowering plants add interesting color to the urban scene. The trees provide shade and cooler temperatures during the summer and subdue adjacent street noise.

At night, the park is bathed in soft, warm, light from lanterns and ground lights. The waterfalls, water column, and pools are also lighted and provide a spectacular show.

The park itself is located between two turn-of-the-century buildings that were restored and renovated and have become prestigious addresses for downtown businesses. As open space in the business district, Steinman Park is a quiet setting removed from the traffic and noise of the city streets. Shoppers and workers also take advantage of this mid-block short-cut from the Central Parking Garage to the farmer's market and downtown businesses.

The Beginning

In 1978, the Steinman family, owners of Lancaster Newspapers Inc. and a number of Colonial and Victorian style commercial buildings in the vicinity of the Steinman Park site, decided to restore these properties and have plans prepared for the park site. The firm of McCloud, Scatchard, Derck, and Edson (the firm that survives today as Derck & Edson Associates) prepared the park sketches, drawings, specifications, and directed the project's construction through

completion. Root's Nurseries was the landscape contractor.

Design commenced in the early 1980s. The vision for the park included creating a living tribute to John Frederick Steinman and James Hale Steinman that would survive the tests of time and heavy usage. The park design was also a response to the renewed vitality of downtown Lancaster for the enjoyment of the people of Lancaster County, Pennsylvania.

The Park Today

The flexibility of the space makes the park an excellent spot for recitals and other types of artistic events. Chamber music is often heard coming from the park, most notably during the Lancaster Summer Arts Festival. During the holiday season, the park sparkles with lights that decorate the trees, creating an impressive holiday attraction.

Most of all, the park has become a mecca for alfresco brown bag lunchers and for simple relaxation for tired shoppers. The adjacent Pressroom Restaurant also utilizes the inner park for dining from mid-May through mid-September. Steinman Park is a fitting memorial to James Hale Steinman and John Frederick Steinman and gives the public a beautiful park for their enjoyment.

Beyond the embrace of the local community, the park has also received national attention. In May of 1984, Steinman Park received recognition at a White House ceremony for outstanding landscape design in an urban setting. The National Landscape Award was presented by First Lady Nancy Reagan to Caroline Steinman Nunan and Beverly (Peggy) Randolph Steinman of Lancaster Newspapers, Charles E. Edson and Robert I. Derck of McCloud, Scatchard, Derck, and Edson, and J. Clyde Root of Root's Nurseries. The park was selected for its design that provides ample seating for cultural events and includes special features such as lighted waterfalls, a water column, and pools surrounded by beautiful plantings.

A recipient of the National Landscape Award sponsored by the American Association of Nurserymen, Steinman Park has matured gracefully while maintaining its unique character.

Steinman Park was also honored by the American Society of Landscape Architects with the 1999 Medallion Award for making a significant contribution to the quality of life in Lancaster and for standing as a notable example of American landscape architecture.

The popularity and use of this site is a true testament to its timeless quality. It is, in all respects, the people's park.

CHAPTER 26

MIAMI BEACH, OTHER CITIES, SHORE UP THEIR COASTLINES

Lindsay Isaacs

Coastal communities are experiencing unprecedented population growth, and, at the same time, the land on which they are built is disappearing. Sea levels are rising — some say because of global warming — storms are carving away at shorelines, and millions of homeowners are facing the possibility of watching their property wash out to sea. Consequently, it has become more important than ever for coastal communities to develop strategies for maintaining the beaches that attract so many of their residents.

A report prepared by the Washington, D.C.–based H. John Heinz III Center for Science, Economics and the Environment, a non-profit research institute, indicates the extent of the coastal erosion problem in the United States. The report, prepared for the Federal Emergency Management Agency and released in June, states that the Atlantic coast is losing an average of two to three feet per year, and some areas on the Gulf Coast are losing as much as six feet per year. The Heinz report predicts that one out of four homes within 500 feet of a coast will be lost to erosion during the next 60 years.

With 3,600 people moving to them every day, coastal communities are searching for effective methods of maintaining their beaches — their most valuable resource. "We have a moral responsibility to save our beaches," says Reese Musgrave, mayor of Pine Knoll Shores, N.C. "[The alternative is to let things go], and, if we did that, half of our tax base would fall into the water."

Arming the Coast

Communities have a number of options to manage beach erosion, most of which fit into two categories: hard solutions and soft solutions. Hard solutions include groins, seawalls and breakwaters, and soft solutions include beach renourishment, dune construction and property retreat.

Groins are built perpendicular to the shoreline and are extended into the water to catch drifting sand. They have been used frequently, particularly on the New Jersey coast, but they are falling out of favor as primary solutions to erosion because they interrupt the flow of sand to neighboring beaches.

Seawalls, also known as revetments and bulkheads, are usually built vertically on beaches to protect property, but they have

Originally published as "Shoring Up the Nation's Coastlines," *American City & County*, Vol. 115, No. 13, September 2000. Published by Intertec Publishing Corporation, Atlanta, Georgia. Reprinted with permission of the publisher.

disadvantages also. "You almost always see a lowering of the beach profile next to a seawall, and you get scour and a whirlpool effect on the sides," says Truman Henson, a Massachusetts Coastal Zone Management coordinator. "You may even see these results within one season [of building a wall]."

Alternatively, sloped stone revetments have been used and have shown fewer significant consequences, Henson says. The sloped surface resembles the natural slope of the beach but armors the sand with rocks, which do not wash away as easily as sand. The spaces between the stones in such structures also serve as habitats for small animals.

Breakwaters are structures built off shore, parallel to the beach, to catch waves before they break on the beach. The structures create calm waters on the shore. However, depending on the water depth and the size of the structures, breakwaters may not protect the beach at all, says Rebecca Haney, a Massachusetts Coastal Zone Management coordinator. "It's hard to protect eight miles of beach with breakwaters," says Susan Lucas, chief of coastal planning for the Philadelphia District of the U.S. Army Corps of Engineers. "And some people think they're unsightly."

Because of the problems associated with hard solutions, North Carolina banned them all in 1986. The state encourages homeowners to move their homes away from the shore rather than build solid structures to stop erosion. However, most of the communities on the North Carolina coast are old towns, and residents are reluctant to move, says Tony Caudel, Wrightsville Beach town manager. As a result, towns on North Carolina's coast are trying to implement renourishment solutions.

Economic Ebb and Flow

The U.S. Army Corps of Engineers conducts most large beach renourishment projects because of the cost and the amount of work involved in each project. In 1996, Congress passed the Shore Protection Act and charged the Corps with helping coastal communities rebuild their beaches. The Act established rules for local governments to follow to get federal support from the Corps, and it pledged that the Corps would maintain the beach renourishment projects for 50 years.

Currently, the Corps spends $80 million a year to maintain the nation's coastline. "That's only half of what's needed," says Howard Marlowe, president of the Washington, D.C.–based American Coastal Coalition, a non-profit coastal advocacy group. "The demand for federal money is increasing."

Once the Corps approves a renourishment project, it covers 65 percent of the project's cost; local governments are responsible for remaining costs. Wrightsville Beach, N.C., has participated in federal renourishment projects designed to protect the town against storms since the 1960s, following damage by Hurricane Hazel in 1954. The Corps has recently committed to return to the town every four years — at a cost of $2.5 million per visit — to refill the beaches with sand.

Nearby Carolina Beach and Kure Beach undergo federal renourishment projects every three years, at a cost of $3.2 million and $4.5 million respectively. The state contributes approximately 75 percent of the non-federal share of the costs, and New Hanover County pays the remaining costs with money raised by a county-levied 3 percent room occupancy tax on rental properties. The room occupancy tax is used in many coastal communities, including popular Hilton Head, S.C., so that "the tourists who use the resource most pay to have it maintained," says Clark Alexander, an associate professor at the Skidaway Institute of Oceanography in Savannah, Ga.

For many cities, beaches serve as economic engines. No beaches, no tourists. A 1997 survey conducted by San Francisco State University estimates that beach visits in California generate more than $10 billion in direct spending annually. The study reports that visits to California beaches reached 565 million in 1996 while visits to all of the state's theme parks totaled 26 million. "We really can't afford [to ignore beach erosion]," Marlowe says. "There's an economic loss if we [do]. People will go somewhere else, and regions will lose money to other regions."

Stop Gap Measures

All beaches cannot raise enough money through tourism to pay for renourishment projects. For example, Holden Beach, N.C., a barrier island in Brunswick County, has 990 permanent residents and approximately 10,000 rental property occupants in the summer. Holden Beach raises only $700,000 each year from its 6 percent accommodations tax.

Although the town has saved $1.5 million to pay for beach renourishment, Mike Morgan, town manager of Holden Beach, estimates that it costs $1 million to renourish one mile of sand. The town has five miles of beach that need renourishment, so it has applied for federal aid to support such a project.

Until Holden Beach is approved for federal assistance, which may not happen for another nine or 10 years, it must do whatever it can to maintain its beaches. The town most recently constructed five miles of dunes in 1997 by hauling in 200,000 cubic yards of sand by truck. The dunes were stabilized with plants and sand fencing, but they will have to be rebuilt in a few years.

The town also takes advantage of the Corps allowing communities to use dredged materials for beach reconstruction. The Corps routinely dredges the harbor in Wil-

mington and deposits the dredged sand on two miles of Holden Beach and neighboring beaches.

Renourishment

Just as hard solutions have critics, so does beach renourishment as an erosion control method. Florida beaches have had problems finding enough sand to maintain renourishment projects, says Robert Dean, professor of coastal engineering at the University of Florida. In fact, the Corps is finding that it has to go farther off shore to find sand for beaches than it used to.

For example, Miami Beach, which began renourishing its beaches in 1979, is finding that less sand is available locally to continue its renourishment. The Corps is searching for alternative sources of sand for Miami, and some geologists and coastal engineers have suggested using sand from the Bahamas to maintain the project, says Bruce Henderson, environmental specialist for Miami Beach. The Miami Beach tourism industry, which attracts more than three million visitors to the beach each year, supports that idea.

Others say that renourishment is only a temporary solution to a permanent problem. "Essentially, beach renourishment is treating the symptoms, not curing the disease," said Steven Leatherman, director of the Laboratory for Coastal Research at the International Hurricane Center in Miami during a live online chat on USA Today's web site in July. "It is not a general panacea for beach erosion problems, but it can work in some areas where the erosion rate is low."

Some communities have tried to compensate for the disadvantages of hard and soft solutions by using many of them together in one project. For example, Virginia Beach, Va., with help from the Corps, has constructed a seawall, strengthened its boardwalk and dune system, and renourished its beach every three years. The city began planning the $115 million project in 1970. Scheduled for completion next year, the combined measures are intended to protect Virginia Beach from hurricane damage.

Attention Increasing

Although coastal communities are finding some success combining erosion control methods, they may soon have more effective alternatives. The Corps has organized the National Shoreline Erosion Control Development and Demonstration Program, a six-year effort to study new shore protection devices, designs and methods. The Coastal Engineering Research Board, an appointed advisory board, is selecting seven sites where it will evaluate test structures for stability, long-term performance and ability to withstand extreme events.

Beach erosion control methods have not changed much in recent years, but the importance of implementing the methods has increased dramatically. In 15 years, 27 million more people will be living on the coast, and coastal communities still will be grappling with disappearing shorelines.

Until new solutions are devised, communities will continue using groins, seawalls and breakwaters to fight erosion, and they will continue rebuilding dunes, dredging sand and moving their homes away from the shore. "Unfortunately, man has altered the natural resources by moving to the coast in droves," Morgan says. "If we didn't like it, we should have stopped it 50 years ago."

CHAPTER 27

MINNEAPOLIS AND SAINT PAUL, OTHER CITIES, GUIDE GROWTH TO IMPROVE THE ENVIRONMENT

Jim Miara

Suburban sprawl, endless traffic jams, air and water pollution, and dwindling open space are 21st-century evils descending like an implacable plague on major metropolitan centers. After ignoring warning signs that have been mounting for decades, urban planners and public officials everywhere now are scrambling to find short-term and long-range strategies to battle the cumulative effects of uncontrolled growth. And many of them are looking northward for guidance.

Minnesota's Twin Cities area is one of the first U.S. metropolitan regions to formally recognize that haphazard growth is a serious threat to its quality of life and then take steps to combat it. In 1967, the Minnesota legislature created a regional agency called the Metropolitan Council and gave it the authority and tools to help shape the metropolitan area's future.

To advocates of regional planning, the Met Council, as it is called, is a model of enlightened government, with the authority to conduct long-range planning for an area that includes Minneapolis and Saint Paul and the surrounding seven counties of Anoka, Carver, Dakota, Hennepin, Ramsey, Scott, and Washington. The vast metropolitan region comprises 189 municipalities and 2.4 million residents.

A major weapon in the Met Council's planning arsenal is its ability to review the comprehensive plans of all communities within its jurisdiction to ensure that they are in concert with regional goals. It also has the authority to plan for transportation needs and guide regional development, including air travel; water quality and supply; housing; and parks and open spaces.

Following a 1994 legislative mandate to merge with three other regional agencies, the Met Council gained an operational component, which manages the regional wastewater collection and treatment system, the regional transit system, and the Metropolitan Housing and Redevelopment Authority (HRA). The council — with 3,700 employees and an annual budget of nearly $500 million — is financed with funds from a local property tax, user fees from the wastewater

Originally published as "Council, My Council," *Urban Land*, Vol. 60, No. 4, April 2001. Published by the Urban Land Institute, Washington, D.C., Reprinted with permission of the publisher.

treatment system, and the transit system, plus supplemental state and federal funds.

The Met Council gained its widespread authority because it was clear that resolving the multifaceted problems created by growth requires comprehensive planning. The development of transportation (highways and airports) must be coordinated with the transit system. Residential development must be channeled to areas where the infrastructure to support it is in place. And all planning must consider environmental and quality-of-life issues.

"The Metropolitan Council seeks to meld three ideas — economic growth, environmental preservation, and fiscal conservatism, which means maximizing use of existing infrastructure," says Ted Mondale, who was appointed chairman of the Met Council in February 1999, by Minnesota Governor Jesse Ventura. "The problem is fairly simple: 500,000 more people are expected to be living in the Minneapolis/Saint Paul metropolitan area by 2020. Mondale said, "How far should the area spread, and will such population growth lead to unprecedented congestion?"

Mondale, the son of former U.S. vice president Walter Mondale and himself a former state senator and candidate for governor of Minnesota, believes it is the Met Council's job to make sure that does not happen.

"The council creates a framework for regionalism. There is a whole set of services that can be done on a regional scale that can't be done at the local level," he says. "We avoid competition [among cities] because we look at development decisions around systems — transportation, parks and open space, and air and water quality."

This regional framework aligns the council's policies and investments for transportation and sewers to support regional growth objectives. In the Twin Cities, the Met Council is using a combination of incentives, seed money, and design tools for communities to serve as smart growth models.

Unique and Controversial

Curtis Johnson, who served as the council's chairman from 1995 to 1999, points out that the Met Council "is an authentic regional government, one of only two in the country." (Portland, Oregon, is the other.) Since 1994, when the Met Council was reconfigured, he says, "It has done a good job of creating an integrated whole. It conducts planning and operations well, which is difficult. The council has done a good job balancing the two, and the synergy created has been effective."

But Johnson, who now runs Citistates, a Minnesota-based consulting firm that provides advice to regional planners, says that the Twin Cities model would be difficult — if not impossible — to duplicate in other areas. In 1967, when the Met Council came into being, the privately owned bus system was languishing; the wastewater treatment system was inadequate, resulting in pollution of local rivers and lakes; and suburbs were mushrooming with haphazard growth, leading to traffic congestion. In other words, conditions were ripe for an expansion of regional responsibility, and local turf wars — the bane of regional governments — were kept to a minimum. In typical Minnesota fashion, no one perceived the council as a threat, even though it added a nonelected layer of government that superseded the authority of local officials.

Sounding like Garrison Keillor of Lake Wobegon on National Public Radio, Johnson says, "The Twin Cities are cursed by an absence of crisis; nothing bad ever happens here. We have steady growth, a diversified economy, and the unemployment rate has been half the national average for ten years. As a result, it's hard to arouse people over problems, particularly long-range problems."

By 1994 it was clear that traffic congestion and pollution needed a regional remedy. Johnson says the Met Council was accepted as a necessary nuisance, even though some elements of the council's character are highly controversial. The most contentious debate concerns whether the chair and the 16-member board should be elected. Currently, members are appointed and serve at the pleasure of the governor, although they are confirmed by the state senate in consultation with local elected officials. Opponents of the current system note that the regional government in Portland is elected, and the Met Council, which has taxing power and enormous authority, should be, too. "Taxation with representation" is a common cry among those advocating change.

"The Met Council is the only regional planning board in the country that has taxing power," notes Karen Anderson, mayor of Minnetonka, an affluent town of 53,000 located in the western suburbs of Minneapolis. "And there are tax disparities — a 1972 state law provides for sharing of tax proceeds among communities, although the Met Council does not directly administer this program. It's a big deal and people don't like it." Even so, she says that the majority of her constituents support the Met Council in its present form as long as it is monitored closely.

"Minnetonka has always contributed more money that we have gotten in return, but we approve of what the council is doing. We just have to be proactive to make sure there are no greater disparities," says Anderson, who has been in office for seven years. When it comes to the ongoing elected-versus-appointed battle, Anderson, like many in the Twin Cities area, is conflicted. "I have changed my mind several times, but I come back to the appointive system," she says.

Johnson also has come down in favor of the appointive system after initially favoring elections. "I can see it both ways; there are

distinct advantages in each," he explains. With an appointed board, he says, it is possible to recruit qualified people who otherwise would not run, and they are more likely to think districtwide. An elected board, on the other hand, would have more legitimacy, and candidates could make the council's agenda part of their campaigns. In the end, he says, "Electing the council is probably not the best idea, but I think elections will be inevitable."

Mondale clearly favors the appointed body. "Elected officials sometimes end up being complaint-takers from constituents. Now, we have a council that is leading, rather than responding to pressure." He also notes that developers, who have enormous interest in the council's decisions, likely would be huge contributors to district campaigns.

The Twin Cities are unique in that all the pluses and minuses of a given metropolitan area are multiplied by two. There are two urban centers, two symphony halls, two downtown arenas, and two rush-hour commuting patterns. Sixty percent of Minnesota's population lives in the Met Council region, and most of the state's cultural and political institutions are located there as well.

Considering the extensive scope of the council's jurisdiction and the fact that it has the third-largest budget of local governments in the state, some Minnesota legislators have voiced concern that it could challenge the legislature's authority. Jim Solem, who served as the Met Council's regional administrator from the time of the merger of public agencies in 1994 until last year, points out that even though the council is not elected, it is extremely sensitive to the need to build support for its actions — in the districts, in the legislature, and, most important, with the governor.

"The first thing the council has to do is to sell the governor," Solem explains. "Fortunately, the current governor [Jesse

Ventura] is very supportive. When he was running for office, he questioned the need for the council, but now he is very supportive." Indeed, Ventura is so convinced of the council's value that he has given Mondale cabinet-level status.

Regional Planning Successes

Both its opponents and its supporters agree that, over the past seven years, the Met Council has made progress in several key areas. For example, the rivers, lakes, and streams are cleaner. As Johnson, the former council chair, says, "Today, you can fall into the Mississippi without taking a toxic bath. You couldn't ten years ago." Also, urban services are delivered more efficiently and cost-effectively than they were before. Furthermore, rural areas and the nationally acclaimed Twin Cities regional park system have been protected and the number of affordable housing units has increased significantly.

Most observers consider reform of the region's wastewater treatment management system as one of the council's most significant accomplishments. Administered by local boards prior to 1967, the multiple and antiquated wastewater treatment systems strained under the pressure of the suburban population spurt of the 1950s and 1960s. The region's many waterways were being polluted, endangering the quality of life considered to be one of the Twin Cities's major assets. "One of the reasons we supported the creation of the Met Council," says Mayor Anderson, "was [because] Lake Minnetonka was suffering pollution due to the many western suburbs that had poor wastewater treatment systems. Something had to be done."

When the Met Council was created, however, changes came quickly. From 1970 to 1985, some 33 smaller wastewater treatment plants scattered across the region were consolidated into a regional system of nine larger and more efficient plants. More system improvements were made, and in the late 1990s, facing strong opposition from unions, the council nevertheless restructured the workforce. As a result, the operating budget was reduced by $20 million per year over three years. At the same time, it made repairs to the system, started construction of new wastewater treatment plants, and reduced rates for local communities. "It was no longer a situation where a small local board got overwhelmed by unions," explains Solem, who as regional administrator was in the thick of the battle. "The council initiated competition and set cost parameters. There was a little fuss and feathers along the way, but we made the changes."

Transportation

In the 1940s, the Twin Cities region bustled with public rail transportation. Mass transit was so good, in fact, that some urban historians contend that the easy access to rail transport made feasible the development of low-density, single-family homes, which fostered suburban sprawl. But as the popularity of the automobile began to grow in the 1950s, the Twin Cities, like most other metropolitan areas, shifted focus from mass-transit systems to superhighways. As a result, much of the old rail system was neglected and eventually removed. Today, virtually none of the old rail lines are in service.

The Met Council has begun to reverse the situation. In January, ground broke on the $675 million Hiawatha Light-Rail Transit Line, which will extend 11.6 miles from downtown Minneapolis to the Minneapolis/Saint Paul International Airport. Scheduled to open in 2004, the Hiawatha Line is expected eventually to carry 24,800 passengers a day.

"Once this is up and running, there

will be an uncritical rush for everyone to have their own line," says Mondale. "It's a high-quality amenity. When there's a big snowstorm, would you like to get to the office in 12 minutes or sit in traffic for a couple of hours?" Adds Todd Paulson, a Met council board member from Brooklyn Center, "We weren't just breaking ground on a light-rail system, we were breaking ground on regional planning. We are integrating the transit system with community redevelopment, affordable housing, and environmental protection. All the elements have to be coordinated."

Light rail also is a catalyst for development. Mary Hill Smith, a council member representing the western suburbs of Minneapolis and the chairwoman of the council's transportation committee, outlined how integrating the transit system with community redevelopment, affordable housing, and environmental protection is part of the transportation investment. "All elements are interrelated in terms of policies and investments," she says.

Not everyone has welcomed the prospect of the new rail service, however. More than 150 community meetings have addressed abutters' concerns about the Hiawatha Line's disruptive effects. "The light-rail line will affect a lot of people, so we needed to build a consensus," explains Natalio Diaz, the Met Council's transportation planning director. "It required a lot of dialogue and education. We tried to make it explicit that transportation systems are integral to growth."

Smart Growth

Expressed in the simplest terms, says Mondale, the Met Council's goal is to preserve the area's quality of life through smart growth. A no-growth strategy is impossible and uncontrolled growth creates chaos; the only logical alternative, therefore, is to guide growth in directions acceptable to the community.

In an address to a conference on smart growth last year, Mondale said, "We've had a debate in our region for a long time about whether we want to be Mayberry or whether we want to be New York City. If we continue where we're going, we're going to be L.A. or Atlanta, and that's not the kind of place we want to be. The smart growth approach is the way to get out of that either/or debate."

In 2000, the Met Council launched a regional initiative called Smart Growth Twin Cities that engages regional residents in the urban design process by asking them to voice their thoughts about how they want the Twin Cities to look in the future. With a grant from the McKnight Foundation, the council hired Calthrope Associates, a San Francisco, California–based urban design firm, to facilitate the process.

In workshops to be held this spring, residents will consider development preferences for local sites. In fall 2001, the council will host regional workshops considering issues such as the environmental and economic impacts of current and planned growth and debate alternative land use plans. Six test "opportunity sites" have already been chosen. The Met Council hopes these sites will allow for compact, efficient development "that is walkable and transit-friendly and will serve as models for other communities planning smart growth." Residents will participate in small teams of business people, city officials, and developers to create detailed, feasible plans. Local officials have welcomed the initiative. "This gives us a wonderful opportunity to work with our citizens to see where our future may go," says Mayor Myrna Kragness of Brooklyn Center, one of the opportunity site host communities.

The Livable Communities Act, passed by the state legislature in 1995 and coauthored by then state senator Ted Mondale, has become one of the Met Council's most effective tools in implementing smart growth policies. The law authorizes the council to provide grants to communities to develop projects that include a mix of housing and create a community that is more walkable and transit-oriented while preserving green space. Other goals include expanding affordable housing and cleaning up polluted sites for redevelopment to accommodate housing, business, and jobs. Last year, the Met Council awarded $19.2 million to 24 communities and two counties for smart growth projects.

The livable communities program has garnered commitment from communities for an estimated 76,000 units of affordable housing by 2010. About 16,000 units have been built to date by participating communities.

"When we passed the Livable Communities Act in 1995, people thought we were speaking Chinese," recalls Mondale. "We had to look for development sites to clean up, but now we have hundreds of applications. Communities are seeing how they can revive used lands and turn them into vibrant community centers."

In keeping with the council's incentives philosophy, new grant criteria now before the council call for expansion of affordable housing by giving participating cities and counties a chance to earn a higher priority for regional investments in community development, transportation, and environmental projects.

"The council is committed to a regional growth strategy that sustains this region's competitive advantage in the future. We do this by making connections among jobs, housing, transportation, land use, and our region's environmental assets," adds Mondale.

Eye to the Future

In the end, proponents of the Met Council say, the objective is to prepare for the half-million new residents who will inhabit the Twin Cities region in just 20 years — and to do it in a way that preserves the area's cherished quality of life. Accomplishing this requires a comprehensive approach that factors in variables such as economic and social vitality, the best use of land and resources, and the preservation of parks, waterways, and other environmental amenities. At the same time, growth should take place in a way that enhances the urban centers and older neighborhoods.

"The future of the Twin Cities," says Mondale, "depends on the strength of the whole, not just some of its parts. I think the Met Council is on the verge of building a consensus — and it is happening before we reach a crisis point. Florida started taking action only after the Everglades were seriously harmed. Maryland moved only after the Chesapeake Bay was polluted. We want to do things before anything here collapses."

CHAPTER 28

NEW YORK CITY'S OLD RAILROAD TRACKS BECOME HIDDEN GARDEN

Asher Price

The last train to trundle through Manhattan's West Side on the High Line bore a modest cargo. Frozen turkeys, three carloads of them, made their frosty way along the elevated rail route to their appointed end in the city's meatpacking district.

That was in 1980. The High Line then fell dormant, less a conduit for turkeys than a bed for seedlings. Flowers, weeds, and saplings burst up about the dank steel. Drains clogged, leaving storm water rivulets to meander between the rail ties, and birds nested in the rusty shade. Now the High Line is on the verge of conversion to park space, forcing planners to determine whether it should be cultivated and opened to the public or closed off to protect the native plant life that has flourished in the cracks industry left behind.

Construction of the High Line began under the West Side Improvement project soon after the onset of the Depression, signaling the muscled development projects of the New Deal that would soon follow. Elevated two stories above street level, the line was designed to alleviate congestion and ac-

cidents along Tenth Avenue, known as "Death Avenue" for its fatal confluence of pedestrians, trains, and automobiles. The line's operator, the New York Central Railroad Company, delivered nearly half of the city's cream and milk, much of it along High Line. It is thus doubly fitting that when finished in 1934, the High Line was touted as the "Life Line of New York."

But the High Line began limping toward obsolescence by the 1950s. The compact Mack truck provided a more flexible and efficient method for delivering goods to Manhattan buildings. In the 1960s, the southern chunk of the line was destroyed. In 1993 another stretch was torn down.

The last spur of the High Line, a 1.5-mile stretch that wends through Manhattan's artsy Chelsea district, was set to be dismantled in 2001. Thirty feet off the ground, ranging in width from 25 to 40 feet, it runs primarily along Tenth Avenue from 34th Street south to Gansevoort Street. Complaints from local property owners that the line cast a gloomy shadow throughout the neighborhood, combined with the prohibi-

Originally published as "Manhattan's Hidden Garden: What to Do with the Highline?" *The Next American City*, Issue 4, October 2004. Published by The Next American City, Inc., New York, New York. Reprinted with permission of the publisher.

tively expensive maintenance costs borne by CSX, the Richmond-based rail company that owns the structure, sounded the death knell of the High Line.

But in an urban irony befitting New York, the High Line's very dereliction seems to have saved it. Now grassed over, it has suddenly become relevant to a city preoccupied with developing parks. The High Line has its own wild ecosystem framed by old industrial warehouses — and its green and grimy allure seems not wholly unrelated to the chic value of the pricey lofts and galleries that now inhabit those warehouses. Purple aster, Queen Anne's lace, ailanthus trees, apple tree saplings, and Black-eyed susans are a sample of the flora that have taken root — alongside littered broken bottles and trash — atop the abandoned rail bed. The space may become a model for a new breed of urban park reclaimed from industrial use.

A neighborhood group, Friends of the High Line (FHL), was formed in 1999 to save the line from destruction. In keeping with its Chelsea digs, the group enlisted a fashionable and politically connected cadre to stave off challenges from developers and local businesses. The High Line has quickly become a cause *célèbre* that counts actor Edward Norton and fashion designers Todd Oldham and Diane von Furstenberg among its supporters. The growing efforts of the group have met with some success: in a series of court skirmishes last year, FHL successfully halted demolition plans negotiated during the Giuliani administration.

An opposing group, known as the Chelsea Property Owners, has argued that the Line, which once accelerated industrial development, has now choked it. Douglas Sarini, who heads the group, has said that his company, Edison Parking Corporation, has had to turn away offers to purchase its site beneath the High Line for manufacturing development and a new movie studio. "Money doesn't grow on trees. And the last time we checked, it wasn't growing in the weeds of the High Line, either," reads one flyer distributed by the group.

But FHL counters that the High Line could be an economic boon for the city. A nearby park would boost property values, which would, in turn, generate new tax revenues. In December 2002, the city — now under the reign of a new mayor who has championed the project — announced its agreement with FHL. In filing a claim with the federal Surface Transportation Board, the city requested that the High Line be granted a Certificate of Interim Trail Use. If the claim is successful, the space will be eligible for a process called "rail-banking," which allows inactive rail corridors to be reused as recreational trails.

Estimates for the cost of converting the High Line to a park run as high as $65 million. But last July, the New York City Council announced a plan to devote $15.75 million over the next three years to revitalize the High Line. Presumably it did not hurt that Gifford Miller, the speaker of the Council, was a college roommate of Robert Hammond, one of the founders of FHL.

"We believe we can turn this space into one of New York's great places," Deputy Mayor Daniel L. Doctoroff told *The New York Times* in July. "This is the spine, truly the vital link, that connects three rapidly evolving and exciting neighborhoods."

Joshua David, the other founder of FHL, says his organization is now poised to take control of the line and prepare it for public access.

But determining the best use for the High Line may be more of a challenge than saving it. David notes that two camps have developed. One wants to make it as accessible as possible for the public; the other is clamoring to preserve the space as if it were a precious wetland. While the High Line affords a lovely and unusual view that juxtaposes the Hudson River and an industrial landscape, it also shelters a scraggly, fragile ecosystem, valuable because it has developed untouched.

Joel Sternfeld, a photographer who has published a book about the High Line, compared it with New York's most famous open space while touring the site with a reporter from *The Independent*. "Central Park is really cosmetic in many ways. [The High Line] is a true time landscape, a railroad ruin. The abandoned place is the place where seasonality resides... This is what spring in New York actually looks like when it's left up to spring."

Maintaining that "true time landscape" and, at the same time, encouraging public access is the challenge that now falls to High Line planners.

"There's no way to keep it pristine and have people up there," says David.

How the High Line debate plays out may instruct other cities in how to reclaim disused urban structures as active park space. This past summer saw a design competition, featuring work from more than 700 architects from nearly 40 counties. The nonbinding competition held out contradictory trophies: one award to the architect who imagined the most accessible space and another to the architect who best preserved the natural flora.

"In order to keep that as a sublime space and yet to enable it to become a public park, you have to do quite a lot," says Laura Pollak, winner of the prize for site preservation. The goal, she said, is to make the space both natural and social. In their design, Pollak and her team employed raised paths to allow public access but limit trampling. Their vision also calls for a flatbed rail car to serve as a community garden and an "opportunistic landscape" that favors forest succession.

The High Line's likely conversion is not without precedent. FHL points to Paris' *La Promenade Plantée*. Located in the 12th *arrondissement*, in a formerly seedy part of town, the 1.5-mile promenade stands on the site of an elevated rail line that operated from 1852 to 1969. The promenade—built between 1988 and 1998—cost $187 million. The investment seems to have paid off with a local development boom: its street level archways, which once sheltered trash bins, now house the shops of artisans. In another example, Seattle opened Gas Works Park, designed by Richard Haag, in 1973. The nineteen-acre space includes many of the leftover structures from the Washington Natural Gas Company's coal gasification plant, which had closed in 1956 after half a century of operation.

These two sites both follow the model of providing maximum public access. The concern for natural preservation makes the issue of access to a reclaimed space like the High Line more complex.

Some among the competition organizers hold out hope that a design might balance the impulse to preserve a site's ecology with the wish to exhibit its natural growth to the public. The reclamation of the High Line should not aim to segregate humans from nature, says Robert Breunig, director of the Lady Bird Johnson Wildflower Center, which sponsored the preservation prize at the design competition. "The High Line probably could support a strict ecological restoration project, but its design can respect the natural world as much as it does the built environment ... [the High Line] reflects the healing of a landscape that was there before the city was there."

It may seem odd that so many people take the overgrowth along the High Line as a serious natural phenomenon. But its wild park stands as a refreshing counterpoint in a city for which planning and development is a sort of obsessive-compulsive behavior. It is a truer park, in a way, than the city's signature green space, Central Park, which has been carefully rusticated in a bid at planned disorder.

And in a wider sense, the High Line is novel because it not only evaded redevelopment but was forgotten altogether. The superheated real estate market of Manhattan now has parallels in Chicago, where mixed-use skyscrapers are replacing abandoned industrial land on the fringes of The Loop, in Washington, where vast downtown parking lots are subject to massive bidding wars, and in other cities. In the coming years, left-behind spaces in those cities may also become celebrated for their quiet survival.

Those cities may look to the High Line as a valuable guide in preserving odd survivors of real estate competition.

As government agencies close in on a deal to save the High Line, at least one of the grand prize-winning designs has drowned the debate. An Austrian architect laid out her plans to convert the High Line into a mile-long swimming pool. Call it precious blue space.

CHAPTER 29

NORTHAMPTON COUNTY COMBINES ECONOMIC DEVELOPMENT WITH ENVIRONMENTAL PROTECTION

Lance Metzler, Mary Lechner, and *Timothy Hayes*

Economic development and environmental protection often are viewed as competing interests at best and mutually exclusive at worst. Clean air and water, protection of wildlife, and resource conservation often are pitted against jobs and business expansion. Proposals for new industry may be met with cries of "not in my backyard" because of fears of pollution and negative community impacts.

Despite this seeming incompatibility, Northampton County, Virginia, has opened the first phase of a new kind of industrial park in which waste streams are cycled into revenue streams and industrial processes are based on the designs of natural systems. This "ecological industrial park" is part of an innovative county strategy whereby economic development is protecting valuable environmental assets and environmental protection is fostering development of a sustainable economy.

The Land Between Two Waters

Venture across the Chesapeake Bay from the mainland of Virginia to the southern tip of the slender finger of land known as Virginia's Eastern Shore and you will find Northampton County. With the Chesapeake on the west and the Atlantic on the east, Native Americans referred to this Virginia treasure as "the land between two waters."

Northampton County is a place rich in natural and historic resources, including miles of pristine beaches, a string of preserved barrier islands, thriving marshes and tidal creeks, fish and shellfish, birds and wildlife, open land and clean water, small towns and historic villages, woodlands, and farms. Recognizing the global importance of this ecosystem, the United Nations has designated much of Northampton County and the surrounding region as a World Biosphere Reserve.

In sharp contrast to the county's nat-

Originally published as "Economic Development and Environmental Protection: The Northampton County, Virginia, Experience," *Government Finance Review*, Vol. 18, No. 1, February 2002. Published by the Government Finance Officers Association, Chicago, Illinois. Reprinted with permission of the publisher.

ural and historic wealth, many of its people live in severe economic poverty. The closure of nearly all of the area's seafood and agricultural processing plants during the 1980s resulted in the loss of more than 1,500 jobs. By the early 1990s, 28 percent of the population was living in poverty, while 10 percent of the county's homes lacked plumbing and 12 percent lacked adequate sanitary facilities.

Having declined economically to become one of the poorest communities in Virginia and in the nation, the county began to wrestle with difficult, seemingly contradictory questions. Should the environment be sacrificed for economic development? Should a stagnant economy, lack of jobs, and poverty be accepted as the price of protecting a unique environment? Should the county try to strike a balance between economic development and environmental protection that would provide for "manageable" levels of both poverty and pollution? None of these scenarios was acceptable.

Triple Bottom Line

Rather than compromising the local economy for the environment or vice versa, the county instead decided to pursue a strategy that would simultaneously maximize both the economy and the environment for the benefit of the entire community. As one member of the Northampton County Board of Supervisors put it: "We must do business today in a way that won't put us out of business tomorrow."

The community and its elected governing body came to understand that they were trustees of a valuable portfolio of natural, cultural, and human assets. Consequently, they began to explore ways to invest in and protect these assets in order to build a strong and lasting economy and to preserve one of the last truly exceptional unspoiled environments on America's Atlantic coast. Success would be measured in terms of a triple bottom line: economy, environment, and equity.

Sustainable Development Action Strategy

In 1993, the county formally began its sustainable development initiative with a mission to "build a strong and lasting economy by capitalizing on and protecting Northampton's rich natural, cultural, and human assets." The commitment was to develop in a manner that would simultaneously benefit business, the environment, and all of the county's people both now and in the future.

Through a partnership with the National Oceanic Atmospheric Administration and the Virginia Coastal Program, the county hired the nation's first local director of sustainable development. With funding from the NOAA, VCP, and other partners, this individual organized the Department of Sustainable Development and led Northampton in formulating a vision for the county's future and a strategy to achieve that vision.

What came to be known as the Sustainable Development Action Strategy was developed through an intensive, collaborative process involving community workshops, task forces, meetings, and events. The county involved a broad cross section of its diverse citizenry in the strategy development process, leveraging their combined experience to identify industries with realistic, significant, immediate, and ongoing potential for development. As a result of this process, Northampton decided to target the following industry sectors: agriculture, seafood/aquaculture, heritage tourism, research/education, arts/crafts, local products, and sustainable technologies. The community also identified the vital natural, historic, and community assets that would need to be preserved and capitalized on to develop and sustain these targeted industries. The final step in the process was the formulation of an action plan for implementing the strategy. In June 1994, the Board of Supervisors adopted the strategy as the county's official development policy and immediately kicked off its implementation.

One of the keys of the Sustainable Development Action Strategy was to leverage private investment in the county in ways that would achieve the integral goals of building an economic base and protecting natural and cultural assets. It was clear that public financial resources would have to be carefully focused to achieve the greatest possible return for each dollar invested. It was also clear that Northampton's strategy would need to be phased in over time using major impact projects as long-term building blocks. As such, county officials had to determine which course of action would yield the highest economic and environmental return in the shortest period of time. The decision: an ecological industrial park to be known as the Sustainable Technology Park and to be located in the Town of Cape Charles.

America's First Ecological Industrial Park

As it began planning the infrastructure to facilitate business and industrial development, Northampton set its sights on an industrial park that would truly be world class. The goal was to provide an "environment for excellence" that would attract and produce companies that would share the county's high business, environmental, and human equity standards. The vision was for a "green" industrial park — green as in the color of the environment and green as in the color of money.

Economically, the consensus vision was for a park that would help build a strong and diversified economic base by attracting and growing new companies and by retaining and expanding existing companies. The companies in the park would provide quality jobs with competitive wages and benefits and opportunities for training and advancement.

Environmentally, the park would preserve natural and cultural resources, protect habitat and water quality, and strive to eliminate waste and pollution. It would showcase green technology companies and maximize efficient use of resources through "industrial symbiosis." Industrial symbiosis is the notion that the byproducts of one industrial process or company can serve as the raw material for another industrial process or company.

FUNDING

Northampton County and its Department of Sustainable Development raised more than $8 million of local, state, and federal funding to develop the first phase of the eco-industrial park. This funding included a $2.5 million bond issue approved by local voters. To date, this public investment has leveraged another $8 million from private companies locating in the first phase of the park. This funding provided the means to achieve the initial objectives of the county's Sustainable Development Action Strategy.

The public funding covered everything necessary to open the facility as a world-class eco-industrial park, including master planning, community involvement, covenants and sustainability standards, environmental assessments, land purchase, engineering, permits and approvals, infrastructure construction, multi-tenant green building construction, a solar electricity system, natural area purchase, construction of lakes and wetlands, trails, amenities, marketing, legal costs, and the leasing of initial corporate tenants.

Private investment accomplished tenant improvements for office, research/development, and manufacturing space, as well as partial funding for the solar energy system. In addition, $7.8 million has been committed for development of a wind farm within the park that will produce more electricity than used by the entire county. The county has contracted to export this wind electricity to utilities within the northeastern United States energy grid.

MASTER PLAN

A master plan for the park was created through an intensive three-day community design workshop known by architects as a "charette." The plan carefully integrated the park with the historic town of Cape Charles and the natural landscape adjacent to the Chesapeake Bay. The site centered on redevelopment of former industrial land surrounding the town's harbor. The specifics of the plan included roads, utilities, water, sewers, water and stormwater management, and wetland tertiary treatment for water recycling. Fully half of the site was reserved for "ecological infrastructure," including the Chesapeake Bay Coastal Dune Habitat Preserve, natural and created wetlands, and historic/archaeological sites. As an ecological industrial park, its facilities are based on the designs of natural systems. Electricity is generated from sunlight. A water reuse and recovery system is planned to recycle water for industrial use. Porous paving reduces stormwater runoff, which is collected and filtered by constructed wetlands.

MANAGEMENT STRUCTURE

The community formed its own development company to manage the park. Known as the Sustainable Technology Park Authority, the entity's legal name is the Joint Industrial Development Authority of Northampton County and Towns. The Authority is a political subdivision of the Commonwealth of Virginia. Its seven-member board of directors is appointed by the governing bodies of Northampton County and

the towns of Cape Charles, Cheriton, and Exmore.

LAND ASSEMBLY

Slightly more than 200 acres of land was acquired in five transactions between 1995 and 1998. This included 30 acres adjacent to the Chesapeake Bay to be permanently preserved as a Coastal Dune Natural Area Preserve within the park. The land also included 45 acres of brownfields, including a former town dump and abandoned industrial land adjacent to Cape Charles Harbor. The United States Environmental Protection Agency funded environmental assessments that documented the lack of any hazardous materials or pollution problems associated with the site.

INFRASTRUCTURE

Detailed engineering designs were created based on the vision and plans of the original community charette. Construction documents were subsequently prepared for the first phase of roads, utilities, and other infrastructure to serve the park. Local, state, and federal permits and approvals were obtained through a streamlined process, as representatives of most of the agencies involved had participated in the community design charette. Ground was broken on October 17, 1996, in a ceremony during the second national eco-industrial roundtable in Cape Charles. The first phase of roads and utilities was completed in 1998.

SUSTAINABLE TECHNOLOGY INCUBATOR

Completed in January 2000, the showpiece of the Sustainable Technology Park's first phase is a 31,000-square-feet multi-tenant manufacturing/office building. The building meets the U.S. Green Building Council's standards as a "green" building. It features an integrated solar photovoltaic roof system that converts sunlight into 42,000 watts of electricity. With the building operating at full capacity, this will provide up to half of the building's total annual electrical demand.

Other sustainability features include skylights for natural-day lighting, a common meeting and conference center, enhanced insulation, interior environmental sensing, carbon monoxide sensors and alarms, low-energy lighting, low-water fixtures, porous parking lot paving, and native non-irrigated landscaping. The building, which was constructed primarily from local materials, has enhanced structural strength and a longer life span than typical designs. Interior space can be divided flexibly to accommodate up to eight companies for the purposes of manufacturing, research and development, office space, and other uses.

The building's features are designed to not only reduce energy and resource demands, but also to reduce operating costs and to increase occupant productivity and health. As such the building is expected to be superior economically as well as environmentally.

Ecological Infrastructure

In addition to the more traditional infrastructure of roads, utilities, and buildings, Northampton County and its partners integrated key natural resources into the Sustainable Technology Park. A local/state/federal funding package of more than $727,000 was used to fund the park's "ecological infrastructure." Included is a natural preserve, beaches and dunes, a critical migratory bird habitat, constructed wetlands and ponds, a system of trails and boardwalks, more than 4,000 new trees, and a total of 90 acres of protected natural area.

This ecological infrastructure created a win-win-win synergy among the economic development, environmental protection, and community improvement objectives of the park. The natural amenities have enhanced economic development efforts by helping to attract the corporate tenants the county has targeted. Without the projected financial income produced by the corporate tenants of the technology park, it would not have been possible to fund protection of the natural areas or construction of the trails, wetlands, and ponds. The community, meanwhile, has gained a new natural area park, which has proven to be popular among joggers, birdwatchers, and families alike.

Economic Results

The sustainable technology strategy already has attracted several diverse companies to Northampton County and its eco-industrial park. The Norwegian-based company, Hauge Technologies, develops and manufactures "pressure exchanger" equipment that significantly reduces the cost and energy demands of converting sea water to fresh water. This technology promises to make safe drinking water more affordable and available to more people worldwide. Transforming Technologies is another start-up company in the park. It is developing computer security and identification devices. ProVento America, Inc., is a subsidiary of a German wind energy developer that has initially leased offices for 12 employees and expects to grow to 50 employees within five years. ProVento also has leased sites for six wind turbines that will produce 7.8 megawatts of electricity to be sold into the national power grid. The park also has provided land for the expansion of the county's largest manufacturer, Bayshore Concrete Products Corporation, which employs more than 400 people.

In addition to the companies on site in the park, Northampton's sustainable development efforts have attracted several companies that have located throughout the county and its towns. One of these companies, Atlantis Energy Systems, is the successor of a Swiss firm that produces "architecturally integrated photovoltaics." These are commercial and residential roofing, siding, windows, and skylights that generate electricity from the sun. Scientific and Environmental Associates is a consulting firm that provides coastal resources management services to government and corporate clients the world over. The company moved its headquarters to Northampton because of its commitment to sustainable development. Delisheries is a homegrown company using space in the park's incubator to produce gourmet cookie mixes.

A total of 800,000 square feet of building area is planned for future phases of the park, which will provide space for 200 or more companies and 1,200 to 1,500 jobs. The park's first incubator building includes 31,000 square feet of space to accommodate its first four to six companies and as many as 100 employees. Depending on market conditions, buildout of the park will occur over the next two or three decades, providing a long-term public framework for private investment.

In the year since the park opened, these companies have combined to create more than 50 new jobs, a significant impact given Northampton's rural economy. Over the next two years, they are expected to create an additional 50 jobs and to bring $15 million in direct real estate and equipment investment to the county. Cape Charles Wind Farm alone is valued at $7.8 million and will generate $120,000 annually in business personal property, machinery, and tools taxes.

Annual debt service for the park is approximately $200,000, with annual operating and maintenance expenses of about $100,000. As soon as the first building is fully leased it will generate an annual rental income of $180,000. Combined with annual tax revenues of $120,000, the park's direct revenues and expenditures are balanced for the first phase. The financial sustainability of the park will remain a key measure of success as development continues.

Toward a Sustainable Future

Building on the success of the eco-industrial park, Northampton already is aggressively moving forward with the next phase of its sustainable development strategy. One key project is the reclamation of the county sanitary landfill as a "seaside ecological farm." The goal is to turn trash into treasure by transforming an economic and environmental challenge into a valuable community asset. The county landfill will reach capacity within two years, at which time it will have to be closed and capped. It forms the highest point in the county and affords breathtaking views of the Atlantic Ocean, coastal wilderness marshlands, and a string of barrier islands. Conceptual development plans include a network of hiking trails, a high-point observation platform, and the restoration of ponds, wetlands, forest, and other bird habitat.

The seaside ecological farm project already has been selected as a Brownfield Redevelopment Showcase by the United States Environmental Protection Agency, which has committed $400,000 to support the project. In addition, the National Oceanic and Atmospheric Administration has committed $10,000 to fund partner workshops for project planning. The county also has entered into a Rebuild America partnership with the United States Department of Energy to develop the renewable energy components.

The county is investigating the potential of a renewable energy farm that would harvest methane from the landfill, bio-fuels from soybeans grown on the county's farms, and wind energy from the strong coastal winds. The six wind energy turbines planned for the landfill property will produce 7.8 megawatts of clean renewable electricity to be exported to the northeastern United States power grid. Early financial projections indicate that tax revenue from these turbines will offset a significant portion of the debt service required to fund the multi-million dollar landfill closure costs. The county has applied for a grant/loan from the United States Department of Agriculture for construction of a waste transfer station.

Northampton's strategic plan also focuses on ways to further support the county's growing aquaculture industry, which involves cultivating fish and shellfish for harvest. The most profitable species being grown in Northampton's aquaculture farms is the famous Cherrystone Clam, which has grown from a less than $1 million dollar industry in 1990 to more than $20 million in 2001. Other fish and shellfish species also are being developed for commercial aquaculture farming. And by integrating aquaculture with agriculture, the county hopes to create eco-industrial synergies whereby soy-diesel byproducts serve as fish food and fish farm effluent provides nutrient-rich agricultural fertilizer. Virginia Tech, The Nature Conservancy, and Cornell University's Work and Environment Initiative have provided initial support for this work.

Conclusion

Northampton's Sustainable Technology Park is living proof that economic development and environmental protection are not mutually exclusive and that these goals can be pursued simultaneously to enhance a community's overall quality of life. Although the county has a long way to go to completely overcome its severe poverty and to rebuild a healthy economic base, its experience demonstrates that integrating asset development and protection in an action-oriented, community-based plan is a powerful strategy for success. An extensive local, state, and federal partnership for project financing has been key to leveraging private investment in Northampton's development strategy thus far and will continue to be relied upon as the county continues its course toward a sustainable future.

CHAPTER 30

PETALUMA REORIENTS ITS DOWNTOWN AROUND A RIVER

Charles Lockwood

Petaluma, California, is used to making planning history. A quarter century ago, it became the second American city (after Ramapo, New York) to enact growth controls. Later, those controls were the first to be tested in the courts — and upheld as a legitimate use of municipal authority.

Located 40 miles north of San Francisco, Petaluma began jumping after U.S. Highway 101 was widened in 1956. The city's population almost doubled — from 14,000 to nearly 25,000 — in the 1960s, schools began double shifts, and city services were strained. In 1972, in an effort to contain growth, Petaluma began limiting residential development to 500 new housing units a year.

That 500-unit ceiling — called the Residential Growth Management System — is still in effect and still popular. "It allows us to plan all of our community facilities and our capital improvements at a pace that is manageable and financeable," says Pamela Tuft, Petaluma's planning director.

Regulations have their limits, however. Despite its growth controls, Petaluma now has 50,000 residents and is plagued by sprawl — with fringe residential and commercial development devouring surrounding farmland and traffic snarling streets and highways. The city is now close to its urban limit line, unchanged since 1969. Next month, a 20-year urban growth boundary plan will appear on the city ballot. The measure is expected to pass easily.

Meanwhile, about a quarter of the city's central area remains vacant or underused. But now that picture is changing with a new plan that could once again put Petaluma on the map.

A River Runs Through It

When it comes to redevelopment of the central area, Petaluma has many advantages, including the Petaluma River, which has been the focus for commercial and industrial development since the town's founding in 1833. It also has an active rail corridor, historic commercial buildings, a circa-1910 train station, and progressive residents willing to try new things.

However, the central area is cut in half

Originally published as "Pioneering Petaluma," *Urban Land*, Vol. 59, No. 7, July 2000. Published by the Urban Land Institute, Washington, D.C. Reprinted with permission of the publisher.

by the Petaluma River, and each side of the river has a distinct identity. The west side — used by director George Lucas as the setting for his classic 1973 movie, *American Graffiti* — is a healthy pre–World War II district with a mix of housing, industry, and commerce. The east side, which has developed less densely in recent decades, consists largely of residential subdivisions.

The problem is what lies between, Central Petaluma is a sparsely developed district of nearly 400 acres at the geographical heart of the city. With its scattering of residential properties and low-density strip commercial, industrial, and institutional uses, Central Petaluma lacks a clear identity.

What to Do

Recent development proposals haven't helped matters. "We were getting piecemeal proposals for projects, like a drugstore in the middle of a parking lot, that were not conducive to a true downtown environment," says planning director Pamela Tuft. "So we decided to get more proactive, to create a plan, and to offer the community the opportunity to participate in developing the plan."

The city council began the process in 1996 by appointing a 26-member advisory committee that includes two city council members, two planning commissioners, a representative of the Petaluma Downtown Association, the executive director of the Chamber of Commerce, property owners, developers, and interested residents. The group met monthly in 1996, and that summer the committee helped to write an RFP for the Central Petaluma specific plan.

In 1997, the advisory committee chose the ROMA Design Group of San Francisco to prepare the new plan, noting that the document would have to support and complement an existing river enhancement and

access plan and the city's 1986 general plan. Among other things, the general plan directs growth to the city center and the river. Refinements to the specific plan are now in the works, and it is expected to be adopted within the next few months. "Our approach," says Bonnie Fisher, a principal at ROMA, "is to provide the structure to knit downtown Petaluma together and complete the urban fabric."

River and Rail

The specific plan makes the Petaluma River downtown's major organizing elements. Thus the plan supports riverbound industrial uses while also orienting new development projects to the river. Entertainment and leisure-based businesses will be sought for the turning basin, where big ships turn around to sail back to San Francisco Bay.

In addition, "the specific plan is very pedestrian-oriented," says city councilman David Keller, "with a wide range of, and connections to, transit facilities, including the railroad, boats, cars, bicycles, buses, and transit." The city's historic train depot will provide rail service as well as local and regional bus service, and the station will serve as a gateway to the pedestrian-oriented downtown. Two light rail transit stops have been included in the plan in the hope that Sonoma County voters will approve a light rail line in next month's election.

Other projects outlined in the plan include tree-planting, a fourth river crossing, and a traffic circle to relieve congestion and create a gateway into Central Petaluma. In addition, the city is buying the 32-acre Mc-Near Peninsula, adjacent to the turning basin, for a regional park with pedestrian, car, and transit connections to Central Petaluma sites.

New commercial and entertainment uses are to be introduced to Central Petaluma on both sides of the river. And because the west side-based Downtown Association is concerned that new development on the east side of the river will steal away their cachet and customers, the advisory committee has worked hard to allay that fear.

To prevent the development of a new, rival downtown, the specific plan calls for integrating redevelopment into the existing downtown through pedestrian and view orientation, architectural design guidelines, parking, and transportation connections. The specific plan also encourages recycling Central Petaluma's many underused properties by developing mixed-use projects that complement the west side's commercial district.

Where It Stands

Central Petaluma is about to bloom with restaurants, a small cineplex, specialty shops, and food marketplaces showcasing Sonoma county's various specialty crops. The cornerstone for redevelopment in the area, says city councilman David Keller, is a "wasted resource" called the Golden Eagle, a seven-acre shopping center dating from the 1960s that backs onto the river. Keller says the Golden Eagle is fully leased and its owner has no financial incentive to redevelop it, but "he is very amenable to redoing the shopping center if other owners and developers begin implementing the specific plan."

High-density housing will also help to create a vibrant downtown core. The specific plan calls for a mix of live/work studios and apartments, low-income units, and elderly housing. A total of 400 housing units is anticipated.

"The plan tries to do away with regimented zoning" by accommodating a combination of housing, office, and commercial uses, says Vincent Smith, a planner with the city.

Public hearings on the specific plan are scheduled to begin this fall. Members of the planning department and the advisory committee say they expect easy adoption. Officially, implementation is likely to begin in early 1999, but privately driven redevelopment activity has already begun. Several property transactions for major downtown blocks are under way.

In addition, the city's advisory committee has already endorsed the preservation and renovation of the historic downtown rail station and continued use of the existing rail lines — key elements in the specific plan. Roadways and circulation, open space, and bicycle access plans have also been approved.

"Any city can be a sprawling, freeway-centered community," says David Keller. "We are trying to steer Petaluma in another direction. If we do it right, we can have a thriving downtown that will last for generations and preserve Petaluma's character and rich sense of community."

CHAPTER 31

PHILADELPHIA AND CAMDEN RESTORE THEIR RIVERFRONTS

Roshi Pelaseyed

Hundreds of municipalities in the U.S. were developed along waterways to facilitate industrial development and transport of goods. The location helped these communities prosper, but also left them scarred with hundreds of abandoned, contaminated sites. Federal legislation and state efforts have helped many to reverse this trend and reuse these waterfront areas. The list of famous locales that have undertaken riverfront brownfield redevelopment includes Brooklyn, Pittsburgh, Richmond, Virginia, Memphis, Cincinnati, Reno, Nevada, and more recently Los Angeles. Numerous smaller municipalities also have used creative financing and federal and state resources to reinvigorate their waterfronts.

The Philadelphia Metropolitan Region provides a case study of the latest trends in brownfield redevelopment. Brownfields, as defined by the U.S. Environmental Protection Agency, are "abandoned, idled, or under-used industrial and commercial facilities where expansion or redevelopment is complicated by real or perceived environmental contamination." This broad definition encompasses any contaminated property from a local dry cleaner to a massive industrial site.

The biggest hurdle in bringing these properties to better and higher uses is the perceived risk of contamination and the fear of liability for clean-up. Yet, redevelopment of these sites makes economic sense in the face of the nationwide efforts to stop sprawl and to make use of existing infrastructure, for in-place infrastructure reduces the cost of redevelopment. In recent years, the EPA has helped communities overcome these barriers to redevelopment by providing financial assistance through grants and revolving loan funds and by publicizing brownfield redevelopment efforts.

As the fourth largest metropolitan region, the Philadelphia Metropolitan area is home to more than 6 million people and numerous brownfield sites. According to the 2000 U.S. Census, it was the slowest growing large metropolitan area in the '90s. The city has lost most of its population to its suburbs, where a 3 percent population growth has led to a 33 percent increase in development of greenfields. According to the Metropolitan Philadelphia Policy Center, a nonprofit policy research organization, approximately one-fourth of the nation's population and consumer buying power lives within one day's drive of the area.

Originally published as "Riverfront Brownfield Redevelopment," *The Commissioner*, Winter 2003. Published by the American Planning Association, 122 South Michigan Avenue, Suite 1600, Chicago, Illinois 60603-6107. Reprinted with permission of the publisher.

The region is also home to hundreds of abandoned industrial sites, the legacy left by industries. To turn this around, the region is taking advantage of the available financial tools to convert these brownfields into ratables, such as luxury waterfront townhouses to multipurpose community centers. It is no surprise that President George W. Bush chose Conshocken, a community just on the border of Philadelphia on the Schuylkill River, to announce his new brownfields legislation last February. The Small Business Liability Relief and Brownfields Revitalization Act will double available funds for brownfield redevelopment for fiscal year 2003 to $200 million.

The City on the Delaware

Philadelphia, despite its historic significance and its strong prominence in the health-care and pharmaceuticals industries, has struggled to become competitive with most metropolises around the nation. Although the city is home to two rivers, the Schuylkill and the Delaware, most of the city's redevelopment efforts ignored that potential, leaving the riverfront areas to trash, crumbling factories, and other unwanted uses. But times have changed. In November 2001, the city unveiled plans to create an American Venice in the tradition of great European cities.

The city soon unveiled plans for redevelopment of two riverfront areas. The City Planning Commission has developed a plan for an 11-mile expanse along the Delaware River to convert this underutilized area into residential and recreational uses, allowing the public greater access to the water.

The proposal includes an incremental clean-up strategy, including phytoremediation. This is remediation technique using plants to remove or stabilize contaminants thereby transforming the blighted landscape into flowering fields. Other innovative techniques that will be used in this area include use of porous pavements on roadways, wetland/vegetated swales along the roads, green infiltration trenching along street, bike trails and parking areas for water quality improvement that will reduce the need for wastewater treatment infrastructure. The cost of clean-up for the area is estimated to be at least $250 million.

The visions for the North Delaware Riverfront include:

• A trail and a linear river park.
• A river road with public access to the river.
• Thousands of new residential and commercial units.

This will require zoning changes and incentives to entice suburban developers. The plans have already captured the EPA's attention. In March 2002, the EPA announced its intention to provide technical assistance and guidance through its regional Smart Growth Agreement with the City of Philadelphia. The city has committed funding from its neighborhood economic stimulus fund to bring to fruition.

In addition to these plans, the Schuylkill River Development Council also has outlined similar plans for the western part of the city. The goal is to create a river trail that connects the existing popular Kelly Drive path to Center City, Philadelphia's downtown district, to encourage further development.

"Two Cities, One Exciting Waterfront"

Nearly a dozen New Jersey towns share the Delaware River with Philadelphia, affording spectacular views of Philadelphia's skyline. Camden, once a bustling industrial port, is home to RCA and Campbell Soup Company. Camden is the poorest municipality in New Jersey, and among the poorest in the nation, with an annual unemployment rate of 12 percent and a median household income of $23,421. In its heyday, the Camden riverfront, known as Cooper's Ferry, served as a tourist destination. The area boasted hotels, taverns, pleasure gardens, and residences. With the economic shift from manufacturing to service and river transport giving way to other alternative modes of transportation, Camden slid into decline.

Camden's salvation came in 1984 with the establishment of the Cooper's Ferry Development Association by the city, the Campbell Soup Company, RCA, and other private companies, and government and civic leaders. Since then, the waterfront has been transformed into an entertainment mecca with the infusion of millions of public dollars. Just seven years after the State of New Jersey's announcement of $52 million funding for its development, the New Jersey State Aquarium opened in 1992. It is now one of the five most visited attractions in the region. The addition of a four-acre $9 million horticultural playland, the Children's Garden, made this destination even more attractive. Other new attractions on the Camden waterfront include the Tweeter Center — a $56 million indoor-outdoor entertainment facility that can seat up to 25,000 people, and a minor league baseball stadium, Campbell Fields.

While Cooper's Ferry has made the plans for the rebirth of Camden's waterfront, the Delaware River Port Authority of Pennsylvania and New Jersey, a regional transportation and economic development agency, and owner and operator of four of the river bridges, has financed most of the developments. It has invested more than $200 million in waterfront projects on both sides of the river. Just last summer, it provided $2.5 million for the completion of the pier and visitors center for USS *New Jersey* battleship, one of the latest tourist attractions in Camden. Another high-priced investment is the $32 million tram to link

Philadelphia's Penn's Landing to the Camden waterfront.

As Camden has made steady progress in redeveloping this side of the waterfront, plans on the other side have been at a virtual standstill. Philadelphia's plan for Penn's Landing is a family entertainment center to house, among others, the Please Touch Children's Museum. Since 1997, the city has relied on the promise of one developer to create this magnet. Yet not a single brick has been laid due to continued delays in starting construction. The city is attempting to get construction started by March 1, 2003.

Despite the setbacks with the planned developments in Philadelphia, plans for capitalizing on the tourism potential of the area are in full gear. The Delaware River Port Authority, the agency that has created many of the existing tourist attractions along the river, recently announced the development of a new nonprofit agency to coordinate all tourism marketing efforts.

A Public-Private Partnership

The Borough of Paulsboro also has tackled brownfield redevelopment. This 2.1-square-mile borough of 6,535 residents ranks 20 on the list of 100 most stressed municipalities in New Jersey with 21 percent of the population living below poverty level in 1990.

The borough maintained a relatively small industrial base, with BP and Essex Chemical as two of its major industries. Paulsboro suffered an economic blow when these two entities ceased operation due to stricter environmental regulations. The closing of the Mobil plant in a neighboring town has further eroded employment. Lack of developable land is another impediment to Paulsboro's economic growth as most land use is residential.

The 150-acre BP property, the largest

available land for industrial/commercial development is located directly across the Delaware River from the Philadelphia International Airport. The property, better known as tank farm, served as an oil storage and distribution center. Several years ago, BP, in an effort to dispose of unused properties around the nation, started investigating the possibility of alternative uses for the property. The company retained an engineering firm to conduct a market feasibility study to determine the highest and best use for the property. At the same time, BP initiated discussion with Essex Chemical about the adjacent property that was used as a gypsum landfill. Essex was receptive to BP's suggestion for redevelopment of the area and pledged its willingness to follow suit with BP plans.

From the start, BP approached the borough about its plans. Because of the location of the site, one of the initial thoughts was to develop the site as a niche port. It was also important to make adequate provisions for public access to the waterfront. The recommended site development plan includes:

- **Waterfront Port Development**, including a 900-foot wharf structure that can accommodate mid-sea ocean-going vessels up to 800 feet in length. The wharf has upland storage of 30 to 40 acres. The location of the borough and an analysis of river traffic indicate the site could be partially developed as a port facility. Paulsboro is among the four South Jersey municipalities under consideration for the Port Inland Distribution Network.
- **Industrial/Commercial Development** at the south end of the project site, adjacent to existing industrial uses (five-acre parcels, to be used individually or combined).
- **River Gateway**, a commercial/retail development with public access to the riverfront.
- **Open Space** provision consists of a green buffer to separate the industrial uses from

the surrounding neighborhood and creation of a neighborhood park.

One of the most innovative components of this project is the building of a solar plant on the Essex-owned former gypsum landfill. The plant, the largest thin-film solar plant in the Northeast, will generate power for the operation of the on-site environmental remediation equipment. While the original plan called for the location of the plant on a more pristine portion of the site, known as the employee ballfield, to increase the development potential of the site, it was decided to move the plant to the landfill, which meant an additional $250,000 for its construction.

The most challenging part of the project is creating access to the site. To reach the riverfront from Interstate 295, the north-south highway which connects the town to the Northeast U.S. market, traffic has to go through a residential neighborhood. To connect the site directly to I-295, an overpass would be needed. This part of the project has proven to be challenging. In addition to the $25 million price tag, the project has to make the list of the transportation improvement plan created by the regional metropolitan planning agency. The borough was able to secure funding from the same agency for initial studies. The construction of the overpass and the site's development are still several years away.

The Feds to the Rescue

One of the brownfield tools the federal government has made available to localities is the grant program. The EPA Brownfield Pilot grants provide $200,000 to municipalities and counties to conduct an inventory of the brownfield areas and investigate the extent of contamination in order to determine a remediation plan and future end uses. More than 300 localities have used these grants. In the Delaware Valley, all suburban counties in Pennsylvania have been awarded an EPA Pilot grant to identify potential brownfield sites for development. On the other side of the river, the Township of Pennsauken in Camden County received a pilot grant. The township has 700 acres of vacant and underused property along its seven miles of riverfront on the Delaware River.

Since 1980, Pennsauken Township has undertaken an aggressive economic redevelopment strategy that targets the riverfront. First, it designated the entire area as a waterfront management area under New Jersey environmental guidelines that limit certain types of development and preserve open space. Then it acquired 230 acres of tidal marshland.

The township has identified several properties suitable for redevelopment. Among them is Petty's Island, a 450-acre island in the Delaware River between Camden and Philadelphia. Once an oil storage and distribution facility, the island presently hosts only a container cargo shipping operation. Another major site is a 137-acre inactive landfill used for construction debris and home to a warehouse. The area also includes 17 acres of scattered smaller sites. The township has used the EPA grant to investigate the contamination level at the sites to ensure their suitability for future development.

Pennsauken hopes that with the completion of the pilot project it can embark on an aggressive marketing effort to redevelop its waterfront. With two fiber-optic lines serving the area, and the completion of a light rail line by New Jersey Transit, Pennsauken's waterfront should be an attractive magnet for development for commercial, entertainment, and recreational uses. As in Paulsboro, site access remains a challenging issue that must be addressed along with cleanup and acquisition.

Pennsauken has faced some resistance from the site owners. For example, site vis-

its for the EPA grant project have been refused by one owner. In the meantime, the township officials learned about possible negotiations between the land owner and the operator of a cogeneration plant to locate a plant on the site; this development would be inconsistent with the township's current plan. More recently, as the township was preparing to embark on the last steps of the acquisition process of another site, the site owner decided to resume operation of the site as an oil storage and distribution facility.

Other Waterfront Dreams

A number of other Delaware River municipalities have plans. Gloucester City, New Jersey's 12th poorest municipality, is another recipient of an EPA Pilot grant; it has been planning for waterfront revitalization for 25 years. With the help from state grants, the city improved its waterfront park with various active and passive recreational opportunities. Future plans include development of brownfields on the southwestern edge of the city.

In the summer of 2002, Gloucester County, where Paulsboro is located, rolled out its brownfields program at Riverwinds, a 1,200-acre multi-use facility erected on a former brownfield site in West Deptford. Using New Jersey's 1992 Local Redevelopment and Housing Law, the county developed a countywide redevelopment plan to reuse old industrial sites and blighted areas, targeting some 14 municipalities. Burlington and Salem counties, New Jersey, as well as Chester and Bucks counties, Pennsylvania, also have expressed interest in riverfront redevelopment. Further south, Wilmington, Delaware, has been rebuilding the waterfront and redeveloping on its brownfield sites.

Developing housing, shopping centers, office complexes and recreational facilities on once-contaminated land is no longer viewed as undesirable. In densely populated areas, it may be the truly feasible option for development. Despite myriad financial in-centives and tools, brownfield development has not yet received complete acceptance as a planning strategy.

CHAPTER 32

PHOENIX, OTHER CITIES, USE GIS TO PREVENT URBAN SPRAWL

Anya Sostek

The blue blob starts innocently enough. Then it slowly starts to grow. As the seconds fly by, it picks up momentum, expanding in lumpy spurts. Eating into its red background, the blue blob seems to be truly alive. And in a way, it is: The "blue" is actually the Phoenix metropolitan area in a Landsat satellite image. The red is the surrounding vegetation. And the animated geographic information system (GIS), showing the city's growth from the 1970s through the 1990s, paints a textbook picture of sprawl.

In Gallatin County, Montana, hundreds turn out to see an animated aerial "video" of their landscape. The video, which appears to be shot from a plane, shows the mountains of Big Sky country littered with houses. But the picture isn't actually a video, and most of those houses aren't actually there — yet. Under the county's projected growth model, they will be in 20 years if policies limiting sprawl are not adopted. And the "video" is an animated computer image generated from digital still photographs and topographical data.

In state and local governments across the country, public officials are using GIS to help the public understand the concept — and impact — of sprawl. While planners and information technology workers have used GIS to develop land use policy since the term "sprawl" was coined, the spread of the technology into the public arena has blossomed more recently. GIS has spread from techies all the way to governors, such as Maryland's Parris Glendening and Wyoming's Jim Geringer, who personally use the technology in presentations on growth.

Nowhere is GIS taught to the public more than at the Metropolitan Council, a regional agency that determines land use, wastewater and transportation issues for the seven-county area surrounding and including Minneapolis and St. Paul. "I think the concept is largely a discussion among the development community, builders, local units of government, banks, academics, designers and law firms," says Ted Mondale, chair of the Metro Council. "I don't think it's a debate that's been put before the public. You don't walk up to someone and say, 'Let's debate smart growth.'"

In terms of growth policy, the Twin Cities area is better off than most. For more

Originally published as "Bringing Sprawl to Life," *Governing*, Vol. 15, No. 3, December 2001. Published by Congressional Quarterly Inc., Washington, D.C. Reprinted with permission of the publisher.

than 25 years, the council has had a policy in effect using the sewer lines as a guide for allowing growth. But as the area has grown, the sewer district has proved something of an inefficient boundary, permitting growth in illogical places and contributing to the proliferation of septic tanks in outlying areas. So to change the region's "Blueprint" plan, officials are taking their case to the public, educating residents about sprawl and soliciting their views on how they want the region to grow. In each of the literally hundreds of meetings planned to bring the smart-growth debate to the public, the audience is treated to a GIS show. "A picture is worth a thousand words," says Eli Cooper, the Metro Council's director of planning and growth. "Every public meeting that the Metro Council holds has included a backdrop of no less than 10 to 15 display maps."

Depending on the type of meeting, Metro Council has different maps. Some show natural resources, such as rivers, lakes and slopes. Others show growth in rural areas, or highlight development zones and brownfields in urban settings. One general map tracks housing-lot size by date on a parcel-by-parcel basis. By analyzing the GIS data, planners have determined that the region's average lot size has doubled since World War II. For the Metro Council, the meetings and maps have not only informed the public but also helped the agency. "They love it," Mondale says. "People think this is the best thing we've ever done."

For the Twin Cities area and elsewhere across the country, there are a few basic ways to model sprawl. One is by isolating one particular indicator and watching how that has changed over time. Depending on the location, that indicator could be houses, or traffic, or even wells or septic tanks. Landsat images of vegetation provide another way to get a general picture of sprawl. This method simply requires animating, or displaying on a shot-by-shot basis, infrared aerial photographs from different years.

Even if cities or counties don't have good internal GIS data, this method is relatively easy because Landsat images have been available from the federal government since 1972.

Governments can also use digital orthophotos — pictures taken from the air with distortion eliminated to form a perfect map — to point out how specific areas look physically different than they once did. Combined with topographic data, these photos can create 3-D maps, providing a recognizable landscape for citizens. Such data exist for nearly 60 percent of the country.

Growth modeling is one of the most advanced ways to demonstrate sprawl, enabling officials to show not just how their community has changed over the years but how it will change in the future. A computer model is used to input characteristics, and the model can extend the data out for decades to show how the landscape is likely to change. The model can work for growth policy as a whole, or for individual policy decisions, such as whether to put a hospital at a particular intersection or build over a wetland.

Growth models produce some of the most dramatic maps at public meetings. While even standard GIS images produce what Cooper calls "the wow effect" when shown to the public, growth models can take public reaction one step further. "There's some four-letter words," says Wil Orr, director of the NASA Sustainability and Global Change Program at Prescott College, who has run growth models for numerous governments, including Maui, Hawaii; Santa Barbara, California; and Door County, Wisconsin.

When Orr traveled to Gallatin County to run his model, the response was overwhelming. The county, home to the city of Bozeman, has been transformed in recent years from a rural mountainous border of Yellowstone National Park to a playground for the rich, full of ski resorts and enormous second homes known as "starter castles." The 2,500-square-mile county is the fastest-growing in Montana, jumping more than 30 percent from 50,000 to 68,000 people in the past 10 years. And in conservative Montana, where countywide zoning is unheard of, any growth policy is very controversial.

At the Museum of the Rockies, where the presentation was shown, the parking lot ran out of spaces. Organizers had intended to run one demonstration for up to 250 people, but ended up having to do the presentation twice when 500 showed up. The growth models displayed different scenarios: one showing the current policy, one showing a policy developed by environmentalists and one showing an approach developed by farmers. "Some were appalled, some were excited, all were informed," says Dale Beland, an independent consultant and former Gallatin County planning director.

The models — and the public input — helped the county planning board develop an ambitious open-space-preservation plan and a controversial system for market-based development credits, which was later rejected by the county council. "GIS has been an effective tool in helping people understand the depth and scope of sprawl issues," Beland says. "With a county so large, people have such a parochial knowledge."

Although growth modeling is currently available only through consultants or other outside agencies, communities all over the country may soon be able to utilize it. A partnership encompassing the nonprofit conservation organization NatureServe, the GIS software developer ESRI, the U.S. Geological Survey and Academia is developing a package of software tools to help localities plan for growth, including environmental checkpoints, growth-modeling software and

a "town meeting module" to help produce GIS graphics for presentations. The software is currently in a pilot phase in the Yellowstone National Park area, the Gulf Coast Plain in Florida and Georgia, and Napa County, California.

"The point of this is not to tell people what to do but to give them the tools to step back and better think about and articulate their vision for their community," says NatureServe President Mark Schaefer, a former deputy assistant secretary of the U.S. Interior Department.

Growth modeling is not perfect, and it does not pretend to depict an exact replica of what a community will look like 50 years down the line. The models are simply visualizations of existing transportation or population models, which can be seriously flawed. Orr says that his presentations always include the caveat that the models shown only represent a best guess at the future. And GIS itself is not always exactly on target. As multiple types of data are layered on, important details may become obscured. "GIS as a tool has potential for misunderstanding," says Beland. "It can acquire a life of its own if it's not explained carefully."

Overall, however, the benefits of GIS and growth modeling seem to outweigh the drawbacks, as long as the analysis is performed and explained carefully. Whether it's through an image as simple as a vegetation picture, or as complicated as an animated growth model, GIS is becoming an invaluable tool for helping the public understand sprawl. And as citizens start to become aware of the ramifications of uncontrolled growth, GIS can help them control it. "We try to leave people saying that this is where you're headed, but you have the capacity to change it," says Orr. "You don't have to accept this as your future."

CHAPTER 33

PORT ARANSAS, OTHER CITIES, BENEFIT FROM WILDLIFE CONSERVATION TRAILS

Elaine Robbins

Like many beach towns, Port Aransas, a sleepy fishing village on the Texas coast, always bustled with beachgoers in the summertime, only to slip into near hibernation after Labor Day.

In the off season, "you could roll a bowling ball down the main street and not hit anybody," says Mike Hall, co-owner of the local Family Center IGA supermarket.

Then three years ago, the New Great Texas Coastal Birding Trail put this quiet community on the map. Now thousands of visitors a year flock to Port Aransas each February for the town's whooping crane festival, a celebration of the endangered, five-foot-tall bird that winters in nearby Aransas National Wildlife Refuge. More visitors show up during the spring and fall migrations to watch birds at nearly a dozen nearby viewing areas along the trail.

Birding has given such a boost to business that Port Aransas (pop. 3,370) plans to set aside an additional 1,500 acres for a new park with wildlife observation posts. "It's not something that happened overnight," says Hall. "But there's no doubt in my mind

that the birding trail has brought new business to town at a time of year when we need it."

Things are looking up along the 700-mile coastal birding trail. A few miles north, in Fulton-Rockport (pop. 8,500), local businesses are taking in $4.5 million a year from birders, $1 million of that during their annual Hummer/Bird Festival, when thousands of hummingbirds arrive to drink sugar water from dozens of backyard feeders. In the Lower Rio Grande Valley on the Mexican border — a region that in 2001 had the lowest per capita income in the U.S. — birders from all over the world spend $100 million a year to see such dazzling subtropical species as the chachalaca and the green jay.

By all accounts, the trail has been a win-win proposition. It offers outdoor recreation for the growing number of people who enjoy watching wildlife, gives a boost to small towns that have lost jobs and population in the decades since World War II, gives landowners a way to diversify farm and ranch income, and provides an incentive for habitat conservation while building a con-

Originally published as "Driving Them Wild," *Planning*, Vol. 69, No. 12, December 2003. Published by the American Planning Association, 122 South Michigan Avenue, Suite 1600, Chicago, Illinois 60603-6107. Reprinted with permission of the publisher.

stituency for conservation. Touted as a model of sustainable tourism, the trail won the prestigious British Airways Tourism for Tomorrow Award in 2001, beating out 115 entries from 47 countries.

After the soaring success of the Great Texas Coastal Birding Trail, new wildlife-viewing trails are popping up faster than bluebonnets in springtime. This year the Texas Parks and Wildlife Department opened two new trails: The Panhandle Plains Wildlife Trail and the Heart of Texas Wildlife Trail, leading travelers to terrific bed-and-breakfast places along green, cypress-lined rivers. The state's fourth wildlife-viewing trail, the Prairies and Pineywoods Trail, is due to open at the end of next year.

Now some 20 other states are jumping on the bandwagon in an effort to replicate Texas's success. Florida's Fish and Wildlife Conservation Commission has opened two segments of its Great Florida Birding Trail, a 2,000-mile driving route that connects established birdwatching spots and lesser known sites. Virginia has completed the Virginia Coastal Birding and Wildlife Trail and the Mountain Trail through the Appalachians; a Piedmont Trail is in the works. Trail projects are under way or have recently opened in Oklahoma, Louisiana, Washington, Wisconsin, Georgia, and Kentucky.

These projects tap the growing number of people who enjoy watching wildlife. In the last 20 years, the number of birdwatchers has more than tripled, from 21 million to 69 million, according to a 2000 survey by the U.S. Forest Service. A 2001 study, by the U.S. Fish and Wildlife Service, found that 66.1 million Americans engage in observing, feeding, or photographing wildlife, compared with 34.1 million who fish and 13 million who hunt.

A vast number of Americans participate in wildlife-related recreation, from those who view birds (33.5 percent) and other wildlife (45.9 percent) to those who go to see wildflowers and natural vegetation (45.5 percent) and natural scenery (60.9 percent), according to the Forest Service survey. Although hunters and fishers spend twice as much as wildlife watchers — buying everything from hunting gear to fishing guides — wildlife watchers spent a considerable $38.4 billion on their activities in 2001, $8.2 billion of that on wildlife-related trips.

The Secret of Its Success

Ted Eubanks and Madge Lindsay couldn't have predicted how the coastal birding trail would take off when they first came up with the idea in 1993. Eubanks, president of the nature tourism consulting firm Fermata, Inc., had just served on a task force whose job was to develop a nature tourism plan for then Texas governor Ann Richards. At a wildlife conference at the Texas coast, he began talking over a beer with Lindsay, who worked in Texas Parks and Wildlife's Nongame Wildlife Program, about ideas for putting nature tourism goals to work. Their initial idea was simple: Use federal transportation dollars — ISTEA and later TEA-21— to build a wildlife driving trail.

First, Eubanks and Lindsay wrote a grant and in 1994 won $1.4 million in federal and state funds, including transportation enhancement funds and 20 percent matching funds from TxDOT, the Texas Department of Transportation.

Next, they held a series of public meetings that brought together communities, local businesses, private citizens, land managers, and government agencies. In the beginning, says Linda Campbell, nature tourism coordinator at Texas Parks and Wildlife, Eubanks and Lindsay "had to do a lot of talking to make sure people understood this would be beneficial to their economy and they would benefit from the nature-based tourism business coming through." Communities that were used to competing with their neighbors for tourist dollars also had to be sold on the idea of cooperating on a regionwide project.

That initial groundwork proved to be worth the effort. "I think that was the key to our success — this grass-roots effort of involving the public," says Campbell. "Some states use a top-down approach because a lot of their wildlife sites are public. But in Texas we look carefully at a grass-roots approach because we're a private land state — 94 percent of the land is privately owned. It's very important that we work with communities and get their buy-in and support. It's their job to promote it, because they are the ones that will benefit ultimately."

After the communities were on board, Eubanks and Lindsay spent the next three or four years in his Chevy truck, driving around to evaluate sites and plan the trail. Using mile markers and his truck's odometer, they marked off sites on a state highway map. To create a trail that linked together more than 300 sites along 700 miles of coastline, Eubanks designed a main route with 46 separate driving loop routes that would each take a long weekend to explore. "A lot of the things that are being done in other states are now accepted as the rule — I literally made that stuff up on the fly," says Eubanks.

At some sites, they put in improvements like hummingbird and butterfly gardens. At others, they built boardwalks and observation platforms that overlooked wetlands. They landscaped parks with native plants and put in parking areas along roadsides.

Once the site descriptions were approved, they printed beautifully illustrated maps — one each for the upper, central, and lower coasts. Each site description included driving directions, species to be seen, and best times of year to view them. Finally, they installed highway signs emblazoned with a black skimmer motif to help travelers navigate the trail.

Although marketing is essential to make tourism trails a success, the Texas Parks and Wildlife Department has simply used its usual channels of communication to market the coastal birding trail in the last three years. With Texas's reputation as the nation's number one birding destination, serious birders spread the word quickly. Located on two major flyways, Texas boasts 622 documented species, more than any other state. The Lower Rio Grande Valley is a great place to see subtropical species of birds as well as butterflies: Texas has 40 percent of the butterfly species recorded in the U.S. and Canada.

While much of the original formula is being replicated in the new trails, funding sources may have to change. TEA-3, the next version of the federal transportation law, is now making its way through Congress, with highway enhancements in dispute. The states may need to find alternative funding sources, from foundation grants to other state agency funds.

Another change involves technology: We've come a long way from odometers and highway maps. "Now we probably go to 1,000 to 2,000 sites every year," says Eubanks. "Our guys are out there with laptops and digital cameras and handheld GPSs. It's just dramatically different."

The Next Big Thing

Many of the new trails go beyond birds to create a larger nature experience of a place. "Whereas the Great Texas Coastal Birding Trail was purely a birding trail, we quickly moved from birds to general nature," says Eubanks. "Lately we've been very aggressive about integrating history into it as well. So now it's really an experiential trail — using nature as a way of framing culture and history."

In the future, Eubanks dreams of vast "landscape trails" that would link existing state wildlife-viewing trails to create driving routes that stretch across vast regions of the nation. In the first of these trails, Fermata plans to create an experience of the Great Plains.

"We're literally going from southern Manitoba, Alberta, and Saskatchewan all the way through the heartland of America down into the grasslands of northern Mexico, which are very much extensions of the Great Plains," he says. Although the landscape has been transformed from the wilderness it once was, these trails will give travelers a glimpse of wild places far from the madding crowds — and provide a strong incentive to conserve what's left along the way.

CHAPTER 34

PORTLAND PROTECTS
ITS OPEN SPACES

Bruce Stephenson

Portland is a premier "green city" whose quality of life is consistently ranked among the highest in the United States (Chapman & Starker, 1987; Friedman, 1993; Partners for Livable Communities, 1994). In an era when government planning is viewed as a problem, not a solution, Portland provides a rare model for melding environmental protection and a booming economy (Artibise, Moudon, & Seltzer, 1997; Easterbrook, 1995; Egan, 1996). "Even more shocking," wrote columnist E. J. Dionne, Jr., "the planning system — in place since 1973 — is popular" (Dionne Jr., 1997, p. A27). Yet, even in this planning Mecca, half a century lapsed before citizens moved toward the regional city Lewis Mumford had envisioned. Exploring the slow realization of Mumford's vision not only opens another chapter in Portland's planning history (Abbott, 1983; Blackford, 1993; MacColl, 1979); it may also help other metropolitan regions trying to replicate the Oregon growth management model.

Portland lines both sides of the Willamette River just south of its juncture with the Columbia River. The surrounding landscape is a scenic mix of bucolic farmland, evergreen forests, and commanding moun-

tain peaks. Historically, Portland's economy centered on timber and agriculture, which made the landscape a common bond in the life of residents and a central concern for numerous plans (Artibise, Moudon, & Seltzer, 1997). The longstanding effort to systematically preserve the northern Willamette Valley's scenic and productive landscape is due, in part, to a "moralistic political culture (Abbott, 1994, p. 207) that values the public good over the individual. Since 1970, Portlanders have generally accepted the notion that government should enforce a system of public planning and land-use controls to guide private land developers toward collective goals (Abbott, 1994). While a unique political culture underlies Portland's growth management system, good fortune has also contributed.

The creation of Forest Park, the largest wilderness preserve in an American city, typifies the Portland experience. In 1903, John Olmsted, Frederick Law Olmsted's stepson, recommended establishing a linear park along the Tualatin Ridge on the west side of Portland. The Parks Board executed only a portion of the Olmsted plan, and almost all of the Tualatin Ridge remained in private hands. In 1915, subdividers platted

Originally published as "A Vision of Green: Lewis Mumford's Legacy in Portland, Oregon," *Journal of the American Planning Association*, Vol. 65, No. 3, Summer 1999. Published by the American Planning Association, Chicago, Illinois. Reprinted with permission of the publisher.

1,400 acres along the ridge and investors were soon secured. Road building, however, proved too difficult on the steep slopes and the project collapsed. The City gained title to the property, but Olmsted's proposal remained buried until the City hired Robert Moses in 1943 to delineate public projects for postwar development. Moses rejuvenated the idea of a "Forest Park," recommending "that the steep wooded hillsides located on the westerly border of the City be placed in public ownership" (Moses, 1943, p. 38). After the war, a "Committee of Fifty" championed Moses' proposal and, in September 1948, the City Council dedicated 4,200 acres to create Forest Park (Houle, 1988). Today this 5,000-acre preserve lies in the midst of one of the nation's faster growing urban regions, a product of vision, perseverance, and luck. Like the Olmsted blueprint for Forest Park, Lewis Mumford's summons for a green, regional city waited for decades until finally resurrected in the late 1980s.

Lewis Mumford's Vision of Green

In his first book, *The Story of Utopias* (1922), Mumford introduced the concept of *regionalism*, a philosophic template to guide modern city-building around the constructs of nature (Luccarelli, 1995; Thomas, 1990). All individuals and societies hold utopian notions of a better life, but without a vision that incorporates limits as well as aspirations, he wrote, "the outlook for our civilization is almost as dismal as Herr Spengler finds it in *Der Untergang des Abendlandes*" (Mumford, 1922, p. 268). Science and technology were remaking the world, but Mumford feared that if these forces were not channeled into "human patterns," individuals would be cut off from nature and become as standardized as the modern city's growing proliferation of machines. He ad-

vocated regional surveys as the means to focus scientific studies on the needs of the local community, while the Garden City concept provided the model for building *utopias*—"good places" that "spring out of the realities of our environment" (Mumford, 1922, p. 307).

In 1927, in his keynote address at the National City Planning Conference, Mumford challenged the nation's planners to adopt a regional perspective. He chastised the profession's bent for viewing cities as machines designed for production rather than biological organisms capable of reproduction. "City planning can do nothing on this basis which cannot be done just as well as a matter of engineering technique, and just as blindly from the social standpoint, in the … municipal engineer's office" (Mumford, 1927, p. 47). Unless planners recognized regional environmental constraints, cities would pass "the limits of functional size and use" (p. 48). Mumford recounted a sequence of deterioration that occurred when past urban civilizations exceeded natural limits. Periods of excessive growth were followed by ecological catastrophe and then the collapse of cities and civilization. The "necropolis" or dead city, Mumford cautioned, was the fate of any society that promoted unlimited growth (p. 48). Another decade elapsed, however, until his ideas gained national attention.

In 1938, Mumford's career reached its apex. After a grueling 2-year writing schedule, he published *The Culture of Cities* to laudatory reviews. In this rich study, Mumford analyzed the evolution of the modern city and critiqued American civilization. The world's first consumer economy had no bounds. Given the capabilities of modern technology, the nation's rapid urbanization posed a special problem: America's frontier heritage had created a culture that excelled at exploiting nature's bounty, but in their fervor Americans had failed to construct stable or well-designed communities. The accelerated expansion of urban America during the 1920s testified to the efficiency of mass production techniques, but standardized projects followed a factory-style regimen that lacked personal or cultural functions. Just as the factory was designed to assemble and mobilize workers, the modern city was becoming a center for assembling and mobilizing consumers. Since his first book, Mumford had written of urban dwellers evolving into robots, removed from nature, dependent upon artificial means for survival, and programmed to consume. In *The Culture of Cities*, he argued that the city was no longer a place to live, but a place to buy. "A rootless world removed from the sources of life: a Plutonian world, in which living forms become frozen into metal: cities ... defiling their own nest, reaching into the sky after the moon: more paper profits, more vicarious substitutes for life" (Mumford, 1938b, p. 255).

In 1938, Mumford's appearance on the cover of *Time* not only attested to his stature as a writer, but to his growing influence in the ongoing experiments to restructure American life. In contrast to most of the intellectual left, Mumford's vision of a better society was tinted with green rather than red. His environmentalism had a revolutionary edge, as he pushed "to transcend the machine, and to create a new biological and social environment" (Mumford, 1938b, p. 492). But he eschewed radical change for an orderly transformation that would bring urban civilization into harmony with evolutionary and organic patterns (Luccarelli, 1995; Miller, 1989). The New Deal greenbelt towns outside Milwaukee, Cincinnati, and Washington, DC, put Mumford's theories to the test and, at the same time, augmented his stature as America's leading urbanist.

Regional Planning in Portland

The acclaim that greeted *The Culture of Cities* afforded Mumford the luxury to travel and explore new possibilities. Out of a flood of offers, he accepted requests from Honolulu and the Northwest Regional Council (NRC), a nonprofit regional planning group, to work as a consultant for the first time (Miller, 1989). *The Culture of Cities* was "causing young men to see visions and old men to dream dreams," the NRC's Ben Kizer wrote to Mumford. After this "tremendous task of composing *The Culture of Cities*, new scenes, new aspects of human effort and human folly might rest and refresh the spirit" (Kizer, 1938, p. 4). The opportunity to visit a region long associated with Eden attracted the weary author. The offer to study "what the government is doing with the Columbia, that great river of power, beauty and greatness" (p. 3) ensured his services.

In 1937, the opening of the Bonneville Dam had given regional planning its first foothold in Portland (Robbins, 1997). "The Bonneville Dam was ... a fine piece of planning," Earl Riley, Portland commissioner and future mayor, stated in his address to the 1937 Oregon Planning Conference (Oregon State Planning Board, 1937, p. 15). The 300 planning advocates gathered in Portland were united by the belief that the new energy source offered the means to stimulate the economy and reduce "haphazard growth" (p. 17). A wave of migration from the Dust Bowl had diminished the supply of affordable land, but with the Bonneville complex, stated Walter Blucher, executive director of the American Society of Planning Officials, "new growth ... can be the deliverance or the destruction of the area, depending on how it is controlled.... This is the only place in the United States new enough so that you can make it become a land flowing with milk and honey.... I hope you won't spoil it" (p. 18).

That summer, Portland's Reed College hosted a follow-up meeting to discuss creating an agency for disseminating research on regional issues and coordinating planning efforts. The mix of academics, planners, and resource managers agreed that "only an impartial agency, free from political influence, and financially independent of special interest groups could fill the need" (NRC, 1943, p. 8). A steering committee organized the NRC's first conference and garnered a 3-year, $74,000 Rockefeller Foundation grant to establish a three-person staff in Portland (NRC, 1943).

After the NRC opened its new office, Kizer wrote Mumford imploring him "to make a swift reconnaissance of this region ... and discuss our plans with us, criticizing and helping us develop them" (Kizer, 1938, p. 2). It was a unique opportunity. In *The Culture of Cities* Mumford had concentrated on replanning mature regions, but "here," as Kizer put it was "a new land, with new possibilities of development, with virgin resources" (p. 2). Mumford agreed to spend 2 weeks touring the Northwest and to deliver a series of lectures on the prospects for regional planning.

Like many before him, the worldly traveler was transfixed by Oregon's landscape. "What I have seen with my eyes has been fabulously beautiful: the Great Douglas firs" and the "snow swept crest of Mt. Hood, rising above rim after rim of stark mountains" (Mumford, 1938d, p. 3). The logging operations, however, amounted to a "massacre" (Mumford, 1938e, p. 2). The wasteful practices of these "hard-bitten businessmen" did not stem from greed, Mumford believed, but from the desire for power: "for nothing testifies to power like the ability to destroy" (p. 2).

The picturesque Columbia River Gorge east of Portland especially intrigued him. The "abrupt rocks and water falls" reminded him of the "great Chinese paintings of the classic era. Esthetically, perhaps, the great-

est landscape I have ever seen," he wrote, "surpassing in intensity even ... Hawaii" (Mumford, 1938d, pp. 3–4). Encroaching industrial development, however, marred this natural masterpiece. This preyed on Mumford. A local historian wrote that his response, delivered to Portland's City Club, "set the narrow-minded business community on their ear" (DeMarco, 1991, p. 129).

In his speech to the City Club, Mumford proposed that Portlanders could "do a job of city planning like nowhere else in the world" (Mumford, 1938a, p. 26). But after encountering the "neglect in letting this fine land with its wonderful scenic beauty get away from you, it made me wonder," he asked, "if you are good enough to have it in your possession? Have you enough intelligence, imagination, and cooperation among you to make the best use of these opportunities?" (p. 26). He summoned business leaders to "control more vigorously" (p. 26) the land along the Columbia because industry had already decimated some of the most scenic sites.

After this engagement, Mumford's trip devolved into a fast-paced, perfunctory exercise, "even speaking, God save me," he confided in a personal letter, "to the [Seattle] Chamber of Commerce!" (Mumford, 1938e, p. 3). "Out of it all much will ... come" (p. 3), but he was unsuited for the "role of honored authority" (Mumford, 1938c, p. 2). While this role was gratifying, he felt rushed, "empty," and yearned for the "whole life" (p. 2). "A week of rest on my native soil," he wrote a friend, "will cause me to put forth green shoots again" (Mumford, 1938d, p. 5).

Regional Planning in the Northwest

Mumford's "green shoots" sprouted when he penned *Regional Planning in the*

Northwest that fall. The 20-page memorandum outlined an alternative to the "false ambitions and stultifying slogans" that constituted Portland's "melancholy plan" (Mumford, 1939a, p. 2). He advocated a "change of direction" (p. 3) in planning to coincide with the new power-generating capacity of the Bonneville complex. Mumford adhered to an "energy utopianism," a belief that once regions switched energy sources, the potential for change would dramatically accelerate. In the Northwest, the new power system was the means to decentralize population into garden cities and reduce pollution in city centers (White, 1995).

Mumford envisioned Portland branching into a series of "urban inter-region[s]" (Mumford, 1939a, p. 11) that balanced function and aesthetics. He recommended greening the city's central core and enhancing the industrial and cultural base of smaller towns to foster the "reforestation" of urban culture and stem "social erosion" (p. 20). Directing growth into a system of interconnected "greenbelt towns" would ease congestion, while new development would spread around, not over, the Willamette Valley's fertile land and scenic sites. Funds spent on "urban rehabilitation" and garden city design, Mumford concluded, "would obviate the very need for grandiose engineering experiments to which we are all by sheer inertia and fashion, too easily committed" (p. 19).

To institute this vision, a "regional authority" needed "to plan, to zone, to purchase and to dispose of land" (Mumford, 1939a, pp. 14–15). Its "first duty" would be to channel development "into points of maximum advantage ... without infringing upon the original beauties of nature" (p. 13). The authority should also "carry out the details" of planning and have the power to over-ride "short-sighted local opposition" (p. 15). These "collective democratic controls" would inhibit property rights, but Mumford forecasted corresponding reduc-

tions in "disorder ... foul building practices, ... duplicated railroad systems, abandoned logging towns, and dead mining camps" (p. 7). In addition, greenbelt towns with affordable housing and integrated transportation systems would "provide a special invitation to settlement by new industries" (p. 11).

Mumford remained a utopian at heart. "What Christianity expressed in terms of heaven," he pictured "in terms of daily living" (Mumford, 1938b, p. 378). He sought to revive the "organic community" (Blake, 1990, p. 200), a traditional form balancing work, nature, and civic responsibility, in a region blessed with a landscape of "overpowering beauty" (Mumford, 1939a, p. 1). A renaissance would ensue, he hoped, once nature became an active component of culture, and culture, in turn, harmonized around nature. Once "people ... know in detail where they live and how they live; they will be united by a common feeling for their landscape, their literature, and their language" (Mumford, 1938b, p. 386). Then the northern Willamette Valley would offer a place to live Mumford's cherished "good life,"[1] rather than merely pursuing the goods of life.

The NRC printed 1,500 copies of *Regional Planning in the Northwest* and circulated all but 20. Mumford anticipated returning to Portland in May 1940, to deliver the commencement address at Reed College and to reexamine the region. He cancelled the engagement, however, because his interest in planning and architecture seemed "the most pusillanimous act in the world" with the threat of "Hitlerism triumphant" (Mumford, 1939b, pp. 1–2). In a "world ... getting blacker" (p. 1), Mumford turned his attention to preparing the nation for a monumental crusade.

Mumford never returned to Portland, and the immediate impact of his work was negligible. The weakness of *Regional Planning in the Northwest*, like all Mumford's writing on regional planning, was his politics. His goal was a society of cultured citizens, but experts had to direct the "groping intelligence and under-lying desires of the majority" (Blake, 1990, p. 283) towards new ideals. Politics for Mumford, Casey Blake writes, "rested on demonstration, not argument, on expert guidance, not popular participation, and on assent, not consensus" (p. 283). The NRC promoted Mumford's vision, but it never moved beyond academia and New Deal agencies. By 1943 the NRC ceased operations because it failed to gain backing from the private sector. That same year, at the urging of business leaders, the City hired New York's Robert Moses (who labeled Mumford "an outspoken revolutionary" [Caro, 1975, p. 471]) to plan Portland's postwar transition (Abbott, 1993).

For the most part, Moses' plan reiterated projects, such as Olmsted's Forest Park proposal, outlined in earlier plans. He did, however, expand the role of public facilities and the auto (MacColl, 1979). "What triumphed in wartime Portland was a conception of planning as a prelude to civil engineering," wrote Carl Abbott (1983, p. 144). Rather than Mumford's complex of garden cities, Robert Moses' "engineered city" would guide planners in Portland after World War II.

The "Oregon Experiment" in Portland

In the decade after 1945, planning rarely moved beyond the realm of traffic engineering or public works in greater Portland. Except for Forest Park, Moses' major civic improvements were never realized, and the quest for suburban land often made design guidelines superfluous. For instance, grocer Fred Meyer, the region's leading retailer, moved his projects outside of Portland if they were constrained by planning regulations. The region's rapid suburban growth paralleled the national experience, but a distinct uneasiness also took hold. "Jerked by

the war from an Arcadian existence among flowers and firs, it looks back longingly ..." Richard Neuberger wrote in his exposé on Portland for the *Saturday Evening Post* (1947, p. 23). Residents wanted "their Eden undisturbed" (p. 23) and in the midst of an economic boom this gave the city "a split personality" (p. 23), according to the future Oregon senator. While Neuberger expressed Portlanders' reluctance to see their city become "a swashbuckling, industrial giant" (p. 23), the threat of urban sprawl would later engender similar feelings.

In 1969, exploding urban growth in the Willamette Valley pushed Governor Tom McCall to make land use planning a "statewide, not merely local, concern" (MacColl, 1995, p. 205). Urban pollution, the loss of rich farmland to "leap-frog" subdivisions, and a fear that the state's renowned "livability" was in decline all fueled Oregon's planning revolution (Abbott, 1983; MacColl, 1995). McCall, a maverick Republican, voiced the concerns of both the rural and urban constituents who "thought land was too valuable" to let "the ticky-tacky treadmill of development" destroy Oregon's natural resources (Walth, 1995, p. 246). During his first term (1966–1970), McCall pushed Oregon into the forefront of environmental reform, and, in 1969, Senate Bill 10 established the nation's first comprehensive planning act. In his second term (1970–1974), McCall renewed his planning crusade in the opening address to the 1973 State Legislature. The former journalist touched a common nerve among Oregonians, especially those west of the Cascades, by denouncing the "coastal condomania and the ravenous rampage of suburbia in the Willamette Valley" (DeGrove, 1984, p. 237). Compiling plans was not enough to rein in the "grasping wastrels of the land," who "mock Oregon's status as the environmental model for the nation" (p. 237). The Legislature followed McCall's lead and in 1973 passed Senate Bill 100 (SB 100), which required local governments to formulate comprehensive plans that met state-mandated goals.

The new act led to the establishment of statewide goals, one of which required designated territorial limits for each city. In Portland the regional Metropolitan Services District (Metro) was directed to manage and design an Urban Growth Boundary (UGB), encompassing 24 cities and portions of three counties.[2] The implementation of SB 100 coincided with a deep recession in the Oregon economy. During this period of slowed growth, consensus building in Portland faced relatively little pressure from development interests. In 1978 voters approved a new charter that gave Metro formal powers for regional planning. This referendum made Metro the nation's only directly elected regional government, consisting of a 12-member board and an executive officer (DeGrove, 1992; Poulsen, 1987). A year later, the State accepted Metro's UGB (which contained 364 square miles), and Portland would become the one American metropolis that could be described, in James Kunstler's words, as "Lewis Mumford's dream come true" (Kunstler, 1993, p. 205).

SB 100 revolutionized the planning process, but a number of obstacles remained before Portland could become the green city Mumford had envisioned. The UGB protected farmlands and forests from urban encroachment, but within the UGB little had been done to safeguard the natural landscape. Goal 5, one of the 14 State goals for planning, requires local governments "to conserve open space and protect natural and historic resources for future generations" (Oregon State Planning Goals, 1994, p. 300). SB 100, however, failed to require standardized inventories or methods of data collection, resulting in plans of wildly divergent quality. Goal 5 also orders a "balancing" between economic and environmental factors in the review of development proposals, but without guidelines, local governments showed broad discretion in their decisions. Planning departments often relied on volunteers to inventory natural areas and even monitor sites after conditions were placed on development projects in environmentally sensitive areas.

Metropolitan Greenspaces: Renewing the Vision

As Portland's economy surged to life in the late 1980s, growth pressures mounted and Goal 5 became the rallying point for activists seeking to protect the region's natural beauty and ecology (Ketcham, 1994). Portland Audubon, the region's most influential environmental organization, took the lead in inventorying natural areas for Goal 5. In the early 1980s, Mike Houck, Audubon's urban naturalist, noticed that the remaining natural corridors matched many sites identified in the Forty-Mile Loop Trust's plan to complete the Olmsteds' original system of parkways. Houck, however, could barely pursue this finding because of his time commitments as head of a coalition trying to protect the region's remaining natural areas.[3]

In 1983, the Clackamas County Commission sold Deep Creek Park, a 76-acre wilderness, to a logging company for $400,000. The Commission claimed the park represented a "luxury" (Kohler, 1983, p. D1) the county could no longer afford, and proceeds from the sale funded improvements for the county's remaining parks. After this defeat, Houck realized that Portland's "green city" status did not immunize citizens from the contentious land use issues that drive local politics throughout the United States (M. C. Houck, personal communication, April 24, 1995).

The next year, Oaks Bottom, a 160-acre wetland on the Willamette River, seemed destined for a similar fate. Portland had acquired the willow and cottonwood swamp 25 years earlier to create a park in a heavily developed area, but the city was considering turning the site into either a motocross course or a yacht harbor. Houck employed a campaign of stealth and education to keep Oaks Bottom natural. First, he made 40 "Oaks Bottom Wildlife Refuge" signs and placed them throughout the property. Then, at countless public meetings, Houck's advocacy inspired conservationists, key politicians, and even reluctant business interests to believe that this riparian wetland represented a "providential gift" (Collins, 1990, p. 14). The persuasive naturalist also led scores of field and canoe trips to introduce citizens and politicians to the 140 species of birds nesting near the central city. In 1988, Mayor Bud Clark, who became a heron enthusiast after a Houck canoe trip, led the City Council in designating Oaks Bottom as a wildlife refuge (Pierce, 1990).

After this victory, a local foundation awarded Houck a grant to set up a Metropolitan Wildlife Refuge System. For citizens intent on preserving urban natural areas, Houck was a "Modern-day Moses" (Collins, 1990, p. 14) with a vision of "the promised land of Portland's future" (p. 14). Houck, however, made it clear that before attempting to secure the future, civic leaders needed to revisit the past. In a speech to the City Club in 1989, he called on his audience to renew an old mission, not invent a new one. Natural corridors were essential for enhancing biodiversity, but as Olmsted and Mumford argued, an interconnected system of natural landscapes also enhanced *human* life (Houck, 1989). In an age of communal dissolution, greenways offered a means, Houck argued, "to link people together. We need to cultivate — or renew — a feeling of the landscape. We need to rediscover what living here means to us on an intuitive, visceral level" (Collins, 1990, p 11).

After Houck's address, Metro's planning staff investigated linking the region's natural areas with a series of greenways. Metro had shown little interest in open-

space planning until a 1986 study found that local governments had generally failed to address the acquisition of wilderness preserves or to inventory natural areas. In 1989, Metro completed a regional park study which found that "there was no regional coordination in natural area parks and preserves" (Metro, 1992, p. 42). This problem manifested itself when a revitalized economy spurred growth rates in the late 1980s. By 1990, only Orlando and Atlanta, among metropolitan areas with populations over one million, were growing faster than Portland. In 1990, Metro projected 500,000 new residents by 2010, which would push the region's population to 1.7 million. Caught off guard by the population surge, residents feared that "the region's unique identity" and its "livability" would be "compromised" (Houck & Poracsky, 1994, p. 254).

In response to these concerns, Metro hired Joseph Poracsky, a geography professor at Portland State University, to map the region's natural lands.[4] The study team mapped 3,600 natural sites totaling 119,000 acres in a 602-square-mile area. After Poracsky found that only 8.5% of the natural land acreage was protected, he cowrote a position paper, *Recommendations for a Regional System of Natural Areas*, that set the guidelines for what became a Metro initiative, Metropolitan Greenspaces (Houck & Poracsky, 1994).

Metro worked closely with Houck in promoting its new program. The agency provided Houck with office space to conduct public outreach and network development after he helped the agency obtain a $1.1-million grant from the Interior Department to establish the Greenspaces Program, one of two national demonstration projects. Houck remained on loan from Audubon and the Wetlands Conservancy from 1989 to 1992. He maintained his independence from Metro so that he could continue to serve as an advocate and critic of the Greenspaces Program (Howe, 1998). In 1991, the first

Greenspaces brochure introduced the concept of linking "a mosaic of natural areas into greenspaces, preserving wildlife habitat and crafting greenways for animals, plants, and people" (Metro, 1991). Metro staff also traced the genesis of this initiative to the Olmsteds and Lewis Mumford:

> These wild lands are our legacy, remnants of the native landscape enjoyed by past generations. But very little remains. The metropolitan area's burgeoning population ... could result in the extinction of our most wondrous experiences. Nearly a century ago, the Olmsteds, the renowned landscape architects, proposed for us an ambitious scheme of interconnected parks. Three decades later, planning visionary Lewis Mumford advocated a natural areas system for the region.... Metropolitan Greenspaces is that renewed vision. (Metro, 1991)

In their advocacy of greenspaces, some enthusiasts lost track of time and history. After nearby Vancouver, Washington, decided to design a greenway system in conjunction with Portland, the project coordinator claimed his inspiration came from "Lewis Mumford, Portland planner, the first to have a dream of a regional system of greenways back in 1903" (Richards, 1991, p. B2). Even if planners had difficulty distinguishing between Olmsted and Mumford, they had finally come to appreciate their solutions for protecting and enhancing the region's natural beauty.

In 1992, Metro published *A Guidebook for Maintaining and Enhancing Greater Portland's Special Sense of Place* (Ribe, 1992), crafted by a team from the University of Oregon's School of Landscape Architecture. The study reprinted Mumford's challenge to the City Club, and followed his recommendation to design a "new urban pattern ... providing a proper distribution" of the three essential landscapes: "the primitive, the rural, and the urban" (Mumford, 1939a, pp. 18–19). The guidebook presented 10 illustrated planning principles to "harmonize

growth patterns with regional landforms" (Ribe, 1992, p. 5). The team also recommended a slow expansion of the UGB to ensure that future development followed "quality growth patterns" (p. 51).

That July, Metro completed the Greenspaces Master Plan. Based on the discipline of landscape ecology, the plan sought to protect and restore the "green infrastructure" through land acquisition and regulation (Metro, 1992). It took 3 more years of consensus building, however, before voters passed a $138.8-million bond measure to fund a natural land acquisition program.[5] In 1992 voters also approved a home rule charter for Metro that gave it a new political legitimacy, including the authority to write functional plans to which city and county plans had to conform.

In 1994, the Metro Council adopted the *Region 2040* concept to "set the course" (Metro, 1995, p. 1) for regional planning over a half century. In the future, the region's development would follow a more compact form to lessen dependence on the automobile and to preserve open space networks. In 1995, the Council debated three growth concepts to guide *Region 2040*: Expand the UGB by 25%; keep the UGB intact and funnel development into centers and corridors with high transit use; or channel new growth into satellite cities outside the UGB (Metro, 1994). The Metro Council rejected the Mumfordian concept of satellite cities and voted to focus development within a single UGB. Although part of his plan was ignored, "the revival of interest in regional land use planning indicates the continuation of Mumford's legacy: the importance of reorienting 'place' as a means of social and environmental reform," writes one Mumford scholar (Luccarelli, 1995, p. 220). Toward this end, activists have embraced Mumford's vision to move their community in a new direction. Perhaps more than his plan, it is Mumford's conception of life connected to community and nature that led Neil Goldschmidt, former Portland mayor and governor of Oregon, to conclude that "Portland is a better city thanks in large part to the wisdom and foresight of Lewis Mumford" (Haar & Kayden, 1982, p. 16).

Today, Metro oversees an evolving, regional city: Wilderness and agricultural greenbelts mark growth boundaries; coherent architecture defines commercial centers; 140 miles of trails and greenways connect natural lands and neighborhoods; and a system of buses, trolleys, and light rail lines offers transportation alternatives to the automobile. By the end of 1997, Metro had acquired half the lands listed on the 1995 bond measure while using only one third of the approved revenues (Hunsberger, 1998). The amenities of this green city are matched by its "silicon forest's" lucrative economic landscape. Portland offers an evolving prototype in a nation struggling to accommodate growth (DeGrove, 1994). But even here, half a century elapsed before regional planning took hold, and questions about its viability remain.

The economic dynamism of the region's silicon forest and its pleasing lifestyle are spurring a heavy in-migration that is unlikely to slow in the foreseeable future. At the same time, development interests are demanding the expansion of the UGB to counter rising urban land values (Ehrenhalt, 1997).[6] The increase in land values has placed open space at a premium, and despite Metro's land acquisition program, these sites are being lost at an unprecedented rate. According to Howe (1998), "the fact that no one can say just how much has been lost highlights a fundamental weakness in Metro's planning agenda" (p. 67).

In part, Metro is a victim of its own success. The progress made in land acquisition could lead to the perception that natural resource protection is a moot point, when, in fact, metro is struggling to implement the Metropolitan Greenspaces Plan.

In *Region 2040*, planners designated 16,000 acres of environmentally sensitive land as unbuildable. Yet, until Metro adopted provisions for protecting floodplains and water quality (Title 3 of the Urban Growth Management Functional Plan) in June 1998, there were no regulatory means to enforce this directive, and local governments were given 18 months to realign their plans to fit Metro's vision. Since 1990, 1,100 housing units have been constructed on floodplains within the UGB. With the region's development pressures, construction on sensitive habitats will continue unless funds and technical assistance are invested to implement the Metropolitan Greenspaces Plan. "Metropolitan Portland faces the very real prospect," Howe (1998) contends, "of becoming a densely developed region that is devoid of wildlife and subject to the vagaries of nature including floods and mudslides" (p. 71).

The problem plaguing Metro parallels the inherent weakness of Mumford's regionalism: Regional planning postulated by experts cannot succeed without a reciprocal effort at the local level. Activists such as Mike Houck helped Metro set a new agenda, but the Portland model will remain in question until the "critical problem," which Mumford identified in 1939, becomes more central to the local and regional planning process. "The critical problem is redistributing population in places of maximum advantage for life: in sites that are physically healthy and stimulating, with a sufficient underpinning of natural resources, with a sufficient supply of social facilities and cultural institutions" (Mumford, 1939a, p. 18).

Despite its limitations, Mumford's genius remains relevant because he tied human well-being to the mystery of life. He floated many thoughtful abstractions, but his basic theorem never extended too far from reality. In an age devoted to consumption, technology, and engineering, Mumford advocated the art of design to solve the complex problems of urbanization and to initiate a renewal of American culture. Communities designed around the constructs of nature can sustain ecological health while humans confront a complexity, balance, and force they can neither replicate nor fully comprehend. In its essence, Mumford's conception of regional planning offers the "myth of life" (Williams, 1990, p. 45). This option still remains viable, Mumford wrote in his first book, provided "we ignore all fake utopias and social myths that have proved either so sterile or disastrous" (Mumford, 1922, p. 300).

Notes

1. Mumford's concept of the "good life" came from the tradition of public humanism dating back to Aristotle. "'Men come together in cities,' said Aristotle, 'in order to live: they remain together to live the good life'" (Mumford, 1938b, p. 492).

2. Regional planning reappeared in Portland in 1957 when planners and office-holders in the three metropolitan counties in Oregon (Multnomah, Clackamas, and Washington) and Clark County, Washington, formed the voluntary Portland Metropolitan Planning Commission (1957–1966). The Commission's cooperative efforts garnered federal funds for studies, but it remained primarily a research organization with little power. For more on the history of regional planning in Portland, see Poulsen (1987) and DeGrove (1992).

3. Houck and Esther Lev were instrumental in organizing the Friends and Advocates of Urban Natural Areas (FAUNA). Members represented watershed protection groups advocating the preservation and enhancement of open spaces and fish and wildlife habitat in the areas where they lived. Houck also was responsible for organizing four "Country in the City" symposiums at Portland State University between 1988 and 1991. Over 2,000 people listened to experts in the fields of ecology, recreation, planning, and landscape architecture share their knowledge of how to design programs to preserve and enhance urban natural areas.

4. Natural areas were defined as self-sustaining plant and animal communities largely devoid of man-made structures. "Working landscapes" such as tree plantations, golf courses, and agricultural areas were not included.

5. In November 1992, a referendum to secure $200 million in general obligation bonds for acquiring sites identified in the Metropolitan Greenspaces Plan failed. After the defeat, Metro initiated a $138.8-million bond campaign for land acquisition. The late Bill Naito, a leading developer, headed a "blue ribbon" committee to promote the initiative. This time the acquisition sites were listed and prioritized on the ballot. The measure passed in 1995 with over 60% of the vote.

6. In 1997, Metro voted to designate as urban reserves 18,000 acres of land outside the UGB (equivalent to 8% of the land within the current boundary). The urban reserves will be incorporated into the UGB in the near future; 5,359 acres were so added in December 1998, to comply with state law requiring that UGBs contain a 20-year supply of buildable land. For more on this issue, see Egan (1996) and Ehrenhalt (1997).

References

Abbott, C. (1983). *Portland: Planning, politics, and growth in a twentieth century city*. Lincoln, NE: University of Nebraska Press.

Abbott, C. (1993). *The metropolitan frontier: Cities in the modern American West*. Tucson, AZ: University of Arizona Press.

Abbott, C. (1994). The Oregon planning style. In C. Abbott, D. Howe, & S. Adler (Eds.), *Planning the Oregon way: A twenty-year evaluation* (pp. 51–84). Corvallis, OR: Oregon State University Press.

Artibise, A., Moudon, A. V., & Seltzer, E. (1997). Cascadia: An emerging regional model. In R. Geddes (Ed.), *Cities in our future* (pp. 149–174). Washington, DC: Island Press.

Blackford, M. G. (1993). *The lost dream: Businessmen and city planning on the Pacific Coast, 1890–1920*. Columbus, OH: Ohio State University Press.

Blake, C. N. (1990). *Beloved community: The cultural criticism of Randolph Bourne, Van Wyck Brooks, Waldo Frank, and Lewis Mumford*. Chapel Hill, NC: University of North Carolina Press.

Broder, D. (1998, July 15). Pioneering livability. *The Oregonian*. p. M2

Caro, R. A. (1975). *The power broker: Robert*

Moses and the fall of New York. New York: Random House.

Chapman, N. J., & Starker, J. (1987). Portland: The most livable city? In L. Price (Ed.), *Portland's changing landscapes.* (pp. 191–207). Portland, OR: Portland State University Press.

Collins, C. (1990, August 26). The greening of Portland. *The Oregonian,* pp. 10–17.

DeGrove, J. (1984). *Land, growth, and politics.* Chicago: American Planning Association Press.

DeGrove, J. (1992). *The new frontier for land policy: Planning and growth management in the United States.* Cambridge, MA: Lincoln Land Institute.

DeGrove, J. (1994). Following in Oregon's footsteps: The impact of Oregon's growth management strategy on other states. In C. Abbott, D. Howe, & S. Adler (Eds.), *Planning the Oregon way: A twenty-year evaluation* (pp. 227–244). Corvallis, OR: Oregon State University Press.

DeMarco, G. (1991). *A short history of Portland.* Portland, OR: Lexikos.

Dionne, E. J., Jr. (1997, March 21). Government planning that keeps Portland green. *The Washington Post,* p. A27.

Easterbrook, G. (1995). *A moment on the earth: The coming age of environmental optimism.* New York: Viking.

Egan, T. (1996, December 30). Drawing the hard line on urban sprawl. *New York Times,* pp. A1, A14.

Ehrenhalt, A. (1997, May). The great wall of Portland. *Governing, 10,* 20–24.

Friedman, E. S. (1993). *The facts of life in Portland, Oregon.* Portland, OR: Portland Possibilities.

Haar, C. M., & Kayden, J. S. (1982). *A tribute to Lewis Mumford.* Cambridge, MA: Lincoln Land Institute.

Houck, M. C. (1989, October 13). Protecting our urban wild lands, renewing a vision. Address to the City Club of Portland.

Houck, M. C., & Poracsky, J. (1994). The Portland metropolitan urban natural resources program. In R. Platt (Ed.), *The ecological city: Preserving and restoring urban biodiversity* (pp. 251–267). Amherst, MA: University of Massachusetts Press.

Howe, D. (1998). Metropolitan Portland's greenspaces program. In *Creating sustainable places symposium* (pp. 67–71). Tempe, AZ: Hershberger Center for Design Excellence, Arizona State University.

Houle, M. C. (1988). *One city's wilderness: Portland's Forest Park.* Portland, OR: Oregon Historical Society.

Hunsberger, B. (1998, January 12). Metro gives itself an "A" for land buys. *The Oregonian,* p. E1.

Ketcham, P. (1994). *To save or to pave: Planning for the protection of urban natural areas.* Portland, OR: Portland Audubon Society.

Kizer, B. (1938, May 17). Kizer to Lewis Mumford. Lewis Mumford Papers, University of Pennsylvania Special Collections.

Kohler, V. (1983, April 29). Clackamas County sells 76-acre Deep Creek Park. *The Oregonian,* p. D1.

Kunstler, J. H. (1993). *The geography of nowhere.* New York: Simon and Schuster.

Luccarelli, M. (1995). *Lewis Mumford and the ecological region.* New York: Guilford Press.

MacColl, E. K. (1979). *The growth of a city: Power and politics in Portland, Oregon 1915–1950.* Portland, OR: The Georgian Press.

MacColl, E. K. (1995). The battle to control land use: Oregon's unique law of 1973, In R. Lowitt (Ed.), *Politics in the post-war West* (pp. 203–220). Norman, OK: University of Oklahoma Press.

Metro. (1991). Metropolitan greenspaces [Brochure]. Portland, OR: Author.

Metro. (1992). *Metropolitan greenspaces plan.* Portland, OR: Author.

Metro. (1994). *Concepts for growth.* Portland, OR: Author.

Metro. (1995, Spring/Summer). To the citizens of the region. *2040 Framework.* 1. Portland, OR: Author.

Miller, D. L. (1989). *Lewis Mumford: A life.* New York: Weidenfeld and Nicolson.

Mumford, L. (1922). *The story of utopias.* New York: Boni and Liveright.

Mumford, L. (1927). The next twenty years in city planning. *Proceedings of the nineteenth national city planning conference* (pp. 45–58). Washington, DC: American Institute of City Planning.

Mumford, L. (1938a, July 22). Are you good enough for Oregon? *Portland City Club Bulletin, 18,* 26.

Mumford, L. (1938b). *The culture of cities.* New York: Harcourt, Brace, and Company.

Mumford, L. (1938c, July 3). Mumford to Sophia Mumford. Lewis Mumford Papers, University of Pennsylvania Special Collections.

Mumford, L. (1938d, July 17). Mumford to

Josephine Strongin. Lewis Mumford Papers, University of Pennsylvania Special Collections.

Mumford, L. (1938e, July 27). Mumford to Josephine Strongin. Lewis Mumford Papers, University of Pennsylvania Special Collections.

Mumford, L. (1939a). *Regional planning in the Pacific Northwest: A memorandum.* Portland, OR: Northwest Regional Council.

Mumford, L. (1939b, September 4). Mumford to Josephine Strongin. Lewis Mumford Papers, University of Pennsylvania Special Collections.

Neuberger, R. E. (1947, March 1). The cities of America: Portland, Oregon. *The Saturday Evening Post, 219,* 22–24, 104–108.

Northwest Regional Council. (1943). *A summary of the history of the Northwest Regional Council.* Portland, OR: Author.

Oregon State Planning Board. (1937). *Proceedings of the Oregon planning conference.* Portland, OR: Author.

Oregon state planning goals. (1994). In C. Abbott, D. Howe, & S. Adler (Eds.), *Planning the Oregon way: A twenty-year evaluation* (pp. 300–304). Corvallis, OR: Oregon State University Press.

Partners for Livable Communities. (1994). *America's most livable communities.* Washington, DC: Author.

Pierce, N. (1990, April 29). Portland pioneers urban natural areas. *The Oregonian,* p. M2.

Poulsen, T. M. (1987). Shaping and planning Portland's metropolitan development. In L. Price (Ed.), *Portland's changing landscapes* (pp. 86–98). Portland, OR: Portland State University Press.

Ribe, R. (1992). *Ten essentials for a quality regional landscape: A guidebook for enhancing greater Portland's special sense of place.* Portland, OR: Metro.

Richards, L. (1991, December 24). Dream taking shape as network of green. *The Oregonian,* p. B2.

Robbins, W. G. (1997). *Landscapes of promise: The Oregon story 1800–1940.* Seattle: University of Washington Press.

Thomas J. L. (1990). Lewis Mumford, Benton MacKaye, and the regional vision. In T. P. Hughes & A. C. Hughes (Eds.), *Lewis Mumford: Public intellectual* (pp. 66–99). New York: Oxford University Press.

Walth, B. (1995). *Fire at Eden's gate: Tom McCall and the Oregon story.* Portland, OR: Oregon Historical Society.

White, R. (1995). *The organic machine: The remaking of the Columbia River.* New York: Hill and Wang.

Williams, R. (1990). Mumford as Historian of Technology. In T. P. Hughes & A. C. Hughes (Eds.), *Lewis Mumford: Public intellectual* (pp. 43–65). New York: Oxford University Press.

CHAPTER 35

PORTLAND PURSUES BALANCE BETWEEN ITS ECONOMY AND ENVIRONMENT

Timothy Grewe, Susan Anderson, and *Laurel Butman*

The word "sustainability" is becoming an increasingly common word in the public policy lexicon. The concept behind the word, however, is not widely understood. Simply put, sustainability is the notion that current economic and consumption patterns should not reduce opportunities for future generations by depleting or impairing resources.[1] Put another way, sustainability is the process of creating balance among the environment, the economy, and social equity. The concept is derived from the recognition that the earth's natural capital is limited and that pollution and wastefulness are a drain on the economy.

Government finance officers understand well the consequences of imbalance among the environment, the economy and social equity. Many cities have been forced to spend hundreds of million of dollars to remedy the legacies of past generations. Urban sprawl from shortsighted land-use planning, water pollution from combined sewer systems, overflowing landfills from heavy waste loads — these are just a few of many examples of how the unsustainable actions of past generations can prove costly to succeeding generations.

Although the national and international debate over environmental policy and legislation is interesting, the rubber hits the road at the state and local levels. Problems created by imbalances between the environment and the economy often result in regulations and resource drains at the local level. Ultimately, local government officials are the ones who must devise solutions to address the environmental issues plaguing their communities.

A profound, understandable concern for the welfare of future generations is focusing increasing attention on sustainability, causing many organizations to rethink the way they conduct business. Scientific research confirms that human activity is causing a buildup of greenhouse gases in the atmosphere that already is altering the world climate. Left unchecked, climate change could undermine the delicate system that sustains life on earth. Conducting business as usual, without regard for its impact on the environment, is simply no longer an option.

Originally published as "Portland, Oregon: A Case Study in Sustainability," *Government Finance Review*, Vol. 18, No. 1, February 2002. Published by the Government Finance Officers Association, Chicago, Illinois. Reprinted with permission of the publisher.

By now, most people have either heard or read about global warming. Recent reports by the United Nations and the National Academy of Sciences offer some startling glimpses into the future.[2]

- Temperatures on earth are expected to rise between 2.5 and 10.4 degrees Fahrenheit by the end of the 21st century, almost twice as much as 1995 predictions and far exceeding the 1 degree temperature increase of the 20th century.
- By 1996, 25 percent of the world's approximately 4,630 mammal species and 11 percent of the 9,675 bird species were at significant risk of total extinction.
- Costs for extreme weather damage reached $608 billion in the 1990s, exceeding the aggregate costs of the previous 40 years.
- Every day, Americans generate 125 pounds of waste per capita. Annualized, this translates into a total annual waste flow of 250 trillion pounds, only 5 percent of which is recycled.
- Every 100 pounds of product manufactured in the United States generates at least 3,200 pounds of related waste.
- Hazardous chemical exposure is suspected of causing a litany of adverse human health impacts — from birth defects to cancer. Global pesticide use results in 3.5 to 5 million acute poisonings a year.
- The United States is responsible for 25 percent of the world's carbon dioxide emissions. To stabilize atmospheric carbon dioxide levels and curb the trend of global warming, these emissions must be reduced by 70 percent in the coming decades.

Altering this course by adopting principles of sustainability will require dramatic changes in current social and economic systems. Many local governments, however, already are meeting this challenge by integrating environmental, economic, and social goals toward a sustainable future. Among these governments is the City of Portland,

which was recently recognized as one of three international cities doing the most to achieve sustainability. This article describes Portland's efforts and identifies some of the most salient considerations for other governments to consider in formulating their own strategies for a sustainable future.

Rising to the Challenge

Despite the success of its sustainability initiative, Portland is hardly alone in this regard. Other cities throughout the world also are making significant progress. More than 400 cities, for example, have adopted global warming plans. Worldwide, local governments are taking the lead in applying sustainability concepts. Government finance officers stand to gain much from one another by sharing their experiences in developing options and implementing needed initiatives. Two brief examples illustrate the kinds of innovative sustainability solutions that have been implemented by local governments across the globe.

With a population of just greater than 16,000, the City of Arcata, California, relies on marsh plants to decontaminate wastewater and to provide secondary sewage treatment. The Arcata Marsh and Wildlife Sanctuary was constructed as an alternative to a regional facility that would have required a 70 percent rate increase. In addition to treating Arcata's wastewater, the facility provides wildlife habitat and public park land. The total cost to build the integrated facility was $7.1 million, far less than the $25 million estimated for a conventional system. The benefits of this innovative facility, however, extend far beyond mere sewage treatment.

Similarly, the City of Curitiba, Brazil, has been a pioneer in sustainability for almost 30 years. Before 1970, Curitiba was a rapidly growing city with sprawling "favelas" or slums. Narrow or nonexistent street networks in the favelas prevented the effective circulation of refuse collection trucks. To prevent the health problems associated with the accumulation of solid waste, the city distributed recycling bins around the favelas, offered transit tokens in exchange for separate and recyclable trash, and provided surplus food in exchange for organic waste. The savings from recycling and fewer refuse trucks are used to pay for the transit tokens. Local farmers, meanwhile, convert the organic waste into fertilizer.

Today, most families and businesses in Curitiba pre-sort their refuse, 70 percent of which is either recycled or composted. The program has simultaneously enhanced the economic situation of the city's poor and the city's own waste management and recycling efforts. Curitiba's sustainability program has expanded to include an extensive park and lake system that doubles as flood protection, more than 1.5 million street trees planted by citizen volunteers, small-scale affordable housing distributed equitably throughout the city, and a bus system that accommodates more passengers than New York City's. The city is prosperous, clean, and beloved by its citizens, most of whom would not live anywhere else.

The Portland Story

Although all cities are different, some core principles and tools for integrating sustainability into government emerge from an examination of one city's experience. Today's ecological and intergenerational challenges are as prevalent in Portland as they are elsewhere. What makes Portland unique is its institutionalization of sustainability as a core business driver. The city's sustainability program has evolved from the focus of a single department to become a way of life for the entire organization.

Portland is a city of about 500,000 at the confluence of the Willamette and Co-

lumbia Rivers. The Willamette River runs through the heart of the city, which is the cultural and natural center for 24 government entities that share both a regional government and a 20-year-old urban growth boundary. Portland has had a preoccupation with planning and a tradition of strong civic involvement since the passage of Oregon's state land-use laws in the 1970s. Those laws recognize citizen involvement as a primary goal and require urban areas to develop long-range land-use and facilities plans. They also direct jurisdictions to consider the impacts of future plans on 19 statewide goals, including energy, housing, economy, and transportation.

Portland citizens and businesses have worked with city government to envision a land-use pattern that works for the local environment, economy, and community. By keeping urban development out of the fertile farmlands surrounding the region, the urban growth boundary was an important first step toward sustainability. Designed to contain sprawl and promote the efficient delivery of urban services, the urban growth boundary is a well-known extension of the community's original vision. Less well known are the plans for what lies within the urban growth boundary. Portland's land-use plans call for the creation of a network of regional and town centers — linked by public transit — in which residential and commercial activity are concentrated. A supporting regional vision includes a connected network of trails, parks, and greenspaces.

This pattern works for businesses because it provides certainty about the location of future development. It works for the environment because it reduces pollution from transportation and relieves development pressure on sensitive areas. It works for the community because it creates healthy neighborhoods where people can walk or bike to the services they need — a feature that is particularly important for lower-income residents. And it works for government because it makes efficient use of existing infrastructure.

GRASSROOTS BEGINNINGS

In 1988, a nonprofit organization called 1,000 Friends of Oregon took an important step forward in advancing the city's vision for a sustainable future. In response to a plan for a new bypass highway to reduce traffic congestion, 1,000 Friends of Oregon conducted an influential study comparing various alternatives for addressing population growth. The study demonstrated how a land-use pattern of moderate density and pedestrian-friendly neighborhoods along a regional transit network could reduce driving and improve air quality. As a result of this study, local decision makers abandoned the highway plans in favor of the more sustainable alternative.

This example illustrates several key sustainability concepts. First, it sought a solution that addressed the cause of the problem. Second, it was more than a simple "no" strategy; it provided a viable alternative to highway construction that met the community's needs. Third, it resulted in environmental, economic, and community benefits.

PORTLAND TAKES ACTION

A similar approach is now being applied to other areas of municipal interest. Stormwater runoff is a growing concern because of flooding, erosion, and overflows from the combined sewer system. The traditional approach to stormwater was to pump or pipe it away, requiring major infrastructure construction and maintenance. To avoid these costly fixes, the city began searching for a more cost-effective and sustainable alternative that would address the cause of the problem, not just the symptoms.

One root cause of the problem was the proliferation of impervious surfaces (e.g., rooftops, streets, and sidewalks) that accelerate water flow and prevent it from perco-lating into the ground. Although the traditional engineering solution to this problem is to install more or bigger pipes, Portland is pursuing a package of "green solutions" that use vegetation to control stormwater.

- Through partnerships with public and private landowners, the city is restoring degraded stream banks and upland areas with native vegetation. For the past two years, this program has restored nearly 300 acres per year.
- The city is purchasing property in flood plains and restoring wetlands or other natural features.
- The city provides financial incentives to encourage private-sector projects that demonstrate environmental building techniques. These projects include the use of vegetated rooftops ("eco-roofs") and parking lots to facilitate evaporation and drainage.

These alternatives have proven less expensive than the added infrastructure required to transport stormwater runoff. More importantly, they provide benefits that surpass efficient stormwater management, including additional open space, increased neighborhood livability, improved air quality, summer cooling, and habitat. Many alternatives are easy to implement, regardless of a jurisdiction's size.

ADOPTING POLICIES TO SUPPORT SUSTAINABLE ALTERNATIVES

Since the early 1990s, Portland has adopted policies to support and encourage sustainable alternatives. In 1993, for example, Portland became the first United States city to adopt a carbon dioxide emissions reduction plan. This action was followed by the adoption of Sustainable City Principles in 1994. These initial efforts culminated in the creation of the Office of Sustainable Development, which coordinates the city's sustainability efforts.

In early 2001, Portland adopted a green building policy requiring that all new construction and major remodeling of city buildings, as well as city-funded commercial property and affordable housing projects, meet environmental standards established by the U.S. Green Building Council. Responding to concerns about the potential costs of conforming to green building standards, the city commissioned a life-cycle cost/benefit analysis. The study confirmed that over their useful lives, the benefits of structures built to these standards exceed the costs. One unexpected outcome of the study was evidence that green buildings provide healthier and more productive work environments. Features such as increased day lighting, reduced toxic materials, and better air handling all enhance workplace health and safety. Similar studies have demonstrated much higher student test scores in schools designed with day lighting.

Policies need not be as dramatic as the adoption of green building standards to positively impact a jurisdiction's overall sustainability efforts. For example, Portland requires recycling and waste reduction in its operating bureaus. To facilitate compliance, the city provides paper recycling receptacles for each employee and battery recycling collection service for each bureau. Residents are following the city's lead, evidenced by the fact that 54 percent of all waste is recycled. Other efforts to reduce paper waste include the required use of procurement cards and online bidding (and bond sales).

MOVING TOWARD A COORDINATED APPROACH

Many cities are responding to environmental mandates requiring them to clean up waterways polluted by previous generations, restore air quality, and protect wildlife endangered by human activity. These mandates present a major resource challenge to local governments. Until 1999, Portland had separate programs to address the requirements of the Endangered Species Act, the Clean Water Act, Superfund listings, and

other federal and state mandates. The result was a litany of diffuse programs using competing resources to address these mandates as separate problems.

River Renaissance, a program focused on the health of the Willamette River, is addressing the requirements of these mandates through an integrated, proactive approach. Through coordinated watershed planning, River Renaissance facilitates collaboration between city bureaus. This approach promotes the efficient use of resources to comply with environmental mandates. River Renaissance has become a nexus for community volunteerism among the disparate mandates. In addition, it has spawned new community dialogue about the kind of city Portland hopes to become.

Formulating a Sustainability Strategy

There are as many approaches to sustainability as there are municipalities. Although federal, state, and local regulations will shape sustainability efforts to some extent, governments should devise a strategy suited to their particular circumstances. Still, there are a number of factors that any government should consider in developing a sustainability strategy. These factors are discussed below.

INTERNALIZING ENVIRONMENTAL COSTS

Many businesses are realizing that environmental costs are becoming internalized through regulation. For example, consider an electric utility that generates significant amounts of greenhouse gas emissions at its generation plants. Although those emissions are not currently regulated or taxed, the company is preparing for their possible regulation in the future by investing in wind power and in forestry projects that offset the impact of the company's emissions. Today's free pollution is tomorrow's financial liability.

For local governments, some environmental costs already are internalized. Pollution may be free to a housing or police agency, but it is a very real cost to an environmental or health agency. Jurisdictions need only look to the past for guidance. Lead paint, for example, was legal until 1978. Current generations are now paying the costs for that unfortunate policy. To avoid the repetition of such mistakes, local governments should survey their business practices to identify opportunities for making them more environmentally friendly.

LIFE-CYCLE ANALYSIS

Life-cycle analysis is a systematic tool for assessing the total cost (or impact) of an investment over its useful life. Sustainable alternatives often make economic sense when viewed through the lens of life-cycle analysis. The purchase price of an alternative fuel vehicle, for example, may be more than that of a traditional vehicle. Over the life of the vehicles, however, fuel savings in the former almost always compensate for the initial price difference. Reduced emissions from the alternative fuel vehicle, which negate the need for costly federal mandates, also should be considered in the analysis. Sustainability demands a long-term, holistic approach to decision making that goes beyond mere acquisition costs. In the end, this approach will enhance financial stability.

At its wastewater treatment plant, Portland is working with an organization called the Zero Waste Alliance to develop a chemical management system. In addition to the costs of the treatment chemicals used, officials are projecting other costs associated with the use of chemicals. Hazardous substances often create higher costs for storage, employee training, protective clothing, disposal, and insurance. Over their life cycle, chemicals also pollute the environment.

When all of these factors are included in the equation, pollution prevention is usually an excellent investment.

INSTITUTIONALIZING SUSTAINABILITY

Incorporating sustainability into a government's core business practices requires much more than applying a new standard or adopting a new program. Governments should integrate sustainable development into their organizational systems instead of creating parallel bureaucracies. Portland's evolution illustrates this important distinction.

In 1990, Portland established the City Energy Challenge Program with a goal of saving $1 million annually through energy conservation. Resources for the program were provided by city bureaus, each of which contributed 1 percent of their energy bills. None of this money was used for capital investment. Among other things, it paid for an energy efficiency manager who worked with the bureaus to assess opportunities, provide technical expertise on new technologies, and identify financial incentives such as utility rebates, grants, and loans. Over the past decade, Energy Challenge savings have totaled nearly $10 million. Successful projects range from single lighting retrofits to a sewer gas fuel cell at the wastewater treatment plant.

Developing a citywide commitment to sustainability is Portland's current focus. The city is working to build energy and sustainability goals across bureaus. For example, the Office of Management and Finance is completing a strategic plan that includes sustainable business practices and performance measures among its core strategic actions. Similarly, the Water Bureau is developing a sustainability program that integrates sustainability into its business plan. City bureaus have come to recognize that to be most effective, sustainability must take hold within the workplace culture.

COMMUNICATION AND EDUCATION

Integrating sustainability goals across city functions requires broad understanding and participation across organizational divisions. Portland communicates sustainable development concepts to employees and managers in a variety of ways, including the following:

- Every two weeks, the city e-mails a "green tip" to all employees, effectively sharing ways to apply principles of sustainability both at home and at work. These e-mails raise awareness and reinforce the city's own sustainability efforts.
- A volunteer team sponsors a "green fair" for city employees featuring environmentally preferable products and a sustainable fashion show.
- A local chapter of the nonprofit organization Natural Step provides training on its framework for assessing the sustainability of specific actions. The Water Bureau's management team, which has already received training on this methodology, is developing a plan to engage the rest of its employees in the program.

THIRD-PARTY CERTIFICATION

Third-party certification is emerging as an important tool in promoting sustainable practices. Just as product testing laboratories vouch for the safety of the products they test, a number of organizations have developed sustainability standards. A national example is the U.S. Green Building Council's Leadership in Energy and Environmental Design (LEED) standards. A building that is LEED certified has met standards for resource efficiency, air quality, and the use of environmentally preferable materials.

Similarly, Portland's auto shops are certified by a pollution prevention program established by the State of Oregon and a number of local governments. The Parks Bureau is working with an organization called Salmon Safe to develop standards for urban parks. This certification program will provide better stream protection in parks and enhance accountability. Compliance with these kinds of standards demonstrates the city's commitment to the environment and promotes accountability and credibility.

EVALUATING SUSTAINABILITY

Sustainable strategies are marked by three key characteristics: (1) they create economic advantage; (2) they positively impact the environment; and (3) they meet community needs. Solutions that address only one of these three characteristics are generally not sustainable.

Sustainable solutions treat the cause of the problem, not the symptoms. Using eco-roofs to accelerate the evaporation of stormwater, for example, is a fundamentally different approach than remediating runoff through infrastructure repairs. Portland's efforts are designed to reduce or eliminate problems before they jeopardize future generations. Portland's bikeway program is providing a sustainable solution to automobile emissions.

Conclusion

Governments today are spending hundreds of millions of dollars to remedy the shortsighted decisions of the past. Because of these experiences and continued environmental degradation, more and more governments are coming to understand the importance of sustainability — that delicate balance among the environment, the economy, and social equity. Portland and many other cities worldwide are taking proactive steps to provide a more livable future. Sustainability efforts do not have to be large to make a difference. Simple changes in purchasing and waste management practices, for example, can yield significant results. In light of the many creative solutions to environmental challenges, some of which are discussed in this article, governments should take great care to ensure that their business practices do not mortgage the future of coming generations.

Notes

1. Lisa S. Nelson, "Community Sustainability and Land Use," *Public Administration Review* 61 (2001): 6, 741–746.

2. See Intergovernmental Panel on Climate Change, *Third Assessment Report of Working Group I* (2001) and United Nations Environment Programme, *Global Environment Outlook* 2000 (2000).

CHAPTER 36

RIVERHEAD AND MATTITUCK TAKE STEPS TO PROTECT NATURE

Joe Haberstroh

Their daughter Gayle was waiting for them, and she was anxious. "Mom, you've got to do something—the bay is brown," Gayle said. "It turned brown overnight."

Jean walked over to the stream where the Marriners kept their 23-foot sailboat, *Fun*, then out to the nearby shore of Peconic Bay. As far as she could see, the usually sparkling waters of the Peconic were the color of weak coffee.

"Fifteen days earlier," she recalled, "it had been Peconic blue."

The Peconic Estuary—also called the Peconic Bay complex or, simply, the Peconics—spreads across more than 100 shallow bays, harbors and tidal creeks between the north and south forks of eastern Long Island, about 80 miles east of New York City.

Along its shores are former whaling villages, summer communities, working potato farms, and well-tended vineyards. It is a place of $1 million vacation homes and deep water sailboats, but also of old Long Island ways. Here, in flat-bottomed skiffs built by local craftsmen, dwindling ranks of commercial "baymen," as they are known, rake for clams and scallops and trap fish.

On the very day she arrived home in Mattituck, Jean Marriner, who owned a public relations agency, telephoned one of her friends in the League of Women Voters. She eventually joined forces with Jean Lane, a local art historian and Sierra Club activist.

The two Jeans learned that the bay's troubles stemmed from aggressive algae that soon would be known as "brown tide." A botanical cousin to red tides and other harmful algal blooms that have shadowed waters elsewhere in the world in the past two decades, brown tide was choking off the Peconics' lucrative beds of clams and scallops. The shellfish weren't spawning as they once did. The scallops came up in the dredges dead, their shells open.

An annual harvest valued at $7 million at the dock was in peril, but the problem was more than just economic. Brown tide struck at the very heart of regional identity of eastern Long Island. It's as if Kansas couldn't grow wheat or oranges were banished from Florida.

Originally published as "Turning the Tide," *Planning*, Vol. 70, No. 8, August/September 2004. Published by the American Planning Association, 122 South Michigan Avenue, Suite 1600, Chicago, Illinois 60603-6107. Reprinted with permission of the publisher.

Shocked into Action

The devastating appearance of brown tide and the determination to get rid of it triggered a sustained regional planning effort that has transcended the plight of the shellfish. With lobbying by local activists such as Jean Marriner and celebrities such as pop singer Billy Joel, the U.S. Environmental Protection Agency in 1993 designated the Peconic Estuary a "national estuary of significance." That unlocked federal funding, and it created the Peconic Estuary Program, which continues to operate 19 years after brown tide first bloomed.

The sprawling program has not been a panacea: No zoning changes have resulted, and development moratoriums remain intensely controversial. But land preservation has boomed, millions have been spent on laboratory research into brown tide, and a deeper understanding has emerged of the close connection between upland development and water quality.

The federal government is involved through its National Estuary Program, which was created in 1987 when the Clean Water Act was amended. With local and state partners, the program preserves and rehabilitates estuarine systems, the semi-enclosed coastal areas where marine waters mix with fresh water. Estuaries provide critical habitat for birds and mammals and nursery areas for fish. Brackish wetlands also act as important filtering zones between the land and sea. Since 1987, Congress's annual funding for the program has been about $15 million.

Today, the EPA helps to oversee the protection of 28 estuaries, from Albemarle-Pamlico Sounds in North Carolina to Puget Sound in Washington State. On Long Island, local managers of the Peconic Estuary Program must submit annual "implementation reviews" to the EPA to show their efforts are on track.

On Long Island, the Peconic program has erected a planning framework to help local communities safeguard the watershed that surrounds the bay system. Broad strategies have been adopted to preserve land, reduce fertilizer use, and redirect stormwater run-off. And specific land-use tools have been suggested to local planners in the trenches of subdivision review.

"One of the things that emerged was just the idea of protecting 100 feet around a wetland, and trying to maintain natural vegetation, as opposed to vegetation that requires extensive application of fertilizers," says Valerie Scopaz, AICP, planning director for the Town of Southold, one of the five towns of eastern Long Island.

Town Power

Under New York state law, towns, run by elected supervisors and boards, are given many of the powers that in other places in the U.S. fall to counties — in particular, decisions on land use. Towns in New York encompass villages, cities, and unincorporated areas.

Because of the power of New York towns, local planners such as Scopaz have been central to the Peconic Estuary effort, with local and county planning professionals serving on the program's technical advisory committee (Scopaz among them).

The program area falls within Suffolk County, and county planners have built a regional database for land use in the Peconics region — an electronic inventory of some 5,000 parcels. The Suffolk planners have also churned out maps using geographic information system maps to delineate Peconic Bay's groundwater-contributing areas.

"I think the program has been very successful," says DeWitt Davies, chief environmental analyst for the Suffolk planning agency. "It's a well-respected technical effort, and it serves as a good example for other efforts that could or should be taken along our coastlines, and along the North Shore of Long Island."

The planners' GIS (Geographic Information System) maps helped to cement the case that the Peconics' main problems were not smokestack industries, or even a proliferation of towering sewage plants. Instead, what ails the bay is nonpoint source pollution: toxic chemicals traveling underground to the bay from heavily fertilized farms, manicured yards, and oily asphalt roads.

Now in its fifth year since a Comprehensive Conservation and Management Plan program was passed, the estuary program addresses six key issues: brown tide; nutrient pollution (primarily in the form of nitrogen from agricultural and residential fertilizer usage); living resources and habitats; pathogens that force the closure of shellfishing waters (such as bacteria from human and dog waste); toxics in the system (a relatively small issue because there is no heavy industry in the area); and the protection of critical lands.

The management plan is ambitious: It lists 340 actions to be taken, and more than half have been started. Some of the projects are big and sophisticated, such as the $3 million, 1996–2001 Brown Tide Research Initiative, a university-based research program. Other projects have a low-key approach, such as the annual "Go Organic" fair organized by the North Fork Environmental Council, or the work by Cornell Cooperative Extension to teach residents how to cultivate shellfish.

The Right Blend?

Overall, the programs' achievements have blended policy, construction project, and public outreach:

- The five eastern Long Island towns that surround the Peconic Bay complex agreed to a no-discharge rule, under which boaters have their onboard toilets emptied by EPA-funded pump-out boats, or at such facilities at the dock. The rule won critical support from the local Association of Marine Industries only when estuary program officials promised business interests that boat toilets would not be portrayed to the public as a major contributor to poor water quality — and they have not been.

- With $8 million from the EPA and the New York Department of Environmental Conservation, the sewage treatment plant at Riverhead was modernized to reduce the amount of nitrogen it unleashes into a section of the Peconics called Flanders Bay.

- Cornell University's extension office, which operates out of Southold, New York — along the shores of the bay — has built the world's first greenhouse to propagate eel grass, the marine plant vital to protecting juvenile scallops from hungry crabs and fish. Using old photos and new interviews with aged baymen, Cornell has also tried to verify how much eel grass once grew throughout the system, and where.

- The Nature Conservancy has created 10 spawner sanctuaries where more than 100,000 scallops and clams have been poured into the water to increase shellfish density and jump-start reproduction.

- This summer, the program unveiled a carefully negotiated, voluntary agreement with 35 golf clubs to reduce the amount of nitrogen they apply to their courses.

"We pledged from the beginning that everything we do would be based on considerable science and a tremendous effort at complete inclusion," says Vito Minei, who directs the estuary program from his position as director of the Suffolk County Division of Environmental Quality. "We pledged that the state Department of Environmental Conservation was not going to ram this down everyone's throat and that we, at the county level, were not going to run all these environmental regulations."

Minei's promises notwithstanding, the idea of an EPA–supervised estuary program at first inspired little enthusiasm. At least in the public mind, the connection had not yet been made between land-use practices in the Peconics' 128,000-acre watershed and water quality in the bay itself.

"Our sailing friends thought it was a bunch of environmentalists who were going crazy," Marriner says. "They didn't want to have anything to do with it. We decided we would persevere because the bay and the creeks meant so much to us."

Water-dependent businesses such as marinas were also wary — primarily of federal government involvement — and yield-oriented farmers did not appreciate what impact their upland pesticide use had on the bay's water quality. Even the EPA was unconvinced. The agency already had two estuary programs nearby, for Long Island Sound and for the New York–New Jersey harbor.

Most important, local town officials weren't accustomed to sharing land-use planning responsibilities with other towns, much less Washington, D.C. Efforts in the 1980s to encourage town cooperation on solid-waste management issues had failed.

Most local officials also "operated within their own fiefdoms," says Kevin Mc-Donald, vice-president of Group for the South Fork, an environmental organization in Bridgehampton. "But we did have a few supervisors at the time who were quite progressive. They began to make the case that the Peconics are a big bathtub. We all swim in it, we all bathe in it, we all fish in it, and we'd all better take care of it."

It required the return of brown tide in 1986, 1987, and 1988 before opinion coalesced around the idea that something had to be done.

The Big Guns

In 1989, Jean Marriner formed Save the Peconic Bays, Inc., a nonprofit advocacy group. She charged $10 for a membership. Soon, she was escorting Long Island native Billy Joel around the halls of Congress to get the EPA to include the Peconics in its program. Joel, a native of Hickville, Long Island, had a summer home in East Hampton and had begun to advocate on behalf of traditional baymen in the South Fork area known as the Hamptons and also in the Peconics. His 1989 song, "The Downeaster 'Alexa,'" was his bittersweet tribute: "I was a bayman like my father was before. Can't make a living as a bayman anymore."

Joel is emotionally invested in a part of Long Island that outsiders may not know about. For many, Long Island is associated with the Gold Coast mansions of the Great Gatsby era, or the middle-class developments like Levittown that mushroomed after World War II. Yet even as three million people have settled on the island, the main freeway eventually notching 71 exits, there has always been another Long Island. This is the leafier place locals call the East End, where 100,000 people are spread among five waterfront towns.

On the South Fork, the Hamptons come alive in the summer, as Hollywood stars and New York celebrities remove to beachfront saltboxes and splashier compounds behind high privet hedges. On the more rural North Fork, where fishing and whaling villages were built among rolling farms, the style is plainer and the pace slower.

Between the North and South forks lies the Peconic Bay complex, with 340 miles of heavily indented coastline. There are white beaches lined with broken scallop shells, wooded bluffs, and lonely marshes where egrets wade for a meal. More than 100 endangered or threatened species of wildlife thrive in the Peconics. Sea turtles paddle in from the ocean each summer on their northern migration from the Caribbean, lobster scuttle along the rocky ledges, and osprey glide along the water's surface, occasionally diving for flounder or weakfish.

Southerly winds that average 15 mph and protected inland waters make the area a sailor's heaven. It is no wonder that the Nature Conservancy has designated the Peconics as one of the Western Hemisphere's "Last Great Places."

Settlers first arrived 350 years ago. At first, traditional ways held sway. The baymen dug clams and scallops from the soft bottom of the bays and caught striped bass in traps held together with oak posts hacked from the coastal woods. Upland, farmers grew potatoes and planted apple orchards that to this day help to make Suffolk County the state's number one agricultural county in terms of revenue. The farm economy has also been powered in the past 25 years by the development of 52 vineyards on the North Fork.

As Long Island matured, development pressure rose in the Peconics area. Asphalt roads began to grid the old farms. Rain swept oils from passing vehicles into the ground. Septic systems were buried alongside new houses. Growing communities built sewage treatment plants and directed the effluent into the bay.

Beginning in the 1950s, agricultural fertilizer use soared. In the decades that followed, residents moving into new homes dumped fertilizers on their new lawns. Land was cheaper in the Peconics than elsewhere on Long Island, so development continued to gobble up open space. As the wetlands disappeared, roads, driveways, and parking lots channeled tainted groundwater into the bays.

Turning Point

If Long Islanders began to sense they were in a growing battle to preserve the Peconics, the collapse of the scallops served, says Minei, as the effort's "crystallizing event." Although people could not agree on the cause of the scallops' demise — was it just water quality or perhaps a resource stressed by over-fishing? — no one disputed the profound implications for a region whose livability and future hinged on the health of the marine environment.

Moving swiftly, the Suffolk County Office of Ecology completed a brown tide comprehensive assessment in 1987. At the same time, the county began a daily water quality monitoring program throughout the bay complex. The assessment allowed local leaders and planners to make the case that the area should be included in the National Estuary Program. The monitoring produced a key set of data for the various marine biologists from across the U.S. who waded into the as-yet unsolved mystery of brown tide.

Over the past decade, EPA funding in the program has exceeded $6 million. Suffolk County has spent about $800,000 in the same period and raised about $7 million for environmental restoration work with a quarter percent increase in the sales tax. In addition, the program received about $15 million from the 1996 passage of a $1.75 billion statewide bond act to pay for environmental efforts.

Perhaps most important, the program benefits from a real estate transfer tax approved by eastern Long Island voters in 1999. That tax — two percent on the sale of property — has raised $163 million for the purchase of open space in the Peconics watershed. The money is spent almost as quickly as it is collected.

With such healthy funding, an effort originally directed to revive the scallop industry has addressed a wider range of environmental and development issues affecting the bay and the communities on its shores. Open space around the shoreline was quickly seen as one key to preserving the bay's health, and county and local planners were central to identifying existing land uses, how much land was left to develop, and other land-use trends.

Suffolk County planners used GIS software to produce highly detailed maps that dramatically illustrated how the once sleepy Peconics had come under unprecedented development pressure. Now, years later, the planners' maps continue to guide town boards in choosing which sensitive lands to set aside with the public's open space money.

"Previous to that, the land-use maps that were generated here were much more generalized and individual lot lines were not shown," says Davies, the analyst at the Suffolk County planning department. "So, when we had this GIS computer capability, we could get more and more fine analysis of what was happening in the watershed area. We did a land-use inventory of all five eastern townships. The original data set that was used to discuss open space acquisition was based on those original maps."

Over the years, county planners have become a sort of think tank for the estuary program. They have filed numerous analyses, providing a foundation for policy makers. They produced a report on land available for development under current zoning. They researched the study area's existing population, trends, and build-out population. They catalogued water-dependent uses in the five East End towns, and undertook a sweeping historical analysis of land-use changes that had occurred from the mid-1970s to the mid-1990s.

The land-use map is digital and can be accessed through the Internet. The planners commissioned a new set of aerial photographs to work from, but they also fanned out and conducted site visits to confirm the photos. "You see a structure on a photograph, but you don't necessarily know what it is," Davies says. "We had to actually go out and verify the land-use codes we had."

Bottom Line

For all the activity swirling around the Peconic Estuary Program and what Suffolk County describes as the program's "holistic approach to improving and maintaining the estuary and its watershed," the bay scallop crop has never recovered. The annual harvest, once 250,000 pounds, has fallen to roughly 3,000 pounds. A harvest that once took the baymen from October through the following spring now lasts a day or two. Peconic Bay scallops have become almost a delicacy. Since the 1980s, their price has risen from about $5 per pound to $19.95 in retail seafood markets.

Meanwhile, brown tide, which laid the scallops low, has not been seen in the Peconics for six years.

"The failure to date, in the absence of brown tide, is that we haven't seen the restoration of the scallop industry," Menei says. "That is a nagging, persistent shortcoming. That's what we set out to do."

Even with millions of dollars available to pay for land acquisition, the towns of eastern Long Island sometimes have struggled to make deals with farmers who can fetch higher prices from developers. From 1995 to 2001, some 3,500 acres were lost to developers within the Peconics' watershed, leaving 25,000 acres of open space in the five eastern towns. The Peconic Estuary Program does not have veto power over any particular development.

Still, the program's influence can be felt in subtle ways. Kevin McDonald recalls discussions about the inconsistent way the towns allowed developers to remove native vegetation from building sites. Some towns had a standard, some did not. The idea arose for a "unified watershed clearing restriction."

"Just as we spoke of this," McDonald says, "the towns of Riverhead and Southold started including watershed-clearing restrictions as they worked on their comprehensive planning updates."

As for Jean Marriner, she has moved elsewhere in New York State. She is proud of her early work in getting the National Estuary Program to recognize the Peconics as a place worth saving. At the same time, she has watched as many developments have been built, which she believes is contrary to the spirit of the original grass-roots effort. She wishes elected leaders had used the important work of planners such as DeWitt Davies to guide development more aggressively.

Why does she believe the Peconic Estuary Program has even more work ahead of it? "I think it's a lack of political will somehow, and the education of the public about these issues," she says. "It takes time, I know. I guess if we had another brown tide, people would sit up and really take notice."

CHAPTER 37

SAINT LOUIS PARK CREATES A NEW COMMUNITY GREEN DOWNTOWN

Sean Stowell

The city of St. Louis Park, Minn., through a community wide visioning process created a plan for redeveloping an eight square block area into a vibrant space for living, shopping and working. Told Development was selected by the city to make the vision a reality and subsequently hired Damon Farber Associates to develop a comprehensive site plan that would reflect the upscale nature of the development and the vision of the community.

The focal point of the development is a two block long community green. A 500-person Veterans' Memorial Amphitheater provides a space for community events and also provides ADA access to the park. The partnership between private development and public open space resulted in an area that reflects the vision of the community.

A Look at St. Louis Park

St. Louis Park is an established community of 10.8 square miles located southwest of Minneapolis. According to city data, in a little more that 115 years, it has grown from a village of 45 families to a community of 44,126 residents. In August 1886, 31 people signed a petition asking county commissioners to incorporate the village of St. Louis Park. The petition was officially registered on November 19, 1886. By incorporating, these citizens hoped to turn this small community into a boomtown.

Explosive growth came after World War II. In 1940, 7,737 people lived in St. Louis Park. By 1955, more than 30,000 residents had joined them. Sixty percent of St. Louis Park's homes were built in a single burst of construction from the late 1940s to the early 1950s.

Today, most of St. Louis Park is developed, and much of the focus has shifted from building infrastructure to improving it, and part of that improvement is seen in the community green and the amphitheater.

Community Green

"The community green is really a link between the amphitheater and Wolfe Park to the main street in the city," said Damon Far-

Originally published as "Adding Character to a Suburb," *Landscape Architect and Specifier News*, Vol. 20, No. 3, March 2004. Published by Landscape Communications, Tustin, California. Reprinted with permission of the publisher.

ber, president of Damon Farber Associates. "This is a public space on which a mixed use development fronts. This is very urban in character."

Elements such as decorative street lighting, banners, seasonal planters, public art, comfortable benches, arbors, fountains and decorative pavers reinforce the pedestrian atmosphere and promote the image of a vital community destination.

Known as Excelsior and Grand, the project is a mixed-use redevelopment project designed to create a new downtown for this first-ring Minneapolis suburb. The multi-phased project will eventually create a focal point and city center of eight to 10 buildings, including apartments, offices, retail shops and restaurants. The focal point of the development is a two block long Community Green.

Borson Construction company completed phase one, which includes four separate multi-housing/retail mix buildings with 342 units of rental housing and 65,000 square feet of retail space, as well as two parking ramps that accommodate 852 vehicles.

"This project has really given this place some character," Farber said. "This was a strip mall suburb and the town green gives everybody a physical focus within the community. It feels like a downtown which they never had in this city and it really enhances the sense of place."

The major challenge for this portion of the project was the intermingling of pedestrian and automobile traffic. He said the design used a variety of paving materials as a traffic-calming device.

"We used speed bumps at pedestrian crossings and introduced interlocking concrete pavers into the roadway system where we wanted traffic to slow and where we wanted to accent pedestrian movement."

One of the keys to success for this project, according to Farber, was the community involvement.

Adding Character

While he admits this isn't always the case, Farber said the community of St. Louis Park really feels a sense of ownership when it comes to their town and that came across in design meetings. This project was 15 years in the making when the city came to the citizens and proposed pulling the downtown area into one large usable space.

While Damon Farber Associates was not involved in those early meetings, they later sat in on many community meetings, looking at various design schemes and visual images of the proposed designs.

"There were a number of meetings and the character of the green is a result of those meetings," Farber said. "It was a very inclusive and very positive process."

Other elements within the area of the Community Green include a brick paved star pattern in one of the turnabouts, and historic themed lighting that marries the historic character of the area with a more contemporary feel. Also there is a Haddonstone produced fountain and an arbor designed by Damon Farber Associates to complement it.

Veterans' Memorial Amphitheater

This 500 person amphitheater provides a unique public open space for community events and allows handicap access from adjacent Wolfe Park to the new retail and housing development. Within this amphitheater is a memorial wall dedicated to the citizens of St. Louis Park who have served the United States in times of war.

According to Damon Farber Associates vice president Tom Whitlock, a 10 foot tall cast-in-place concrete wall features three wall-mounted flagpoles representing POW/MIAs, the state of Minnesota and the United States. Two plaques between the flags represent the American Legion and Veterans of Foreign Wars. Also on the wall are bronze medallions for each of the five branches of the armed forces and a silhouette of the Iwo Jima Memorial.

The most unique aspect of this amphitheater is the ADA accessibility of the facility.

"We have a serpentine path that winds through the amphitheater," Whitlock said. "There is ADA seating at every level. It turned out to be a simple, graceful solution to what could have been a really tough problem."

Accessible concrete paver pathways wind through the theater giving visitors access to the grassy terrace. The lowest terrace allows wheelchair users to occupy cut out areas so that their companions may sit side-by-side.

"The challenge was to get from top to bottom without looking like a handicap ramp," Farber said. "The path spirals like a nautilus shell."

The seating is all modular block according to Whitlock, along with the steps. A new gateway piece has been added to the top of the amphitheater along with an information kiosk, bike racks and a seating wall.

The city has programmed this area well with concerts virtually every night in the summer and ice sculptures in the winter along with other community related activities and events. The amphitheater holds large Memorial Day activities as well.

The amphitheater is enhanced with a variety of plantings. The backdrop to the amphitheater has a row of little leaf lindens in a half arc behind the stage. The top of the amphitheater has a row of white ash that has distinctive purple foliage in the fall. A hedge of aster sits on the back edge of the amphitheater while hydrangeas slope to the front row of the amphitheater. The upper plaza features serpentine rows of maple and juniper that form the area around the gateway, creating a buffer between the upper plaza and the bike path. Along with the linden behind the stage are massings of junipers and stella de oro.

For a suburban area that lacked much character beyond a strip mall, St. Louis Park residents have taken pride in their city, making it an attractive place to live, shop, work and play.

"This is really a lesson in how to make a high quality design with a limited budget," Farber said. "We did that by using materials in different ways. The people in St. Louis Park have really felt a sense of ownership in their city and they have risen to the occasion."

CHAPTER 38

SAINT PAUL REVIVES ITS INNER-CITY RIVERFRONT AREA

Frank Edgerton Martin

In the late 1980s, Saint Paul's Mississippi riverfront exhibited the decline evident in many Midwestern river cities. Office towers and retail areas turned their backs on the river, and waterfront industries that had flourished for decades became increasingly stagnant, even though Minnesota's service economy was booming.

Following the flight to the suburbs of downtown's primary anchor, West Publishing, in 1992, Saint Paul's leaders recognized that something had to be done. They hired architect Benjamin Thompson, a Saint Paul native son who had gone on to serve as design architect for the revitalization of Boston's Fanueil Hall Market and Baltimore's waterfront, to create a new vision for downtown, expecting him to produce a massive report detailing economic and urban design strategies. Instead, Thompson came back a few months later with a simple but daring panoramic sketch of a reforested stretch of the Mississippi Valley that transformed the city's sense of possibility. The broad river valley, with the tops of houses and steeples showing through the tree canopy, suddenly seemed like a place where people could live again, a network of neighborhoods replacing old industrial facilities and empty lots.

Thompson's image appeared on television and in newspapers throughout Minnesota, generating genuine enthusiasm for the idea that the forgotten river might hold the key to Saint Paul's future. In 1995, the Saint Paul Foundation created a nonprofit organization, Greening the Great River Park, to oversee replanting the valley forest. Although Thompson did not specify tree types, the involvement early on of ecologists and landscape architects led to a focus on restoration of the native ecological community. But the real story of the rescue of Saint Paul's riverfront began when this vision of trees was turned into a public/private partnership between the city and the developers to create new houses, jobs, and cultural attractions in the valley.

Creating a Frame for Thompson's Picture

To begin the transition from a watercolor landscape painting to urban development, the city hired architect Ken Greenberg of the Toronto-based architecture and planning firm Urban Strategies, who had overseen development in the mid–1990s of

---

Originally published as "Saint Paul's New Riverfront Urban Villages," *Urban Land*, Vol. 60, No. 4, April 2001. Published by the Urban Land Institute, Washington, D.C. Reprinted with permission of the publisher.

a new master plan for the Twin Cities campus of the University of Minnesota. City officials were impressed with the common-sense urbanism of the design, which called for making the campus more pedestrian friendly and reopening connections between Northrop Mall and the Mississippi River. Working with Close Landscape Architecture of Saint Paul and Applied Ecological Services of Brodhead, Wisconsin, Urban Strategies completed its plan, the Saint Paul on the Mississippi Development Framework, in June 1997.

As stated at the beginning, the "Development Framework is based on an implicit understanding that quality of life — the ability of a city to effectively balance economy, environment, and society — provides a primary competitive advantage in an increasingly globalized world." The framework specifically called for formation of an agency to steward riverfront projects over the long term, and in 1997, with significant grant money from regional foundations, the Saint Paul Riverfront Corporation was created to fulfill that role. Working closely with the Riverfront Corporation is the Saint Paul on the Mississippi Design Center, which includes staff from nearly all city departments who meet regularly to discuss new projects with developers and architects.

The framework has served as the philosophical touchstone for every development project that has gotten underway in downtown Saint Paul and along the river since its completion. The city government's ongoing, interdepartmental agreement to follow the policies outlined in the framework is one of the most significant factors in Saint Paul's success. Ten basic framework principles (see box) that have served as the basis for building the urban environment now are being refined as site-specific guidelines for developing new urban villages along both sides of the river.

Saint Paul on the Mississippi Development Framework Principles

- Evoke a sense of place
- Restore and establish the unique urban ecology
- Invest in the public realm
- Broaden the mix of uses
- Improve connectivity
- Ensure that buildings support city building goals
- Build on existing strengths
- Preserve and enhance heritage resources
- Provide a balanced network for movement
- Foster public safety

Activity Day and Night

With the emphasis on supporting and working with developers, rather than simply responding to individual proposals, the Saint Paul Riverfront Corporation now is stewarding projects ranging from housing, to new banking and software company facilities, to museums and other cultural attractions that draw evening and weekend activity. The Science Museum of Minnesota is a major addition to the downtown side of the river that draws thousands of visitors and school groups each year. Following Thompson's early sketch, the building, designed by Ellerbe Becket of Minneapolis, steps down the limestone bluff from the uplands on which downtown is built to lowlands near the river's edge. The museum building, with its terraces overlooking the valley, can be thought of as a metaphorical "staircase" that connects the city to the river. Around the base of the museum, Great River Greening (formerly Greening the Great River Park) has planted hundreds of native trees that eventually will extend to the adjacent Upper Landing Park.

Upper Landing Park, whose concept was designed by Close Landscape Architecture, will include a limestone riverside amphitheater shaded by a soaring canopy and exhibits from the Science Museum. A large commons will accommodate festivals, and a river balcony and promenade are planned, along which permanently moored boats will provide concessions, rentals, and educational and restroom facilities to minimize the impact on the fragile floodplain site. One of the most unusual Upper Landing projects will be the restoration of the headhouse of the former Harvest States grain elevators for commercial uses such as cafés, waterfront taverns, and galleries.

The Upper Landing Urban Village

Just to the west of Upper Landing Park, a new mixed-use neighborhood will front a new regional trail along the north bank of the river. The 17-acre project, which is being developed by Dallas-based Centex Corporation, will include open space and seven blocks of condominiums, townhouses, and apartments. The Saint Paul city council made the surprising decision in 1997 to reserve the highly contaminated site — once slated for a plastics plant — to create one of the urban villages envisioned by the development framework. Centex will coordinate site cleanup with $4 million in financing from the Metropolitan Council — the Twin Cities' regional government — and $11 million in tax increment financing. Centex will invest an additional $3 million for site landscape architecture and another $2.5 million to bury power lines on the site.

The $140 million project will include for-sale housing ranging from condominiums costing $200,000 to two-story townhouses in the $600,000 range to be developed by Rottlund Homes. Rental units will range from $800 to $2,100 a month. One of the project's most innovative components is a mixed-use city block that includes housing and 23,000 square feet of mostly on-grade retail and restaurant space facing the river at the Upper Landing's front door to downtown. Construction is estimated to take three years, with completion expected before 2005.

Bridging the River

For decades, the area south of the Mississippi known as Harriet Island and the West Side Flats languished, beset by flooding problems that stymied development. In the early 1990s, the Army Corps of Engineers began a massive project to protect the floodplain area, developing a linear dike that offered an ideal opportunity to create a new promenade extending from Harriet Island to the Lafayette Bridge, located near downtown's eastern edge. Upriver, directly linking downtown to Harriet Island, the Wabasha Bridge recently was rebuilt with new railing, paving, and lighting to draw pedestrians from downtown across the river to Harriet Island and the neighborhoods that Saint Paulites call the "West Side."

Now designated a regional park, Harriet Island serves as the centerpiece of a 3,000-acre riverfront park system that stretches from the University of Minnesota to the city's southern boundary. This citywide network of parkways and recreational trails is a boon for city residents because, with its sinuous route, no neighborhood is more than three miles from the river.

The West Side Flats: A Model for New Urban Villages

A second urban village is planned directly east of Harriet Island in the West Side Flats to complement the Upper Landing project. Working to translate the framework plan into real-world development, Hammel, Green and Abrahamson, Inc. (HGA), a Minneapolis architecture/engineering firm, is creating an overall plan for housing, open space, and a hydrological system on the sensitive Flats site. Ultimately, developers Sherman & Associates, Jerry Troyen, and KKE Architecture will implement these ideas for the 45-acre area.

A market analysis conducted by Zimmerman/Volk Associates, Inc., of Clinton, New Jersey, looks beyond local comparables to encourage a mix of high-density housing for the West Side Flats: "Given the potential nonresidential uses — ranging from retail to entertainment — that may occur on the site, an overall residential density of approximately 20 to 25 units to the acre should be achievable." The report goes on to say that a target mix of approximately 1,000 housing units could be broken down into multifamily rental units (58 percent), multifamily for-sale units (24 percent), and single-family, attached, for-sale units (17 percent).

Zimmerman/Volk envisions target households for the West Side Flats as a mix of urban and suburban, older and younger families with an affinity for urban life. A majority of these households might include professionals, small business owners, software and computer specialists, and office workers.

Serving as consultant to HGA, urban designer Rich McLaughlin has been involved with the southern bank of the river, where the West Side Flats is located, since 1995. He recalls the early conflicts between landowners who wanted a themed entertainment complex built on the site and the city, which, following the framework plan, wanted an urban neighborhood with multiple uses and a variety of owners. Five years later, no theme park plan has surfaced, leaving open the opportunity for the urban alternative.

"I see it as an opportunity to reactivate the riverfront with restaurants and nightclubs, hot dog and ice cream stands, that reflect a traditional urban neighborhood scenario," says McLaughlin. HGA's urban planner, Nick Koch, takes a broader view of the potential new neighborhood: "West Side Flats is really becoming a rich blending of corporate employment, housing density, and significant investment in the public realm of parks, streets, and even stormwater retention," he argues. "It's an unprecedented multiuse project for our region ... and it makes sense both physically and economically."

The West Side Flats and much of Harriet Island lie in lowlands protected by the Army Corps of Engineers' recently completed levee, which also serves as a riverfront esplanade linking the two districts and offering views of downtown. Future residents of West Side Flats will be able to make use of riverfront trails and Harriet Island's improved open space.

The Saint Paul River Corridor Urban Design Plan, developed by Close Landscape Architecture, calls for extending the adjacent grid of streets through the new development rather than creating superblocks divorced from the city. An existing rail corridor that snakes through the neighborhood and over the river will be treated as an opportunity to frame a central park and accommodate a new trail. To establish a strong urban streetscape, mansion-style apartment buildings and condominiums, along with other types of housing, will be built with clear setback requirements to guarantee consistent street edges. Regular setbacks and relatively consistent housing massings are seen throughout Saint Paul neighborhoods, part of the urban fabric that the city's new urban designers see as worth emulating.

Because the West Side Flats was once floodplains, the site-specific guidelines now being developed encourage the preservation of native riparian landscapes and the integration of stormwater management elements

with "green fingers" of open space that channel and filter runoff. HGA and Sherman &
Associates currently are gathering market research on "comparable" three- to four-story
urban housing projects to show interested
developers that low-rise, mixed-price housing has been successful in other cities.

When he presented the Saint Paul on
the Mississippi Development Framework to
residents in 1997, Mayor Norm Coleman,
with an instinct for ecological as well as political benefit, spoke of the riverfront and its
connection to every neighborhood in the
city. The Saint Paul River Corridor Urban
Design Plan argues that the river and its
reaches are more than a "thin ribbon
through the city." Instead, it says, the "river
corridor should be viewed as a watershed
model, an entity that incorporates elements,
communities, and patterns from well beyond the river itself." These elements include both ecological and culturally significant elements such as sacred Native
American sites and historic riverboat land-
ings and commercial areas. Several projects
have been undertaken to preserve the city's
riparian resources and integrate them into
the built environment.

The Lower Phalen Creek Watershed
Restoration Project is a neighborhood-
driven effort to enhance the habitat along
this small creek, improve trails, and recon-
nect the neglected strand of green space with
surrounding neighborhoods. Further to the
north, the Phalen Corridor Initiative is a
large-scale strategy to bring new industries
to deteriorated East Side neighborhoods.
One unusual component of the initiative
was the replacement of the declining Phalen
Shopping Center with a wetland intended to
filter and improve the quality of runoff
water headed for the Mississippi.

The Saint Paul Riverfront Corporation
is supporting the Renaissance Project, a network of greenways, streetscape improvements, and parks that will extend the river
valley's reach into downtown and older

neighborhoods. The project is envisioned as
flexible, changing as necessary to meet new
market needs and take advantage of development opportunities. To date, the project
has supported 92 acres of new or improved
parks, five miles of new trails, and eight
miles of improved streetscapes, along with
overlook terraces and viewpoints. Heeding
the development framework plan's call for
connected infrastructure and integrated
transportation modes, the Renaissance Project is funding two new stair towers that will
link the new Wabasha Bridge to parklands
below.

Taking a Long-Term View

When riverfront work began in 1994,
Patrick Seeb, then deputy mayor, and
Mayor Coleman realized that they would
have to be patient, setting ten years as a
benchmark for tangible progress. Although
Coleman has announced that he will not run
for a third term, advocates such as the Saint
Paul Riverfront Corporation will continue
to raise money from the private sector and
foundations for riverfront planning.

To celebrate the tenth anniversary of
work along the river, the Riverfront Corporation is staging the Grand Excursion 2004,
a steamboat flotilla that will bring passengers
from Rock Island, Illinois, to Saint Paul.
The event marks the sesquicentennial of an
earlier expedition, the 1854 steamboat jour-
ney of 1,200 people from Rock Island to
Saint Paul. The excursionists, one of whom
was former President Millard Fillmore, were
considered by the *Chicago Tribune* to be "the
most brilliant ever assembled in the West,
statesmen, historians, diplomats, poets, and
the best editorial talent in the country."

As a result of the publicity generated by
the 1854 junket, millions of dollars were invested in the region and Minnesota was cat-
apulted into statehood. A century and a half
later, Mississippi River towns ranging from

Dubuque, Iowa, to Wabasha, Minnesota, have passed resolutions supporting the 2004 excursion. The Mississippi river — which urban visionary William Morish once described as "America's fourth coast" — is poised for rediscovery.

When the river towns were founded in the 19th century, the Mississippi meant everything to the mining, manufacturing, and milling industries, which depended on the river to transport raw materials and finished products. Today, the historic and cultural landscapes left behind by these industries are being integrated with restored upland and floodplain forests. The excursionists of 2004 will not see a purely "native" river valley in Saint Paul. What they will see is the beauty of a working river where shipping and service industries thrive, thousands of people live, and the complex river ecology that existed in President Fillmore's time is coming back to life.

CHAPTER 39

SAN FRANCISCO TRANSFORMS INDUSTRIAL SITE INTO OPEN SPACE AND TRAILS

Jodie Carter

The Mission Bay Redevelopment

Mission Bay in downtown San Francisco, Calif., is undergoing a 300-acre urban redevelopment that aims to create a thriving mixed use community with a master plan that includes more than 5 million square feet of commercial and industrial space, a 500-room hotel, 850,000 square feet of retail space and 49 acres of parks and recreational areas, including a newly constructed 3.5-acre waterfront park that runs along Mission Creek.

The Catellus Development Corporation, a San Francisco–headquartered real estate investment trust, is developing Mission Bay on a former industrial site that sits on the city's waterfront, an area known as China Basin. The 300-acre area is being developed as a public-private partnership between Catellus and the master developer and majority property owner, under agreements with the San Francisco Redevelopment Agency and the city. Those agreements not only create new commercial space, but also provide public benefits, including new

housing and an open connected park system. Those agreements not only create new commercial space, but provide public benefits, including new housing.

Designs for Mission Bay began in the late '80s, with EDAW, Inc., a San Francisco based design, land planning and environmental analysis firm, creating the original master plan. Since then, several other firms (most recently Skidmore Owings & Merrill LLP) have contributed to new and revised master plans for the promising site. In 1999, EDAW's Jacinta McCann, principal designer, and Michael Cannon, senior designer, took over the Mission Creek Park design.

Construction on the Mission Bay development site began in 1999 with an estimated completion date of 2050. Considering that hefty timeline, to say that the development is forward-thinking is an understatement. The needs and wants of future users seem to have been considered in every detail from the construction of public facilities to infrastructure, including a state-of-the-art, all-fiber-optic network. Incorpo-

Originally published as "Making Room for the Long-Term Legacy of Mission Creek Park," *Landscape Architect and Specifier News*, Vol. 20, No. 3, March 2004. Published by Landscape Communications, Tustin, California. Reprinted with permission of the publisher.

rating these cutting-edge data infrastructures should make Mission Bay even more of a destination for the next generation of city-dwelling technology users.

The ambitious redevelopment is predicted to be an employment engine for San Francisco, eventually representing approximately five percent of the city's job base at full build-out, and promising 6,000 new residential condominiums and apartments to house the eager workers. Considering the projected growth of Mission Bay, the redevelopment could be the equivalent of an urban "field of dreams," promising that as Catellus builds, *they* will come; "they" meaning the projected community of 11,000 residents and 31,000 workers expected to inhabit the new space by its 2050 completion date.

Part of Mission Bay's draw is the new University of California San Francisco media and research campus; the largest biomedical university expansion in the country. The new campus, which is expected to employ 9,100 people within its 43-acre site, should also attract technology-based companies sure to find a prestigious home within the 300-acre Mission Bay development. More than 450,000 square feet of the $1.5 billion campus space has already been built and another 900,000 are under construction with an expected full build-out in 15 to 20 years.

Mission Creek Park

At the forefront of the Mission Bay redevelopment is Mission Creek Park, a 3.5-acre oasis of grass, trees, granite footpaths, benches and a café overlooking the San Francisco waterfront area called the Central Basin. The park represents the first installment of a 15-acre park connected to Mission Bay's network of smaller parks, greenbelts and biking and jogging trails. "The park is a very important first piece of the development of open space at Mission Bay because it functions as a gateway into the bay," says McCann. "It also shows the community the quality of the future park system planned at Mission Bay and should encourage future investment in the bay."

McCann and Cannon, who led the park's site design, began drawings in late 1999, on a fast track to complete the initial design concepts by mid–2000, with construction completed in the fall of 2003. "The city wanted to provide public open space before they began selling residential, because this area is on the edge of the city — there's not a lot down there; ball fields, parking lots and industrial sites," recounts Cannon.

Walking through the park today on a winding creek-side path flanked with flowing grasses and the soft bend of willows, it's hard to imagine the previous condition of the Mission Creek Channel. "This site was just horrible to begin with," avowed Cannon. "For years the creek had been a junkyard with old tires and beams and pieces of concrete sections and riprap along the creek — it was awful."

Transforming this former industrial site into a progressive waterfront park full of open space and a healthy ecological habitat meant taking advantage of the natural assets of the site. With this in mind, the landscape features passive recreational space oriented toward the creek, using materials and curving lines to create a soft natural interface with the restored creek edge.

The park's long-term mission, to create a sense of place for its future community, also provides one of its greatest landscape design challenges. "The park must be flexible enough to change as this development moves forward," says Cannon. To do this "we had to balance the needs of the developer, the redevelopment agency and the community."

The park is invaluable to the community because it plays a significant role in reestablishing the habitat and the ecology of the creek channel. McCann and Cannon's design of the park restored the creek edge to a more natural bank configuration by removing junk materials like broken asphalt and riprap, remnants of the site's industrial heritage. The site was regraded and planted with a mix of native plants suited to the tidal environment of the bay.

Finding the right plants for this environment was essential, so McCann and Cannon developed a plant palette in association with an ecologist who specialized in San Francisco's environment. The resulting mixture of plant material stabilized the creek, minimizing riprap.

Of course, the grading plan had to take into account these tidal inundations as well. "The channel has a difference in water height at high tide of about 12 feet," explains McCann. "We worked with an engineer to develop the grading plan, then the old concrete and other materials were removed. The bank was regraded and new riprap was brought in where the bank needed protection."

While the park undoubtedly has improved the ecological health of Mission Creek Channel, it also offers a refreshingly open scenic space within a densely populated urban environment. "It's where a business person or a resident can go for a breath of fresh air and momentary respite from the everyday world," offers McCann.

Michael Cannon echoes her sentiments, "What we set out to do was to design a park that could accommodate these uses; retail, commercial, and residential. We tried to not make the park too stuffy or too busy; to accommodate a range of passive recreation activities; to not presume too much — to be very flexible in the way it could be used."

The Major Design Elements

The Mission Creek Park offers trails that follow the creek, curved landscape steps that form a natural, outdoor amphitheater, a small glass pavilion and café for sipping cappuccino and an open lawn that rises with sweeping knolls.

TRAILS

Three park trails parallel Owens Street, which runs the length of the park. The two upper trails, one a sidewalk, the other a bike path, stretch like twin sidewalks flanking the street. Both upper trails are made of asphalt and are 12 feet wide. "The bike lane was dyed with a tan mix to set it apart from the sidewalk, making it look more park-like and less vehicular," noted Canon. The bike trail is an important part of the park's integration within the larger Mission Bay area because "it will connect, at future stages, to other bike paths that will extend through Mission Bay, connecting along the streets to parks and other development areas," states McCann.

The lower trail, made of decomposed granite, is a more informal walkway that allows visitors to get close to the water as it meanders along the renewed creek edge, swinging by the landscape steps and café. "We picked decomposed granite because we wanted to make it a more casual path and have it tie in with the more natural edge that we restored along the channel," noted McCann.

LANDSCAPE STEPS

To create a natural outdoor amphitheater, McCann and Cannon staggered three tiers of 75-foot-long curved concrete benches, embedding them as parallel arcs set into a small berm. "We wanted to create a space that could be ready for a performance or just a place for people to gather and sit and enjoy the view," says Cannon. "We didn't want anything too flashy, so we tucked the seats into the berm so they really felt like part of the park. It's a place where people can sit and have a view of the park, looking over the creek and into the San Francisco skyline."

These partially embedded lawn steps use concrete as a band for seating, with round fluorescent lights subtly recessed into each end of each step. The curved concrete adds a little industrial flair to the design, says Cannon.

GLASS PAVILION AND CAFÉ

The architecture firm of Tom Eliot Fisch collaborated closely with McCann and Cannon in the design of the park pavilion, a contemporary 1,000-square-foot glass, metal and block structure complete with indoor café, created as a "destination" for local residents. The glass walls of the transparent pavilion present a sanctuary from the elements on windy days while retaining a nice view over the creek and into the city skyline. Food services, restrooms and seating are offered inside the pavilion. Extending from the exterior pavilion, a paved, outdoor plaza offers seating underneath a canopy of Chinese tallow trees. Forward-thinking design is demonstrated in future plans (around 2009) to build a pedestrian bridge over Mission Creek, connecting the park plaza to residential areas on the northern side of the channel.

LAWN

Cannon and McCann came up with a creative way to maximize the lawn while working around a budget constraint. "We were going through the budgeting process and we couldn't get a playground, so we really wanted to create some playful mounds that kids could run around on. We built a cone shaped mound and a big, long, linear mound that kind of replicated what was underground — the buried underground channel," says Cannon. "We wanted to give reference to things emerging underneath the

ground — to call attention to the three-dimensional movement of the earth."

The east lawn enables visitors to sit on the lawn and overlook the creek and city skyline. The knolls also function to screen out the cars from the adjacent roadway. The lawn design functions as a passive recreational space, where visitors have ample open room to throw a Frisbee, read a book or just take in the view of the city skyline.

PLANTINGS

The concept behind the overall planting design was to "plant things in large masses to give a stronger feel to the park, punctuating it with a few specimen trees," states Cannon. Within that concept plantings were chosen with seasonal considerations in mind. "In San Francisco, even in winter, you can sit out on the terrace and the sun will be out; so we were conscious of selecting trees that looked good all year round." Punctuating the lawn, Chinese scholar trees will keep their beautiful structure throughout the winter months.

Evergreens like Indian laurel, Victorian box and cajeput tree offer year-round color while serving double duty, by screening out street noise as well. A few Yoshino flowering cherry trees near the meandering granite path complement the park with subtle color in spring. Because this can be a seasonally windy site, ornamental grasses like Mexican feather grass, maiden grass and big blue liriope bring movement to the landscape. Quick-growing Chinese tallow trees, standing in perfect groups near the glass pavilion, offer contrasting seasonal color, with leaves that turn red in the fall.

Along Owens Street, double rows of lemon-scented gum trees form a refreshing canopy for the bike path and sidewalk underneath. Coolibah trees (*Eucalyptus microtheca*), an evergreen from Australia, run nearest to Owens Street.

McCann and Cannon consulted with Wetland Research Associates to develop a palette of native plants to restore the direct edge of the channel. Yellow-twig, western and red-twig dogwoods along with several willows, including weeping willow, arroyo willow and corkscrew willow, were planted along the channel bank. This shoreline vegetation attracts birds seeking refuge in the foliage. Pilings placed in the channel are reminiscent of the industrial history of the site while providing a resting place for seagulls, as typically happens along waterfronts.

OUTDOOR AMENITIES

The park is scattered with numerous amenities, including urban benches, curved lines, a modern bike rack, trashcans, lights and signs. All the "furniture" at Mission Bay adheres to a modern European style. "All the architects got together and advised Catellus and came up with Mission Bay standards, which designated the theme of the park's amenities; stating the details of things like the color, texture and finish of sidewalks," recalls Cannon. "We just tried to simplify, simplify, simplify, and eventually we got down to what the core elements were. We had a rigorous review with the San Francisco Redevelopment Agency on the proposed standards for every bench and bike rack: Even the utility covers in the sidewalk — they were all thought through."

Complications

This was a fast-track project requiring extensive coordination between the agencies, the community and other stakeholders. McCann and Cannon had a window of five to six months to create design development and construction drawings — a very ambitious pace considering the level of co-

ordination needed between the city, engineering teams and the Catellus Development Corp. "It's a small park, but it was very complicated," asserts Cannon. There was an existing 7- by 7-foot boxed sewer line running underneath the ground that could not be disturbed. "We weren't sure of its precise depth. It was built in the 1930s, and we weren't sure how accurate the surveys were at that time." The channel location worked out perfectly in the end — it was buried deep enough to allow a smooth grade transition down to the channel.

The other complication, according to Cannon, was that the entire area is in a liquefaction zone. "Probably the biggest technical challenge was designing for settlement," states McCann. "Depending on the weight of materials, settlement happens at different rates. We had to make sure we could plan the plaza so that it could connect seamlessly to the pedestrian bridge — planned to cross over the channel at a future date — to make sure that the building would connect to the path with a safe relationship."

Completion of the First Phase

The first phase of the park was completed in October 2003. "There will be a second phase of the park, which will proceed when it's triggered by the development at Mission Bay," states McCann.

Overcoming a site's challenges on a fast track project of this complexity and importance is taxing, but the legacy this park will offer its future users will be worth it. "This was a fun project," says Cannon. "The client was really great — they wanted to make positive change and build a community."

CHAPTER 40

SAN JOSE, OTHER CITIES, INITIATE CORRIDOR PRESERVATION

Michael Davidson

To ask why a transportation corridor should be planned and preserved is like asking why planning should exist at all. Plans for transportation corridors have become as commonplace as those for neighborhoods and downtown districts. Today, rural jurisdictions such as Sheboygan County, Wisconsin, are as likely to undertake a major corridor study as nearby urban neighbors like Milwaukee.

Corridors are the gateways to and the connectors between our towns and cities. They preserve and protect our scenic landscape, support community image, manage traffic, help communities function effectively and efficiently, and generate business for commercial enterprise. More specifically, corridors benefit local governments by providing developers with a reliable canvas on which to create environmentally appropriate and conducive developments. Corridor preservation ultimately alleviates the confusion of developers and provides for more orderly land-use management. It can help relieve local planning departments of the headaches caused by unorganized development on fragmented transportation systems. Poorly designed corridors can destroy the landscape, exacerbate congestion, create safety risks, pollute the air, repel pedestrians, and stifle business productivity.

Corridor planning is more than just an attractive transportation concept; it is now mandatory under the Intermodal Surface Transportation Efficiency Act of 1991 (ISTEA). States and regional agencies are required to include corridor preservation in their long-range transportation strategies. Future thoroughfares that are believed to be in the public interest should be identified and equipped with an established protection plan.

With the recent enactment of the Transportation Equity Act for the 21st Century (TEA-21), the basic transportation and planning requirements specified under ISTEA remain in place. Metropolitan and statewide provisions concerning fiscal constraint, planning horizon, and public involvement will continue. Freight shippers and public transit users have been added to the list of specified stakeholders. The most

Originally published as "The Road to Be Traveled: Planning and Preserving Transportation Corridors," *PAS Memo*, July 1998. Published by the American Planning Association, 122 South Michigan Avenue, Suite 1600, Chicago, Illinois 60603-6107. Reprinted with permission of the publisher.

notable difference with the new legislation is the consolidation of 16 metropolitan and 23 statewide planning "factors" into seven general "areas." Each must be considered in both the metropolitan and statewide transportation plans. More information on TEA-21 can be found at

In 1996, the Federal Highway Administration (FHwA) released a two-volume study on corridor preservation: *Volume I, Corridor Preservation: Case Studies and Analysis Factors in Decision-Making*; and *Volume II, Corridor Preservation: Study of Legal and Institutional Barriers*. The study addresses corridor preservation as a planning and implementation strategy for transportation programs and provides a framework that states, metropolitan planning organizations, and local agencies can follow to build an understanding of the corridor preservation process and then use for the enhancement of local and regional transportation systems.

This chapter is based partly on the FHwA study in so far as it is an examination of the latest developments in corridor planning. Examples and case studies from other sources are also used to help define corridors, determine why preservation is important, identify risks, and lay out measures that are most useful for overcoming those risks.

What Is Corridor Preservation?

For most planners, corridor preservation involves managing development, access, landscaping, and signage along major arterial roads or limited access highways. It may also involve protecting and preserving views and open space along scenic highways. But before such practices occur, the land on which future transportation corridors are to be established needs to be identified, mapped, and protected from inconsistent development. The American Association of

Priority Checklist for Corridor Preservation

☑ **Importance of the Corridor:** Is the corridor needed to serve development patterns in the next 20 years?

☑ **Immediacy of Development:** Is the threat of development imminent? Will strategic parcels be lost if nothing is done?

☑ **Risk of Foreclosing Options:** If development does occur in the potential alignment, what corridor options will be foreclosed?

☑ **Opportunity to Prevent Loss of the Corridor:** Are planning tools available — other than outright acquisition of right of way — that can be employed to protect the corridor?

☑ **Strength of Local Government Support:** Will the affected communities do their fair share to help? Do they have the needed tools at their disposal?

State Highway and Transportation Officials (AASHTO) Task Force on Corridor Preservation defines corridor preservation as "a concept utilizing the coordinated application of various measures to obtain control of or otherwise protect the right-of-way for a planned transportation facility."

The FHwA study identifies the two types of corridors and the fundamental planning objective:

• Proposed corridors are those yet to be designed, but which state and regional agencies have determined to be needed in anticipation of future growth and development, and that they are considering in the preparation and adoption of long-range transportation plans.

• Existing corridors, for which capacity needs to be maintained, preserved, increased, and for which development adjacent to the corridor needs to be modified, or improved in some way (e.g., by addressing access management, development densities, landscaping, or other traditional corridor planning elements).

Planners Talk Corridors

At a November 1997 Chicago-area conference, "Successful Corridor Planning: From Concept to Implementation," cosponsored by the Northwest Municipal Conference and APA's Chicago Metro Section, municipal planners discussed the obstacles encountered with corridor planning and preservation. Of most concern to conference participants were issues related to traffic flow, including safety, efficiency, and access; policy decisions about intergovernmental agreements and municipal ordinances supporting the corridor plan; aesthetic issues relating to signage, landscaping, gateway planning, and lighting; and the impacts of various land-use decisions on the corridor. For example, land-uses adjacent to a roadway corridor, which may differ in character and transportation need, are an important consideration when labeling a corridor commercial, residential, industrial, or otherwise.

A Bump in the Corridor

Planners face many challenges in preserving corridors. Daniel Mandelker, Stamper Professor of Law at Washington University in St. Louis and attorney Brian Blaesser of Robinson and Cole in Hartford — authors of Volume II of the FHwA study — list inadequate regulations, funding limitations, inadequate acquisition and condemnation powers, environmental requirements, and property rights as the legal and institutional barriers to corridor preservation facing jurisdictions today.

Mandelker and Blaesser offer several suggestions for overcoming such barriers:

- Adjusting to intergovernmental conflict is necessary because federal, state, and local government corridor preservation roles and responsibilities often conflict or overlap with one another.
- Effective corridor preservation requires local governments to adopt sophisticated development controls and procedures for administration (e.g., density transfers, transferable development rights, and development exactions).
- Local governments should be careful not to assume all of the management responsibilities.
- Local governments must be willing to cooperate with private developers on land dedications and other contributions to avoid takings challenges.
- Environmental clearances should be planned for and timed in such a way as to not jeopardize the corridor preservation measures, preferably at the mapping stage.
- Uncertainties that exist in the implementation of corridor preservation, such as responsibilities of each level of government, environmental clearances, and legal risks of takings, should be acknowledged up front so measures can be taken to minimize the consequences of these uncertainties.
- The sophistication in the design of corridor programs requires that staff, especially at the local level, are aware of the takings clause and are fluent in the use of land regulation and acquisition powers.
- Insufficiencies in the federal legislation supporting transportation programs may demand changes in program requirements and policies.
- An alternative strategy needs to be considered in the event that corridor preservation is blocked by legal constraints or the failure of governments to cooperate.

The corridor preservation programs highlighted in the study begin in advance of acquisition. This distinguishes them from standard right-of-way protection measures, which are typically taken through acquisition and regulation before the commencement of project construction, in that they occur in advance of acquisition.

To Build a Corridor

What processes shape a successful corridor planning or preservation strategy? Jurisdictions must first decide what type of corridor planning is necessary. Measures to determine this are numerous. For example, chaotic strip commercial development, problems with traffic access and management, and capacity deficiencies are all potential indicators that change is needed. For future corridors, periodic traffic projections, analyses of future systems deficiencies, population and economic projections, projected growth patterns and location, major development proposals, project approvals, and construction permits along the corridor are measures of planning and preservation needs for future corridors.

Mandelker and Blaesser divide corridor planning measures into four fundamental categories: local land-use planning and development controls, corridor mapping laws, access management, and land acquisition.

Local land-use planning and development controls. Land-use and development controls for corridor preservation are typically managed at the local level rather than by the state or federal governments. Ideally, a community's comprehensive plan and zoning ordinance will both guide corridor development and be the foundation for land-use regulation.

The transportation element of a local comprehensive plan can be key in the corridor preservation process because the plan is the formal document for identifying transportation corridors that require preservation, and local development controls used

for corridor preservation are based on the plan. The zoning ordinance, as the chief tool for implementing the comprehensive plan, can be used to maintain a level of land-use intensity that is compatible with corridor designation. Montgomery County, Maryland, zones corridor lands for the least intensive use that is found in adjacent zones, but allows for interim uses in the zone that can be removed when the roadway is eventually developed.

Another land preservation technique, density transfers, is employed by local governments to protect development from obstructing corridor land. Planners in San Jose, California, used density transfers to "shift" permitted housing densities to sites outside of the corridor in order to keep the land needed for the proposed expressway free of development until the municipality could acquire the property. Lacking the funds for immediate acquisition, the city thought it imperative to work closely with developers whose projects might have threatened development of the corridor.

Density bonuses were part of a 1980s strategy to preserve the Olive Boulevard corridor in Creve Coeur, Missouri. Site consolidations were taken in exchange for the density bonuses. Planners approved specific high-traffic businesses, such as service stations and restaurants, only when they were included as part of a planned development that was three acres or larger.

Interim land uses are often allowed along corridor properties to discourage potentially long-term developments and save the land for future corridor use. The West Valley Corridor near Salt Lake City remained protected for more than 10 years before the corridor was completed. Local jurisdictions arranged deals with developers, allowing them to place particular — but removable — interim uses on the properties around the corridor. West Valley City even gave tax breaks to property owners who retained agricultural uses.

San Jose planners encouraged such interim uses as ground-level parking garages, storage areas, golf driving ranges, and nurseries until public funds could be acquired and corridor planning could proceed. Fortunately, this measure was not challenged by local developers. Officials claimed that the need for the corridor was strong enough to dissuade legal action. The corridor's current success as a contiguous system of roadway and light rail is largely attributed to the local government's cooperation with developers.

Overlay zoning is a technique that planners have incorporated into planning strategies for existing corridors around the county. In the 1980s, in Hilton Head, South Carolina, the aesthetic character of the resort community was threatened by development pressures. This prompted local officials to implement a corridor overlay district to protect Hilton Head's primary arterials from visual decay. The overlay district, which had statutory support from the state, was incorporated into the Hilton Head comprehensive plan. The plan encouraged viewshed protection — classifying them as natural, scenic, or rural — and set forth policies for signage and community gateways. Design review was also established as part of the comprehensive plan.

Rigorous design controls, such as those in Hilton Head, are not always necessary. Creve Coeur alleviated some of the design burdens simply by requiring parking lots to be sited behind buildings. The city implemented other land-use controls along its corridor, including the conversion of single-family residences to office space in a specific section. Standards for this area include "appropriate" signage, parking in the rear, and efforts to retain the residential character of the structures.

Land-use controls in Naples, Florida, are geared toward preserving the area's two largely natural corridors rather than retrofitting sections through new sign requirements or parking changes. Preventative

measures were taken to preserve the corridor's open space and historic landscapes. On developed sections, strict buffering is required to conceal walls that line the perimeter of the corridors.

When preservation is lost, retrofitting can occur to reclaim previous land. A section of the Phalen Boulevard Corridor, in St. Paul, Minnesota, is undergoing a $4.2 million restoration of wetlands and a lake on the site of a failed shopping center. The poor performance of the 200,000-square-foot mall, its status as an environmental hazard, and an ongoing neighborhood revitalization effort made the property a natural choice for restoration.

Corridor Mapping. Mapping is a valuable tool that provides visual conceptualization of corridor land development. Stakeholders, including transportation agencies, local planners, and private developers, use the maps to plan for land uses on parcels of property adjacent to the corridor.

Mapping allows for predictability of land uses and permits jurisdictions to reserve vacant parcels of property for later taking under eminent domain. Once a map is adopted, the local government has the right to prohibit development within the specified land area. These measures prevent costly repurchasing of developed land and minimize the number of developed properties that have to be moved. According to Mandelker and Blaesser, state legislation authorizing the use of mapping in corridor preservation is essential. A model state corridor mapping act has been developed by APA.

Access Management. In the context of corridor preservation, access management means protecting the capacity of existing routes and systems by controlling access rights from adjacent properties (e.g., limiting curb cuts). Although its use for the purposes of corridor preservation is relatively new, it can play a key role in managing capacity and preventative maintenance for transportation systems. If done properly, it may even alleviate the need for the construction of new roadways.

Access management programs are managed by the state. States classify highways according to their access needs and set standards for the intervals at which access will be allowed (e.g., one access point per mile). Developers and property owners are required to apply for a permit to construct an access point from their property to the roadway. Coordination between the state and local governments is essential because access management can have a major effect on local land-use planning.

Aside from corridor preservation, access management is more commonly used to meet goals of improving traffic flow and safety by removing raised medians, street widening, adding turn lanes, better traffic signal coordination, and traffic incident management.

Acquisition. Acquiring land for public ownership is important to corridor planning and preservation because it protects corridor property from development, minimizes land costs, and helps to prevent a taking of property. Land for corridors is most often obtainable through voluntary agreement with the owner. However, property occasionally is acquired through involuntary measures.

Mandelker and Blaesser suggest that corridor planners consider several factors during the land acquisition process. Among these considerations are the legal, financial, and administrative roles played by federal, state, and local governments. Corridor stakeholders need to be aware of the acquisition powers held by each level of government, as well as the limitations they bring to the process.

Land acquisition can arouse a complex, but solvable, set of problems, say Mandelker and Blaesser. For example, inadequate legal authority could be corrected if legislation favored advance acquisition in corridor programs. Poor management skills can be strengthened with guidance and training from the FHwA.

Also, funding requirements need to be established, approved, and provided by Congress with relative consistency for FHwA-approved advance acquisition programs. A state-mandated statute to support additional funding, perhaps through a special levy tax, for advance acquisition by state and local governments would arm the jurisdictions with more authority.

Corridor land acquisition is subject to intense and time-consuming environmental controls. Environmental review should be done at the corridor designation stage to shorten the lengthy environmental review process. FHwA needs to promote cooperation between agencies on issues such as environmental assessments, Clean Water Act requirements, and other federal standards.

The Tie That Binds

In Illinois, intergovernmental decision making about transportation issues is handled effectively because transportation councils have been established to facilitate successful corridor planning. The councils consist of governmental bodies that have entered into a legal partnership to address land use, transportation, environment, design, and boundary agreements for one of the six specified corridor projects in the northeastern region of the state. The councils are governed by the Intergovernmental Cooperation Act and the Local Land Resource Management Planning Act. This approach to corridor planning, which is promoted by the Northeastern Illinois Planning Commission (NIPC), ensures intergovernmental cooperation in the region.

Nowhere is the relationship between governmental entities nurtured more than in suburban Lake County, Illinois, north of Chicago. The Corridor Planning Council of Central Lake County (CPC) was established to provide a forum for coordinated planning of the Route 53 extension corridor.

According to a 1996 NIPC report, the planning goals of the member jurisdictions included discussions about overloading public facilities, possible environmental damage, and "destructive" intergovernmental competition. To meet these goals effectively and efficiently, and to define CPC's role in developing the environmental impact statement (EIS), the council collaborated with the Illinois Department of Transportation (IDOT). The agreement specified the transportation alternatives to be considered for the EIS, it established the steps in the EIS process that would eventually lead to the study results for the council to review, and it committed IDOT to consider the planning and environmental standards adopted by the council members.

As a protective planning measure, and one that could provide consistency to planning and development regulations around the corridor, the CPC developed its principles of agreement. The agreement consists of 24 standards that address relevant issues like stormwater management, arterial access, open space preservation, and the management of land-use conflicts. IDOT and the Illinois State Toll Highway Authority have agreed to honor the standards, and local jurisdictions have incorporated them into development ordinances.

The Corridor Planning Council of Central Lake County was the first such transportation endeavor in the region. Its success may serve as a model for similar corridor planning projects in northeastern Illinois.

Conclusion

Although the concept of planning and preserving transportation corridors is nearly two decades old, many systems have still fallen victim to political, economic, and land-use forces that have left transportation networks in disarray. ISTEA and TEA-21 may help this by essentially forcing jurisdictions to look at transportation systems. The good news is that the resources to tackle this complex issue have increased. There is a growing consciousness among drivers who want a safer, more efficient, and attractive commute to their destinations, which may make corridor planning a higher priority.

CHAPTER 41

SAN RAFAEL, OTHER CITIES, RESTORE URBAN PARKS WITH PRIVATE DONATIONS

Terra Hargett

When Charles McKinney was hired as the administrator of Riverside Park in New York in 1981, he was in charge of a once great park that had changed dramatically. When the 316-acre park was created in the 1870s, the four-mile stretch of land attracted residents from each of the communities along its border. Residents used the area to meet with friends, have picnics or play sports. Like many urban parks, it was a refuge from the bustling city. However, in the two decades before McKinney was hired, inadequate funding had left the Parks Department understaffed, and area residents rarely used park facilities, causing the park to deteriorate.

Situations like that of Riverside Park are all too common. Across the country, parks departments have been encouraged by local governments to concentrate on sports and recreation programming, leaving little money for maintenance or improvements for basic facilities in urban parks, says Kathy Madden, director of the Urban Parks Institute at the New York–based Project for Public Spaces (PPS).

In turn, residents stay away from the parks. Residents stop using a space for a variety of reasons, says the PPS publication "How to Turn a Place Around." According to the book, the space may be unused because residents feel that it is unsafe or simply because it does not have the facilities that the community needs.

To bring residents back to those spaces, many parks directors are using previously untapped resources. Riverside Park, for example, has undergone a dramatic restoration over the past 20 years. By partnering with Riverside Park Fund, a non-profit formed by concerned residents, McKinney has garnered financial and volunteer support from residents, who have led the way in improving facilities and increasing attendance at the park.

Like McKinney, many parks directors are finding it necessary to use unique partners or methods to revitalize urban parks. They are asking residents to offer ideas, volunteer time or even contribute funds. In several cities, parks departments have been supported by mayors and other city officials

Originally published as "Restoring Urban Parks: New Life in Old Spaces," *American City & County*, Vol. 116, No. 14, September 2001. Published by PRIMEDIA Business Magazines & Media Inc, Atlanta, Georgia. Reprinted with permission of the publisher.

who have led the revitalization effort by connecting city departments, school districts and businesses to revitalize deteriorated urban parks.

See and Say

When faced with the task of improving deteriorated parks, parks directors must determine if the parks are meeting the needs of their communities. According to "How to Turn a Place Around," observing how the parks are used is the first step in revitalizing a park.

When McKinney and his staff began evaluating Riverside Park, they examined park use, condition and design history, and interviewed park users. While assessing the park, the staff found that many facilities were not being used frequently or correctly.

"When we saw any facility that was not being used, we looked at unmet demand. We had people playing soccer on lawns because there were no soccer facilities, kids skateboarding on benches and people using other areas improperly," McKinney says.

After identifying unused areas, park staff worked to improve them. For example, one area of the park had been devoted to square dancing, but, since that activity had declined in popularity, the park staff replaced the existing dance floor with a sand volleyball court that is now frequently used by residents.

Assessing parks also means asking the communities what they need from the areas. "The important starting point in developing a concept for any public space is to identify the talents and assets within the community. In any community, there are people who can provide a historical perspective, valuable insights into how the area functions, and an understanding of the critical issues and what is meaningful to people," according to "How to Turn a Place Around."

As New York did with Riverside Park,

San Rafael, Calif., relied on community input to revive deteriorating Albert Park. "[The park] is in the central downtown area, and surrounding it is one of the oldest parts of the city. In the mid–1990s [the park] had fallen into disuse and become a hangout for transients. Facilities were not attractive to the community, and [residents] stopped visiting the park," says Carlene McCart, director of the city's Community Service Department.

Sharon McNamee, then director of the park, spearheaded an effort to get resident input. "We found partners and community groups that were interested in components of the new master plan," McCart says. "We hired a consultant and had a series of public meetings. We heard a lot of different ideas, which were reviewed by the Parks and Recreation Commission."

Several unique facilities sprang from residents' requests. The park bordered an area of town populated by the descendants of Italian immigrants who settled the city, and San Rafael had a sister city in Italy. To reflect those ties, residents wanted the park to include Italian bocce courts and a formal Italian garden.

The city provided seed money to begin construction of the courts, and the Marin County Bocce Federation was formed to help raise additional money. Six bocce courts were built in a brick patio area, with a wheelchair-accessible building providing a public restroom and kitchen, and an administrative office for the federation. The courts attract between 400 and 600 people a week to the park.

Howdy Parkner

In addition to observing park use and asking what communities need in their parks, parks departments should consider partnering with other groups to help with the revitalization effort, Madden says. Residents in many communities have formed non-profit organizations dedicated to revitalizing parks. In New York, the groups range "from unstructured friends groups that [clean up] empty lots to highly structured, highly funded organizations, such as the Central Park Conservancy," Madden says.

One of those groups, the Riverside Park Fund, was started to perform a variety of functions. "The initial desire to form the organization came because people felt a great sense of caring and were very concerned about [the park's] condition," says James Dowell, executive director of the Riverside Park Fund. "The fund was founded to, first of all, show public officials that this was a park that was important to people; to go in as volunteers and do something for the park; to raise private money to leverage public funds; and to accelerate improvement."

McKinney welcomed the help because the park's budget had been decreasing each year since he was hired. "Six hundred thousand [dollars] became $500,000, and that became $400,000, so we had to build on our other strength, which was community involvement," he explains. "The Riverside Park Fund [is composed of] positive helpers who work to raise public funds and to increase volunteerism."

The fund boasts 4,000 member families who make yearly contributions. "The vast majority [of members] are people who live within six blocks of the park and use it on a regular basis," Dowell says. The Riverside Park Fund has become an umbrella organization, supporting the park's playground and tennis associations, among other subgroups.

In addition to financial support from residents and area businesses, the fund has culled a workforce from the community through a program called "Adopt the Park." The program lets residents adopt a section of the park that is important to them, such as a garden, playground or tennis court.

"Most people in the area don't have backyards, but they may have an urge to cultivate, so we let them adopt gardens," McKinney says.

"Some people tell me that [gardening in the park] is the only thing that keeps them sane," Dowell says.

Like the Riverside Park Fund, the resident-led Albert Park Renovation Committee in San Rafael worked with city staff to identify what park facilities would help the community, who would use the park and what funding methods were available. "Without [the partnership, the park] wouldn't be where it is today," McCart says. "If the city had to fund improvements, it would have taken a long time to get where we are today. By parceling out our master plan and phasing it in, working with one non-profit at a time, it has moved us closer to completion."

Official Seal of Approval

In addition to forming partnerships with resident groups, parks directors can try enlisting the help of mayors or other local government officials who can pull departments together to revitalize deteriorated public areas. "Mayors are realizing that parks need to be defined more broadly and that they aren't just for recreation," Madden says. "Park-type improvement — such as taking little intersections that have traffic islands and turning them into mini-parks — give value to these cities and urban areas. Mayors have taken on the task of improving the city's public spaces so that the definition of parks evolves to include public space."

For example, Chicago parks have gotten a major facelift with the help of Mayor Richard Daley, who has made it a goal to live up to the city's motto, *urbs in orto*, or city in a garden. Daley has brought the Chicago Park District, Chicago Public Schools, as well as other departments together to "green" the city. "No [one] city department is concerned exclusively with quality of life and attractive public spaces," Daley said at a PPS conference last July. "So all of them have to be. And it's the mayor's responsibility to keep them on the same page."

Chicago's Campus Park Program tears up asphalt lots at city schools and replaces them with grass and trees. So far, the city has created 80 campus parks, which added 200 acres of park area to the city, and 20 more parks are planned for completion next spring. Another initiative, the Neighbor Space Program, pulls together several departments to turn tax-delinquent lots and river edges into small parks and gardens. The program has acquired 21 acres of underused property and converted them into 72 community gardens and parks.

Other city officials also are taking charge of their community's parks. In Philadelphia, Malcolm X Memorial Park suffered from vandalism and drug activity, and residents of the 3rd District had had enough. A non-profit group, Friends of Malcolm X Memorial Park, contacted Councilwoman Jannie Blackwell with its concerns. Blackwell made revitalizing the park an official project of her office, encouraging partnerships with the Children's Hospital of Philadelphia, as well as city departments and area businesses. "It was really a neighborhood venture," Blackwell says. "My job was to be in touch with all of the [organizations]."

Now, the park has chess tables, playgrounds and basketball courts, and it has become a regular gathering place for the community. "It is a total change from what it was," Blackwell says.

Whether through observation, community meetings or partnerships, parks directors have several tools to aid in park revitalization. "Form partnerships with other institutions, like cultural institutions, planning departments or whoever would be involved in parks in [your] city," Madden advises. "[Parks departments should] view themselves more holistically as the facilitators creating a city's public space. They need to form partnerships and to try, in a sense, to market parks as the glue that holds a city together, as the thing that makes a city more livable and improves the quality of life."

CHAPTER 42

SEATTLE, OTHER CITIES, ENCOURAGE DEVELOPMENT OF "GREEN" BUILDINGS

Ellen Perlman

Hardy alpine plants — species that thrive in the extreme temperatures and poor soil of rocky mountainsides — are alive and well and growing in an unexpected place: the rooftop of a three-story commercial building in Portland, Oregon.

It's a nice aesthetic touch for tenants working in a renovated warehouse that's located in an industrial area near the Willamette River. But that's not why the developer hauled alpine flora to the site. Rather, it's because Portland provides incentives to prod private-sector builders into developing "green" buildings. In this case, the vegetative rooftop is an environmental plus. The plants and soil catch the rainwater and hold it longer than a regular rooftop does. When the rainwater finally flows off the roof, it's cleaner — it hasn't picked up pollutants from the asphalt of a more traditional roof — and it doesn't gush with high velocity into stormwater drains, along with water from streets and sidewalks. The flora-planted roof also lowers energy costs over the life of the building. The plants protect the roof from damaging ultraviolet light and temperature extremes, reducing heating and cooling needs.

The ecoroof, or vegetative roof, is not all that makes this century-old brick structure a "green" office building. There are also energy-saving lights and skylights as well as ample parking spots for bicycles. In addition, during the renovation of the building, more than 95 percent of the brick, timber and other original warehouse materials were either reused or recycled. In short, the building is green because it has less of an adverse impact on the environment, conserves more resources and provides healthier indoor working conditions than a conventional building.

Portland's not alone in pushing the construction of environmentally sensitive buildings. The movement is coming of age in several major cities around the country, although evidence of progress is slow to surface. Building projects take many years from conception to completion, so while green-building policies are in place — many states and localities passed green-building ordinances a year or two ago — and green-building plans are on the drawing boards, only a few projects are up and functioning.

States and localities have taken two ap-

Originally published as "A Tree Grows Through It," *Governing*, Vol. 15, No. 4, January 2002. Published by Congressional Quarterly Inc., Washington, D.C. Reprinted with permission of the publisher.

proaches to pushing "green" buildings. One is to lead by example by implementing policies that call for their own agencies and departments to meet specified green standards when building new facilities. This past spring, for example, Maryland Governor Parris Glendening signed an executive order mandating that all new state facilities meet certain green criteria. One of those requirements, for instance, calls for having at least 6 percent of the energy used to run new state buildings come from renewable sources, such as solar panels or wind turbines.

The other tack — the one Portland is taking — is to push the private sector to build green. In part, Portland made the decision based on where development activity was greatest. The city itself didn't have many municipal buildings on the drawing board. The city has a policy for new municipal facilities to meet green-building criteria — and buildings such as a new control center for wastewater treatment will be green. But as Rob Bennett, manager of the Green Building Division of the Office of Sustainable Development, put it, "when we reviewed how the program should be developed, it was clear the private sector was where the building was going on."

Seattle used similar reasoning to come to the opposite conclusion. At the time it adopted its green-building policy, the city was undergoing the biggest municipal building boom since the Great Fire of 1899. With the local government itself adding many new facilities to the cityscape, it made sense to be the trailblazer on building green.

It's a course of action that many are following and one that dovetails with the private-sector approach. The idea is that by diving in first, Seattle hopes to persuade the private sector to follow its lead. "What we're seeing in most local governments and states is they're trying to encourage green building by setting an example first," says Peter Templeton, a program manager with the U.S. Green Building Council, a coalition of business groups working to promote green building.

Governments also push green criteria in their own building plans for another reason: long-term costs. Although the initial upfront investment is higher, it is less expensive in the long run to own and operate an energy-efficient building. And, as governments move forward and set a positive example, the price for materials and equipment could fall. "If technologies such as photovoltaic panels for solar energy and fuel-cell technology gain acceptance as mainstream, costs come down," Templeton says.

The features of green buildings are many and varied. Designers look at positioning the buildings to take advantage of the sun and natural lighting, but they also take care to avoid flooding the interior with sunlight during the hottest part of a summer day. Builders use non-toxic adhesives in laying carpets and other flooring so indoor air quality is not compromised. They load up on insulation to keep energy costs lower throughout the life of the building. And they use such resource-saving devices as automatic faucets in restrooms. These faucets can save about 50 percent of water use in office buildings since regular faucets run unnecessarily while people soap their hands.

There are other ideas. A plan for a green building in Arlington County, Virginia, proposes to collect rainwater from the roof and use it for landscaping and for flushing toilets so potable water isn't wasted. The developer also plans to contract with a local manufacturer so that the materials for the building don't have to be transported long distances, another energy saver.

Since the upfront costs of building green tend to be higher than those of constructing a conventional building — not only are the prices for materials often higher but there are additional costs due to the involvement of extra design teams and engineers who specialize in building green — developers aren't always keen to take on such projects. So several states are trying to entice private companies to build green by offering monetary, tax and density incentives that can turn the green-building idea into a more appealing business proposition. Last year, for instance, Maryland approved $25 million for 10 years' worth of green-building tax credits, effective July 1, 2002. A similar tax credit was approved in New York.

The city of Portland's program is called "G-Rated Buildings Suitable for All" and was approved a year ago. "The heart of the effort is to offer people incentives to get started," says Mike O'Brien, a green-building specialist in the Office of Sustainable Development. The city promises to provide leadership and guidance to encourage green-building practices in private-sector development.

Some of that encouragement comes in the form of cash. Builders can get $15,000 for meeting a minimum level of green-building criteria, as defined by the U.S. Green Building Council, and $20,000 for a higher level. The money cannot be used for materials. It is designated for soft costs, such as waste-management consulting or learning from designers how to build green.

There are lesser amounts available for developers whose buildings are too small to qualify for the full amount or who are remodeling rather than starting from scratch. The city hopes the money can get builders who have been wary of the "green" idea to come around. "It's partly a psychological thing, fear of the unknown," O'Brien says of the reason developers drag their feet. "They haven't dealt with it before. The money can cause someone to say, 'Let's give it a shot.'"

The shot was heard around the city. Within a few weeks of announcing the program, the city had allocated all of the money appropriated for the program, with $260,000 going to 13 different building projects. Portland also is gathering technical expertise and information about green buildings and holding workshops and training for the building industry. And it is working on resolving code and other regulatory issues that conflict with green-building practices and on expanding market demand by educating residents and businesses.

Seattle, on the other hand, is spending a huge amount of its capital budget on building municipal facilities, which fall under a green-building policy adopted in February 2000. It says that all capital-improvement projects over 5,000 square feet must be built to a certain green standard, called the silver level by the standards-setter, the U.S. Green Building Council.

Seattle has 12 green-building projects in the design or construction phase, including a new city hall, a justice center, which will have a vegetative roof, and a library—all within a few blocks in the downtown. In all, 2.7 million square feet is going green. "It's a way we can provide leadership to the private sector," says Lucia Athens, manager of the Sustainable Building Program. "We can get projects on the ground that people can look at." When the buildings are up and running, Seattle will be the largest owner of certified green buildings in the country—at least for the time being.

All of which pleases Athens, who sees merits beyond the usual virtues of green buildings. Creating a healthier, more pleasing work environment, she suggests, can increase employee retention. What's more, the local salmon will benefit as well. There is a fish run that courses through the city. Improving water quality and reducing the peak flows from storm runoff will help protect the salmon's habitat.

Like Portland, Seattle is offering up to $20,000 to a commercial-sector project to pay for soft costs associated with green building. The city also is looking to expand its building program to the affordable-housing sector and is considering a design resource center that would be a one-stop shop for information and technical assistance.

But some of the barriers to green buildings go beyond expertise. When Portland's green-buildings experts sat down with developers, they found that builders who wanted to put up an ecoroof, for instance, were not able to find a contractor who was willing to do both the roof membrane and the landscaping. When developers have to hire an extra contractor to do the jobs separately, it makes the project more complicated. That's where government incentives play a role: They can help fight the developers' tendencies to walk away from green projects.

Arlington County, Virginia, has what may be a unique program for keeping developers interested. It doesn't offer tax incentives but allows for more density if builders meet the silver-level standard for green buildings. Extra density, which can translate into more tenants, is a big selling point for some companies. The larger rent roll can offset the higher upfront costs of building green.

That comes into play for a company that builds what are known as "merchant" buildings. This is when the developer builds the building, leases space to tenants and then sells the building to an insurance company or real estate investment trust. The developer does not experience energy savings over the life of the building, and may have difficulty selling the project because it was more expensive to build that a standard one. But if the building has a higher density than would otherwise have been allowed, the project can make economic sense for the developer.

So far, one builder in Arlington County has applied for the program, which sunsets in three years. The Navy League is building a 200,000-square-foot commercial project with retail and office space. The project will be allowed 5 percent of additional space if it meets the green-building standards the county has set. The county hopes more builders will apply for the program so it will have good data to analyze after three years to find out if green building is better in the long run.

But just as important, the community needs to gain a better understanding of just what green buildings are. There have been some misconceptions that green buildings are noticeably different. "We want to build buildings but not have them be weird," says Joan Kelsch, a county environmental planner. "It's not, 'I work in that building made of recycled tires,' but 'I work in this great building with great windows or good acoustics.' They are buildings that feel better but also have economic implications for the building owner."

CHAPTER 43

SEATTLE HIGHWAY IS DESIGNED TO PROTECT WILDLIFE

Elaine Robbins

Drive 53 miles east from Seattle, and you'll soon find yourself in the cool elevations of the Cascade Range, in a recreation area called Snoqualmie Pass.

Some 24,000 cars and trucks a day travel through the scenic mountain pass on Interstate 90, Washington's major east-west interstate, on their way to and from Seattle. To accommodate the growing traffic, the Washington Department of Transportation (DOT) plans to expand the highway on the eastern side of the pass from two lanes to four.

They know it will not be a standard-issue road expansion project. That's because Snoqualmie Pass is an important travel corridor not only for humans but also for deer, elk, pine martens, bobcats, coyotes, and other animals that must travel through the bottleneck of the mountain pass to reach larger wilderness areas to the north and south. The expansion of I-90 will create a formidable barrier for these animals.

"We identified this area as one where we wanted to focus on improving habitat connectivity," says Paul Wagner, the biol-

ogy program manager for the Washington State DOT. "We asked, 'What kind of design-related response do we need?'"

Transportation planners across the country are asking similar questions as they recognize the serious impact of highways on wildlife. About one million animals are killed on U.S. roads each day, according to the Humane Society. Just as worrisome to wildlife biologists are that large animals often avoid roads altogether, making the nation's four million miles of roads a major contributor to the problem of habitat fragmentation.

Harvard landscape ecologist Richard T. T. Forman, author of *Road Ecology*, estimates that while roads cover just one percent of the U.S. landscape, their ecological impact is actually close to 20 percent. But transportation planners and wildlife biologists in the U.S. and in Europe, Canada, and Australia are sharing what they learn in the search for solutions. Employing a toolkit that includes wildlife crossing structures and statewide habitat connectivity plans, they hope to increase the wildlife "permeabil-

Originally published as "No More Road Kill," *Planning*, Vol. 69, No. 2, February 2003. Published by the American Planning Association, 122 South Michigan Avenue, Suite 1600, Chicago, Illinois 60603-6107. Reprinted with permission of the publisher.

ity" of highways, particularly in sensitive areas.

"We're out of the era where we were building tons of roads, and we're into a phase of maintaining and improving existing roads," says Amanda Hardy, wildlife biologist at the Western Transportation Institute at Montana State University. "In the process, we're realizing that maybe we didn't do too well the first time around. We're thinking how we can improve our existing infrastructure the second time around."

Such activities have increased markedly since 1998, when federal TEA-21 funds became available for wildlife mitigation. Under TEA-21, 10 percent of the $217 billion in funding for surface transportation programs was allocated for 12 "enhancement" categories, among them wildlife crossings on new and existing roads as well as habitat connectivity measures. Transportation departments and conservation groups such as Defenders of Wildlife are lobbying for similar funding levels when TEA-21 comes up for reauthorization in fall 2003.

Wildlife Crossing Here

Although transportation experts use a variety of tools to design "green highways," the primary tool is the wildlife crossing structure. In the past 30 years, an estimated 100 to 200 underpasses and six overpasses have been built on highways in North America. When used in conjunction with roadside fencing, these "critter crossings" have proved effective in significantly reducing roadkill and providing safe passage for wildlife.

Banff National Park in Alberta, Canada, has become an international model of wildlife-crossing design. There, the Trans-Canada Highway, Canada's major east-west thoroughfare, crosses the national park in a place where grizzly bears, black bears, deer, elk, moose, wolves, coyotes, and bighorn sheep travel through the Bow River Valley. As early as the 1970s, animals attempting to cross the highway after dusk often were killed.

"We had an exceptionally high kill rate," says Bruce Leeson, senior environmental assessment scientist for Parks Canada. "We were getting in excess of 100 large animals a year killed on the highway."

As traffic increased in the late '70s, transportation planners proposed a highway expansion. The proposal provoked a debate. Why, critics asked, should Canada's flagship national park have a highway running through it in the first place? Eventually, the road expansion was approved, but only "with exceptional measures to protect wildlife and to solve the problems that already existed," says Leeson. "So here we were faced with this challenge and duty to solve this problem."

Over a 20-year period starting in the 1980s, Canada spent millions of dollars on 24 crossing structures along a 28-mile stretch of highway. In addition to 22 underpasses, two 164-foot-wide overpasses were built.

Planted with native trees and shrubbery, they provide cover for everything from black bears to chipmunks and an open view that grizzly bears, elk, and deer prefer. To keep wildlife off the highway and direct them to the crossings, engineers installed eight-foot-high fencing along both sides of the highway. In the last section of work, they buried a section of chain-link fence in the ground "to deal with the diggers — primarily wolves and coyotes," says Leeson. "We discovered that these animals would dig under the fence and get between the two fences and become even more vulnerable."

Since the crossings were installed, wildlife roadkill has been reduced by 80 percent — and as much as 96 percent for collisions involving ungulates (hooved animals such as deer and elk). But wildlife structure design is still an evolving science as experts learn what works and what doesn't. Wildlife biologists have found, for example, that black bears and mountain lions prefer underpasses, while grizzly bears, wolves, and ungulates like the openness of overpasses where they can get a wide view. All these animals tend to avoid structures that are too close to human activity such as hiking, biking, and horseback riding.

Bill Ruediger, the ecology program leader for highways and roads for the U.S. Forest Service, has seen the biggest failures on projects where state transportation departments take minimum mitigation steps to save money. "If we put $150,000 into a structure that doesn't work, I don't find that to be a cost-effective approach," he says. "It might cost $300,000 or $400,000 to design a structure for a big animal that is much more effective."

The location of a crossing structure is another factor critical to its success. Before making siting decisions, planners should research where wildlife prefer to cross, the location of wildlife connectivity zones, and future land-use build-out scenarios, say Scott Jackson and Curtice Griffin in *A Strategy for Mitigating Highway Impacts on Wildlife*. The authors suggest a few components of a practical, comprehensive approach:

- Avoid highway fencing and Jersey barriers when not used in association with wildlife passage structures.
- Use small (2' × 2') amphibian and reptile passages wherever roadways pass along the boundary between wetlands and uplands.
- Use oversized culverts and expanded bridges at stream crossings.
- Selectively use viaducts instead of bridges at important stream and rivers crossings.
- Use landscape-based analyses to identify "connectivity zones" where a variety of mitigation efforts can be concentrated to maintain ecosystem processes.
- Selectively use wildlife overpasses and large wildlife bridges with "connectivity zones."

- Monitor and maintain plans to ensure that mitigation systems continue to function over time and that knowledge gained from these projects can be used to further refine mitigation techniques.

Highways and Habitat

Transportation planners know that highway crossings alone won't help wildlife. "We need to manage adjacent lands appropriately," says Ruediger. "It means that you don't build a Wal-Mart on the other side of a highway crossing — or a condominium or a high-density bike path."

Habitat connectivity was a major goal of the Washington DOT in planning the Snoqualmie Pass highway project. "We studied where crossings would be most effective, where they would line up with connectivity land-management schemes," says Wagner. The DOT worked with the U.S. Forest Service, which had been consolidating its holdings in the Snoqualmie area by swapping land with Plum Creek Timber Company.

The Forest Service plans to manage this land as linkage areas for wildlife. When construction begins in another year or two, I-90 will include crossings aligned with wildlife corridors, fencing to direct wildlife to the crossings, and stream crossings that both remove barriers to fish passage and allow animals to travel along riparian areas.

"From the standpoint of planning, the issue of the surrounding land use is critical," says Wagner. "We don't want to end up in a place where transportation agencies are doing a lot of careful work and spending a lot of public money on these things when there's not the interest or long-term commitment to protecting corridors. That's why we felt like starting where we did made such sense."

The goal, according to Wagner, is to conduct environmental analyses earlier in the planning process. "Now what we're doing is earlier analysis for the 20-year transportation plan," he says. "Is the project in a wetland area? Is it in an area that's typical habitat for certain species, particularly endangered species? Is it within a buffer area of a stream that will be supporting listed salmon species?"

The Washington DOT plans to develop more partnerships with other government agencies as well as private organizations like land trusts — groups that purchase conservation easements on biologically significant lands. "We could fix a lot of the problems that exist with the highways if we had partnerships," says Wagner. "Ideally, you'd have all these players working off the same habitat connectivity plan."

Florida's Road Less Traveled

Florida is at the forefront of a movement to incorporate wildlife protection earlier in the planning process. With a booming population and a rich diversity of wildlife — including the endangered Florida panther and threatened black bear — Florida faces serious roadkill rates and habitat fragmentation challenges.

By all accounts, the Florida DOT has embraced the challenge. "We thought we needed to better implement the planning of transportation, land use, and environmental issues," says C. Leroy Irwin, the environmental manager in the planning office of the Florida DOT. "So we brought together the federal and state agencies and agreed to basically blow up our process and develop a new process that would work for all of us."

The result was the Efficient Transportation Decision Making (ETDM) process, developed in 2000 and set to be fully implemented in 2004. The new process calls for two screenings of environmental data that will automatically highlight potential wildlife problems before a project shows up on the drawing board. The first screening,

known as the planning screen, is conducted every three to five years during the development of the long-range transportation plan. At this stage, the DOT conducts an environmental analysis and sends it to 24 governmental agencies for review.

The second step, known as the programming screen, is run each year by the DOT for Florida's 25 metropolitan planning organizations on priority projects that are being considered for the five-year work program. "The programming screen provides more detailed information about the project," says Irwin. "Each agency has a responsibility to respond back to the MPO or the DOT. If the agency handles endangered species or habitat, they have the responsibility to tell us at that stage what the problems are."

Under the ETDM process, potential wildlife problems are resolved before a project can move forward. "If the need is great, then the project will move forward, but we can make a commitment at that time to building a wildlife crossing or do further study," he adds.

The ETDM process, which has been praised by conservation groups, has several advantages for DOTs as well as wildlife, according to Irwin. "Rather than being in a reactive mode, we're in a proactive mode," he says. "We can design the project *for* the environmental issues. It also gives us a much better funding scenario. We know what's got to be done, and what we can put more funding into."

A Road Map for the Future

From an ecological perspective, there is no such thing as a "green highway." That's why the first rule in transportation planning is to avoid building or expanding roads in sensitive ecological areas — and when unavoidable, to minimize their impact.

In an effort to more accurately target

the areas worth protecting and predict the impact of road projects on these areas, more DOTs and conservation groups are using a new tool: ecological mapping.

In Florida, the DOT contracted with the University of Florida's Landscape Ecology Program to develop a GIS tool that could be used to identify and set priorities for potential roadkill areas. The model allows them to look at everything from species distribution to land use on existing roads to use as a basis for future road project decisions. These road maps to the state's ecological resources provide the data that make the development of the new planning process possible.

In California, the Nature Conservancy and other conservation groups have done mapping to identify more than 300 different corridors used by wildlife in the state. The California Nature Conservancy, which shares this information with Caltrans and effected change in the agency's wildlife mitigation policy, lists the general advantages of these eco-maps:

- Avoid or minimize transportation impacts.
- Focus transportation enhancement and mitigation funding on high-priority landscapes.
- Encourage better land use.
- Leverage multi-site outcomes.

There are advantages for the transportation agencies as well:

- Enhanced project delivery and time and money savings.
- Shared biological or other resource data.
- Help with land acquisition.
- More environmentally responsible projects.
- Better environmental image.

Washington State's DOT developed a GIS modeling tool to evaluate multi-species, large-carnivore habitat connectivity in the region (Washington, Idaho, and British Columbia). The model is designed to help planners identify major highway segments that intersect habitat linkage areas — and to calculate landscape permeability ratings for specific areas.

This "big-picture" model includes data on land cover, roads and highways, population density and land ownership, topography, and hydrology. These maps have provided a tool for transportation planners to make better informed, long-range planning decisions.

Defenders of Wildlife, which has a Habitat and Highways campaign, recommends that planners in states that lack extensive mapping resources instead use their state biodiversity conservation plan as a tool for identifying high-priority areas for protection. (States must complete these plans by October 2005 in order to keep receiving state wildlife grants from the U.S. Department of the Interior.)

Another new tool is the "road-effect zone" maps designed by Richard Forman to help transportation planners identify the ecological effects of proposed roads, from the impact of traffic noise on birds to channelization of streams. Forman names several key priorities for transportation planners, including directing rural traffic to existing primary highways and avoiding the conversion of rural, secondary roads to medium- or high-traffic usage.

In Florida, where rural roads are rapidly giving way to suburbanization, State Road 46 is a roadkill hotspot in a state where more than 100 black bears have been killed each year over the last few years. The problem is particularly bad in November, when the bears are on the move around Ocala National Forest at dawn and dusk, searching for food as they build up fat stores for the winter. Residents and travelers head through the forest on their way to Orlando to the south or Daytona Beach to the east.

Salvation lies in a simple, dirt-floor culvert — a mere 24 feet wide and 47 feet long, planted with pines to direct bears to the entrance — where black bears, bobcats, gray foxes, and whitetail deer cross under the road and get to the other side.

CHAPTER 44

SILVER SPRING, OTHER CITIES, TURN OLD RAILROAD CORRIDORS INTO PUBLIC TRAILS

Terra Hargett

When transportation funds are mentioned, most community leaders think of building highways and interstates, but a growing number of cities and counties across the United States are setting a different trend. Residents are telling their legislators and city representatives that they want alternatives to concrete and congestion. Those communities are using abandoned rail corridors, which normally sit unused or are sold off in sections, to create trails. Railtrails can be used for bicycling, walking, in-line skating, cross-country skiing or horseback riding. Some rail-trails preserve historic landmarks, and others help preserve wildlife.

Rail-trails are not new, but since the 1980s the number of trails has increased because of federal and state legislation allowing for alternative transportation spending. According to Karen Stewart, director of communications at Washington, D.C.–based Rails to Trails Conservancy (RTC), more than 1,200 rail-trails, totaling about 11,000 miles of converted track, have been completed since the 1960s. The trails have been built in rural and urban areas alike,

using a variety of funding and construction methods.

ISTEA Refreshes Growth

Because transportation funds have traditionally been used to build highways and transportation systems, trail supporters have had a difficult time convincing some government officials to allocate funds for alternative transportation methods. The Intermodal Surface Transportation Efficiency Act (ISTEA), signed into law in 1991, has made it easier by giving state and local governments latitude in spending the money. Additionally, the legislation includes language mandating that recipients spend 10 percent of their surface transportation dollars on transportation enhancement activities. City transportation enhancement funds can be used to build trails as long as 20 percent of the project budget is raised locally.

Longleaf Trace Trail, a converted rail corridor that stretches 39 miles from Hattiesburg, Miss., to Prentiss, Miss., benefits from that provision. In 1994, two retired at-

Originally published as "Rail-Trails Gather Steam," *American City & County*, Vol. 116, No. 1, January 2001. Published by the Intertec Publishing Corporation, Atlanta, Georgia. Reprinted with permission of the publisher.

torneys, Stone Barefield of Hattiesburg and Bobby Garraway of Bassville, wanted to use federal funds to convert an abandoned Illinois Central rail line into a trail. The lawyers worked to pass a bill in the state legislature that would allow counties and cities in Mississippi to form recreational districts, which would qualify for ISTEA funding.

Supporters of the bill hoped that recreational districts would be able to raise the 20 percent of funds that were necessary to use ISTEA money for trail construction. After the bill was passed in 1994, several residents worked to encourage the formation of a recreational district between the four cities and three counties that ran along Longleaf Trace Trail.

James Moore, trail advocate and owner of a bike shop, became the lead spokesperson for forming a recreational district and building the trail. "The trail was a much needed addition to the area," Moore says. "We are not a very bike-friendly area. There are no bike lanes or trails. We have a state park, but, as far as getting into nature quickly, this met that need."

Moore traveled through the counties, giving speeches to civic and business organizations. From those organizations and other private entities, the group raised $160,000 before it approached cities and counties to ask them to form the recreation district.

The four cities and three counties along the rail line agreed to join the coalition and invest public funds in the venture. Each county agreed to contribute a total of a quarter of a mil for the trail. With the $160,000 already in hand, the counties' contributions brought the total amount to $520,000, giving the $2.5 million project the 20 percent in local funding it needed to use ISTEA funds.

The Mississippi Department of Transportation purchased the rail line from Illinois Central and leased the land to the recreation district. The trail, which opened on Labor Day 2000, took nearly two years to complete. Its opening brought a surge of tourism to the area.

"All of a sudden, towns with 300 and 1,200 people have new businesses," Moore says. "It was difficult, but in the end it was so worthwhile. When I go out there, I see kids and mothers with their children. It is a place where they feel safe. We have had nothing but positive feedback, and it has been very much worth the hard work."

Banking on the Right-of-Way

In many cases, railroads are supportive of rail-trails because they allow the rail corridor to remain intact should the railroad ever need it in the future. Railbanking, a process that grants a trail group temporary control of an abandoned corridor, has become a common practice since it was established through 1983 amendments to the National Trails System Act.

A railroad company may sell, donate or lease an inactive corridor to a trail agency that will assume taxes, legal liabilities and maintenance of the corridor. According to the act, the rail-banked lines will remain intact because they are treated as if they had not been abandoned. The Surface Transportation Board retains control of the railroad right-of-way.

Congress passed the act to protect the corridors for future rail lines, which would take precedence over the interim trails built on the corridors. Because of increased freight traffic, a few railroad companies have repossessed rail corridors that have been railbanked.

Georgia took advantage of railbanking when the state Department of Transportation paid $7 million for a 57-mile railbanked trail that runs through Cobb, Paulding and Polk counties. The counties partnered with the Georgia Department of Natural Resources, which leased the land on which the counties created a state trail.

"In the past, a railroad would abandon a corridor, and farmers would buy it piece by piece," says Ed McBrayer, executive director of Atlanta-based PATH, a non-profit organization that promotes greenways. "Suddenly, it is strips of land instead of a continuous corridor."

The counties created the Silver Comet Trail to preserve the corridor and to provide recreation resources for their residents. (The trail is named for the Seaboard Coast Line passenger train that operated in the corridor.) Construction began in 1993, and 37½ miles have been completed. Ultimately, the trail will reach Anniston, Ala.

Trail Controversy

Despite their popularity with preservationists and railroad companies, rail-trails have been known to spark conflict. Because valuable land is in question, with many groups and individuals claiming rights to the outcome of the land, controversy is inevitable.

When the B&O Railroad abandoned an 11½ mile corridor in 1985, many groups, including an historical society that wanted to preserve the rail line and another group that wanted to install a light-rail line, had plans for the unused corridor. The Coalition for Capital Crescent Trail in Silver Spring, Md., lobbied for a trail. The process was not easy.

Residents who lived near the rail line had expressed concern about traffic and crime if a trail were built. "Neighborhood communities tend to be nervous with anything they are not familiar with," says Wayne Phyillaier, president of the coalition. "The key is to get them on board, show them a vision and give them an opportunity to express their views and participate in the process."

The coalition took steps to garner support for the trail. Members visited local communities and civic associations to present their vision of the trail and showed 40 to 50 slides of other trails and pictures of the right-of-way in its current condition.

With the help of RTC and the Washington Area Bicyclist Association, the trail coalition lobbied the National Park Service and the Montgomery County government to build the trail. Convinced that the idea was worthwhile, Montgomery County purchased the railbanked corridor from Silver Spring to the D.C. line in 1988 for $10.5 million. The following year, a local businessman acquired the remaining land and leased it to the National Park Service, which purchased it in 1990.

Local utility Potomac Electric Power and Project Open Space, a non-profit organization in Montgomery County, joined other groups to provide 20 percent of the project budget; the county also received $867,000 in ISTEA funds. The Washington, D.C., section of the trail was constructed and is managed by the National Park Service.

Seven miles of the Capital Crescent Trail have been paved and completed. The trail connects two national park trails — the C & O Canal and the Rock Creek Park Trail. Because the trail also connects Washington, D.C., with its suburbs, commuters use it. "The trail is a good alternative to being stuck in the busy streets," Phyillaier says.

What happens to the remaining three miles is a hotly contested issue between those who want to extend the pedestrian/bike trail and those who want to install a light rail line. While officials are determining its fate, the stretch is serving as an interim trail.

Despite the conflict and hard work involved, communities that attempt rail-trail projects are rewarded for their hard work, Phyillaier says. "When we first built the trail, people were worried," he says. "Now, people have found that it is a great recreational asset."

Communities that want to preserve rail lines and provide additional recreation opportunities for their residents are continuing to build rail-trails; about 1,200 projects are currently under way. Although the trails require hard work and innovation, communities attest that the end result is well worth the effort.

Rails-to-Trails Resources

Rails to Trails Conservancy, Washington, D.C., offers information for communities interested in building rail-trails. Visit the organization's Web site (www.rail trails.org) to get information on existing trails; to obtain technical information and resources for building trails; or to obtain information about federal funds available for rail-trail development.

Additional articles about rail-trails can be found in American City & County's online archives at www.americancityand county.com.

CHAPTER 45

WEST DES MOINES TURNS FLOODPLAIN INTO REGIONAL PARK AND OPEN SPACE

Sally Ortgies and *Edwin Slattery*

A 770-acre former sand-and-gravel mine has been transformed into the crown jewel of West Des Moines, Iowa's parks program. It is now the site of Raccoon River Park.

Thanks to the vision of the West Des Moines Parks and Recreation Department and a cooperative effort with the Iowa Department of Natural Resources (IDNR), a variety of recreational opportunities are available to the residents of West Des Moines and to the nearly 500,000 residents of the Des Moines metropolitan area.

Years of planning, followed by a phased development program, have changed this large area that was once primarily disturbed land into a major leisure-time destination for softball, soccer, swimming, fishing, boating, hiking, bicycling, picnicking, nature study, special events, and relaxation.

The Setting

The park site, located in the floodplain of the Raccoon River and inside the city of West Des Moines's corporate boundaries, lies next to expanding West Des Moines neighborhoods and within minutes of downtown Des Moines. It is bounded by the Raccoon River and a levee on the south and east and by a railroad line along the north and west. Here, the river's meanderings have created rich deposits of sand and gravel in the bottomlands that have formed the park site.

Sand and gravel mining operations started on the site about 1950, ending in 1991. Long-term removal of the sand and gravel created a 250-acre lake and many smaller ponds and wetlands. Most other parts of the site have had their topsoil removed or have had their natural features altered in some way by moving or reshaping the soil. In this way, areas of higher ground have risen from the construction of haul roads, deposits of spoil material, levees, and processing stations.

Before development, open space — comprising a combination of water, landforms, and vegetation — was the dominant characteristic of the site. Mining activities

Originally published as "Underneath It All: Raccoon River Park," *Public Management*, Vol. 85, No. 3, April 2003. Published by the International City/County Management Association, Washington, D.C. Reprinted with permission of the publisher.

had left vegetated piles of overburden and excavated depressions that created extensive wetlands. The site was heavily vegetated with species normally present in highly disturbed areas.

About a dozen small, shallow, but permanent ponds and wetland areas are located on the site, with no clear pattern of drainage between or among them. Provisions for interconnecting these wet areas by culverts in order to promote free circulation of water within the lake system are included in the park development plan.

Along the edge of the park for more than two miles flows the Raccoon River, whose banks are steep in most places and range from four to 12 feet high. A levee was constructed by the mining company along the shoreline of the river to keep high river water from flooding the site, and though it has deteriorated in places, it still provides an excellent foundation for recreational trails.

As might have been expected on mining premises, there was little mature vegetation on the undeveloped site. Canopy-type trees were virtually absent, except along the river and in other isolated areas.

New growth like small trees and low-growing plants had occurred on the higher ground, along haul roads and spoil banks above the 10-year flood level. Other places featured scrub/shrub vegetation, providing extensive wildlife habitat. A marked absence of aquatic vegetation in the lake and ponds reflected the steepness of the bank, the depth of the water, and the lack of nutrients in the sterile sand bottom.

Waterfowl and deer have been the most frequently found inhabitants. Deer are substantial in their numbers and distributed over the entire park, as they have benefitted from sufficient cover and availability of browse (grazing vegetation).

Waterfowl and shore birds are the most conspicuous users of the ponds and lake. Blue heron, double-crested cormorants, and Canadian geese are evident, while mallards, teal, and wood ducks are also abundant. An ecological survey performed in the summer of 1989 by the IDNR reported 44 species of birds seen at the site.

Active Participants in the Development

By earlier arrangements, the IDNR had obtained ownership and responsibility for the lake and adjacent areas from the mining company. The department had conducted studies of the lake and its surroundings and concluded that a valuable recreational resource could be developed. IDNR, however, was unwilling to develop and manage this resource without the support and cooperation of other levels of government. It was at this time that West Des Moines decided to join forces with the state in developing the site.

Even though recreational facilities had shown significant growth in West Des Moines in recent years, demand for organized sports facilities and open space still outstripped supply. The West Des Moines Parks and Recreation Department recognized the potential for developing a major complex for a number of sporting events and general recreational activities. To help bring this potential to reality, the city had bought two tracts of land totaling 112 acres as far back as 1987.

In 1988, an agreement was signed by the city and the IDNR that formalized their common interest in acquiring, developing, and managing land in Raccoon River Park. This agreement recognized the potential public benefit of the park facilities and identified the separate and joint responsibilities of each public participant.

Master Plan

In 1991, to realize the dream of a major recreational facility, a master plan was completed by Stanley consultants to determine:

1. Recreational and reclamation activities appropriate to the site.

2. Circulation, utilities, and services necessary to support these activities.

3. Best sequence and order of site development.

A matching of the characteristics of the site with the recreational needs of the community uncovered some unusual and exciting opportunities for development. An awareness of site constraints, site opportunities, and community needs became the basis for generating a realistic set of goals for the project, which included:

- To develop recreational and educational facilities and opportunities for the residents of West Des Moines and its surroundings.
- To restore and reclaim land disturbed by sand and gravel excavation and make it into an attractive environment.
- To identify land uses and recreational activities compatible with the floodplain character of the site.
- To relate uses of Raccoon River Park with compatible and complementary facilities in nearby Brown's Woods and Walnut Woods, the linear Jordan Creek Park, and countywide greenbelts along rivers and streams.
- To achieve a design that could be developed in stages; would make maximum use of existing features; could be constructed within the financial limits of the project sponsors; could be operated and managed in a cost-effective manner; and would make an aesthetic and functional statement that this was a premier local and regional facility.

Recreational Plan

Among the first park components desired and addressed were soccer facilities. The soccer complex now is located in one of the previously undisturbed sections of the park, which had been pasture land. Because this area was already grassed and relatively flat, it was ideal for immediate soccer use and in fact was used for league play by the West Des Moines Soccer Club after construction of the park facilities.

Ultimately, this portion of the park will be graded by the soccer club to provide improved soccer fields, with the possibility of irrigation. Some of the fields may also be lighted. Adjacent to them are restrooms and a concession stand, with parking for 418 cars.

The softball-field complex contains five ASA–regulation softball fields, each with 10-foot-tall outfield fences 300 feet from home plate. Each field is automatically irrigated and uses a manufactured clay in parts of the infield to minimize rutting. Subdrains are found around the infields. High-mast lighting illuminates each field, with provisions to upgrade each field's lighting level to "tournament" standards. Each field has two dugouts equipped with drinking fountains, plus bleachers for the fans. In the center of the complex are buildings that house maintenance equipment, concessions, restrooms, equipment storage, tournament administration, and an umpire's lounge. Parking is available for 408 cars.

The 250-acre Blue Heron Lake offers high-quality boating and fishing opportunities. A double-lane boat ramp with a central courtesy pier allows boaters with trailers to enter and leave efficiently. Paved and lighted parking accommodates 46 vehicles with trailers. Boats on the lake must be operated at a no-wake speed, while certain areas are restricted to boats with electric motors only.

The beach was developed to offer a variety of waterside activities. With a developed shoreline of 750 feet and a dry sand area of more than two acres, the beach is ideal for "catching" tanning rays and summer breezes. A beach house is proposed that would house shower and changing facilities, administration, and concessions. Parking for 200 cars is available at this facility.

Substantial grading was required to construct the beach. The preexisting shoreline was steep, with nearly vertical banks in places. More than 37,000 cubic yards of earth was moved into the lake, so that the final beach slope, both above and below water, ranged from 5 to 6 percent. The mining operation had done a thorough job of removing the sand from the lake, leaving little sand for beach development. As a result, nearly 25,000 tons of specially graded sand had to be imported to build a two-foot-deep beach.

In the future, a boating concession will be developed that will rent canoes, sailboats, and paddleboats to park users. And eventually, fishing piers will extend from the shoreline into the lake. Combined with a paved walkway, these facilities will allow fishing access for the physically challenged.

Picnics and Much More

Innumerable sites along the lake can be used for picnicking. Acres of grass, combined with views of the lake, woods, or activities, give ample opportunity to spread out a blanket and relax. Picnic tables will be located throughout the park to provide additional picnicking opportunities. Three shelters have been built that are sized to accommodate groups of up to 200 people and are equipped with lights, electrical outlets, and grills. More shelters are planned.

This project has offered a unique opportunity to demonstrate wetlands management and to illustrate techniques for remaking disturbed and mined lands into high-quality wildlife environments. The presence of a hands-on laboratory with potential for demonstration projects in the midst of an urbanizing area will be a rare asset to the community.

The site provides easy access for students and teachers throughout the metropolitan area for nature study in the field. The Nature Lodge, with a naturalist on staff, is located next to the lake and adjacent to one of the parking lots to afford the physical resources necessary to advance nature study programs. The facility also contains space for community rentals.

A system of asphalt and aggregate-surfaced trails has been developed in the park, with a 3.2-mile loop trail running around the lake as its focus. Important to this trail system will be connections to regional bicycle paths at the Grand Avenue entrance and near the Jordan Creek greenway. Paved trails will be mostly 10 feet wide and will accommodate bicyclists, rollerbladers, and pedestrians.

Development Staging and Costs

The park master plan, which was written in July 1991, intended to guide the development of 770 acres of land from a raw state into a premier park that would serve the entire Des Moines metropolitan area. The scope of the improvements and the magnitude of the costs outlined in the plan have forced the adoption of a staged approach to construction of the park and facilities. This work began in 1994 and continues to this day.

In 1991, the estimated cost to construct the park was $11.6 million, an amount intended to cover the major funding requirements for a park, recreational facilities, and wildlife area that would be ready for public use. As more amenities have been added to the park, more detailed estimates and schedules have been developed as preliminary and final designs were planned and constructed.

As of this writing, more than $12 million has been spent. During the next 10 to 15 years, an additional $7 million is budgeted to develop new facilities and to bring the park site to full development.

Part III
The Future

CHAPTER 46

THE ECO-ECONOMIC
REVOLUTION IS HERE TO STAY

Lester R. Brown

Today's global economy has been shaped by market forces, not by the principles of ecology. Unfortunately, by failing to reflect the full costs of goods and services, the market provides misleading information to economic decision makers at all levels. This has created a distorted economy that is out of sync with the earth's ecosystem — an economy that is destroying its natural support systems.

An economy is sustainable only if it respects the principles of ecology. These principles are as real as those of aerodynamics. If an aircraft is to fly, it has to satisfy certain principles of thrust and lift. So, too, if an economy is to sustain progress, it must satisfy the basic principles of ecology. If it does not, it will decline and eventually collapse. There is no middle ground. An economy is either sustainable or it is not.

The market does not recognize basic ecological concepts of sustainable yield, nor does it respect the balances of nature. For example, it pays no attention to the growing imbalance between carbon emissions and nature's capacity to "fix" carbon, much less to the role of burning fossil fuels in creating the imbalance. For most economists, a rise in carbon dioxide levels is of little concern. For an ecologist, such a rise — driven by the use of fossil fuels — is a signal to shift to other energy sources in order to avoid rising temperatures, melting ice, and rising sea level.

An eco-economy would be one that satisfies our needs without jeopardizing the prospects of future generations to meet their needs. Creating such an economy is not a trivial undertaking; it is nothing less than an Environmental Revolution.

Ecology Over Economics

Ecologists understand the processes that support life on Earth. They understand the fundamental role of photosynthesis, the concept of sustainable yield, the role of nutrient cycles, the hydrological cycle, the sensitive role of climate, and the intricate relationship between the plant and animal kingdoms. They know that the earth's ecosystems supply services as well as goods and that the former are often more valuable than the latter.

A sustainable economy respects the sustainable yield of the ecosystems on which it depends: fisheries, forests, rangelands, and

Originally published as "The Eco-Economic Revolution: Getting the Market in Sync with Nature," *The Futurist*, Vol. 36, No. 2, March/April 2002. Used with permission of the World Future Society, 7910 Woodmont Avenue, Suite 450, Bethesda, MD 20814. Telephone: 301/656-8274; FAX: 301/951-0394; and homepage: http://www.wfs.org.

FIGURE 1
Today's Economy vs. Tomorrow's Eco-Economy

Today's Economy	*Eco-Economy*
Shaped by market forces.	Respects principles of ecology.
Unsustainable: Maximizes profit regardless of consequences to the ecosystem.	Sustainable: Respects carrying capacity of systems; e.g., does not exceed sustainable oceanic fish catch.
Disregards nature's services.	Recognizes ecosystems' natural services.
Consumes dwindling supply of fossil fuels.	Relies on renewable resources such as wind, solar, and geothermal energy.
Pollutes the environment and destabilizes climate.	Minimal pollution, climate-neutral.
Carbon-based auto industry dependent on oil from politically unstable Middle East.	Hydrogen-based fuel-cell auto industry not reliant on specific country source.
Contributes to noisy, congested, and polluted cities.	Will create rail-centered, bicycle-friendly cities that offer less stress and pollution, more exercise.
Likely to decline in not-too-distant future as natural supplies deteriorate.	Will create major new industries; e.g., the wind industry will bring income and jobs from manufacturing, installation, and maintenance.

Source: Eco-Economy

---

croplands. A particular fishery can sustain a catch of a certain size, but if the demands on the fishery exceed the sustainable yield by even 2% a year, the fish stocks will begin to shrink and will eventually disappear. As long as the harvest does not exceed the sustainable yield, it can be sustained in perpetuity. The same is true for forests and rangelands.

Nature also relies on balances. These include balances between soil erosion and new soil formation, between carbon emissions and carbon fixation, and between trees dying and trees regenerating.

Nature depends on cycles to maintain life. In nature, there are no linear flow-throughs, no situations where raw materials go in one end and garbage comes out the other. In nature, one organism's waste is another's sustenance, and nutrients are con-tinuously cycled. This system works. Our challenge is to emulate it in the design of the economy.

Ecologists appreciate the role of photosynthesis, the process by which plants convert solar energy into the biochemical energy that supports life on the earth. Anything that reduces the photosynthetic product, such as desertification, the paving of productive land, or the acidification of lakes by acid rain, reduces the productivity of the earth in the most fundamental sense.

Despite this long-standing body of ecological knowledge, national governments have expanded economic activity with little regard for sustainable yields or the fragile balances in nature. Over the last half century, the sevenfold expansion of the global economy has pushed the demand on local ecosystems beyond the sustainable yield in country after country. The fivefold growth in the world fish catch since 1950 has pushed the demand of most oceanic fisheries past their ability to produce fish sustainably. The sixfold growth in the worldwide demand for paper is shrinking the world's forests. The doubling of the world's herds of cattle and flocks of sheep and goats since 1950 is damaging rangelands, converting them to desert.

An ecologist not only recognizes that the services provided by ecosystems may sometimes be worth more than the goods, but that the value of services needs to be calculated and incorporated into market signals if they are to be protected. Although calculating services is not a simple matter, any reasonable estimate is far better than assuming that the costs are zero, as is now the case. For example, a forest in the upper reaches of a watershed may provide services — such as flood control and the recycling of rainfall inland — that are several times more valuable than its timber yield. Unfortunately, market signals do not reflect this, because the loggers who are cutting the trees do not bear the costs of the reduction in services. National economic policies and corporate strategies are based largely on market signals. The clear-cutting of a forest may be profitable for a logging firm, but it is economically costly to society.

Another major failure of the market to provide reliable information comes when governments subsidize the depletion of resources or environmentally destructive activities. For example, over several decades the U.S. Forest Service used taxpayer money to build roads into national forests so that logging companies could clear-cut forests. This subsidy only artificially lowered the costs of lumber and paper, and it led to flooding, soil erosion, and the silting of streams and rivers. In the Pacific Northwest, it destroyed highly productive salmon fisheries. And all this destruction was underwritten by taxpayers.

In a world where the demands of the economy are pressing against the limits of natural systems, relying on distorted market signals to guide investment decisions is a recipe for disaster. Historically, for example, when the supply of fish was inadequate, the price would rise, encouraging investment in additional fishing trawlers. When there were more fish in the sea than we could ever hope to catch, the market worked well. Today, with the fish catch often exceeding the sustainable yield, investing in more trawlers in response to higher prices will simply accelerate the collapse of these fisheries.

A similar situation exists with other natural systems, such as aquifers, forests, and rangelands. Once the climbing demand for water surpasses the sustainable yield of aquifers, the water tables begin to fall and wells go dry. The market says drill deeper wells. Farmers engage in a competitive orgy of well drilling, chasing the water table downward. On the North China Plain, where 25% of the country's grain is produced, this process is under way. In Hebei Province, data for 1999 show 36,000 wells, mostly shallower ones, being abandoned during the year as 55,000 new, much deeper wells were drilled. In Shandong Province, 31,000 were abandoned and 68,000 new wells were drilled.

In an eco-economy, drilling additional wells would be banned once a water table showed signs of falling. Instead of spending money to dig deeper wells, investments would be channeled into measures to boost water efficiency and to stabilize population in order to bring water use into balance with the sustainable supply.

Evidence is accumulating that our global economy is slowly undermining itself on several fronts. If we want economic progress to continue, we have little choice but to systematically restructure the global economy in order to make it environmentally sustainable.

Imagining the Scope of Change

Converting our economy into an eco-economy is a monumental undertaking. There is no precedent for transforming an economy shaped largely by market forces into one shaped by the principles of ecology.

The scale of projected economic growth outlines the dimensions of the challenge. The growth in world output of goods and services from $6 trillion in 1950 to $43 trillion in 2000 has caused environmental devastation on a scale that we could not easily have imagined a half century ago. If the world economy continued to expand at 3% annually, the output of goods and services would increase fourfold over the next half century, reaching $172 trillion.

Building an eco-economy in the time available requires rapid systemic change. We will not succeed with a project here and a project there. We are winning occasional battles now, but we are losing the war because we do not have a strategy for the systemic economic change that will put the world on an environmentally sustainable development path.

Although the concept of environmentally sustainable development evolved a quarter century ago, not one country has a strategy to build an eco-economy — to restore carbon balances, to stabilize population and water tables, and to conserve its forests, soils, and diversity of plant and animal life. We can find individual countries that are succeeding with one or more elements of the restructuring, but not one that is progressing satisfactorily on all fronts.

Nevertheless, glimpses of the eco-economy are clearly visible in some countries. For example, 31 countries in Europe, plus Japan, have stabilized their population size, satisfying one of the most basic conditions of an eco-economy. Europe has stabilized its population within its food-producing capacity, leaving it with an exportable surplus of grain to help fill the deficits in developing countries. China — the world's most populous country — now has lower fertility than the United States and is moving toward population stability.

Denmark is the eco-economy leader. It has stabilized its population, banned the construction of coal-fired power plants, banned the use of nonrefillable beverage containers, and is now getting 15% of its electricity from wind. In addition, it has restructured its urban transport network; now 32% of all trips in Copenhagen are on bicycle. Denmark is still not close to balancing carbon emissions and fixation, but it is moving in that direction.

Other countries have also achieved specific goals. A reforestation program in South Korea, begun more than a generation ago, has blanketed the country's hills and mountains with trees. Costa Rica has a plan to shift entirely to renewable energy by 2025. Iceland, working with a consortium of corporations led by Shell and Daimler-Chrysler, plans to be the world's first hydrogen-powered economy.

So we can see pieces of the eco-economy emerging, but systemic change requires a fundamental shift in market signals — signals that respect the principle of ecological sustainability. Unless we are prepared to shift taxes from income to environmentally destructive activities, such as carbon emissions and the wasteful use of water, we will not succeed in building an eco-economy.

Restoring the balances of nature in energy production depends on shifting from a carbon-based economy to a hydrogen-based one. Even the most progressive oil companies, such as BP and Royal Dutch/Shell, that are talking extensively about building a solar/hydrogen energy economy are still investing overwhelmingly in oil, with funds going into climate-benign sources accounting for a minute share of their investment.

Reducing soil erosion to the level of new soil formation will require changes in farming practices. In some situations, it will mean shifting from intense tillage to minimum tillage or no tillage. Agroforestry will loom large in an eco-economy. Restoring forests that recycle rainfall inland and control flooding means reversing decades of tree cutting and land clearing with forest restoration, an activity that will require millions of people planting billions of trees.

Building an eco-economy will affect every facet of our lives. It will alter how we light our homes, what we eat, where we live, how we use our leisure time, and how many children we have. It will give us a world where we are a part of nature, instead of estranged from it.

Restructuring the Economy

We can now see what an eco-economy looks like. Instead of running on fossil fuels, it will be powered by renewable sources of energy, such as wind and sunlight, and by

geothermal energy from within the earth. It will be hydrogen-based instead of carbon-based. Cars and buses will run on fuel-cell engines powered by electricity produced with an electro-chemical process using hydrogen as the fuel instead of internal combustion engines. With fuel cells powered by hydrogen, there is no climate-disrupting carbon dioxide or noxious health-damaging pollutants; only water is emitted.

In the new economy, atmospheric carbon dioxide levels will be stable. In contrast to today's energy economy, where the world's reserve of oil and coal are concentrated in a handful of countries, energy sources in the eco-economy will be widely dispersed — as widely distributed as sunlight and wind. The world's heavy dependence on the Middle East for much of its energy will likely decline as the new climate-benign energy sources and fuel-cell engines take over.

The energy economy will be essentially

FIGURE 2
Declining Industries in an Eco-Economy

Industry	Description
Coal mining	The 7% decline in world coal burning since it peaked in 1996 will continue in the years ahead.
Oil pumping	Projections based on shrinking oil reserves indicate production will peak and start declining in the next 5-20 years. Concern about global warming could bring the decline closer.
Nuclear power	Although public concern focuses on safety issues, it is the high cost that is ensuring the industry's decline.
Clear-cut logging	The rapid spread in eco-labeling of forest products will likely force logging firms to change to sustainable harvesting or be driven out of business.
Manufacture of throwaway products	As efforts to close the materials cycle intensify, many throwaway products will either be banned or taxed out of existence.
Automobile manufacturing	As world population urbanizes, the conflict between the automobile and the city will intensify, reducing dependence on automobiles.

Source: Eco-Economy

a solar/hydrogen economy with various energy sources deriving from the sun used either directly for heating and cooling or indirectly to produce electricity. Wind-generated electricity, which is likely to be the lowest-cost source of energy, will be used to electrolyze water, producing hydrogen. This provides a means of both storing and transporting wind energy. Initially, existing natural gas pipelines will be used to distribute hydrogen. But over the longer term, both natural gas and oil pipeline networks can be adapted to carry hydrogen as the world shifts from a carbon-based to a hydrogen-based economy.

The transport systems of cities have already begun to change. Instead of the noisy, congested, polluting, auto-centered transport systems of today, cities will have rail-centered transport systems, and they will be bicycle- and pedestrian-friendly, offering more mobility, more exercise, cleaner air, and less frustration.

Urban transport systems will have the same components as they do today: automobile, rail, bus, and bicycle. The difference will be in the mix. As more city planners recognize the inherent conflict between the automobile and the city, cleaner and more efficient transport systems will develop. Urban personal mobility will increase as automobile use and traffic congestion decline.

The materials sector of the eco-economy will look far different, too, as it shifts from the linear economic model, where materials go from the mine or forest to the landfill, to the reuse/recycle model, yielding no waste and nothing for the landfills.

One of the keys to reversing the deforestation of the earth is paper recycling; the potential here has been only partly realized. A second key is developing alternative energy sources that will reduce the amount of wood used as fuel. In addition, boosting the efficiency of wood burning can measurably lighten the load on forests.

Another promising option is the use of carefully designed, ecologically managed, and highly productive tree plantations. A small area devoted to plantations may be essential to protecting forests at the global level. Plantations can yield several times as much wood per hectare as can a natural forest.

In the economy of the future, the use of water will be in balance with supply. Water tables will be stable, not falling. The economic restructuring will be designed to raise water productivity in every facet of economic activity.

In this environmentally sustainable economy, harvests from oceanic fisheries, a major source of animal protein in the human diet, will be reduced to the sustainable yield. Additional demand will be satisfied by fish farming. This is, in effect, an aquatic version of the same shift that occurred during the transition from hunting and gathering to farming. The freshwater, herbivorous carp polyculture on which the Chinese rely heavily for their vast production of farmed fish offers an ecological model for the rest of the world.

A somewhat similar situation exists for rangelands. One of the keys to alleviating the excessive pressure on rangelands is to feed livestock the crop residues that are otherwise being burned for fuel or for disposal. This trend, already well under way in India and China, may hold the key to stabilizing the world's rangelands.

And finally, the new economy will have a stable population. Over the longer term, the only sustainable society is one in which couples have an average of two children.

Creating New Industries

Describing the eco-economy is obviously a somewhat speculative undertaking. In the end, however, it is not as open ended as it might seem, because the eco-economy's

FIGURE 3
Examples of Expanding Industries in an Eco-Economy

Industry	Description
Fish farming	Although growth will slow from the double-digit rate of the last decade, rapid expansion is likely to continue.
Bicycle manufacturing	Because bicycles are affordable, nonpolluting, quiet, require little parking space, and provide much-needed exercise in exercise-deprived societies, they will become increasingly common.
Wind-farm construction	Wind-electricity generation, including off-shore wind farms, will grow rapidly over the next few decades, until wind is supplying most of the world's electricity.
Wind-turbine manufacturing	Today the number of utility-scale wind turbines is measured in the thousands, but soon it will be measured in the millions, creating an enormous manufacturing opportunity.
Hydrogen generation	As the transition from a carbon-based to a hydrogen-based energy economy progresses, hydrogen generation will become a key industry.
Fuel-cell manufacturing	As fuel cells replace internal-combustion engines in automobiles and begin generating power in buildings, a huge market will evolve.
Solar-cell manufacturing	For many of the 2 billion people living in rural Third World communities who lack electricity, solar cells will be the best bet for electrification.
Light-rail construction	As people tire of the traffic congestion and pollution associated with the automobile, cities in industrial and developing countries alike will be turning to light rail to provide mobility.
Tree planting	As efforts to reforest the earth gain momentum and as tree plantations expand, tree planting will emerge as a leading economic activity.

Source: Eco-Economy

broad outlines are defined by the principles of ecology.

What is not so clear is how ecological principles will translate into economic design. For example, each country has a unique combination of renewable energy sources that will power its economy. Some countries may draw broadly on all their renewable energy sources, while others may concentrate heavily on one that is particularly abundant, such as wind or solar energy. A country with a wealth of geothermal energy may choose to structure its energy economy around this subterranean energy source.

Building a new economy involves phasing out old industries, restructuring existing ones, and creating new ones. World coal use is already being phased out, dropping 7% since peaking in 1996. It is being replaced by efficiency gains in some countries, by natural gas in others (such as the United Kingdom and China), and by wind power in others (such as Denmark).

The automobile industry faces a major restructuring as it changes power sources, shifting from the gasoline-powered internal combustion engine to the hydrogen-powered fuel-cell engine. This shift from the explosive energy that derives from igniting gasoline vapor to a chemical reaction that generates electricity will require both a retooling of engine plants and the retraining of automotive engineers and automobile mechanics.

The new economy will also bring major new industries, ones that either do not yet exist or that are just beginning. Wind electricity generation is one such industry. Now in its embryonic stage, it promises to become the foundation of the new energy economy. Millions of turbines soon will be converting wind into electricity, becoming part of the global landscape. In many countries, wind will supply both electricity and, through the electrolysis of water, hydrogen. Together, electricity and hydrogen can meet all the energy needs of a modern society.

In effect, there will be three new subsidiary industries associated with wind power: turbine manufacturing, installation, and maintenance. Manufacturing facilities will be found in scores of countries, industrial and developing. Installation, which is basically a construction industry, will be more local in nature. Maintenance, since it is a day-to-day activity, will be a source of ongoing local employment.

The robustness of the wind turbine industry was evident in 2000 and 2001 when high-tech stocks were in a free fall worldwide. While high-tech firms as a group were performing poorly, sales of wind turbines were climbing, pushing the earnings of turbine manufacturers to the top of the charts. Continuing growth of this sector is expected for the next few decades.

As wind power emerges as a low-cost source of electricity and a mainstream energy source, it will spawn another industry: hydrogen production. Once wind turbines are in wide use, there will be a large, unused capacity during the night when the demand for electricity drops. With this essentially free electricity, turbine owners can turn on the hydrogen generators and convert the wind power into hydrogen, ideal for fuel-cell engines. Hydrogen generators will start to replace oil refineries. The wind turbine will replace both the coal mine and the oil well. Both wind turbines and hydrogen generators will be widely dispersed as countries take advantage of local wind resources.

Changes in the world food economy will also be substantial. Some of these, such as the shift to fish farming, are already under way. The fastest-growing subsector of the world food economy during the 1990s was aquaculture, expanding at more than 11% a year. Fish farming is likely to continue to expand simply because of its efficiency in converting grain into animal protein.

Even allowing for slower future growth in aquaculture, fish farm output will likely overtake beef production before 2010. Perhaps more surprising, fish farming could eventually exceed the oceanic fish catch. Indeed, for China — the world's leading consumer of seafood — fish farming already supplies two-thirds of the seafood, while the oceanic catch accounts for the other third. With this development, new jobs will be created: aquatic ecologist, fish nutritionist, and marine veterinarian.

Another growth industry of the future is bicycle manufacturing and servicing. Because the bicycle is non-polluting, frugal in its use of land, and provides the exercise much needed in sedentary societies, future reliance on it is expected to grow. As recently as 1965, the production of cars and bikes was essentially the same, but today more than twice as many bikes as cars are manufactured each year. Among industrial countries, the urban transport model being pioneered in the Netherlands and Denmark, where bikes are featured prominently, gives a sense of the bicycle's future role worldwide.

As bicycle use expands, interest in electrically assisted bikes is also growing. These bikes are similar to existing bicycles, except for a tiny battery-powered electric motor that can either power the bicycle entirely or assist elderly riders or those living in hilly terrain, and their soaring sales are expected to continue climbing in the years ahead.

Just as the last half century has been devoted to raising land productivity, the next half century will be focused on another growth industry: raising water productivity. Virtually all societies will be turning to the management of water at the watershed level in order to manage available supply most efficiently. Irrigation technologies will become more efficient. Urban wastewater recycling will become common. At present, water tends to flow into and out of cities, carrying waste with it. In the future, water will be used over and over, never discharged. Since water does not wear out, there is no limit to how long it can be used, as long as it is purified before reuse.

Another industry that will play a prominent role in the new economy, one that will reduce energy use, is teleconferencing. Increasingly for environmental reasons and to save time, individuals will be "attending" conferences electronically with both audio and visual connections. This industry involves developing the electronic global infrastructure, as well as the services, to make teleconferencing possible. One day there may be thousands of firms organizing electronic conferences.

New Jobs in the Eco-Economy

Restructuring the global economy will create not only new industries, but also new jobs—indeed, whole new professions and new specialties within professions. For example, as wind becomes an increasingly prominent energy source, thousands of wind meteorologists will be needed to analyze potential wind sites, monitor wind speeds, and select the best sites for wind farms. The better the data on wind resources, the more efficient the industry will become.

Wind engineers will be hired to design customized wind turbines. The appropriate turbine size and design can vary widely according to site. It will be the job of wind engineers to tailor designs to specific wind regimes in order to maximize electricity generation.

Environmental architecture is another fast-growing profession. Among the signposts of an environmentally sustainable economy are buildings that are in harmony with the environment. Environmental architects design buildings that are energy- and materials-efficient and that maximize natural heating, cooling, and lighting.

In a future of water scarcity, watershed hydrologists will be in demand. It will be their responsibility to understand the hydrological cycle, including the movement of underground water, and to know the depth of aquifers and determine their sustainable yield. They will be at the center of watershed management regimes.

As the world shifts from a throwaway economy, engineers will be needed to design products that can be recycled—from cars to computers. Once products are designed to be disassembled quickly and easily into component parts and materials, comprehensive recycling is relatively easy.

Technologies used in recycling are sometimes quite different from those used in producing from virgin raw materials. Within the U.S. steel industry, for example, where nearly 60% of all steel is produced from scrap, the technologies used differ depending on the feedstock. Steel manufactured in electric arc furnaces from scrap uses far less energy then traditional open-hearth furnaces using pig iron. Recycling engineers will be responsible for closing the materials loop, converting the linear flow-through economy into a comprehensive recycling economy.

In countries with a wealth of geothermal energy, it will be up to geothermal geologists to locate the best sites either for supplying power plants or for tapping directly to heat buildings. Retraining petroleum geologists to master geothermal technologies is one way of satisfying the likely surge in demand for geothermal geologists.

If the world is to stabilize population sooner rather than later, it will need far more family-planning midwives in Third World communities. This growth sector will be concentrated largely in developing countries, where millions of women lack access to family planning. The same family-planning counselors who advise on reproductive health and contraceptive use can also play a central role in controlling the spread of HIV.

Another pressing need, particularly in developing countries, is for sanitation-system engineers who can design sewage systems not dependent on water, a trend that is already under way in some water-scarce countries. As it becomes clear that using water to wash waste away is a reckless use of a scarce resource, a new breed of sanitation engineers will be in wide demand. Washing waste away is even less acceptable today as marine ecosystems are overwhelmed by nutrient flows. Apart from the ecological disruption of a water-based disposal method, there are also much higher priorities in the use of water, such as drinking, bathing, and irrigation.

Yet another new specialty that is likely to expand rapidly in agriculture as productive farmland becomes scarce is that of the agronomist who specializes in multiple cropping and intercropping. This position requires expertise both in the selection of crops that can fit together well in a tight ro-

tation in various locales and in agricultural practices that facilitate multiple cropping.

Investing in the Environmental Revolution

Restructuring the global economy so that economic progress can be sustained represents the greatest investment opportunity in history. The conceptual shift is comparable to that of the Copernican Revolution in the sixteenth century. In scale, the Environmental Revolution is comparable to the Agricultural and Industrial Revolutions that preceded it.

The Agricultural Revolution involved restructuring the food economy, shifting from a nomadic lifestyle based on hunting and gathering to a settled lifestyle based on tilling the soil. Although agriculture started as a supplement to hunting and gathering, it eventually replaced these practices almost entirely. The Agricultural Revolution entailed clearing one-tenth of the earth's land surface of either grass or trees so it could be plowed. Unlike the hunter-gatherer culture that had little effect on the earth, this new farming culture literally transformed the surface of the earth.

The Industrial Revolution has been under way for two centuries, although in some countries it is still in its early stages. At its foundation was a shift in sources of energy from wood to fossil fuels, a shift that set the stage for a massive expansion in economic activity. Indeed, its distinguishing feature is the harnessing of vast amounts of fossil energy for economic purposes. While the Agricultural Revolution transformed the earth's surface, the Industrial Revolution is transforming the earth's atmosphere.

The additional productivity that the Industrial Revolution made possible unleashed enormous creative energies. It also gave birth to new lifestyles and to the most environmentally destructive era in human

FIGURE 4
Expanding Professions in an Eco-Economy

Profession	Description
Wind meteorologists	Wind meteorologists will play a role in the new energy economy comparable to that of petroleum geologists in the old one.
Family-planning midwives	If world population is to stabilize soon, literally millions of family-planning midwives will be needed.
Foresters	Reforesting the earth will require professional guidance on what tree species to plant where and in what combination.
Hydrologists	As water scarcity spreads, the demand for hydrologists to advise on watershed management, water sources, and water efficiency will increase.
Recycling engineers	Designing consumer applications so they can be easily disassembled and completely recycled will become an engineering specialty.
Aquacultural veterinarians	Until now, veterinarians have typically specialized in either large animals or small animals, but with fish farming likely to overtake beef production by 2010, marine veterinarians will be in demand.
Ecological economists	As it becomes clear that the basic principles of ecology must be incorporated into economic planning and policy making the demand for economists able to think like ecologists will grow.
Geothermal geologists	With the likelihood that large areas of the world will turn to geothermal energy both for electricity and for heating, the demands for geothermal geologists will climb.
Environmental architects	Architects are learning the principles of ecology so they can incorporate them into the buildings where we will live and work.
Bicycle mechanics	As the world turns to the bicycle for transportation and exercise, bicycle mechanics will be needed to keep the fleet running.
Wind-turbine engineers	With millions of wind turbines likely to be installed in the decades ahead, there will be strong worldwide demand for wind-turbine engineers.

Source: Eco-Economy

history, setting the world firmly on a course of eventual economic decline. The Environmental Revolution resembles the Industrial Revolution in that each is dependent on the shift to a new energy source. And like both earlier revolutions, the Environmental Revolution will affect the entire world.

There are differences in scale, timing, and origin among the three revolutions. Unlike the other two, the Environmental Revolution must be compressed into a matter of decades. And while the other revolutions were driven by new discoveries and advances in technology, this revolution is being driven more by our instinct for survival.

There has not been an investment situation like this before. The amount that the world spends now each year on oil, the leading source of energy, provides some insight into how much it could spend on energy in the eco-economy. In 2000, the world used nearly 28 billion barrels of oil, some 76 million barrels per day. At $27 a barrel, the total comes to $756 billion per year. How many wind turbines, solar rooftops, and geothermal wells will it take to produce this much energy?

One big difference between the investments in fossil fuels and those in wind power, solar cells, and geothermal energy is that the latter will supply energy in perpetuity. These "wells" will not run dry. If the money spent on oil in one year were invested in wind turbines, the electricity generated would be enough to meet one-fifth of the world's needs.

Investments in the infrastructure for the new energy economy, which would eventually have to be made as fossil fuels are depleted, will obviously be huge. These include the transmission lines that connect wind farms with electricity consumers and the pipelines that link hydrogen supply sources with end users. Much of the infrastructure for the existing energy economy — the transmission lines for electricity and the pipelines for natural gas — can be used in the new energy economy as well. The local pipeline distribution network in various cities for natural gas can easily be converted to hydrogen.

For developing countries, the new energy sources promise to reduce dependence on imported oil, freeing up capital for investment in domestic energy sources. Although few countries have their own oil fields, all have wind and solar energy. In terms of economic expansion and job generation, these new energy technologies are a godsend.

Investments in energy efficiency are also likely to grow rapidly simply because they are so profitable. In virtually all countries, industrial and developing, saved energy is the cheapest source of new energy. Replacing inefficient incandescent light bulbs with highly efficient compact fluorescent lamps offers a rate of return that stock markets are unlikely to match.

There are also abundant investment opportunities in the food economy. It is likely that the world demand for seafood, for example, will increase at least by half over the next 50 years, and perhaps much more. If so, fish-farming output — now 31 million tons a year — will roughly need to triple, as will investments in fish farming. Although aquaculture's growth is likely to slow from the 11% a year of the last decade, it is nonetheless likely to be robust, presenting a promising opportunity for future investment.

A similar situation exists for tree plantations. At present, tree plantations cover some 113 million hectares (280 million acres). An expansion of these by at least half, along with a continuing rise in productivity, is likely to be needed both to satisfy future demand and to eliminate one of the pressures that are shrinking forests. This, too, presents a huge opportunity for investment. No sector of the global economy will be untouched by the Environmental Revolution. In this new economy, some companies will be winners and some will be losers. Those who anticipate the emerging eco-economy and plan for it will be the winners. Those who cling to the past risk becoming part of it.

CHAPTER 47

ECONOMIC GROWTH WITHOUT DESTRUCTION

Storm Cunningham

At last, some good economic news: There's a mushrooming new global economic sector that already exceeds a trillion dollars per year — and even restores natural resources. It's called *restorative development*, defined as socio-economic revitalization based on the restoration of our natural and built environments. And it will dramatically reshape our economies, communities, and environments throughout the twenty-first century.

Turning an old-growth forest into a farm, or demolishing a historic building for a shopping mall, is the kind of development we're most familiar with: new development. Decontaminating abandoned industrial property and turning old factories into apartments and stores is another kind of development, one that builds without destroying: restorative development. Returning a distressed old farm to productivity by rebuilding topsoil, removing accumulated salts, and restoring surrounding watersheds is another example of restorative development.

Nations around the globe have accumulated backlogs of needed restoration projects worth trillions of dollars. Meanwhile, hundreds of billions of dollars of new res-

toration needs are added annually, creating perhaps the largest new growth sector of the world economy. What's more, most of the other so-called "new economies," such as hydrogen, biotech, nanotech, and digital, are either a direct outgrowth of the restoration economy, or will find their greatest markets in restorative development.

Restoration Industries

Our current restoration economy comprises eight industries. Four involve the natural environment: ecosystem restoration, fisheries restoration, watershed restoration, and agricultural restoration/rural development. The other four industries, which restore the built environment, are:

• **Brownfields remediation and redevelopment.** Brownfields are lands that are not being used productively as a result of real or perceived contamination. The U.S. Environmental Protection Agency's Brownfields Initiative has awarded more than $140 million in nationwide grants to help communities clean up abandoned, lightly contaminated sites and restore them to productive community use. For example, in

---

Originally published as "Restorative Development: Economic Growth without Destruction," *The Futurist*, Vol. 37, No. 4, July/August 2003. Used with permission of the World Future Society, 7910 Woodmont Avenue, Suite 450, Bethesda, MD 20814. Telephone: 301/656-8274; FAX: 301/951-0394; and homepage: http://www.wfs.org.

> ## FIGURE 1
> ## The Money in Restoration
>
> The following selected initiatives come with a hefty — and worthy — price tag, author Cunningham notes. Total projects exceed $1 trillion in expenditures to revive environments, economies, and aesthetics. Here are 10 current (or recently completed) restorative projects worldwide.
>
> 1. **$100 million** in dam restoration or removal worldwide.
> 2. **$225 million** to restore site around Stonehenge.
> 3. **$450 million** to restore Reagan National Airport in Washington, D.C.
> 4. **$500 million** to restore Istanbul's Golden Horn Waterfront.
> 5. **$700 million** rebuilding of a single highway interchange in Springfield, Virginia.
> 6. **$2.5 billion** to replace the Washington, D.C., area's Wilson Bridge.
> 7. **$3.1 billion** to launch first phase of Russian railway rehabilitation.
> 8. **$12 billion** restoration of a single watershed in China.
> 9. **$15 billion** to rebuild and restore Afghanistan.
> 10. **$52 billion** per year to restore natural disasters, *not* including human-caused disasters or terrorism.
>
> *Source:* The Restoration Economy *by Storm Cunningham.*

Concord, New Hampshire, officials are working to identify contamination in a 440-acre (178-hectare) industrial corridor and develop a remediation and redevelopment plan with the potential to create more than 2,500 new jobs — or 8% of the city's total unemployment.

• **Infrastructure refurbishment and reconstruction.** This aspect of restorative development deals with the flows that connect our built environment: power, sewerage, traffic, water, even garbage. One major infrastructure refurbishment project is the London Underground with an estimated budget of $42 million (£27 million).

• **Heritage restoration.** A community's physical heritage comprises aspects of the built environment that lasted long enough to be a source of community attachment — or where an event occurred that the community considers intrinsic to its identity. Heritage can also be environmental (fisheries) or cultural (indigenous languages).

• **Disaster/war restoration and rebuilding.** Three categories of disasters make up this restoration industry: war, manmade disasters (such as oil spills, nuclear power accidents, and even mudslides due to deforestation), and natural disasters (such as volcanic eruptions and earthquakes). The cost of rebuilding war-torn Afghanistan is estimated at $15 billion. The cost of restoring worldwide disasters is roughly $52 billion per year.

Some of these industries, such as disaster and war restoration, have been around for millennia. Others, such as brownfields restoration, just appeared in the past decade. (New regulations in 1990 made it possible for business people to buy contaminated lands.) But the sudden growth of restorative development and its emergence as a collective economic force can be traced to the convergence of three global crises:

1. The Constraint Crisis: We are out of room. This doesn't mean there are no more wide-open spaces fit to develop, but rather that virtually every developable acre of land — whether it's a farm, a historic battlefield, or a recreational greenspace — already serves a vital purpose that people will fight to protect from developers.

2. The Contamination Crisis. Chemical, organic, and radiological contamination from industrial, agricultural, and military activities have affected ecosystems and supplies of water, food, and air.

3. The Corrosion Crisis. We've been

building practically nonstop since the beginning of the Industrial Revolution, and many of the world's cities are getting very old. In the United States, much of the infrastructure is decrepit: The American Society of Civil Engineers has documented a $1.3 trillion backlog for restoring infrastructure.

These are the same three crises that have brought down civilizations throughout history — and that have sometimes triggered their renaissance. However, we now face all three crises simultaneously on a global scale.

Beyond Sustainability

Restorative development, while benefiting the environment, is not an "environmental message" per se. Rather, restorative development is a strategic path for leaders of businesses, nonprofits, and government agencies that wish to grow economically, or that want to revitalize themselves.

Since the beginning of the Industrial Revolution, our growth assumptions have been based on exploring new geographic frontiers and exploiting new natural resources. Now that the greatest new growth frontier is behind us, we need to reexamine what developed in the past three centuries — and all the natural places we've damaged in the process.

For instance, many cities have no remaining greenfield areas (i.e., land that has never been developed) that they can use for expansion. Some cities, such as Niagara Falls, New York, have discovered that 100% of the buildable land they still possess is contaminated. Meanwhile, cities that do have greenfields are finding increasing resistance to developing them. To grow economically, both types of architecturally challenged cities must redevelop their brownfields instead.

In fact, some of the largest opportunities for restoration industries involve revitalizing the cities we've created during the past 300 years of unfettered growth. That's why developers worldwide are shifting their focus to restorative development. Now when they proposed to restore ugly, abandoned property that generates no tax revenues, the same citizens' groups, historic preservation societies, and environmental agencies that used to fight their new developments are instead supporting them.

However, restorative development should not be confused with sustainable development. Sustainable development — which has yet to be properly defined or measured — usually requires a decade or more to produce an attractive bottom line. Restorative development pays off big, and pays off now.

What's more, the field of sustainable development emerged in reaction to uncontrolled new development, but it doesn't solve the problem. Sustainable development is simply a greener form of new development; it can't repair the accumulated corrosion and contamination, which will only exacerbate the Constraint Crisis. Sustainability is a great concept, but the world needs restoration first. After all, who really wants to sustain the mess we're living in now?

Restorative development should also not be confused with the maintenance/conservation mode of development. Though highly essential, conservation has largely lost the battle against new development. This is why most of the largest conservation groups, such as The Nature Conservancy, have embraced ecological restoration. They're not just preserving our last few pristine ecosystems; they're buying and restoring the damaged land around them so they can actually *expand*.

We've moved from an unsuccessful attempt to slow the decrease of wildlife habitat to a successful strategy of *increasing* wildlife habitat. That's a very different, and much more hopeful, dynamic. Of course, as with any new field, standards are still being set, and not all early attempts are successful. But that, too, is part of the opportunity for academics, engineers, and scientists.

Tomorrow's Restoration Economy

Restorative development is fully capable of replacing new development as the dominant economic growth mode. It's every bit as profitable as new development (often more so), so it offers an attractive path, a natural evolution, away from the old model. In a corporate world that demands dramatic quarterly profits, and a political world that demands results during an election cycle, only restorative development can deliver the goods with bipartisan support.

Integrated partnerships among the public sector, private industry, and non-governmental organizations may be the best long-term vehicles for complex, large-scale restoration projects. They will also likely be the entities that restore nations in decades to come.

With a new economic sector that delivers strong economic, aesthetic, and environmental returns, many new legal tools and investment products will emerge. This will likely include a broad spectrum of restorative real estate investment trusts (REITs). What's more, the opportunities for inventors, entrepreneurs, programmers, and consultants are virtually unlimited: Almost any industry or profession that existed in the dying new development economy will have its analog in the restoration economy.

This is the greatest new frontier for hardware, software, the sciences, economics, art, philosophy, architecture, engineering, academia, and policy makers: Nothing is more urgent, nothing is more important, and nothing is more economically productive than restoring our world. Virtually every major trend and discipline of this century either will be rooted in restorative de-

---

FIGURE 2
The Truth about Brownfields

In the early 1990s, few people had heard of brownfields. Now they're in the dictionary — and already widely misunderstood. Here is the truth about five common brownfield misconceptions:

1. The purpose of brownfields remediation is *not* simply to clean the environment. Unlike Superfund sites — the largest, most-contaminated sites in the United States, selected for cleanup by the Environmental Protection Agency to keep the public safe — the chief goal of brownfields remediation is turning a profit.

2. Brownfields comprise more than just ground and groundwater. Buildings can also be highly toxic with contaminants such as lead paint, asbestos insulation, and mercury that fall under the "hard costs" of brownfields cleanup.

3. Most brownfields are not heavily contaminated. Contamination is often minimal, yet perceived as serious. Abandoned industrial sites, for example, have sat idle for decades because the public falsely assumes they're toxic.

4. Most brownfields are not abandoned. Many contaminated sites are in use, but their contamination has not been assessed. When 30% of industrial acreage in Hartford, Connecticut, was abandoned between 1986 and 1997, much of it was found to be contaminated — which means workers toiled in toxic environs.

5. Brownfields are not restricted to large industrial sites in urban locations. Many are small and rural, such as rural gas stations (abandoned and operational) with leaky underground storage tanks. Further, in 27 states, the EPA cannot prevent a company from putting fuel or chemicals into underground storage tanks that are known to be leaking.

Source: The Restoration Economy *by Storm Cunningham.*

velopment or will converge with it in a way that will transform and revitalize it.

Every city that is currently being touted as a model of rebirth, sustainability, or economic health has already embraced restorative development projects in their new model. For most of them, this was an intuitive, emergent transition: Until recently, they didn't possess the terminology or theoretical structure to talk about or plan for restorative development in a coherent manner.

Now, the dialogue has begun, and this first phase of the restoration economy is about to enter a period of maturation. The concepts and lessons of the past decade must start to be formally incorporated into public policy, university curricula, and business strategies.

Restorative development has already reversed several trends that are taken as gospel by many futurists. Desertification is a good example: We all know that the Sahara has been expanding for decades, right? *Wrong.* Recent analysis of satellite images shows it's been shrinking for about 15 years. Why? The primary mechanism has been restorative agriculture, which was taught to farmers 15 to 20 years ago in about a dozen nations on the edge of the Sahara.

Restorative development already accounts for a major portion of the good economic news on the planet, yet it seldom gets the credit, because we don't measure it. Within the next five to 10 years, it will dominate most development budgets, and will continue to do so for the rest of the twenty-first century.

CHAPTER 48

THE IMPORTANCE OF LANDSCAPING IN THE URBAN ENVIRONMENT

Ignacio F. Bunster-Ossa

Placing open-space concerns at the core of the planning and design of urban areas is a strategy that is quickly becoming important in the health and vitality of cities. It also could lead to a retooling of urban design and a blurring of the boundaries that this discipline shares with architecture, landscape architecture, and civil engineering.

From a formal standpoint, the practice of urban design typically is concerned with building setbacks and orientation, height, scale, and material quality: the characteristics of the "positive" mass that fills the land. It also involves the infrastructure needed to connect this mass to the world, namely utility and circulation systems. A part of this time-tested practice, a standard palette of so-called "negative" spaces — parks, plazas, promenades, courts, and gardens — are normally summoned to provide "soft" relief from the otherwise "hard" agglomeration of streets and buildings. A polarity is thus perpetuated between indoor and outdoor environments, and design style or theme is the only way to physically integrate one with the other.

The pursuit of sustainable urban environments, however, forces a reevaluation of past practices. There is little doubt that green buildings can play an important role in the sustainable development agenda. But to this agenda an equal if not greater contribution can be made through the design of related open areas, especially in denser urban situations in which issues such as water quality, energy conservation (and production), climate mitigation, pollution control, connectivity, and social exchange become amplified. Open space always will need to satisfy people's outdoor gathering and recreation needs while helping to impart a meaningful sense of place. But under a sustainable agenda it must do so as part of a system that integrates ecological, infrastructure, building, landscape, and social functions, engaging the full gamut of spatial typologies — big and small — from gardens to rooftops to sidewalks to streets, parks, and waterways. Owing to its overarching utility, open space is gaining recognition as a sustainability superstructure, or green metastructure, that can directly enhance the economic and environmental viability of urban areas.

Originally published as "Landscape Urbanism," *Urban Land*, Vol. 60, No. 7, July 2001. Published by the Urban Land Institute, Washington, D.C. Reprinted with permission of the publisher.

Much like new branches in science that emerge when separate disciplines coalesce (molecular biology, for example), the landscape-based approach to the planning and design of urban areas is acquiring its own identity. Ecological urbanism, green urbanism, or just plain sustainable design have been associated with this approach. Now, a new term, landscape urbanism, appears to be gaining ground. The University of Chicago, for example, offers a master of architecture concentration in landscape urbanism, in which the landscape is viewed "as an element of urban infrastructure ... in the context of contemporary urban development and public work, as opposed to an art historical genre, an environmental science, or an applied art." Another example is the Architecture Association (AA) in London, a school long known for its avant-garde design outlook and teaching methods. The AA now offers a 12-month, studio-based postgraduate course in landscape urbanism, which is designed for students who wish to "integrate the techniques and modes of operation that historically have been described as landscape design, with the domain of urbanism." At the University of Pennsylvania's Graduate School of Fine Arts in Philadelphia, landscape architecture students habitually participate in design studios where the landscape, as a field of operations, consists of heavy-industrial yards, warehousing and manufacturing districts, working waterfront, and other urban brownfields; landscape urbanism is unofficially used to describe the focus of such studios. Although these academic programs may differ as to the approach and content of the course work, they all focus on the use of open space as a tool for restructuring urban areas.

The following are some of the more significant open-space concerns central to the practice of landscape urbanism:

- *Water quality*: retaining, filtering, storing, infiltrating, or otherwise mitigating the adverse impact of storm runoff. (The use of vegetated roofs, soft ground, and porous paving figures into this equation.)
- *Water recycling*: filtering and storing graywater for irrigation, building cooling, or groundwater replenishment.
- *Energy conservation*: minimizing heat gain or loss through proper block layout and building orientation and through the planting of shade trees, vine structures, and vegetation that can screen or funnel prevailing winds.
- *Energy generation*: using building rooftops, projections, canopies, and other exposed structures as support for photovoltaic sheets or panels, wind turbines, heat coils, and other energy generation devices.
- *Heat-island effect*: using planted areas, shade structures, and surfaces with high reflectivity to help minimize solar absorption as well as to moderate urban microclimate.
- *Airborne particulates*: trapping dust and other particles through the use of greenery around windows and other building openings. Planted terraces and balconies can extend this benefit up a building's floor.
- *Biodiversity*: Creating and enhancing wildlife habitat by introducing complex, ecologically coherent, and self-sustaining landscapes wherever possible, especially along waterways, retention ponds, and wetlands through bioengineering techniques.
- *Urban agriculture*: producing food products for local consumption through the cultivation of community gardens, utility easements, and roof terraces.
- *Transportation*: creating a linked network of spaces that can facilitate bicycling and other modes of alternative transportation. The flexible use of streets and thoroughfares for public gathering and celebrations is part of this mix.
- *Infrastructure*: doubling the use of open space as utility corridors.

- *Recreation*: Integrating any of the above-referenced functions with open-space amenity and recreation needs through the use of paths, playfields, fountains, pools, landforms, open-air structures, furniture, and other landscape features.

All of these concerns relate to some aspect of energy conservation and environmental health. Sustainability, however, also addresses cultural health; that is, how the well-being and identity of particular groups within a larger society are sustained as physical and social change occurs around them. Because the use of space can significantly influence identity, how communities are engaged in the process of planning and designing urban areas is, too, a concern of landscape urbanism. Public outreach and, more recently, public art are two ways in which community issues are integrated with the process of planning and design.

The city of Ventura, California, for example, recently selected an artist-led team of landscape architects and biologists to design trails and paths around the filtering ponds connected to the city's treatment plant, which also provide sanctuary to a host of aquatic birds. When the volume of editorials and letters published in the local newspaper is considered, it can be said that few expenditures of public funds in the city's history have generated as much debate about who Venturans are and how they see their lives in relation to the environment. Multiple public meetings are planned to help elucidate how this project will affect the relationships among sewage treatment, public art, and natural habitat. While no new developments are involved in this project, the public debate nonetheless is directly related to urban growth and the perceived quality of the urban environment.

Whether serving cultural or ecological purposes, the practice of landscape urbanism integrates all of the aforementioned concerns with a given development program. The objective is to create a seamless green urban fabric in which the traditional dichotomies between positive and negative, as well as hard and soft, are rendered obsolete. Fusion, rather than division, is the order of the day.

For decades, a diverse group of visionary thinkers has been challenging the design establishment, advocating integrative approaches to architecture, art, landscape architecture, and urban place making. Among them are architect Peter Cook, of Archigram fame; Frederich Hundertwasser, the Austrian artist/builder; and Anne Spirn, professor at Massachusetts Institute of Technology and author of the *Granite Garden*. Another, James Wines, of Site, Inc., current chair of architecture at Pennsylvania State University, has made a career out of built work that deliberately blurs the line between art, landscape, ecology, and architecture.

More recently, several projects have come on the scene that showcase the precepts that inspired past visions. Reality, it seems, is catching up with utopia. At the DaimlerChrysler headquarters in Berlin's Potsdamer Platz, for example, architect Renzo Piano and landscape architect Herbert Dreiseitl have collaborated to create an intricate symbiosis between building and landscape, with water being the primary unifying element. Through its use of vegetated roofs, cisterns, mechanical tanks, and biofiltering pools, the project helps capture and retain rainwater, provides graywater for toilets and irrigation, cleanses recycled water, and creates new wetland habitat. Little about the design of the water fountains that edge the buildings betrays their function as reservoirs for water conservation, recycling, and purification or their link to the building's cooling system.

In Santiago, Chile, architect Borja Huidobro has designed a corporate office building whose western facade is shielded from the sun by a 15-story screen supporting colorful vines. Separated several feet from the building curtain wall, the screen creates a cool recess between the outside air and the building's interior and reduces the need for air conditioning.

While these examples are building specific, the merits of green architecture can be extended to entire redevelopment districts. In this nascent sustainability age, smart growth has become the guiding principle of public agencies charged with managing regional growth. Most of this growth impinges on previously undeveloped land, or greenfields. However, where growth occurs through the redevelopment of urban land — brownfields — the precepts of smart growth require a finer planning and design grain to uphold the sustainability agenda. At this finer grain, landscape urbanism is proving to be a valuable approach. The master planning of the area adjacent to the upper Mississippi in Minneapolis, Minnesota, illustrates this value.

The land upstream from the St. Anthony Falls in the Mississippi River, north of downtown Minneapolis, consists of about 500 acres of mostly light-manufacturing and industrial land. Prominent uses include a municipal barge terminal and operations yard, a scrap metal plant, and a sand and gravel operation. In 1999, a comprehensive revitalization study of the two-mile waterfront was prepared by a consultant team that included transportation and civil engineers, architects, economists, and ecologists. While city, state, and federal agencies were intimately involved in the process, the lead public agency was the city's park and recreation board.

New development was very much on the agenda, but the overarching goal was to maximize the waterfront lands and the river's appeal as an open-space resource. Specifically, the open space had to accommodate the extension of a river parkway, and provide bicycle paths for downtown commuters, land for active and passive recreation, new floodplain habitat, buffers to existing habitat, and water filtration and retention area. It also had to allow for needed

river access and public facilities necessary to reinforce the social fabric of adjacent neighborhoods — all within an integrated, continuous system.

Over 18 months, scores of meetings — at times contentious — were held to gauge public opinion on the specific program of, and balance between, the open space and new development. Much debate about what the waterfront environment should look like also took place. Only six guidelines were developed to establish a common ground for the public and private realms. The guidelines focused on four key concerns: solar gain, wind protection, river and downtown views, and water filtration. The use of natural technologies in the form of bioengineering was then proposed to create water filtration parks and "living machine" water gardens where aquatic plants could help absorb contaminants, trap silt, and delay and lessen the impact of storms. Water gardens also were located to provide an open-space amenity to specific development nodes. One of them, anchoring several mid-rise office buildings, uses an amphitheater with commanding views of the downtown skyline as a spillway to the river.

In the end, the master plan yielded the following:

- 90 acres of new parkland
- 15 miles of bike lanes and recreation trails
- four miles of restored riverbank
- more than five miles of parkway and boulevard
- 2,500 housing units (overall density of 25 to 30 dwellings per acre)
- 2,000 new jobs (in retail, office, and light-manufacturing facilities), and
- over $10 million in addition tax revenue.

It also yielded a unanimous endorsement from the city council — a rarity. Owing to this and other approvals, developers already have begun to generate detailed designs for some of the available parcels. But this is a long-term plan. Still, influencing the slow process of development are simple yet strategic guidelines that guarantee, through the quality and function of the open space, the upper Mississippi's long-term economic and environmental viability as an urban place.

Some years ago, former U.S. Senator Gaylord Nelson (D–Oregon), the so-called father of Earth Day, methodically painted before a rapt convention of landscape architects in Portland the impact on global resources of the next doubling of the earth's population, which United Nations analysts anticipate happening within seven or so decades. The last doubling of the population occurred since World War II, a time that — in the United States, at least — coincided with a massive transformation of rural areas into urban land.

What is the likelihood that over the next 75 or so years, as the population yet again doubles, the amount of existing urban land also will double? How likely is a doubling of Los Angeles? Phoenix? Dallas? Chicago? Not very likely, of course. A combination of environmental, economic, and social factors already are pointing to a slowing of the "great suburban expansion," a trend that was confirmed recently by a *New York Times* analysis of the 2000 census.

In order to accommodate another 300 million or so inhabitants in the United States, a massive transformation of existing urban land will be necessary, and to this effort quality, accessible, and environmentally sound open spaces are likely to become increasingly important. But such spaces cannot be modeled after the great urban parks of yesteryear. In a world of diminishing resources, efficiency will be a priority. (Besides, what city can afford today to carve out of existing urban land hundreds of acres for new parks?) New models of open space will be necessary, satisfying simultaneous and overlapping functions — especially if clean water, clean air, and affordable energy become as scarce as many predict. One clear function will be the reinforcement of "micro" identities, as communities everywhere seek to distinguish themselves from a growing number of places that are all starting to look the same. Most of their attention will be focused on open space related to infill sites and brownfields.

Driven by the agenda of sustainability, the combination of environmental, cultural, and infrastructure concerns, coupled with traditional needs for amenities and recreation, is likely to change the way communities plan and design urban space. This agenda also is likely to affect the way buildings engage the landscape. Sooner or later, the redevelopment of urban areas will have to depend on the integrative value of a "green metastructure." And in time, the planning and design of such places may well be known by a new name.

CHAPTER 49

URBAN PARKS AND PUBLIC PLAZAS RETURN TO THE INNER-CITY

Nancy Egan and *Paul Nakazawa*

Parks and plazas have long served as the common ground for socialization. Since the mid–19th century, the American model for urban parks has been based on the work of Frederick Law Olmsted, the landscape architect, city planner, and writer on social issues who was responsible for the creation of New York City's Central Park and who passed on an enduring belief that city parks would help to create a more civilized society by bringing together all of a city's diverse cohorts on a common ground.

However, in the last half of the 20th century, urban public space saw a variety of challenges — ranging from lack of funding to privatization — that have led to a reconsideration of both the concept of the public domain and the spaces themselves. After World War II, suburbanization and the decline of large urban centers took a toll on metropolitan parks. The lowest point occurred during the Reagan Administration, when cities no longer had monies allocated to the proper care of parks and other public open space — much less for the design of new projects. As the middle class fled from core urban areas to the suburbs, funding for

the maintenance and security of urban parks disappeared.

By the late 1980s, a significant portion of urban public space — once an amenity for all classes — was left to deteriorate. Instead of spending money to improve parks, playgrounds, and plazas, cash-strapped cities opted for police protection. At the same time, disinvestment in traditional public places on the part of municipal governments created an opportunity for private interests to develop simulated public space in the form of downtown corporate plazas or self-described "town centers" that were essentially retail malls.

The renaissance of urban centers, fueled by a combination of demographic changes and global competition for talent, commerce, and employment, has revalued public space. Urban parks and plazas once again are being promoted as critical components of world-class cities — places where the physical shape and civic programs have been transformed by a global tide that has altered the economies of major American centers. Manufacturing, shipping, and other labor-intensive industries have moved out of the

Original published as "After Olmsted," *Urban Land*, Vol. 63, No.7, July 2004. Published by the Urban Land Institute, Washington, D.C. Reprinted with permission of the publisher.

metropolis, settling in more cost-effective locations in the southern states or offshore. The finance, high-tech, and biotech businesses that replaced them demand improved infrastructure for a new class of highly educated employees. As workplaces morph and urban neighborhoods gentrify, cities, for the first time in decades, must expand the public realm to accommodate a new vision of urban life for a different mix of stakeholders.

Former suburbanites, including young workers and empty nesters, are joining stalwart urbanites in a renewed demand for open space in the city. Although the new metropolitans want to enjoy the pleasures of urban parks as much as the Olmstedian citizens did, they have different expectations of public space based on values formed away from the gritty vitality of urban life. Suburban sensibilities vis-à-vis order, security, personal space, and social behavior often conflict with those of other stakeholders, including young people, diverse ethnic groups, and the urban poor.

What unites the disparate factions is their desire for accessible, usable open space that offers an alternative to the high-density hardscape of the city. More and more, local citizens' organizations are speaking out, not just *against* proposed developments, but also *for* the kind of environments, amenities, and programs that they feel are their due. The challenge for government is how to respond to such demands without the support of strong parks departments, adequate funding, or easily adaptable sites.

The emerging combination of political will, private sector involvement, and innovative thinking is producing a new generation of urban parks, plazas, and other public places. Today, the means and results suggest evidence of an urban model in transition.

Urban cores are dense, land values within them are high, and the outer reaches of most U.S. cities are poorly served by public transit. Locations for new parks have been pushed to disused industrial districts — waterfronts, railyards, and other brownfield sites. "The retreat of the industrial glacier" is providing a promising alternative for urban parkland, points out Toronto-based urban planner Ken Greenberg. From the waterfronts of New York City and Seattle to the riverfronts of Detroit and Denver, more than land is being recycled as the industrial infrastructure is reinvented in the new landscapes. "We are no longer building the green lawns of passive parks," maintains Joe Brown, president and CEO of EDAW, headquartered in San Francisco. "We are creating smart parks that can become the hip, active centers of recreation and celebration as well as catalysts for economic investment."

A master plan for the new Brooklyn Bridge Park, located underneath the Manhattan and Brooklyn bridges, involves the transformation of a nearly 67-acre industrial site stretching some 1.3 miles along the East River piers and waterfront. The plan, developed by Michael Van Valkenberg Associates, Inc. (MVVA), of New York with Greenberg and with Hamilton, Rabinowitz & Alschuler of New York, involves unifying the long, narrow site and mitigating the roar of the Brooklyn–Queens Expressway while creating a financially self-sustaining park with a strong identity as a green landscape.

According to Matthew Urbanski, principal of the New York office of MVVA, the process requires reviving the area's existing infrastructure for new uses. "The Brooklyn piers are modern, dating from the 1950s, and are roughly 200 to 300 feet wide ... a sizable industrial footprint of about five acres that can be used. Because infrastructure is costly in every respect, whether repair or maintenance or removal [is involved], there's a structural economy in capturing space. Also, the piers reach out and connect the park to the multiple thousand-acre ocean that is our borrowed landscape here," he says. Older finger piers such as those at another MVVA project, Pier Park in Hoboken, are in such disrepair that they are being rebuilt in a more playful form, notes Urbanski.

In Washington State, the Seattle Art Museum, in partnership with the Trust for Public Land, purchased downtown Seattle's largest and last undeveloped waterfront to accommodate an 8.5-acre sculpture park, which will involve transforming a former industrial site into new green space beyond the museum's walls. The design of the Olympic Sculpture Park by Weiss/Manfredi Architects of New York connects the city to open waterfront space, a continuous surface that unfolds as a landscape for art, linking three disparate sites currently separated by train tracks and roadways.

Other industrial relics are being reinvented as public places. For example, in New York City, the High Line, an elevated railroad spur, stretches 1.45 miles from the Jacob Javits Convention Center to the Gansevoort Street meatpacking district on the far western edge of Manhattan. Located two stories above the sidewalk, the concrete-and-steel structure — so much a part of the urban landscape that it had long gone unnoticed — is slated to be topped with a public park. A grass-roots organization, the Friends of the High Line, has been mobilizing support for several years and now Mayor Michael R. Bloomberg, city council speaker Gifford Miller, and the city council as a whole have all publicly endorsed the idea of a public park on the railroad bed.

In Boston, where the Big Dig has entailed the dismantling of the Central Artery, municipal officials and the Massachusetts Turnpike Authority are involved in creating an urban parkway, the Rose Kennedy Greenway, in the shadow of the former elevated highway. There also are designs for new parks that are in the final stages of development in the North End, the Wharf District, and Chinatown that connect these parks to the city's larger park and open-space system.

In Los Angeles, the Grand Avenue Project involves creating a recognizable downtown center for the sprawling metropolis. Building on the concentration of civic and cultural uses along, and adjacent to, Grand Avenue, it will include a mix of residential, retail, entertainment, and office projects to be developed concurrently on four prime parcels on Bunker Hill, along with a new 16-acre park, which will be a civic plaza that can be used for citywide events.

Complementing efforts to establish new parks on the skeletons of old transportation systems are others who are trying to rescue existing urban parks from the ravages of modern transportation, especially the car. In San Diego's Balboa Park, landscape architect and planner Mark Johnson, president of Denver-based Civitas, says, "Wear and tear and tension from the overlapping use of spaces — 98 institutions in 23 buildings, including the zoo and the museums, attract 12.5 million visitors a year — is damaging what everyone loves." Johnson is part of a team that is studying how to reclaim parkland from parking lots with a series of parking structures, shuttles, and improved access and roadways.

The aforementioned projects, and dozens of others around the country, suggest a commitment to creating new and revitalized public spaces, not only on the part of communities, but also on the part of cities, states, and private institutions to provide such urban spaces, even in the current economy. Northeastern cities have become living laboratories for the reprogramming of these urban centers. For example, in New York, for the first time it is now possible to conceive of a green waterfront zone running entirely around Manhattan. As old uses fade away, the question becomes how to create new parkland and what amenities will attract users that also will allow the parks to be self-sustaining. "In this new era, the process has to expand," explains landscape architect and planner Van Valkenberg. "Our team for Brooklyn Bridge Park includes economic analysts working on income generation plus experts on the cost of maintaining the park, as well as climate engineers and consultants on leading-edge green concerns, all working together with the design team and the community. It is the new prototype," he adds.

In Boston, the combination of higher education, health care, and corporate research and development in the life sciences, especially around MIT and the Longwood Medical complex, represents an unprecedented spatial concentration of talent and capital. The city is also one where the political power of ethnic working-class neighborhoods is significant. Creating what Robert Brown, a principal with Boston-based CBT/Childs Bertman Tseckares Inc. and the Boston Society of Architects's representative to the Mayor's Task Force on the Central Artery Parks, sees as "not just green space but a place of common ground," requires both vision and a long view. "We are a much more diverse city than we were when the Common and the Gardens were planned," says Brown. "Part of our job is to create a framework that is large enough to encompass the program needs of the neighborhoods and the cultural rituals that are very local, and, at the same time, provide parks that are regional and long lasting in their appeal."

The process can become politicized quickly as diverse stakeholder groups lobby for *their* park, setting the stage for potential conflicts. Empty nesters who desire a pastoral, passive experience versus young parents whose kids need a playground versus teenagers who want performance space for urban sports like skateboarding all jockey for room in parklands less than one-tenth the size of the 840 acres in Central Park. Added to the fray is the development community, which sees a well-maintained, well-used, secure green space as a catalyst for nearby private development that will con-

tribute substantially to the local economy — and there is considerable pressure brought to bear on civic leaders and their planners.

A well-articulated vision helps to keep conflictive uses in balance. "People are [eager] to participate in the success in their community," says Johnson. "We have to give them a clear focus, a future they can imagine. And it needs to be big. Incrementalism kills value." Perceived value, whether for users, the city government, the business community, or developers, is essential to bringing a project to life, he explains. "Money flows upward toward vision," quips Johnson, noting that this is particularly true when the private sector gets involved.

When the Seattle Art Museum decided to purchase the Union Oil of California site, for example, the institution put $100 down and had but six months to raise $16.5 million in private funds. Since then, both private donations and public funding, including monies from the National Endowment for the Arts, the Target Foundation, the King County Council and Arts Commission, the Seattle city council, and the federal government, have pushed the project forward. Well publicized, Olympic Sculpture Park captured the imagination of the citizens of Seattle, including the high-tech philanthropists whose companies have replaced the old industrial giants in the local economy.

The new Millennium Park in Chicago will add 16 acres of parkland to Grant Park. When efforts to raise private donations succeeded beyond expectations, city officials took the opportunity to add top-level amenities to the park, including a band shell designed by architect Frank Gehry, an outdoor sculpture by British artist Anish Kapoor, a pedestrian bridge, a music and dance theater, a public fountain, a year-round garden, a 300-seat restaurant accompanying the ice rink, and a replica of the Greek-columned peristyle. Private donors, including Chicago corporations Ameritech,

William Wrigley Jr. Company, and the Tribune Foundation, are now on track to raise more than $100 million to pay for these additions.

While private funding can make a critical difference in the successful beginnings of new park projects, private sector involvement can blur the already tenuous line between public and private in the use of space. Some stakeholders have begun to question the publicness of public space, noting the increased use of exclusionary architectural details — such as antiskate metal clips called "pig ears" or divots in park benches that discourage skating or sleeping — and security technology. For example, skateboarder and writer Ocean Howell in his essay, "The Poetics of Security: Skateboarding, Urban Design, and the New Public Space," published in *Urban Action 2001*, a publication of the Urban Studies Program at San Francisco State University, sees a new approach to the design of public places where "publicness is perceived as privilege." He makes a case against "simulated public space, produced by surveillance, directed toward profit, and enforced by spikes and guards."

The question of access becomes more complex as communities seek new ways to create parkland. Does the developer who builds on the edge of a public amenity have a voice in decisions about the park? What of the developer who provides park space or a public passage at the heart of a town center development; is it really public space? "Does it matter, as long as users perceive it as civic space?" asks Ronald Altoon, principal of Los Angeles-based Altoon + Porter Architects. "We have been designing projects with squares and courts and parks that give users

a sense of entitlement. They're based on a European model of piazzas and town squares surrounded by private shops and cafés and they attract a diverse audience of users." Will they feel the same if they have to go through security to enter or pay for admission?

The questions remain unanswered as the experiment continues in cities across the country. What is promising is the variety of new voices, processes, and forms that both challenge and confirm Olmsted's vision. A recent exhibit titled "Open, New Designs for Public Space" at New York's Van Alen Institute: Projects in Public Places addressed the issue with a collection of projects as diverse as London's City Hall; a memorial bridge in Rijeka, Croatia; and the Favela-Bairrio Project in Rio de Janeiro accompanied by a catalog of essays by an eclectic group of urban thinkers. In their introduction, Raymond W. Gastil, the executive director of the institute, and Zoe Ryan, the curator of the exhibition, capture the caution and optimism of the municipal officials, community leaders, planners, and architects engaged in the creation and preservation of the public realm.

"This is the worst of times to downgrade our expectations for public life. From concerts in Central Park to protests on the Mall, to politics and performance in the streets and squares of six continents, public space is working," write Gastil and Ryan. "Public spaces allow for shared experiences that can give rise to the mutual respect — however grudging — that is the basis of a thriving metropolitan culture. It may not be the best of times for public space, but it is a compelling era."

CHAPTER 50

NATURE AND THE HUMAN SPIRIT

David Moreno

Nature connects people to the planet. It is an introduction to the environment, the community, and to the cycle of life. People feel enriched in places where nature surrounds them. Parks are centers of activity and celebration; botanical gardens teach people about plants from around the world; canyons fill individuals with awe; mountains reach to the sky and lift people's spirits. Water touches and entertains: the calming sounds of babbling streams, the majesty of the crashing surf, the cooling feel of an Alpine lake. People are changed by their connection to the natural world.

Globalization has caused many of the world's cities to become generic. Nature, however, can be a powerful force for interpreting the unique essence of a host culture, and design can be equally powerful for extracting it to create, for the user, memorable experiences of place.

"People need to feed their souls; experiencing nature does this," explains John Aleksich, senior vice president and design principal of the Jerde Partnership, a Los Angeles-based urban planning and architecture firm. "Urban, mixed-use projects can be designed to solidify a sense of place and identity for cities with metaphors from na-

ture that capture the essence of place. Environments can be designed based on organic forms, patterns, structure, and materials; these analogies are universal and universally understood," he adds. "The space between buildings can be organized to be the most powerful part of the project: this is where people move, flow, and pause."

It is a complex challenge to translate a local culture. Imitation is not a viable option. But a project can speak the language of a culture if it is an organic representation of it — if it has grown from it by deriving metaphors from nature to capture its essence in environments based on organic forms, patterns, and structures. Local conditions must inspire the work. Each project must be singular and appropriate to the site and to the city, and while it shares characteristics with the local context, it also creates a new, potent identity in itself.

Common threads bind humankind together. These threads, in turn, create a communal human spirit. Nature is key to this spirit, eliciting joy, relaxation, calm, drama, and awe. Design that incorporates analogies of nature's patterns, forms, structures, and materials will be universally understood. There is a hierarchy to nature's patterns. In

Originally published as "Design Lyrics," *Urban Land*, Vol. 60, No. 7, July 2001. Published by the Urban Land Institute, Washington, D.C. Reprinted with permission of the publisher.

a leaf, smaller veins lead to a larger, central vein. The same is true with tributaries and rivers. Designs that echo this natural pattern create natural circulation patterns, not rigid, but flowing, where people flow like water through a space. The nucleus of a cell can provide the inspiration for a project's main gathering space. Curves and circles are important natural forms. Canyonlike spaces, hill forms, the bowl, the cave, and undulating planes can be choreographed as design compositions. Movement through these forms triggers one's senses: calms, excites, fascinates. Design can trace nature's movements and changes: a river flowing over rock eventually cuts a canyon exposing horizontal layers of stone; erosion creates patterns and color; wind rounds the shapes of hills and boulders; water never is still — its patterns constantly evolve. Water — its sound, its feel, its beauty — invites active participation and a visceral experience of sound and touch. The following projects are examples of the use of the organic to tap into our communality.

Der Mar Plaza, Del Mar, California. Del Mar Plaza, completed in 1989, is a 2.5-acre mixed-use project in the center of Del Mar, a small seaside community in southern California. Shops, public spaces, and parking are unobtrusively tucked into a hillside facing the Pacific Ocean. The dramatic coastline provides a natural context, as does the site's 40-foot grade differential. Circulation patterns are guided by the topography. Five stepped stone terraces cascade down the hill. On each, clusters of buildings are knit into the hillside, reminiscent of an Italian hilltown, where villages seem to emerge organically from the site. The cascade effect was achieved by excavating the hillside and by paralleling the contour of the visible portion of the buildings with the grade.

In Del Mar Plaza, the natural and the constructed connect seamlessly. The main plaza on the upper level offers a wide vista of the Pacific Ocean and has become Del Mar's communal gathering place. Walls are of local stone and storefronts are constructed of rich wood, giving Del Mar Plaza an of-the-earth quality. A variety of contextual facades make the plaza a natural extension of the surrounding village. Trellis-covered walkways, flagstone-paved paseos, hidden gardens, panoramic ocean views, water, shade, and sun tell a subtle yet rich story of southern California's natural environment.

Canal City Hakata, Fukuoka, Japan. Canal City, completed in 1996, is in what used to be an all-but-abandoned section of downtown. The design is a mix of East and West, of built environment and natural landscape. Japanese and westerners alike appreciate the story of nature told in Canal City. (See "Narrative Urban Landscapes," page 62, February 1998, *Urban Land.*) The canal, carved through the nine-acre site, forms the main armature and ties Canal City to its riverfront location. Planetary metaphors are integrated into Canal City's five districts: Star Court, Moon Walk, Sun Plaza, Earth Walk, and Sea Court. The natural wonders of the universe are introduced in such a way as to be interpreted and experienced individually by each visitor.

The architecture refers to time and nature. The building bases are stone, with vertical faces that rise from the canal, and are clad in horizontal bands of stone and tile, suggesting the way a river over centuries erodes layers on the face of a canyon. The color system is a traditional Japanese palette evolving from the earth. The horizontal banding or striping defines the individual structures as a "family of zebras" — each different, but with a clear fit. The paving at the canal edges varies from rough cut, as if eroded by the water's edge, to softer edges, as if on a tidal beach. Sand, stone, mineral deposits, fossils, and seashells are embedded in the concrete. Water effects within the canal re-create geyser and tidal surges. To a great extent, Canal City Hakata is shaped by movement — the   movement   of   water through the canal, the movement of people through its spaces, and the movement of clouds, sun, moon, and stars in the sky above.

Namba, Osaka, Japan. The project involves a gateway to Osaka, Japan's second largest city, an "urban magnet" in the form of a large mixed-use project. Scheduled to open in 2003, the site is adjacent to the Namba train station, which brings millions of people annually into the business district. The area is an infrastructural hub, one of the few great nodes of arrival and departure in the city.

The design concept was to create a natural landscape relief in contrast to the hard, bustling environment that surrounds the site. The goals were to provide an urban park in a part of the city that lacks a meaningful "green" component; to create a pedestrian corridor connecting the east and west sides of the district with existing urban circulation patterns; and to design a place for leisure-oriented retail and entertainment.

Namba is conceived as a sloping park that rises eight stories from street level, forming a green oasis above multiple levels of urban activity. The sloping green area will provide a refreshing contrast to the relentless pattern of linear buildings — a dramatic, soft vista in an otherwise harsh landscape. Bisecting the project at ground level will be a narrow, canyonesque stone-clad thoroughfare providing 24-hour access through the city center. The Namba "canyon" is designed as an armature that also is an amenity, providing a natural experience in an intensely urban site while connecting the site to urban circulation patterns. The canyon will be busy with office workers, shoppers, park-goers, residents, commuters, and tourists.

The canyon will be intersected at three points with curvilinear bridges connecting multiple levels of retail that form the podium for the sloping park above. A retail model is created where humans and nature can intertwine, their energies merging into a hybrid space inspired by the organic. At select locations on each level, the interior environment flows out onto park terraces. Throughout the project, elements of nature are woven together — groves of trees, clusters of rocks, cliffs, outcroppings, and water features such as streams, waterfalls, and ponds.

Dubai Festival City, Dubai, United Arab Emirates. Conceptual work has begun on a new urban waterfront district in Dubai. The first phase of Dubai Festival City, a mixed-use, urban city center scheduled to open in 2004, is intended to provide a unique and powerful sense of place. Dubai is situated on a tidal inlet, and Dubaians have a tradition of sea trade; the country also has been a center for export trade since the 1880s. The design attempts to capture the essence of Dubai and then to deduce metaphors for the sea and land.

The design concept is a meeting of desert and sea and the interplay between the two. When brought together, these two striking natural features create a language unique to the site. Water is the organizing armature of the master plan. The introduction of bay, lagoon, and canal draws the sea into the built urban form, and waterfalls, springs, cascades, tunnels, and fountains spread water's effect throughout the project.

Patterns are incorporated that echo nature: the curvilinear shape of the creek, the crest of waves, and the undulating sand dunes. The structures reflect a wind-sculpted desert, forming a gentle sweep, highest on the north end closest to downtown and lowest on the south, eventually blending into the horizontality of the land. The architecture is unified by colors inspired by the context. A desert palette derived from the 12 colors of Dubaian sand makes up horizontal bands that tell of the passage of time. Sunrise brings in a soft, warm glow; midday is rich with bright red, yellow, and orange; sunset yields cooler magenta, purple, and blue mixed with deep shadows.

The administration and marketing

center for Dubai Festival City, located on a separate site adjacent to the Al Garhoud Bridge and due to be completed in January, will be the visitor's first impression of the project. The building takes the form of a sand dune rising from the natural landscape. Smooth and rippled textures, the layering of undulating lines, crests, and folds echo the patterns of the surrounding vista. Because the viewing of the crescent moon once a month is an important ritual for Dubaians, the design incorporates a 70-degree window to the west.

Park Haven, Rotterdam, the Netherlands. Rotterdam wanted to connect two city icons — Euro-Mast, a 1,300-foot (400-meter) tower, and DeHeuvel Park — to one another and to the canal and harbor that they face, and to integrate the project into Rotterdam physically and environmentally. The design had to take into consideration the objectives of Spatial Plan Rotterdam 2010, which are, among others, to ensure Rotterdam's position as the center of Holland's south wing, its reputation as an international city, and the significance of its port.

Park Haven is a 1.2 million-square-foot (110,000-square-meter) urban, mixed-use project that incorporates leisure, entertainment, residential, hotel, and office uses in a curvilinear pattern. The design metaphor is "edge," honoring the historic Dutch ability to hold the edge of the land against the sea. "Traditionally, a river's edge is well defined, as is a park edge. But the design blurs these traditional edges so that visitors experience a seamless flow between park and water," notes David Rogers, Jerde senior vice president and project designer. DeHeuvel Park spreads onto and over the lower entertainment level that fronts the harbor. In effect, the park provides an architectural canopy of trees, blending into a vertical architecture. Water is brought directly into the main spaces, extending the canal and connecting the site to its natural context.

El CoraZone, Punta Cancun, Cancun, Mexico. The El CoraZone project engages nature in a new way: nature is the story. The historic downtown core of Cancun is ten miles from the hotel zone — a 14-mile-long island strip originally built up in the 1960s that contains most of the retail and convention facilities. The heart of the city, the CoraZone, is defined by the ocean on one side and a lagoon on the other, an environmentally rich ecosystem of mangroves and other plants native to the Yucatan. Concerned that increased urbanization and infrastructure problems were destroying the lagoon, a group of businessmen wanted a new town center built that would give the area a public realm, a communal gathering place. Restoration of the lagoon would be a primary objective so that its habitat would provide a complementary experience to the ocean beaches, broadening the experience of visitors wanting to encounter the local culture and environment.

The lagoon is the centerpiece of a 350-acre project that is surrounded by five distinct districts: an open-air retail street, a courtyard shopping area, a nighttime entertainment area, an environmental park, and a hotel zone. The districts are linked by a boardwalk that makes accessible the ecology and evocative mystery of the lagoon. Veillike canopy trees alternate with tall, skyline palms to frame views of the lagoon, creating a natural transition from green lawn terraces to the mangroves along the lagoon's edge. Water is a visual element that animates all the districts. The built environment, though modern, is richly articulated in its massing and details, recalling the traditional villages of the Yucatan. Thick walls, wood lattices, landscaped terraces, and trellises enliven the streetscapes. The color palette draws on the cream-colored limestone sand and the bright colors of the Caribbean. The El CoraZone project intends to bring the heart of Cancun back to life, delivering educational and cultural experiences, retail, and entertainment to residents and tourists alike.

Nature and the human spirit are lyrical, not predictable. Nature is timeless, flexible, sustainable, and ever changing. It can inform design with its organic forms, and design can celebrate and embellish the environment. It is the responsibility of designers to find and express a balance between the two.

REGIONAL RESOURCE DIRECTORY

Local government organizations and special district agencies included in the case studies, alphabetized by city, county or agency name.

Chesterfield County, Chesterfield, Virginia
Office of the Director
Planning Department
Main Administration Building
9901 Lori Road
Second Floor, Room 203
Chesterfield, VA 23832-0040
Telephone: (804) 748-1040
FAX: (804) 748-1502
Internet: *http://www.co.chesterfield.va.us*

City and County of Denver, Colorado
Office of the Mayor
City and County Building
1437 Bannock Street
Suite 350
Denver, CO 80202
Telephone: (720) 864-9000
FAX: (720) 865-9040
Internet: *http://www.co.denver.co.us/*

City and County of San Francisco,
 California
Office of the Mayor
City Hall
Room 200
1 Dr. Carlton B. Goodlett Place
San Francisco, CA 94102
Telephone: (415) 554-6141
FAX: (415) 554-6160
Internet: *http://www.sfgov.org/*

City of Camden, New Jersey
Office of the Business Administrator
Department of Administration
City Hall
Room 409
520 Market Street
Camden, NJ 08101-5120
Telephone: (856) 757-7150
FAX: (856) 968-4708
Internet: *http://www.ci.camden,nj.us/*

City of Charlottesville, Virginia
Office of the City Manager
City Hall
605 East Main Street
Charlottesville, VA 22902
Telephone: (434) 970-3101
FAX: (434) 970-3299
Internet: *http://www.charlottesville.org/*

City of Chattanooga, Tennessee
Office of the Mayor
City Hall
101 East 11th Street
Suite 100
Chattanooga, TN 37402
Telephone: (423) 757-5152
FAX: (423) 757-4857
Internet: *http://www.chattanooga.gov/*

City of Chicago, Illinois
Office of the Director
City Hall

121 North LaSalle Street
Room 1000
Chicago, IL 60602
Telephone: (312) 744-2976
FAX: (312) 742-3738
Internet: *http://www.cityofchicago.org/*

City of Atlanta, Georgia
Office of the Mayor
Executive Offices
City Hall
55 Trinity Avenue
Atlanta, GA 30303
Telephone: (404) 330-6000
FAX: (404) 658-7673
Internet: *http://www.atlantaga.gov/*

City of Baltimore, Maryland
Office of the Director
Department of Recreation and Parks
3001 East Drive
Druid Hill Park
Baltimore, MD 21217
Telephone: (410) 396-6690
FAX: (410) 576-9425
Internet: *http://www.ci.baltimore.md.us/*

City of Boston, Massachusetts
Office of the Mayor
1 City Hall Plaza
Boston, MA 02201
Telephone: (617) 635-4500
FAX: (617) 635-3496
Internet: *http://www.cityofboston.gov/*

City of Cambridge, Massachusetts
Office of the City Manager
City Hall
795 Massachusetts Avenue
Cambridge, MA 02139
Telephone: (617) 349-4300
FAX: (617) 349-4307
Internet: *http://www.cambridgema.gov/*

City of Fairfield, Ohio
Office of the City Manager
5350 Pleasant Avenue
Fairfield, OH 45014
Telephone: (513) 867-5350
FAX: (513) 867-5329
Internet: *http://www.fairfield-city.org/*

City of Fort Collins, Colorado
Office of the City Manager
City Hall West
300 LaPorte Avenue
Fort Collins, CO 80521
Telephone: (970) 221-6505
FAX: (970) 224-6107
Internet: *http://www.ci.fort-collins.co.us/*

City of Gainesville, Florida
Office of the City Manager
City Hall
P.O. Box 490, Station 6
Gainesville, FL 32602-0490
Telephone: (352) 334-5010
FAX: (352) 334-2203
Internet: *http://www.cityofgainesville.org/*

City of Grand Forks, North Dakota
Office of the City Manager
City Hall
255 North 4th Street
Room 109
Grand Forks, ND 58206
Telephone: (701) 746-4636
FAX: (701) 787-3725
Internet: *http://www.grandforksgov.com/*

City of Hampton, Virginia
Office of the City Manager
City Hall
22 Lincoln Street
8th Floor
Hampton, VA 23669
Telephone: (757) 727-6392
FAX: (757) 729-3037
Internet: *http://www.hampton.va.us/*

City of Hartford, Connecticut
Office of the Chief Operating Officer
City Hall
550 Main Street
Hartford, CT 06103
Telephone: (860) 543-8520
FAX: (860) 722-6619
Internet: *http://www.ci.hartford.ct.us/*

City of Irvine, California
Office of the City Manager
City Hall

1 Civic Center Plaza
Irvin, CA 92623-9575
Telephone: (949) 724-6246
FAX: (949) 724-6045
Internet: *http://www.ci.irvine.ca.us/*

City of Lafayette, Indiana
Office of the Mayor
City Hall
20 North 6th Street
Lafayette, IN 47901
Telephone: (765) 807-1002
FAX: (765) 807-1024
Internet: *http://www.city.lafayette.in.us/*

City of Lake Worth, Florida
Office of the City Manager
City Hall
7 North Dixie Highway
Lake Worth, FL 33460
Telephone: (561) 586-1600
FAX: (561) 586-1798
Internet: *http://www.lakeworth.org/*

City of Lancaster, Pennsylvania
Office of the Mayor
City Hall
120 North Duke Street
Lancaster, PA 17608-1599
Telephone: (717) 291-4711
FAX: (717) 291-4722
Internet: *http://www.cityoflancasterpa.com/*

City of Mattituck, New York
(See Suffolk County)

City of Miami Beach, Florida
Office of the City Manager
City Hall
1700 Convention Center Drive
Miami Beach, FL 33139
Telephone: (305) 673-7411
FAX: (305) 673-7254
Internet: *http://www.miamibeachfl.gov/*

City of Minneapolis, Minnesota
Office of the Mayor
City Hall
350 South 5th Street
Room 331

Minneapolis, MN 55415
Telephone: (612) 673-2100
FAX: (612) 673-2305
Internet: *http://www.ci.minneapolis.mn.us/*

City of New York, New York
Office of the Mayor
City Hall
31 Chambers Street
New York, NY 10007
Telephone: (212) 788-3000
FAX: (212) 788-2460
Internet: *http://www.nyc.gov/*

City of Petaluma, California
Office of the City Manager
City Hall
11 English Street
Petaluma, VA 94952
Telephone: (707) 778-4345
FAX: (707) 778-4419
Internet: *http://www.ci.petaluma.ca.us/*

City of Philadelphia, Pennsylvania
Office of the Mayor
City Hall
1401 John F. Kennedy Boulevard
Room 143
Philadelphia, PA 19107
Telephone: (215) 686-3000
FAX: (215) 686-2625
Internet: *http://www.phila.gov/*

City of Port Aransas, Texas
(See Great Texas Coastal Birding Trail)

City of Portland, Oregon
Office of the Chief Administrative Officer
c/o City/County Information Center
1221 SW 4th Avenue
Room 110
Portland, OR 97204
Telephone: (503) 823-4000
FAX: (503) 823-5384
Internet: *http://www.portlandonline.com/*

City of Riverhead, New York
(See Suffolk County)

City of Saint Louis Park, Minnesota
Office of the City Manager

City Hall
5005 Minnetonka Boulevard
Saint Louis Park, MN 55416
Telephone: (952) 924-2525
FAX: (952) 924-2170
Internet: *http://www.stlouispark.org/*

City of Saint Paul, Minnesota
Office of the Mayor
City Hall
Room 390
15 West Kellogg Boulevard
Saint Paul, MN 55102
Telephone: (651) 266-8510
FAX: (651) 266-8513
Internet: *http://www.co.stpaul.mn.us/*

City of San Jose, California
Office of the City Manager
City Hall
Room 436
801 North 1st Street
San Jose, CA 95110
Telephone: (408) 277-5849
FAX: (408) 277-3131
Internet: *http://www.ci.san-jose.ca.us/*

City of San Rafael, California
Office of the City Manager
City Hall
1400 Fifth Avenue
San Rafael, CA 94901
Telephone: (415) 485-3070
FAX: (415) 459-2242
Internet: *http://www.cityofsanrafael.org/*

City of Seattle, Washington
Office of the Mayor
City Hall
600–4th Avenue
12th Floor
Seattle, WA 98104
Telephone: (206) 684-4000
FAX: (206) 684-5360
Internet: *http://www.ci.seattle.wa.us/*

City of Silver Spring, Maryland
(See Montgomery County and The Mary-
land-National Capital Park and Planning
Commission)

City of West Des Moines, Iowa
Office of the City Manager
City Hall
4200 Mills Civic Parkway
West Des Moines, IA 50265
Telephone: (515) 222-3610
FAX: (515) 222-3638
Internet: *http://www.wdm-ia.com/*

District of Columbia, Washington, D.C.
(See Washington, D.C.)

Great Texas Coastal Birding Trail, Austin,
Texas
c/o Office of the Executive Director
Texas Parks and Wildlife Department
4200 Smith School Road
Austin, TX 78744
Telephone: (512) 389-4396
FAX: (512) 389-4550
Internet: *http://www.tpwd.state.tx.us/birdtrails*

Metropolitan Council, Saint Paul, Min-
nesota
Regional Administration
Mears Park Center
230 East 5th Street
Saint Paul, MN 55101
Telephone: (651) 602-1000
FAX: (651) 602-1358
Internet: *http://www.metrocouncil.org/*

Metropolitan Service District, Portland,
Oregon
Regional Planning Division
Metro Regional Center
600 NE Grand Avenue
Portland, OR 97232-2736
Telephone: (503) 797-1839
FAX: (503) 797-1911
Internet: *http://www.metro-region.org/*

Montgomery County, Rockville, Maryland
Office of the County Executive
Executive Office Building
101 Monroe Street
Rockville, MD 20850
Telephone: (240) 777-2500
FAX: (240) 777-2517
Internet: *http://www.montgomerycountymd.gov/*

Nelson County, Lovingston, Virginia
Office of the County Administrator
County Administration Building
84 Courthouse Square
Lovingston, VA 22949
Telephone: (434) 263-4873
FAX: (434) 263-7134
Telephone: *http://www.nelsoncountyva.org/*

Northampton County, Eastville, Virginia
Office of the County Administrator
County Administration Building
16403 Courthouse Road
Eastville, VA 23347-0510
Telephone: (757) 678-0440
FAX: (757) 678-0453
Internet: *http://www.co.northampton.va.us/*

Orange County, Santa Ana, California
Office of the County Executive
County Administration Building
10 Civic Plaza
Santa Ana, CA 92701
Telephone: (714) 834-2345
FAX: (714) 834-3555
Internet: *http://www.oc.ca.gov/*

Osceola County, Kissimmee, Florida
Office of the County Manager
County Administration Building
1 Courthouse Square
Suite 4700
Kissimmee, FL 34741
Telephone: (407) 343-2380
FAX: None Listed
Internet: *http://www.osceola.org/*

RiverCentre Authority, Saint Paul, Minnesota
Office of the Executive Director
175 West Kellogg Boulevard
Suite 501
Saint Paul, MN 55102-1299
Telephone: (651) 265-4800
FAX: (651) 265-4899
Internet: *http://www.rivercentre.org*

Riverfront Recapture, Hartford, Connecticut
Office of the President and Chief Executive
  Officer
One Hartford Square West
Suite 100

Hartford, CT 06106-1984
Telephone: (860) 713-3131
FAX: (860) 713-3138
Internet: *http://www.riverfront.org/*

Suffolk County, New York
Office of the Administrator
Riverhead County Center
County Road 51
Riverhead, NY 11901-3397
Telephone: (631) 853-4000
FAX: (631) 853-6399
Internet: *http://www.co.suffolk.ny.us/*

**The Maryland-National Capital Park and
  Planning Commission**, Silver Spring,
  Maryland
Office of the Director
8787 Georgia Avenue
Silver Spring, MD 20910
Telephone: (301) 495-4500
FAX: (301) 495-1310
Internet: *http://www.mc-mncppc.org/*

Town of Harmony, Florida
Office of Public Information
3500 Harmony Square Drive West
Harmony, FL 34773
Telephone: (407) 891-1616
FAX: (407) 891-0459
Internet: *http://www.harmonyfl.com/*

Tri-County Metropolitan Transit District,
  Portland, Oregon
Office of the General Manager
Tri-Met Administration Building
4012 SE 17th Avenue
Portland, OR 97202
Telephone: (503) 962-4831
FAX: (503) 962-6451
Internet: *http://www.tri-met.org/*

Washington, D.C.
District Municipal Government
Office of the City Administrator
John A. Wilson Building
1350 Pennsylvania Avenue, NW
Suites 301 and 302
Washington, D.C. 20004
Telephone: (202) 727-6053
FAX: (202) 727-9878
Internet: *http://www.dc.gov/*

NATIONAL RESOURCE DIRECTORY

Major national professional associations and research organizations serving local and regional governments, as well as environmentally concerned professionals and citizens.

Advisory Council on Historic Preservation
Old Post Office Building
1100 Pennsylvania Avenue, N.W.
Suite 809
Washington, D.C. 20004
Telephone: (202) 606-8503
FAX: (202) 606-8647 or 8672
Internet: *http://wwww.achp.gov*

Alliance for National Renewal
c/o National Civic League
1319 "F" St., N.W.
Suite 204
Washington, D.C. 20004
Telephone: (202) 783-2961
FAX: (202) 347-2161
Internet: *http://www.ncl.org/anr*

Alliance for Redesigning Government
c/o National Academy of Public Administration
1100 New York Ave., N.W.
Suite 1090 East
Washington, D.C. 20005
Telephone: (202) 347-3190
FAX: (202) 393-0993
Internet: *http://www.alliance.napawash.org*

Alliance for Regional Stewardship
785 Castro St.
Suite A
Mountain View, CA 94011
Telephone: (650) 623-3082

FAX: (650) 623-0900
Internet: *http://www.regionalstewardship.org*

American Economic Development Council
9801 West Higgins Road
Suite 540
Rosemont, IL 60018-4726
Telephone: (847) 692-9944
FAX: (847) 696-2990
Internet: *http://www.aedc.org*

American Planning Association
122 S. Michigan Ave.
Suite 1600
Chicago, IL 60603-6107
Telephone: (312) 431-9100
FAX: (312) 431-9985
Internet: *http://www.planning.org*

American Real Estate and Urban Economics Association
Kelley School of Business
Indiana University
1309 East Tenth Street
Suite 738
Bloomington, IN 47405
Telephone: (812) 855-7794
FAX: (812) 855-8679
Internet: *http://www.areuea.org*

American Society for Public Administration
1120 "G" St., N.W.
Suite 700

Washington, D.C. 20005
Telephone: (202) 393-7878
FAX: (202) 638-4952
Internet: *http://www.aspanet.org*

American Society of Landscape Architects
636 Eye St., N.W.
Washington, D.C. 20001-3736
Telephone: (202) 898-2444
FAX: (202) 898-1185
Internet: *http://www.asla.org*

Asset-Based Community Development In-stitute
Institute for Policy Research
Northwestern University
2040 Sheridan Road
Evanston, IL 60208-4100
Telephone: (847) 491-3518
FAX: (847) 491-9916
Internet: *http://www.nwu.edu/IPR/abcd.html*

Association for Enterprise Opportunity
1601 North Kent Street
Suite 1120
Arlington, VA 22209
Telephone: (703) 841-7760
FAX: (703) 841-7748
Internet: *http://www.microenterpriseworks.org*

Brownfields Technology Support Center
U.S. Environmental Protection Agency
1200 Pennsylvania Avenue, N.W.
Washington, D.C. 20460
Telephone: (877) 838-7220 (toll free)
Internet: *http://brownfieldstsc.org*

Building Officials and Code Administrators International
4051 Flossmoor Road
Country Club Hills, IL 60478-5795
Telephone: (708) 799-2300
FAX: (708) 799-4981
Internet: *http://www.bocai.org*

Center for Neighborhood Technology
2125 W. North Ave.
Chicago, IL 60647
Telephone: (773) 278-4800
FAX: (773) 278-3840
Internet: *http://www.cnt.org*

Center for Regional and Neighborhood Action
1009 Grant St.
Suite 203
Denver, CO 80203
Telephone (303) 477-9985
FAX: (303) 477-9986
Internet: *http://www.crna.net*

Committee for Economic Development
477 Madison Avenue
New York, NY 10022
Telephone: (212) 688-2063
FAX: (212) 758-9068
Internet: *http://www.ced.org*

Community Associations Institute
225 Reinekers Lane
Suite 300
Alexandria, VA 22314
Telephone: (703) 548-8600
FAX: (703) 684-1581
Internet: *http://www.caionline.org*

Community Development Society International
1123 North Water Street
Milwaukee, WI 53202
Telephone: (414) 276-7106
FAX: (414) 276-7704
Internet: *http://comm-dev.org*

Congress for the New Urbanism
The Marquette Building
140 South Dearborn Avenue
Suite 310
Chicago, IL 60603
Telephone: (312) 551-7300
FAX: (312) 346-3323
Internet: *http://www.cnu.org*

Corporation for Enterprise Development
777 North Capitol Street, N.E.
Suite 410
Washington, D.C. 20002
Telephone: (202) 408-9788
FAX: (202) 408-9793
Internet: *http://www.cfed.org*

Council for Urban Economic Development
1730 "K" St., N.W.
Suite 700

Washington, D.C. 20006
Telephone: (202) 223-4735
FAX: (202) 223-4745
Internet: *http://www.cued.org*

**Downtown Development and Research
    Center**
215 Park Avenue South
Suite 1301
New York, NY 10003
Telephone: (212) 228-0246
FAX: (212) 228-0376
Internet: *http://www.DowntownDevelopment.
    com*

Ecological Society of America
1707 "H" Street, N.W.
Suite 400
Washington, D.C. 20006-3915
Telephone: (202) 833-8773
FAX: (202) 833-8775
Internet: *http://www.esa.org*

Empowerment Zones
(See U.S. Dept. of Housing and Urban De-
    velopment)

Enterprise Communities Initiative
(See U.S. Dept. of Housing and Urban De-
    velopment)

Environmental Assessment Association
1224 North Nakomis, N.E.
Alexandria, MN 56308
Telephone: (320) 763-4320
FAX: (320) 763-9290
Internet: *http://iami.org*

Habitat for Humanity International
Partner Service Center
121 Habitat Street
Americus, GA 31709
Telephone: (912) 924-6935, Ext. 2551 or 2552
FAX: (912) 924-6541
Internet: *http://www.habitat.org*

**Interactive Economic Development Net-
    work**
1730 "K" Street, N.W.
Suite 700
Washington, D.C. 20006

Telephone: (202) 223-4735
FAX: (202) 223-4745
Internet: *http://www.iedn.com*

**International City/County Management
    Association**
777 North Capitol Street, N.E.
Suite 500
Washington, D.C. 20002
Telephone: (202) 289-4262
FAX: (202) 962-3500
Internet: *http://www.icma.org*

**International Conference of Building
    Officials**
5360 South Workman Mill Road
Whittier, CA 90601-2258
Telephone: (310) 699-0541
FAX: (310) 692-3853
Internet: *http://www.icbo.org*

International Downtown Association
190-17th Street, N.W.
Suite 210
Washington, D.C. 20006
Telephone: (202) 293-4505
FAX: (202) 293-4509
Internet: *http://ida-downtown.org*

**National Academy of Public Administra-
    tion**
1101 New York Ave.
Suite 1090 East
Washington, D.C. 20005
Telephone: (202) 347-3190
FAX: (202) 393-0993
Internet: *http://www.napawash.org*

National Association of Counties
Joint Center for Sustainable Communities
440 First Street, N.W.
Washington, D.C. 20001-2080
Telephone: (202) 393-6226
FAX: (202) 393-2630
Internet: *http://www.naco.org*

**National Association of Development Or-
    ganizations**
444 North Capitol Street, N.W.
Suite 630

Washington, D.C. 20001
Telephone: (202) 624-7806
FAX: (202) 624-8813
Internet: *http://www.nado.org*

National Association of Housing and Redevelopment Officials
630 Eye Street, N.W.
Washington, D.C. 20001
Telephone: (202) 289-3500
FAX: (202) 289-8181
Internet: *http://www.nahro.org*

National Association of Regional Councils
1700 "K" Street, N.W.
Suite 1300
Washington, D.C. 20006
Telephone: (202) 457-0710
FAX: (202) 296-9352
Internet: *http://www.narc.org/narc*

National Association of State Development Agencies
750 First Street, N.E.
Suite 710
Washington, D.C. 20002
Telephone: (202) 898-1302
FAX: (202) 898-1312
Internet: *http://www.ids.net/nasda*

National Association for Environmental Management
1612 "K" Street, N.W.
Suite 1102
Washington, D.C. 20006
Telephone: (202) 986-6616
FAX: (202) 530-4408
Internet: *http://www.naem.org*

National Association of Local Governmental Environmental Professionals
1333 New Hampshire Ave., N.W.
Washington, D.C. 20036
Telephone: (202) 638-6254
FAX: (202) 393-2866
Internet: *http://www.nalgep.org*

National Audubon Society
700 Broadway
New York, NY 10003

Telephone: (212) 979-3000
FAX: (212) 979-3188
Internet: *http://www.audubon.org*

National Business Incubation Association
20 East Circle Drive
Suite 190
Athens, OH 45701-3751
Telephone: (740) 593-4331
FAX: (740) 593-1996
Internet: *http://www.nbia.org*

National Center for the Revitalization of Central Cities
College of Urban and Public Affairs
University of New Orleans
New Orleans, LA 70148
Telephone: (504) 280-6519
FAX: (504) 280-6272
Internet: *http://www.uno.edu/~cupa/ncrcc*

National Civic League
1445 Market Street
Suite 300
Denver, CO 80202-1728
Telephone: (303) 571-4343
FAX: (303) 571-4404
Internet: *http://www.ncl.org*

National Community Development Association
522–21st St., N.W.
Suite 120
Washington, D.C. 20006
Telephone: (202) 293-7587
FAX: (202) 887-5546
Internet: *http://www.ncdaonline.org*

National Congress for Community Economic Development
1030–15th St., N.W.
Suite 325
Washington, D.C. 20005
Telephone: (202) 289-9020
FAX: (202) 289-7051
Internet: *http://www.ncced.org*

National Council for Urban Economic Development
1730 "K" Street, N.W.

Suite 700
Washington, D.C. 20006
Telephone: (202) 223-4735
FAX: (202) 223-4745
Internet: *http://www.cued.org*

National Endowment for the Humanities
1100 Pennsylvania Avenue, N.W.
Washington, D.C. 20506
Telephone: (202) 606-8310
FAX: (202) 606-8600
Internet: *http://www.neh.gov*

National Groundwater Association
601 Dempsey Road
Westerville, OH 43081-8978
Telephone: (614) 898-7791
FAX: (614) 898-7786
Internet: *http://www.ngwa.org*

National Housing Conference
815 Fifteenth Street, N.W.
Suite 538
Washington, D.C. 20005
Telephone: (202) 393-5772
FAX: (202) 393-5656
Internet: *http://www.nhc.org*

National Housing Institute
439 Main Street
Suite 311
Orange, NJ 07050
Telephone: (973) 678-9060
FAX: (973) 678-8437
Internet: *http://www.nhi.org*

National Humanities Alliance
21 Dupont Circle, N.W.
Suite 604
Washington, D.C. 20036
Telephone: (202) 296-4994
FAX: (202) 872-0884
Internet: *http://www.nhalliance.org*

National League of Cities
1301 Pennsylvania Avenue, N.W.
Washington, D.C. 20004-1763
Telephone: (202) 626-3000
FAX: (202) 626-3043
Internet: *http://www.nlc.org*

National Main Street Center
(See National Trust for Historic Preservation)

National Trust for Historic Preservation
1785 Massachusetts Avenue, N.W.
Washington, D.C. 20036
Telephone: (202) 588-6219
FAX: (202) 588-6050
Internet: *http://www.mainst.org*

Natural Resource Conservation Service
(See U.S. Department of Agriculture)

Nature Conservancy
4245 North Fairfax Dr.
Suite 100
Arlington, VA 22203-1606
Telephone: (703) 247-3678
FAX: (703) 841-1283
Internet: *http://nature.org*

Office of Community Development
U.S. Department of Agriculture
Whitten Building
Washington, D.C. 20250-1301
Telephone: (202) 720-3621
FAX: (202) 720-5043
Internet: *http://ocdweb.sc.egov.usda.gov*

Partners for Livable Communities
1429–21st Street, N.W.
Washington, D.C. 20036
Telephone: (202) 887-5990
FAX: (202) 466-4845
Internet: *http://www.livable.com*

Partnership for Regional Livability
2125 W. North Ave.
Chicago, IL 60647
Telephone: (773) 278-4800, Ext. 135
FAX: (773) 278-3840
Internet: *http://www.pfrl.org*

Rails-to-Trails Conservancy
1100 Seventeenth St., N.W.
10th Floor
Washington D.C. 20036
Telephone: (202) 331-9696
FAX: (202) 466-3742
Internet: *http://www.railtrails.org*

Sierra Club
85 Second Street
2nd Floor
San Francisco, CA 94105
Telephone: (415) 977-5500
FAX: (415) 977-5799
Internet: *http://www.sierraclub.org*

Society of Wetland Scientists
1313 Dolly Madison
Suite 402
McLean, VA 22101
Telephone: (703) 790-1745
FAX: (703) 790-2672
Internet: *http://www.sws.org*

The Urban Institute
2100 "M" St., N.W.
Washington, D.C. 20037
Telephone: (202) 833-7200
FAX: (202) 331-9747
Internet: *http://www.urban.org*

Trust for Public Land
116 New Montgomery St.
4th Floor
San Francisco, CA 94105
Telephone: (415) 495-4014
FAX: (415) 495-4103
Internet: *http://www.tpl.org*

United States Conference of Mayors
1620 Eye St., N.W.
4th Floor
Washington, D.C. 20006
Telephone: (202) 293-7330
FAX: (202) 293-2352
Internet: *http://www.usmayors.org*

U.S. Department of Agriculture
14th and Independence Avenue, S.W.
Room 5105-A
Washington, D.C. 20250
Telephone: (202) 720-7246
FAX: (202) 720-7690
Internet: *http://www.nrcs.usda.gov*

U.S. Department of Housing and Urban Development
451–7th Street, S.W.

Washington, D.C. 20410
Telephone: (202) 708-1112
FAX: (202) 401-0416
Internet: *http://www.hud.gov*

U.S. Department of the Interior
1849 "C" Street, N.W.
Washington, D.C. 20240
Telephone: (202) 208-3100
FAX: (202) 208-4833
Internet: *http://www.doi.gov*

Urban and Regional Information Systems Association
1460 Renaissance Drive
Suite 305
Park Ridge, IL 60068
Telephone: (847) 824-6300
FAX: (847) 824-6363
Internet: *http://www.urisa.org*

Urban Land Institute
1015 Thomas Jefferson St., N.W.
Suite 500 West
Washington, D.C. 20007-5201
Telephone: (202) 624-7000
FAX: (202) 624-7140
Internet: *http://www.uli.org*

U.S. Environmental Protection Agency
Ariel Rios Building
1200 Pennsylvania Ave., N.W.
Washington, D.C. 20460
Telephone: (202) 272-0167
FAX: None Listed
Internet: *http://www.epa.gov*

U.S. Fish & Wildlife Service
1849 "C" Street, N.W.
Washington, D.C. 20240
Telephone: (202) 208-4717
FAX: (202) 208-6965
Internet: *http://www.fws.gov*

Water Environment Federation
601 Wythe Street
Alexandria, VA 22314-1994
Telephone: (703) 684-2452
FAX: (703) 684-2492
Internet: *http://www.wef.org*

BIBLIOGRAPHY

Books, monographs, articles, and other sources in the field of cities and nature.

Books

Bailey, John T. *Marketing Cities in the 1980's and Beyond*. Rosemont, IL: American Economic Development Council, 1989.

Barnett, Jonathan. *The Fractured Metropolis: Improving the New City, Restoring the Old City, Reshaping the Region*. New York, NY: Icon Edition, 1995.

_____. *Redesigning Cities*. Chicago, IL: APA Planners Press, 2003.

Berkus, Barry A. *Architecture/Art/Parallels/Connections*. Washington, D.C.: The Urban Land Institute, 2000.

Blakely, Edward J. *Planning Local Economic Development: Theory and Practice*, Thousand Oaks, CA: Sage Publications, 1989.

Bleakly, Ken. *Economic Impact Analysis: Assessing a Project's Value to a Community*. Rosemont, IL: American Economic Development Council, 1993.

Burchell, Robert W., et al. *Development Impact Assessment Handbook*. Washington, D.C.: Urban Land Institute, 1994.

Cisneros, Henry G. Editor. *Interwoven Destinies: Cities and the Nation*. New York, NY: The American Assembly, 1993.

Clemetson, Robert A., and Roger Coates. *Restoring Broken Places and Rebuilding Communities*. Washington, D.C.: National Congress for Community Development, 1992.

Congress for the New Urbanism. *Charter of the New Urbanism*. New York, NY: McGraw-Hill, Inc., 1999.

Downing, Paul B. *Local Service Pricing Policies and Their Impact on Urban Spatial Structures*. Vancouver, B.C.: University of British Columbia Press, 1977.

Eppli, Mark J., and Charles C. Tu. *Valuing the New Urbanism*. Washington, D.C.: The Urban Land Institute, 1999.

Fosler, R. Scott. *Local Economic Development: Strategies for a Changing Economy*. Washington, D.C.: International City/County Management Association, 1991.

Garvin, Alexander. *Parks, Recreation, and Open Space*. Washington, D.C.: The Urban Land Institute, 2000.

_____. *The American City*. New York, NY: McGraw-Hill, Inc., 2002.

Garvin, Alexander, Gayle Berens, and Chistopher Leinberger, et al. *Urban Parks and Open Space*. Washington, D.C.: The Urban Land Institute, 1997.

Hall, Kenneth B., and Gerald A. Porterfield. *Community by Design*. New York, NY: McGraw-Hill, Inc., 2001.

Harnik, Peter. *Inside City Parks*. Washington, D.C.: The Urban Land Institute, 2000.

Harrell, Adele V., and George E. Peterson. Editors. *Drugs, Crime, and Social Isolation*. Washington, D.C.: The Urban Institute Press, 1992.

Hatry, Harry, Mark Fall, Thomas Singer, and Blaine Liner. *Monitoring the Outcomes of Economic Development Programs*. Washington, D.C.: The Urban Institute, 1990.

Herzog, Henry W., Jr., and Alan M. Schlottmann, editors. *Industrial Location and Public Policy*. Knoxville, TN: The University of Tennessee Press, 1991.

Hudnut III, William H. *Halfway to Everywhere*. Washington, D.C.: The Urban Land Institute, 2003.

_____. *Cities on the Rebound*. Washington, D.C.: The Urban Land Institute, 1998.

Katz, Peter. *The New Urbanism*. New York, NY: McGraw-Hill, Inc., 1994.

Kemp, Roger L. *Managing America's Cities: A Handbook for Local Government Productivity*. Jefferson, NC: McFarland & Co., Inc., 1998.

_____. *Main Street Renewal: A Handbook for*

Citizens and Public Officials. Jefferson, NC: McFarland & Co., Inc., 2000.

_____. *The Inner City: A Handbook for Renewal.* Jefferson, NC: McFarland & Co., Inc., 2001.

_____. *Regional Government Innovations: A Handbook for Citizens and Public Officials.* Jefferson, NC: McFarland & Co., Inc., 2003.

_____. *Urban Economic Development: Successful Case Studies from American Cities.* East Rockaway, NY: Cummings & Hathaway, 1995.

Kivell, Philip. *Land and the City: Patterns and Processes of Urban Change.* London, England: Routledge, 1993.

Koepke, Robert L. *Practicing Economic Development.* Rosemont, IL: American Economic Development Council, 1993.

Kolter, Philip, Donald H. Haider, and Irving Rein. *Marketing Places: Attracting Investment, Industry and Tourism to Cities, States and Nations.* New York, NY: The Free Press, 1993.

Ledebur, Larry C., and William R. Barnes. *All In It Together: Cities, Suburbs and Local Economic Regions.* Washington, D.C.: National League of Cities, February, 1993.

Lynn, Laurence E., Jr., and Michael McGeary. Editors. *Inner-City Poverty in the United States.* Washington, D.C.: National Academy Press, 1990.

Massey, Douglas S., and Nancy A. Denton. *American Apartheid: Segregation and the Making of the Underclass.* Cambridge, MA: Harvard University Press, 1993.

McLaughlin, Milbrey W., Merita A. Irby, and Juliet Langman. *Urban Sanctuaries: Neighborhood Organizations in the Lives and Future of Inner City Youth.* San Francisco, CA: Jossey-Bass Publishers, 1994.

McNeeley, Joseph B. *Building for the Future.* Washington, D.C.: Fannie Mae Foundation, November, 1993.

Medoff, P., and H. Sklar. *Streets of Hope: The Fall and Rise of an Urban Neighborhood.* Boston, MA: South End Press, 1994.

Milder, N. David. *Niche Strategies for Downtown Revitalization: A Hands-on Guide to Developing, Strengthening and Marketing Niches.* New York, NY: Downtown Research and Development Center, 1997.

Miles, Mike E., Gayle Berens, and Marc A. Weiss. *Real Estate Development.* Washington, D.C.: The Urban Land Institute, 2000.

Moe, Richard, and Carter Wilkie. *Changing Places: Rebuilding Community in the Age of Sprawl.* New York, NY: Henry Holt and Company, 1997.

National League of Cities. *Accepting the Challenge: The Rebirth of America's Downtowns.* Washington, D.C.: National League of Cities, 1994.

_____ and CH2MHILL. *Working Cities, Winning Ideas: James C. Howland Awards for Urban Enrichment, 1998.* Washington, D.C.: National League of Cities, 1999.

_____ and CH2MHILL. *Working Cities, Winning Ideas: James C. Howland Awards for Urban Enrichment, 1999.* Washington, D.C.: National League of Cities, 2000.

Norquist, John O. *The Wealth of Cities: Revitalizing the Centers of American Life.* Reading, MA: Addison-Wesley, 1998.

O'Neill, David. *The Smart Growth Tool Kit.* Washington, D.C.: The Urban Land Institute, 2001.

O'Neill, David, and Victoria R. Wilbur. *Environment and Development.* Washington, D.C.: The Urban Land Institute, 2002.

Palma, Dolores P., and Doyle G. Hyett. *Accepting the Challenge: The Rebirth of America's Downtowns.* Washington, D.C.: National League of Cities, 1994.

_____. *How to Revitalize Your Downtown.* Washington, D.C.: National League of Cities, 1999.

Peck, Dennis, and John Murphy. Editors. *Open Institutions: The Hope for Democracy.* New York, NY: Praeger, 1993.

Peiser, Richard B., and Anne Frej. *Professional Real Estate Development.* Washington, D.C.: The Urban Land Institute, 2003.

Peterson, George E. *Confronting the Nation's Urban Crisis: From Watts (1965) to South Central Los Angeles (1992).* The Urban Institute Press, 1992.

Pitts, Adrian. *Strategic Planning for Sustainability and Profit.* Washington, D.C.: The Urban Land Institute, 1997.

Porter, Robert R., et al. *The Practice of Sustainable Development.* Washington, D.C.: The Urban Land Institute, 2000.

Porter, Douglas R. *Making Smart Growth Work.* Washington, D.C.: The Urban Land Institute, 2002.

Probst, Katherine N., Don Fullerton, Robert E. Litan, and Paul R. Portney, *Footing the Bill.*

Rusk, David. *Cities Without Suburbia.* Washington, D.C.: The Woodrow Wilson Center Press, 1993.

_____. *Inside Game/Outside Game: Winning Strategies for Saving Urban America.* Washington, D.C.: The Century Foundation, Brookings Institution, 1999.

Schuman, Diane R., D. Scott Middleton, and Susan Giles. *Public/Private Housing Partnerships.* Washington, D.C.: Urban Land Institute, 1990.

Schwanke, Dean, et al. *Mixed-Use Development Handbook*. Washington, D.C.: The Urban Land Institute, 2003.

Simmons, Robert A. *Turning Brownfields into Greenfields*. Washington, D.C.: The Urban Land Institute, 1997.

Sklar, Holly. *Chaos or Community: Seeking Solutions, Not Scapegoats for Bad Economics*. Boston, MA: South End Press, 1995.

Snyder, Thomas P., and Michael A. Stegman. *Paying for Growth: Using Development Fees to Finance Infrastructure*. Washington, D.C.: The Urban Institute, 1987.

Squires, Gregory D. Editor. *From Redlining to Reinvestment: Community Response to Urban Disinvestment*. Philadelphia, PA: Temple University Press, 1992.

Stone, P. A. *The Structure, Size, and Costs of Urban Settlements*. Cambridge, England: Cambridge University Press, 1973.

Sullivan, Mercer. *More Than Housing: How Community Development Corporations Go About Changing Lives and Neighborhoods*. New York, NY: New School for Social Research, 1993.

Taub, Richard P. *Community Capitalism*. Boston, MA: Harvard Business School Press, 1988.

Urban Institute, The. *Special Districts: A Useful Technique for Financing Infrastructure*. Washington, D.C.: The Urban Institute, 1992.

Vidal, Avis C. *Rebuilding Communities: A National Study of Community Development Corporations*. New York, NY: New School for Social Research, 1992.

Weston, Josh S. *Rebuilding Inner-city Communities: A New Approach to the Nation's Urban Crisis*. New York, N.Y.: Committee for Economic Development, 1995.

Monographs

Atkinson, Maureen, Patricia Falch, and John Williams. *Marketing Your Downtown*. Management Information Service Report, vol. 28, no. 6. Washington, D.C.: International City/County Management Association, June 1996.

Austrian, Ziona, and Henning Eichler. *Urban Brownfields Site Survey: Preliminary Analysis*. Cleveland, OH: Cleveland State University, Levin College of Urban Affairs, April 28, 1994.

Bamberger, Rita J., William A. Blazar, and George E. Peterson. "Capital Planning." *Planning Advisory Service Report*, no. 390. Chicago, IL: American Planning Association, September 1985.

Bartik, Timothy J. *Who Benefits from State and Local Economic Development Policies?* Kalamazoo, MI: Upjohn Institute, 1991.

Binger, Gary, and Janet McBride. *Beyond Polemics: A Discussion of "The Cases for Suburban Development" and "Beyond Sprawl: New Patterns of Growth to Fit the New California."* Monterey, CA: Association of Bay Area Governments (ABAG), May 1996.

Black, Harry. *Achieving Economic Development Success: Tools That Work*. Washington, D.C.: International City/County Management Association, 1991.

Black, J. Thomas. *Recycling Inactive Urban Industrial Sites*. Washington, D.C.: Urban Land Institute, 1994.

Bowes, David B. "Creating Globally Competitive Communities." *Management Information Service Report*, vol. 28, no. 11. Washington, D.C.: International City/County Management Association, November 1996.

Bradley, Richard H. *Building the New Framework: A Coordinated Strategic Approach*. Washington, D.C.: International Downtown Association, 1992.

_____. *The Downtown of the 21st Century*. Washington, D.C.: International Downtown Association, 1992.

Broachway, G. P. *The End of Economic Man: Principles of Any Future Economics*. New York, NY: W. W. Norton, 1993.

Canter, Larry, et al. *Impact of Growth: A Guide for Socio-Economic Impact Assessment and Planning*. Chelsea, MI: Lewis Publishers, Inc., 1986.

Center for Community Change. *The HOME Program: A Brief Guide for Community Organizations*. Washington, D.C.: Center for Community Change, 1992.

Darling, David L., Jr. *Setting Community Economic Goals*. Manhattan, KS: Community Development Series (No. L-714), Kansas State University, February 1988.

_____. *Strategic Planning for Community Development*. Manhattan, KS: Community Development Series (No. L-830), Kansas State University, February 1991.

_____. *Understanding Your Community's Economy*. Manhattan, KS: Community Development Series (No. L-776), Kansas State University, October 1988.

Edelstein, M. *Contaminated Communities: The Social and Psychological Impacts of Residential Toxic Exposure*. Boulder, CO: Westview Press, 1988.

Ellis, Brinille Elaine. *Strategic Economic Development*. Management Information Service

Report, vol. 26, no. 2. Washington, D.C.: International City/County Management Association, February 1994.

Frank, James E. *The Costs of Alternative Development Patterns: A Review of the Literature.* Washington, D.C.: Urban Land Institute, 1989.

Kemp, Roger L. "Clifton's Future Vision Project." *Planners' Casebook* (No. 5). Chicago, IL: American Institute of Certified Planners, American Planning Association, Winter 1993.

_____. "Financial Productivity: New Techniques for Hard Times." *Municipal Finance Journal,* vol. 10, no. 4, April 1990.

Kirshenberg, Seth D., and Charles Bartsch. *Brownfields: Options and Opportunities.* Management Information Service Report, vol. 29, no. 5. Washington, D.C.: International City/County Management Association, May 1977.

Kotkin, Joel. *The Future of the Center: The Core City in the New Economy.* Los Angeles, CA: Reason Foundation, 2000.

Leiterman, Mindy, and Joseph Stillman. *Building Community: A Report on Social Community Development Initiatives.* New York, NY: Local Initiatives Support Corporation, 1993.

Lichtenstein, G. A., and T. S. Lyons. *Incubating New Enterprises: A Guide to Successful Practice.* Washington, D.C.: The Aspen Institute, 1996.

Mayer, Virginia M., Marina Sampanes, and James Carras. *Local Officials Guide to the CRA.* Washington, D.C.: National League of Cities, 1991.

McGrath, Daniel T. *An Investigation into the Impact of Hazardous Waste Contamination Liability on Urban Industrial Land Redevelopment in the City of Chicago.* Chicago, IL: University of Chicago, Great Cities Institute, December 5, 1995.

McLean, Mary L., and Kenneth P. Voytek. *Understanding Your Economy.* Chicago, IL: American Planning Association, Planners Press, 1992.

Melaville, Atelia I., Martin J. Blank, and Gelareh Asayesh. *Together We Can: A Guide for Crafting a Pro-Family System of Education and Human Services.* Washington, D.C.: U.S. Department of Education and U.S. Department of Health and Human Services, 1993.

Meyer, Angela D., and Ronald J. Swager. *A Bibliography of Selected Topics in Economic Development Literature, 1987-1993.* Rosemont, IL: American Economic Development Council, 1994.

Moore, Mark H., and Darrel W. Stephens. *Beyond Command and Control: The Strategic Management of Police Departments.* Washington, D.C.: Police Executive Research Forum, 1991.

National Council for Urban Economic Development. *Alternative Approaches to Financing Business Development.* Washington, D.C.: NCUED, 1989.

_____. *Forces in the Economy: Implications for Local Economic Development.* Washington, D.C.: NCUED, 1993.

_____. *Industrial Development Bonds: A Resource for Financing Economic Development.* Washington, D.C.: NCUED, 1994.

_____. *Neighborhood Economic Revitalization.* Washington, D.C.: NCUED, 1994.

_____. *Urban Manufacturing: Dilemma or Opportunity?* Washington, D.C.: NCUED, 1994.

National Conference of State Legislatures. *Breaking New Ground: Community-based Development Organizations.* Denver, CO: National Conference of State Legislatures, 1991.

Nowak, Jeremy, et al. *Religious Institutions and Community Renewal.* Philadelphia, PA: The Pew Charitable Trusts, 1989.

Oakland, William H., and William A. Testa. *Does Business Development Raise Taxes: An Empirical Appraisal.* Chicago, IL: Metropolitan Council and the Federal Reserve Bank of Chicago, January, 1995.

Pierce, Neil, and Carol F. Steinbach. *Corrective Capitalism: The Rise of America's Community Development Corporations.* New York, NY: Ford Foundation, 1987.

Sampson, Robert J. *Crime and Community Social Disorganization: Implications for Social Policy.* Washington, D.C.: U.S. Department of Housing and Urban Development, 1993.

Segal, Bradley, Katherine Correll, and Robert Dubinsky. *Business Improvement Districts: Tools for Economic Development.* Management Information Service Report, vol. 29, no. 3. Washington, D.C.: International City/County Management Association, March 1997.

Schmenner, Roger W. *Energy Costs, Urban Development, and Housing.* Washington, D.C.: Brookings Institution, 1984.

Stillman, Joseph. *Making the Connection: Economic Development, Workforce Development, and Urban Poverty.* New York, NY: The Conservation Company, 1994.

Swager, Ronald J. *A Bibliography of Literature in Economic Development.* Rosemont, IL: American Economic Development Council, 1987.

_____. *Economic Development Tomorrow: A Report from the Profession.* Rosemont, IL: American Economic Development Council, 1991.

Articles

Adams, Gerald D. "Presidio Trust Management Plan, San Francisco." *Planning*, Vol. 70, No. 4, April 2004.

Albanese, Joe, and Scott Martinelli. "Restoration Renaissance." *Urban Land*, vol. 57, no. 12, December 1998.

Andrews, Clinton J. "Putting Industrial Ecology into Place." *Journal of the American Planning Association*, vol. 65, no. 4, Autumn 1999.

Arrandale, Tom. "Developing the Contaminated City." *Governing*, vol. 6, no. 3, December 1992.

_____. "Rocky Mountain Revamp." *Planning*, Vol. 70, No. 1, January 2004.

Atkinson, Maureen, and John Williams. "Managing Downtown Revitalization by District." *Urban Land*, vol. 49, no. 9, September 1990.

Bailey, Richard. "Mall Over." *Urban Land*, vol. 57, no. 7, July 1998.

Banikowdki, J. E., K. E. Thomas, and J. L. Zegarelli. "Cleaning Up Without Getting Cleaned Out." *American City and County*, vol. 109, no. 8, July 1994.

Beatley, Timothy. "Preserving Biodiversity: Challenges for Planners." *APA Journal*, Vol. 66, No. 1, Winter 2000.

Ben-Zadok, Efraim. "Growing Smart Is Hard to Do." *Planning*, Vol. 69, No. 9, October 2003.

Barnett, Jonathan. "Shaping Our Cities: It's Your Call." *Planning*, vol. 61, no. 12, December 1995.

Berger, Renee. "Building Community Partnerships." *National Civic Review*, vol. 73, no. 2, May 1984.

Balck, J. Thomas. "Fort Worth: Maintaining Vitality Downtown." *Urban Land*, vol. 57, no. 2, February 1998.

_____. "People, Power, Politics." *Planning*, vol. 63, no. 2, February 1997.

Berton, Valerie. "Keeping 'Em Down on the Farm." *Planning*, Vol. 68, No. 7, July 2002.

Bogorad, Leonard. "Washington: A New Urbanist Frontier." *Urban Land*, vol. 58, no. 9, September 1999.

Bolan, Lewis, and Eric Smart. "Washington at the Millennium." *Urban Land*, vol. 58, no. 9, September 1999.

Bourne, L. S. "The Roepki Lecture in Economic Geography–Recycling Urban Systems and Metropolitan Areas: A Geographical Agenda for the 1990's and Beyond." *Economic Geography*, vol. 67, no. 3, July 1991.

Boyd, James, and Molly K. Macauley. "The Impact of Environmental Liability on Industrial Real Estate Development." *Resources*, no. 114, Winter 1994.

Boydell, Thomas E., and Douglas R. Porter. "Building Public/Private Collaboration in Puget Sound." *Urban Land*, vol. 56, no. 9, September 1997.

Bradley, Richard H. "Vive Le Renaissance!" *Urban Land*, vol. 58, no. 9, September 1999.

_____. "Downtown Renewal: The Role of Business Improvement Districts." *Public Management*, vol. 77, no. 2, February 1995.

Bray, Paul M. "A New Tool for Renewing the Central City: The Urban Cultural Park." *National Civic Review*, vol. 83, no. 2, Spring-Summer 1994.

_____. "The New Urbanism: Celebrating the City." *Places*, vol. 8, no. 4, Summer 1993.

Breslaw, Jon A. "Density and Urban Sprawl: Comment." *Land Economics*, vol. 66, no. 43, November 1990.

Brown, Lester R. "The Eco-Economic Revolution: Getting the Market in Sync with Nature." *The Futurist*, Vol. 36, No. 2, March/April 2002.

Building Association of Northern California. "Striking at the Heart of Sprawl." *BIA News*, vol. 5, no. 1, March 1996.

Bunster-Ossa, Ignacio F. "Landscape Urbanism." *Urban Land*, Vol. 60, No. 7, July 2001.

Carlson, David A. "Paving the Way to Economic Revitalization: 'Covenant Not to Sue' Stimulates Redevelopment in Economic Target Areas." *Massachusetts Environment*, vol. 1, no. 9, February 1996.

Coe, Barbara A. "Public-Private Cooperation." *Western Governmental Researcher*, vol. III, no. 1, Summer 1987.

Clayton, David. "Las Vegas Goes for Broke." *Planning*, vol. 61, no. 9, September 1995.

Colley, Sharon. "Housing Opens Door to Redevelopment." *American City & County*, vol. 115, no. 4, March 2000.

Corser, Susan Ernst. "From Ranchland to Conservation Community." *Planning*, Vol. 69, No. 8, August/September 2003.

Cox, Robert D. "A New Approach to 'Brownfields' in Central Massachusetts." *Massachusetts Environment*, vol. 1, no. 9, February 1996.

Crewe, Timothy, Susan Anderson, and Laurel Butman. "Portland, Oregon: A Case Study of Sustainability." *Government Finance Review*, Vol. 18, No. 1, February 2002.

Crow, Susan R. and Gail M. Cowie. "Georgia's Pine Mountain Ridge: Lessons for Regional Planning." *The Regionalist*, Vol. 1, No. 4, Spring 1996.

Culbertson, Steve, and Jeff Watkins. "Rebuilding

Philadelphia's Neighborhoods." *Urban Land*, vol. 56, No. 9, September 1997.

Cunningham, Storm. "Restorative Development: The New Growth Strategy for Communities of All Sizes." *Public Management*, Vol. 85, No. 7, August 2003.

Curtis, Peter G., and Michael C. Bianchi. "Turning 'TOADS' into 'PRINCES': Financing Environmentally Impaired Properties." *Massachusetts Environment*, vol. 1, no. 3, August 1995.

Davis, Brett. "Chambers Creek Properties Master Site Plan, Pierce County, Washington." *Planning*, Vol. 70, No. 4, April 2004 .

Dimond, Chris. "Made for Walkin'." *American City & County*, Vol. 113, No. 8, July 1998.

Dorsett, John W. "The Price Tag of Parking." *Urban Land*, vol. 57, no. 5, May 1998.

Drawas, Neal M. "Remediation Liability Management." *Massachusetts Environment*, vol. 1, no. 3, August 1995.

Ehrenhart, Alan. "The Trouble with Zoning." *Government*, vol. 11, no. 5, February 1998.

Farrell, Christopher. "The Economics of Crime." *Business Week*, December 13, 1993.

Enlow, Clair. "Streets as Parks." *Planning*, Vol. 68, No. 5, May 2002.

Eysenbach, Mary. "Learning from City Parks." *Planning*, Vol. 69, No. 10, October, 2003.

Faga, Barbara. "Parks Downtown." *Urban Land*, Vol. 60, No. 7, July, 2001.

Finnemore, Melodyh. "Defining Vision." *Urban Land*, Vol. 59, No. 10, October 2000.

Fishbach, John, and Lucinda Smith. "Climate Protection: Fort Collins Likes the Idea." *Public Management*, Vol. 82, No. 8, August 2000.

Fondersmith, John. "Downtowns in the Year 2040." *The Futurist*, vol. 22, no. 2, March–April 1988.

Fosler, R. Scott. "The Future Economic Role of Local Governments." *Public Management*, vol. 70, no. 4, April 1988.

Foxen, Robert. "Approaching Brownfields: Public, Private Forces Combine to Develop Abandoned Property." *Massachusetts Environment*, vol. 1, no. 3, August 1995.

Frank, Lawrence D., and Robert T. Dunphy. "Smart Growth and Transportation." *Urban Land*, vol. 57, no. 5, May 1998.

Frederick, Charles, Karen Wise, and Natalie Saikaly. "Urban Wetlands." *Urban Land*, Vol. 60, No. 7, July 2001.

Frieden, Bernard J., and Lynne B. Sagalyn. "Downtown Malls and the City Agenda." *Society*, vol. 27, no. 4, July-August 1990.

Froehlich, Maryann. "Smart Growth: Why Local Governments Are Taking a New Approach to Managing Growth in Their Communities." *Public Management*, vol. 80, no. 5, May 1998.

Fulton, William "Are Edge Cities Losing Their Edge?" *Planning*, vol. 62, no. 5, May 1996.

_____, and Morris Newman. "The Strange Career of Enterprise Zones." *Governing*, vol. 8, no. 3, March 1994.

Gallagher, Patrick. "Captivate and Educate." *Urban Land*, vol. 57, no. 2, February 1998.

Gihring, Thomas A. "Incentive Property Taxation: A Potential Tool for Urban Growth Management." *Journal of the American Planning Association*, vol. 65, no. 1, Winter 1999.

Glover, Glenda, and J. Paul Brownridge. "Enterprise Zones as an Instrument of Urban Policy: A Review of the Zones in South Central Los Angeles." *Government Finance Review*, vol. 9, no. 3, June 1993.

Gubala, Timothy W. "The Difference Between Economic Developers and Planners." *Economic Development Review*, vol. 10, no. 2, Summer 1992.

Gurwitt, Rob. "New Alliances." *Governing*, vol. 11, no. 9, June 1998.

_____. "The Rule of the Absentocracy." *Governing*, vol. 5, no. 9, September 1991.

Hahn, Kurt. "When and When Not to Use Incentives to Attract Business or to Retain Existing Businesses." *Government Finance Review*, vol. 12, no. 3, June 1996.

Haider, Donald. "Place Wars: New Realities of the 1990's." *Economic Development Quarterly*, vol. 6, no. 2, May 1992.

Hanan, Fran, and Patricia Vaccaro. "Design 2000." *Urban Land*, vol. 59, no. 1, January 2000.

Hardy, Ruth Ellen. "Citizen Participation." *Planning Forum*, vol. 2, 1996.

Hargett, Terra. "Restoring Urban Parks: New Life in Old Spaces." *American City & County*, Vol. 116, No. 14, September 2001.

_____. "Rails-to-Trails Projects in Regions of Georgia, Maryland, and Mississippi." *American City and County*, Vol. 116, No. 1, January 2001.

Harris, Robert R., and John H. Carman. "Battling the American Dream." *Urban Land*, vol. 58, no. 9, September 1999.

Hayden, Delores. "Using Ethnic History to Understand Urban Landscapes." *Places*, vol. 7, no. 1, Fall 1990.

Henning, Ed. "Business Improvement Districts." *Western City*, vol. LXIX, no. 8, August 1993.

Hill, Gary G. "Paying for New Development: The Urban Structure Program of the City of Lancaster." *Government Finance Review*, vol. 13, no. 3, June 1997.

Hitchings, Benjamin G. "A Typology of Regional Growth Management Systems." *The Regionalist*, Vol. 3, No. ½, Fall 1998.

Hoffer, William. "Using Urban Renovation Experts." *Nation's Business*, vol. 77, no. 1, January 1989.

Holden, Alfred. "Why Toronto Works?" *Planning*, vol. 61, no. 3, March 1995.

Hollis, Linda E. "Baltimore: Washington's Neighbor to the North." *Urban Land*, vol. 58, no. 9, September 1999.

Hornick, Sandy. "Context Is Everything." *Planning*, vol. 56, no. 1, December 1990.

Houstoun, Lawrence O., Jr. "Downtown Managers," *New Jersey Municipalities*, vol. 67, no. 4, April 1990.

Howland, Libby. "Resurgence in Downtown Washington." *Urban Land*, vol. 57, no. 3, March 1998.

Hudnut, William H., III. "Downtown: Still the Heart and the Soul of a Region." *Urban Land*, vol. 57, no. 2, February 1998.

Hughes, Ken. "Ten Ways to Get Back to the Plaza." *Planning*, Vol. 68, No. 12, December 2002.

Innes, Judith E., and David E. Booher. "Consensus Building and Complex Adaptive Systems: A Framework for Evaluating Collaborative Planning." *Journal of the American Planning Association*, vol. 65, no. 4, Autumn 1999.

Isaacs, Lindsay. "Shoring Up the Nation's Coastline." *American City & County*, Vol. 115, No. 13, September 2000.

Jacobson, Thomas. "Suburban Design: One Step at a Time." *Planning*, vol. 64, no. 5, May 1998.

Jarger, Ed. "Rooftop Garden Creates an Oasis for Wellness and Rehabilitation." *Landscape Architect and Specifier News*, Vol. 20, No. 6, June 2004.

Jacobson, Louis. "Tennessee Triumph." *Planning*, Vol. 63, No. 5, May 1997.

Jensen, Peter. "San Diego's Vision Quest." *Planning*, vol. 63, no. 3, March 1997.

Kay, Jane Holtz. "The Hub Is Hot." *Planning*, vol. 64, no. 3, March 1998.

Kelly, Margret C. H. and Matthew Zieper. "Financing for the Future: The Economic Benefits of Parks and Open Space." *Government Finance Review*, Vol. 16, No. 6, December 2000.

Knack, Ruth E. "Go Badgers, Fight Sprawl." *Planning*. Vol. 63, No. 5, May 1997.

Knack, Ruth Eckdish. "BART's Village Vision." *Planning*, vol. 61, no. 1, January 1995.

_____. "Charleston at the Crossroads." *Planning*, vol. 60, no. 9, September 1994.

_____. "Downtown Where the Living Is Easy." *Planning*, vol. 64, no. 8, August 1998.

Kozloff, Howard. "Controlling Growth." *Urban Land*, Vol. 59, No. 8, August 2000.

_____. "Three Rivers Rising." *Urban Land*, Vol. 61, No. 7, July 2002.

Labich, Kenneth. "New Hopes for the Inner City." *Fortune*, September 6, 1993.

Lassar, Terry J. "Bridging a Building Boom." *Urban Land*, vol. 59, no. 2, February 2000.

_____. "On Common Ground." *Urban Land*, vol. 58, no. 10, October 1999.

_____. "Portland's On-Track Development." *Urban Land*, vol. 57, no. 3, March 1998.

Lawson, Quentin R., and John N. Pannullo. "Using Marketing Strategies to Address Local Issues." *Public Management*, vol. 68, no. 6, June 1986.

Leinberger, Christopher. "The Beginning of the End of Sprawl." *Urban Land*, vol. 59, no. 1, January 2000.

_____, and Gayle Berens. "Designing for Urban Parks." *Urban Land*, vol. 56, no. 12, December 1997.

Lindsey, Greg, and Gerrit Knaap. "Willingness to Pay for Urban Greenway Projects." *APA Journal*, Vol. 65, No. 3, Summer 1999.

Lockwood, Charles. "Houston's Turn." *Urban Land*, vol. 59, no. 2, February 2000.

_____. "Retrofitting Suburbia." *Urban Land*, Vol. 57, No. 7, July 1998.

_____. "Pioneering Petaluma." *Planning*, Vol. 64, No. 10, October 1998.

_____. "Let There (Not) Be Light." *Planning*. Vol. 70, No. 3, March 2004.

Lowe, Marcia D. "Alternatives to Shaping Tomorrow's Cities." *The Futurist*, vol. 26, no. 4, July-August 1992.

Luce, Thomas F., Jr. "Local Taxes, Public Services, and The Intrametropolitan Location of Firms and Households." *Public Finance Quarterly*, vol. 22, no. 2, April 1994.

Mahtesian, Charles. "Showdown on E-Z Street." *Governing*, vol. 8, no. 2, October 1995.

_____. "The Stadium Trap." *Governing*, vol. 11, no. 8, May 1998.

Markowitz, Michael. "Riverfront Revital." *Planning*, Vol. 69, No. 4, April 2003.

Marshall, John T. "Rebuilding the American City: Bonds of Friendship as Bricks and Mortar." *Planning Forum*, vol. 1, Spring 1995.

Martin, Frank Edgerton. "Saint Paul's New Riverfront Urban Villages." *Urban Land*, Vol. 60, No. 4, April 2001.

McCormick, Kathleen. "Home, Home on the Ranchette." *Planning*, Vol. 64, No. 2, February 1998.

McMahon, Kathleen and Andrew Cahill. "Get Wired or Left Behind." *Planning*, Vol. 69, No. 7, July 2003.

McGuire, Leslie. "Back to the Grandeur of 1904." *Landscape Architect and Specifier News*, Vol. 20, No. 7, July 2004.

McNeal, Alvin R., and Rosalyn P. Doggett. "Metro Makes Its Mark." *Urban Land*, vol. 58, no. 9, September 1999.

Meyer, Peter B., and Thomas S. Lyons. "Lessons from Private Sector Brownfield Redevelopers: Planning Public Support for Urban Regeneration." *Journal of the American Planning Association*, vol. 66, no. 1, Winter 2000.

Miara, Jim. "Residential Rebound." *Urban Land*, vol. 58, no. 9, September 1999.

_____. "Council, My Council" *Urban Land*, Vol. 60, No. 4, April 2001.

Miller, Robert L. "Narrative Urban Landscapes." *Urban Land*, vol. 57, no. 2, February 1998.

Moon, J. Virgil, and Tom Majors. "An Economic Incentives Ordinance in Cobb County, Georgia, Bears Fruit in a Big Way." *Government Finance Review*, vol. 10, no. 3, June 1994.

Moreno, David. "Design Lyrics." *Urban Land*, Vol. 60, No. 7, July 2001.

Murphy, Linda. "The Land Market: How is EPA Fostering Redevelopment of Abandoned Urban Properties?" *Massachusetts Environment*, vol. 1, no. 9, February 1996.

Nozick, Marcia. "Urban Issues Program Underway." *City Magazine*, vol. 14, no. 4, Fall 1993.

_____. "Urban Issues Program Underway." *City Magazine*, vol. 15, no. 1, Winter 1994.

O'Connell, Kim. "Regionalizating Watershed Management." *American City & County*, Vol. 116, No. 6, June 2001.

Ohm, Brian W. "Conservation Easements Along the Mississippi River in Wisconsin." *APA Journal*, Vol. 66, No. 2, Spring 2000.

Oliver, Gordon. "Portland Revs Up for Action." *Planning*, vol. 60, no. 8, August 1994.

Osborne, John. "Blue Ways." *Planning*, Vol. 69, No. 10, October 2003.

Palma, Dolores P. "Downtown Revitalization." *Municipal Maryland*, vol. 23, no. 4, November 1994.

_____. "Effective Strategies for a Safe Downtown." *Municipal Maryland*, vol. 24, no. 7, February 1995.

_____. "Retaining and Strengthening Existing Downtown Businesses." *Municipal Maryland*, vol. 25, no. 3, October 1995.

_____. "Ten Myths About Downtown Revitalization." *Western City*, vol. LXX, No. 6, June 1994.

_____. "Ways to Revitalize Your Downtown." *American City & County*, vol. 107, no. 11, November 1992.

_____, and Doyle Hyett. "Born Again: Downtown Revivals Offer Salvation for Cities." *American City & County*, vol. 122, no. 8, July 1997.

Pawar, Michelle Wyman, and Christopher Rissetto. "A Tool for Improvement: Environmental Management Systems." *Public Management*, Vol. 83, No. 11, December 2001.

Peiser, Richard B. "Density and Urban Sprawl." *Land Economics*, vol. 65, no. 3, August 1989.

Pender, Robert B., and Frank C. Shaw. "Public-Private Partnerships." *Texas Town & City*, vol. 78, no. 6, June 1990.

Perlman, Ellen. "Downtown: The Live-In Solution." *Government*, vol. 11, no. 9, June 1998.

Pizzano, Arthur. "The Fairfield Village Green: A New Downtown for a Sustainable City." *Public Management*, Vol. 85, No. 11, December 2003.

Platt, Roger. "Recycling Brownfields." *Urban Land*, vol. 57, no. 6, June 1998.

Robbins, Elaine. "No More Road Kill?" *Planning*, Vol. 69, No. 2, February 2003.

_____. "Driving Them Wild." *Planning*. Vol. 69, No. 12, December 2003.

Robinson, Brian. "Curbing Urban Sprawl." *civic.com*, vol. 3, no. 5, May 1999.

Roeder, David H. "Organizing for Economic Development." *Planning*, vol. 59, no. 4, April 1993.

Rosen, Martin J. "Reviving Urban Parks." *Urban Land*, vol. 56, no. 11, November 1997.

Rosenfeld, Jordan M. "Designing Urban Public Plazas." *Urban Land*, vol. 56, no. 12, December 1997.

Roy, Roger. "Orlando: Too Much of a Good Thing." *Planning*, vol. 62, no. 3, March 1996.

Rubin, Herbert J. "Community-Based Development Organizations." *Public Administration Review*, vol. 53, no. 5, September-October 1993.

Russell, Charles. "Environmental Equity: Undoing Environmental Wrongs to Low Income and Minority Neighborhoods." *Journal of Affordable Housing & Community Development Law*, vol. 5, no. 2, Winter 1996.

Russell, Peter. "Brownfields Redevelopment: A Developer's Nightmare or a Dream Come True?" *Massachusetts Environment*, vol. 1, no. 9, February 1996.

Rypkema, Donovan D. "Preserving for Profit." *Urban Land*, vol. 57, no. 12, December 1998.

Salvesen, David, and Craig Richardson. "Keeping

Up with Growth." *Urban Land*, vol. 58, no. 9, September 1999.

Schweiger, Renate. "Seattle Rivitalized." *Urban Land*, vol. 58, no. 10, October 1999.

Searns, Robert M. "Happy Trails: Greenways Put Their Stamp on the Denver Area." *Planning*, Vol. 69, No. 1, January 2003.

Seeger, Nancy. "Greening Chicago." *Planning*, Vol. 68, No. 1, January 2002.

Serrao, Gregory. "Ghost Towns or Downtowns? Saving the Cities." *Journal of Housing*, vol. 48, no. 5, September 1991.

Smirniotopoulos, Peter. "Matriculation Reloaded." *Urban Land*, Vol. 62, No. 10, October 2003.

Smith, Mark. "Civano: Lessons for a Region." *Urban Land*, vol. 57, no. 7, July 1998.

Sostek, Anya. "Bringing Sprawl to Life." *Governing*, Vol. 15, No. 3, December 2001.

Starger, Steve. "Reinventing Downtown Hartford." *CT Business*, vol. 1, no. 4, November-December 1998.

Stephenson, R. Bruce. "A Vision of Green: Lewis Mumford's Legacy in Portland, Oregon." *APA Journal*, Vol. 65, No. 3, Summer 1999.

Stinson, Shauna. "The Air Up There." *Urban Land*, vol. 58, no. 10, October 1999.

Stokley, Jan. "Community-based Economic Development." *Economic Development & Law Center Report*, vol. 15, no. 2/3, March-June 1985.

Suchman, Diane. "Rebuilding Downtown Grand Forks." *Urban Land*, Vol. 57, No. 2, February 1998.

Sweazey, John, and Robert Schwartz. "Urban Community Housing." *Urban Land*, vol. 56, no. 11, November 1997.

Swope, Christopher. "Green Giants." *Governing*, Vol. 17, No. 3, December 2003.

Taylor, Marilyn J. "Newark Turning the Corner." *Urban Land*, vol. 57, no. 2, February 1998.

Turner, Robyne S. "Growth Politics and Downtown Development: The Economic Imperative in Sunbelt Cities." *Urban Affair Quarterly*, vol. 28, no. 1, September 1992.

Twitty, Paul M. "Beach Structures." *Urban Land*, Vol. 60, No. 10, October 2001.

Voith, Richard. "City and Suburban Growth: Substitutes or Complements?" *Business Review*, Federal Reserve Bank of Philadelphia, September/October 1992.

Voorhis, Scott Van. "Betting on Boston." *Urban Land*, vol. 57, no. 12, December 1998.

Wallace, Davis. "Riverfront Reborn." *Planning*, Vol. 64, No. 5, May 1998.

Warrick, Brooke and Toni Alexander. "Looking for Hometown America." *Urban Land*, Vol. 86, No. 2, February 1997.

Warson, Albert. "Toronto's Waterfront Revival." *Urban Land*, vol. 57, no. 1, January 1998.

Wassmer, Robert W. "Can Local Incentives Alter a Metropolitan City's Economic Development?" *Urban Studies*, vol. 31, no. 8, August 1994.

Weitz, Jerry, and Terry Moore. "Development Inside Urban Growth Boundaries: Oregon's Empirical Evidence of Contiguous Urban Form." *APA Journal*, Vol. 64, No. 4, Autumn 1998.

Wolch, Jennifer. "Two By Two." *Planning*, Vol. 69, No. 8, August/September 2003.

Wolfensohn, James D. "A Better World Is Possible." *The Futurist*. Vol. 37, No. 4, July/August 2003.

Woolard, E. S., Jr. "An Industry Approach to Sustainable Development." *Issues in Science and Technology*, Vol. 8, No. 3, Spring 1992.

York, Jim. "Miamians at the Gate." *Urban Land*, vol. 56, no. 5, May 1997.

Youth, Howard. "Silenced Spring: Disappearing Birds." *The Futurist*, Vol. 37, No. 4, July/August 2003.

Other Sources

APA Planners Press and Lincoln Land Institute. *Best of Contemporary Community Planning* (CD ROM Format). Chicago, IL: APA Planners Press, 2003.

Bonnell, Barbara. "Inner-Harbor Development." *Lawyers Title News*. Richmond, VA: Lawyers Title Insurance Corporation, May-June 1986.

Gugliotta, Guy. "Rebuilding a Community from the Bottom Up." *Washington Post*, January 24, 1993, p. A1.

Lemann, Nicholas. "Four Generations in the Projects." *New York Times Magazine*, January 13, 1991, pp. 14, 16-21.

Office of Technology Assessment, United States Congress. *The Technological Reshaping of Metropolitan America*. Washington, D.C.: United States Government Printing Office, September 1995.

Partners for Livable Communities. *In Pursuit of Livability: A Strategic Planning Cooperative*. Washington, D.C.: Partners for Livable Communities, Preliminary Report, 1996.

Prager, Adam J., Philip Benowitz, and Robert Schein. "Trends and Practices in Local Economic Development." *Municipal Year Book*. Washington, D.C.: International City/County Management Association, 1995.

Reisch, Mark. *Brownfields Program: Clean Up Urban Industrial Sites*. Washington, D.C.:

The Library of Congress, Congressional Research Service, April 3, 1995.

United States Congress. Office of Technology Assessment. *The Technological Reshaping of Metropolitan America.* Washington, D.C.: United States Government Printing Office, September 1995.

United States General Accounting Office. *Report to the Chair, Committee on Small Business, House of Representatives–Community Development: Reuse of Urban Industrial Sites.* Washington, D.C.: United States General Accounting Office, June 1995.

ABOUT THE EDITOR AND CONTRIBUTORS

Editor

Roger L. Kemp, Ph.D., has been a city manager on both the West and the East Coasts for over two decades. He is presently city manager of Vallejo, California. Dr. Kemp has also been an adjunct professor over the years at major educational institutions such as the University of California, Golden Gate University, Rutgers University, and the University of Connecticut. He holds a B.S. degree in business administration, both M.P.A. and M.B.A. degrees, and a Ph.D. degree in public administration, and is a graduate of the Program for Senior Executives in State and Local Government, John F. Kennedy School of Government, Harvard University. Roger is past-president of the Connecticut Town and City Management Association (CTCMA), and the Connecticut Chapter of the American Society for Public Administration (ASPA). He has written and edited numerous books and articles on various topics related to municipal management during his career. Dr. Kemp received the designation of *ICMA Credentialed Manager* in 2002.

Contributors

Affiliations are as of the times the articles were written.

Susan Anderson, Director, Office of Sustainable Development, City of Portland, Oregon.

Richard Bailey, Director, Chattanooga News Bureau, sponsored by the Chattanooga Chamber of Commerce and the City of Chattanooga, Tennessee.

Gale Berens, Senior Director, University Education and the Inner City, Urban Land Institute, Washington, D.C.

Lester R. Brown, Chairman of the Board, Worldwatch Institute, Washington, D.C., and President, Earth Policy Institute, Washington, D.C.

Ignacio F. Bunster-Ossa, Principal, Wallace Roberts & Todd (specializing in planning and design), Philadelphia, Pennsylvania.

Michael Burger, Environmental Attorney, City of New York, New York.

Laurel Butman, Program Manager, Office of Management and Finance, City of Portland, Oregon.

Steve Bylina, Deputy Commissioner, Bureau of Forestry, Department of Streets and Sanitation, City of Chicago, Illinois.

Jodie Carter, Regional Editor, *Landscape Architect and Specifier News*, Tustin, California.

Storm Cunningham, Chief Executive Officer, RestorAbility Inc., Alexandria, Virginia.

Glenda Daniel, Urban Greening Director, Openlands Project (a nonprofit organization), Chicago, Illinois.

Michael Davidson, Research Associate, Research Department, American Planning Association, Chicago, Illinois.

Jane Deel, Marketing Manager, Derck & Edson Associates, Lititz, Pennsylvania.

Chris Dimon, Vice President and National Director, Urban Design and Planning, HNTB Corporation, Kansas City, Missouri.

Nancy Egan, Principal, New Voodou Consultants (specializing in image/content development to the real estate and design communities), Santa Monica, California, and Cambridge, Massachusetts.

Donald L. Elliott, AICP, Vice President, Clarion Associates, Denver, Colorado.

Eric Emad, Senior Account Executive, Publicis Dialog (a leading green industry public relations firm), Chicago, Illinois.

Barbara Faga, Chairman of the Board, EDAW

Inc. (an international planning, urban design, and landscape architecture firm), San Francisco, California; and Managing Partner, EDAW Inc., Atlanta, Georgia.

John Fishbach, City Manager, City of Fort Collins, Colorado.

Maryann Froehlich, Director, Office of Policy Development, Department of Planning, Policy, and Evaluations, U. S. Environmental Protection Agency, Washington, D.C.

Timothy Grewe, Chief Administrative Officer, City of Portland, Oregon.

Joe Haberstroh, Reporter, *Newsday*, Long Island, New York.

Terra Hargett, Assistant Editor, *American City & County Magazine*, Intertec Publishing Company, Atlanta, Georgia.

Timothy Hayes, Director of Sustainable Development, Northampton County, Eastville, Virginia.

Lawrence O. Houstoun, Principal, Atlantic Group, Philadelphia, Pennsylvania and Cranbury, New Jersey.

Lindsay Isaacs, Assistant Editor, *American City & County*, Intertec Publishing Corporation, Atlanta, Georgia.

Thomas Jacobson, Director of Planning, Chesterfield County, Chesterfield, Virginia.

Margaret C. H. Kelly, Consultant, Public Finance Program, Trust for Public Land, San Francisco, California.

Terry J. Lassar, Communications Consultant and Writer (on development, architecture, and planning issues), Portland, Oregon.

Mary Lechner, Director of Finance, Northampton County, Eastville, Virginia.

Christopher Leinberger, Managing Director, Robert Charles Lesser and Company, Santa Fe, New Mexico.

Charles Lockwood, Freelance Writer, Topanga, California.

Suzanne Malec, Deputy Commissioner of Natural Resources, Department of Environment, City of Chicago, Illinois.

Frank Edgerton Martin, Campus Planning Coordinator, Hammel, Green, and Abrahamson, Inc., Minneapolis, Minnesota.

Joe McCarthy, Senior City Forester, Bureau of Forestry, Department of Streets and Sanitation, City of Chicago, Illinois.

Lance Metzler, County Administrator, Northampton County, Eastville, Virginia.

Jim Miara, Freelance Writer (on technology and development issues), Needham, Massachusetts.

David Moreno, Senior Vice President, Jerde Partnership International (specializing in urban planning and architecture), Los Angeles, California.

Paul Nakazawa, Principal, Nakazawa Consulting, Boston, Massachusetts.

Kim O'Connell, Freelance Writer (on environmental issues), Arlington, Virginia.

Sally Ortgies, Parks Superintendent, Parks and Recreation Department, City of West Des Moines, Iowa.

Michelle Wyman Pawar, Infrastructure Specialist, Reed Smith LLP, Washington, D.C.

Roshi Pelaseyed, Associate, Triad Associates, Dresher, Pennsylvania.

Ellen Perlman, Staff Writer, *Governing Magazine*, Congressional Quarterly Inc., Washington, D.C.

Arthur Pizzano, City Manager, City of Fairfield, Ohio.

Asher Price, Reporter (covering land-use issues and local politics), *Union-Tribune Newspaper*, San Diego, California.

Jessica Rio, Public Information Officer, Department of the Environment, City of Chicago, Illinois.

Christopher Rissetto, Partner and Head, Infrastructure Group, Washington, D.C.

Elaine Robbins, former Executive Editor of *Texas Parks and Wildlife Magazine*, is a Freelance Writer and Editor, Austin, Texas.

Martin J. Rosen, President, Trust for Public Land, a national nonprofit land conservation organization based in San Francisco, California.

Robert M. Searns, AICP, Consultant (on greenways and trails), Littleton, Colorado.

Edwin Slattery, Principal Environmental Engineer, Stanley Consultants, Inc., Des Moines, Iowa.

Lucinda Smith, Environmental Planner, Natural Resources Department, City of Fort Collins, Colorado.

Anya Sostek, Assistant Editor, *Governing Magazine*, Congressional Quarterly Inc., Washington, D.C.

Steve Starger, Freelance Writer, Portland, Connecticut.

R. Bruce Stephenson, Associate Professor, Environment Studies Department, and Director, Growth Management Studies Program, Rollins College, Winter Park, Florida.

Sean Stowell, Regional Editor, *Landscape Architect and Specifier News*, Tustin, California.

Diane Suchman, Project Director, Grand Forks

Panel, Urban Land Institute, Washington, D.C.

Christopher Swope, Staff Writer, *Governing Magazine*, Congressional Quarterly Inc., Washington, D.C.

Paul M. Twitty, Chief Executive Officer and Founding Principal, Schwab, Twitty & Hanser (STH) Architectural Group, Inc., West Palm Beach, Florida.

Jennifer Wolch, Professor of Geography and Director, Center for Sustainable Cities, University of Southern California, Los Angeles, California.

Matther Zieper, Research Director, Public Finance Program, Trust for Public Land, San Francisco, California.

INDEX